# ARUBA, BONAIRE & CURAÇAO
## ALIVÉ!

# ARUBA, BONAIRE & CURAÇAO

## ALIVÉ!

### 2nd Edition

Susan Brushaber & Arnold Greenberg

**HUNTER**

HUNTER PUBLISHING, INC.
130 Campus Drive, Edison, NJ 08818
732-225-1900; 800-255-0343; fax 732-417-1744
comments@hunterpublishing.com

ISBN 1-58843-259-9

© 2002 Alive Travel Books, Ltd.

*This and other Hunter travel guides
are also available as e-books in a variety of
digital formats through our
online partners, including Amazon.com,
BarnesandNoble.com and eBooks.com.*

This guide focuses on recreational activities. As all such activities contain elements of risk, the publisher, author, affiliated individuals and companies disclaim any responsibility for any injury, harm, or illness that may occur to anyone through, or by use of, the information in this book. Every effort was made to insure the accuracy of information in this book, but the publisher and author do not assume, and hereby disclaim, any liability for any loss or damage caused by errors, omissions, misleading information or potential travel problems caused by this guide, even if such errors or omissions are the result of negligence, accident or any other cause.

Maps by Lissa K. Dailey & Kim Foley MacKinnon
© 2002 Hunter Publishing, Inc.
Index by Elite Indexing
Color images compliments of Curaçao Tourist Board
unless otherwise noted.

# www.hunterpublishing.com

Now you can view Hunter's extensive range of travel guides online, read excerpts from books that interest you, as well as view the table of contents *before* you buy! We post comments from other readers and reviewers, allowing you to get a real feel for each book. All transactions are processed through our secure server.

We have guidebooks for every type of traveler, no matter the budget, lifestyle or idea of fun — from dive guides and hiking books to volumes that inspire romantic weekend escapes!

Our top-selling guides in the *ALIVE!* series include: *The Cayman Islands Alive!; Martinique & Guadeloupe Alive!; Dominica & St. Lucia Alive!;* and *Miami & the Florida Keys Alive!* Click on "Alive Guides" on the website to see other exciting destinations in this series.

Active travelers should check out our ***Adventure Guides***, a series aimed at the independent traveler with a focus on outdoor activities. Adventures can be as mild as beachcombing or hiking a hill, or as wild as parasailing, hot-air ballooning or diving among shipwrecks. All books in this signature series offer solid travel information, including where to stay and eat, transportation, sightseeing, attractions, culture, history and more.

Log on to www.hunterpublishing.com to learn about our other series — *Hunter-Rivages Hotel Guides, Landmark Visitors Guides, Romantic Weekends, Nelles Guidebooks* and *Travel Packs* and more.

## About the Alive Guides

**R**eliable, detailed and personally researched by knowledgeable authors, the **ALIVE!** series was founded by Arnold and Harriet Greenberg.

Arnold has co-authored *South America on $40 A Day*, as well as *St. Martin & St. Barts Alive!* and *Buenos Aires & the Best of Argentina Alive!*

Harriet has co-authored *The US Virgin Islands Alive!* and *St. Martin & St. Barts Alive!* She is currently researching *The British Virgin Islands Alive!* and *Puerto Rico Alive!*

This accomplished travel-writing team also operates a renowned bookstore, **The Complete Traveller**, at 199 Madison Avenue in New York City.

## We Love to Get Mail

**T**his book has been carefully researched to bring you current, accurate information. But no place is unchanging. We welcome your comments for future editions. Please write to us at:

*Aruba, Bonaire & Curaçao Alive!*
c/o Hunter Publishing
130 Campus Drive
Edison, NJ 08818

You can also e-mail us at:
comments@hunterpublishing.com.

# Contents

# Introduction

*F*or many, the Caribbean either stops at Barbados, or doesn't even reach much beyond the Bahamas or Virgin Islands. Little is known about the three leeward islands off by themselves just a few miles north of Venezuela, tucked safely below the hurricane belt. Yet, Aruba, Bonaire and Curaçao, the "A," "B," and "C" of the ABC Islands, offer everything you could ever want from a Caribbean holiday.

The "A" stands both for Aruba and the abundance of world-class restaurants, casinos, and topnotch entertainment you'll enjoy there. The "B" is Bonaire, synonymous with bountiful marine life and bucolic landscapes. The "C," Curaçao, is best known for its cosmopolitan quality and Dutch Caribbean charm.

# The Attractions

Though many have yet to discover the ABC Islands, those who have return again and again. Here are a few of the reasons why:

- ☺ With nary a cloud in the sky, the islands enjoy azure skies and turquoise seas 12 months a year. Temperatures in the low 80s and a constant breeze are a given. Best of all, the ABC Islands are located outside the hurricane belt!

◎ Diving and snorkeling here is the best in the Caribbean. Crystal clear waters reveal pristine reefs and fantastic wrecks. Aggressive protection programs and environmentally conscious dive shops guarantee that they'll stay that way for years to come.

◎ Those same trade winds that propelled the merchant ships of the Dutch West India Company now provide ideal conditions for sailing and windsurfing and keep beachgoers comfortably cool.

◎ Active vacationers have a wealth of activities to choose from on land as well as in the water, including golf, tennis, horseback riding, hiking and biking. Nature lovers and bird watchers won't be disappointed either.

◎ Shopping is first-rate, especially on Aruba and Curaçao, where prices for fine fragrances and designer fashions are as much as 20% less than what they cost at home.

◎ All three islands offer a variety of accommodations, from small bed and breakfasts and country inns to luxurious five-star resorts. Types and prices vary by island, but affordability is better than on other islands in the Caribbean.

◎ Dining on all three islands is first-class, offering a variety of cuisines guaranteed to satisfy even the most discriminating palate.

- 🌀 **A**miable, **B**enevolent and **C**aring best describe the people of the ABC Islands. Warmth and hospitality are national traits.

- 🌀 Compared to other islands, the ABC Islands are relatively crime-free. (No matter where you travel, however, car doors should be locked when leaving the car unattended and valuables should always be placed in a hotel safe) Noticeably absent as well are beach vendors hawking T-shirts and souvenirs.

- 🌀 The islands' unique combination of Dutch Caribbean charm and Latin warmth are irresistible!

# A Capsule History

## The First Inhabitants

The earliest known inhabitants of the ABC Islands were the **Caquetio Indians**, a Caribbean faction of the peace-loving Arawak Nation. The Caquetios were not warriors but fishermen who traveled by dugout canoe to trade with their fellow tribes on neighboring islands. They probably settled on the ABC Islands hoping that they had found a safe haven from the fearless **Caribs**, who were more prevalent in the northern islands. Cannibals and warriors, the Caribs were a bellig-

erent people, who at one point had even driven
Columbus off the island of St. Croix.

## The 15th & 16th Centuries

While Columbus was busy discovering new territories in the northern Caribbean, his lieutenant,
**Alonso de Ojeda**, headed south. Many believe
Ojeda was the first to discover Curaçao in 1499,
before going on to discover Aruba from the shores
of the Cape Roman Peninsula in Venezuela.
Amazed by the size of the Indians living on the islands, Ojeda nicknamed the islands *Islas de los
Gigantes*, the Islands of Giants.

However, it is the Italian navigator **Amerigo
Vespucci** who is officially credited with the discovery of Bonaire and Curaçao in 1499. Not finding gold on any of the islands, the Spaniards
characterized them as *islas inutiles,* or worthless
islands. Rather than leave empty-handed, in 1513
they transported most of the Cachets to Santo
Domingo to work as slaves in the copper mines.
Eventually, the Spanish returned to Aruba and
Curaçao, setting up cattle ranches to be tended by
the Indians they had brought back from Santo
Domingo. The ranches never prospered.

Despite the rampant activities of marauding pirates and British buccaneers throughout the rest
of the Caribbean, life on the ABC Islands was un-
eventful until 1634. In that year, the **Dutch** easily conquered Curaçao, and in 1636, they occupied
Aruba and Bonaire as well.

Throughout the next 150 years or so, attention was focused on Curaçao, while Bonaire and Aruba stayed quietly out of the way.

The **Dutch West India Company** recognized the strategic value of Curaçao's natural harbor, both as a military strong point for its ongoing battles against the Spanish and as a commercial harbor set amidst its trading routes and possessions in the New Netherlands and Brazil. Curaçao soon became an important depot for slaves brought from Africa to work on plantations throughout the Caribbean. It was also a stopping point for South American and Caribbean products bound for Europe, just as it is now.

## Oil Brings Prosperity

The abolition of slavery in 1863 all but devastated the island's economies, forcing many residents to seek employment elsewhere. Prosperity returned in 1915 with the arrival of the **Royal Dutch Shell Refinery** on Curaçao. Shell became the largest employer on the island, attracting workers from Bonaire and other islands as well.

Aruba followed suit nine years later in 1924, with the opening of the Lago Refinery by the **Standard Oil Company** of New Jersey (Exxon). The boom years lasted until 1985, when a declining oil market forced both Shell and Exxon to close their refineries.

# The Islands Today

Luckily for both islands, the days when they were entirely dependent on oil for their livelihood are long gone. Aruba has focused its energies on tourism and is now one of the most popular destinations in the Caribbean. Returning to its roots, Curaçao is quickly becoming both a commercial powerhouse and a vacation paradise.

Bonaire, more low-key than its sister islands has, until recently, stayed more or less out of the spotlight. Since many Bonaireans had looked to the refineries on Curaçao and Aruba for employment, economically Bonaire was strongly linked to the other islands. Nowadays, with the growing popularity of diving, bird watching and ecotourism, Bonaire is holding its own.

## The People

The ABC islanders are descendants of the African slaves, Arawak and other native Caribbean peoples, and the Dutch and Spanish settlers. Their mixed ancestry is a reflection of the islands' history. Forty to 50 different nationalities are represented on Aruba and Curaçao, most of whom are the descendants of laborers who came from neighboring islands, as well as other Dutch colonies and countries around the world, to work in the oil refineries. An increasing number of Dutch retire on the islands.

# Island Government

In 1954, the Netherlands Antilles, Surinam and Holland issued a proclamation promising to cooperate as equal, though independent, partners within the **Kingdom of the Netherlands**. No longer colonies, the Antilles became an autonomous entity within the Kingdom of the Netherlands, responsible for their own internal/inter-island affairs. Defense, citizenship and foreign affairs still fall under the jurisdiction of the government of the Kingdom of the Netherlands, which does not involve itself in the internal affairs of the partners. The capital of the Antilles is **Willemstad**, Curaçao. Surinam left the Kingdom in 1975. Aruba seceded from the Netherlands Antilles in 1986 and is now an independent partner within the Kingdom.

Holland's monarch, **Queen Beatrix**, is at the head of the Kingdom. She appoints **governors** to serve as her representatives on Aruba and in the Netherlands Antilles for a term of six years. The role of the governor is entirely independent of the local governing body. The governor of the Antilles resides in Willemstad. Ministers from Holland, the Netherlands Antilles and Aruba serve on the **Council of Ministers**, which handles matters concerning foreign affairs, national security and Dutch nationality.

Legislative, executive and judicial powers are established according to the standard guidelines of parliamentary democracy. The 22 members of **Parliament** are apportioned among the four islands and elected by popular vote. The majority

*In the 1950s, the islands of the Netherlands Antilles were Aruba, Bonaire, Curaçao, Saba St. Maarten & St. Eustatius.*

Introduction

parties are then asked by the government to form a seven-member Council of Ministers, headed by the Prime Minister, wherein lie the executive powers. Judicial powers rest within the common courts of Aruba and the Netherlands Antilles. The highest court is the **Court of Justice** in the Hague.

Though independent of Bonaire and Curaçao, Aruba's political status within the Netherlands is that of a **commonwealth**. Free to determine domestic policy, her cultural, political and defensive links to Holland and her sister islands are still strong.

# Antillean Cuisine

## A Multi-Ethic Background

Not only is the multi-ethnic heritage of the ABC Islands reflected in the faces of their residents, but also in the local cuisine. When you look through the dining sections pertaining to each island, you'll undoubtedly notice the many international cuisines represented on the list of island restaurants. French, Italian and Continental are familiar to everyone, but authentic Antillean cuisine is not something you're likely to find in your hometown. The cuisine of the Antilles is as rich and flavorful as the islands' history.

## The Arawaks

Sampling the local **krioyo** cooking is one of the best ways to experience the local culture. The earliest inhabitants of the Antilles, the Arawak Indians, were skilled farmers, cultivating potatoes, peanuts and peppers just as they had in their native South America. In addition, they gathered avocado, pineapple, papaya, guava and the *shimaruku* – the West Indian cherry – which they found growing naturally on several of their new island homes. Flavor was added by seasoning foods with many of the plants they found growing wild, including oregano and basil. They cooked the red buds of the annatto in oil to produce a food coloring, which was then added to whatever they were cooking. The Arawaks employed various cooking methods: boiling and steaming; roasting food barbecue-style; or baking on a *comal*, a griddle made of clay.

## The Spanish Contribute

The Spanish, who settled on the island in the 16th century, began to use many of the native foods in their own cooking and introduced their Arawak slaves to **pork** and the use of pig lard. They taught the Indians to cook with sugar instead of honey and introduced them to salt, mango, citron and olives from Asia.

## The African Influence

Soon, African slaves were brought to the islands, and with them came the **plantain**, which is now served with most meals. It is usually fried, though it's sometimes boiled. The slaves also introduced *fungee*, a porridge originally made from sorghum flour. Sorghum is a tropical cereal grass still grown on Bonaire. The Arawaks began to make their own version of this porridge from cornmeal and today it is a staple of the Antillean diet known as *funchi*. Then, as now, *funchi* was cooked in an iron pot brought from Africa and constantly stirred using a *lele*, a three-pointed wooden stirrer, or a *palu di funchi*, a wooden paddle.

## Dutch Flavorings

The Dutch colonists, who arrived in the 17th century, contributed **cheese**, **bacon** and **beans** to the island diet. During the same time, Sephardic Jews fleeing the Inquisition were granted permission by the Dutch to settle in Curaçao. The most affluent among them added a touch of refinement to the Antillean kitchen, often combining sweet and sour flavorings by using capers, raisins, dried prunes, olives and piccalilli in one dish.

With the arrival of the oil refineries in the early 20th century came Dutch laborers, who introduced sandwiches made with cold meats and cheeses, and canned vegetables. During this period, potatoes also acquired a renewed importance in the island diet. A brand-new dimension was added to the local cuisine when Dutch personnel from Indonesia were stationed on Curaçao during World War II. Exotic sounding dishes such as *nassi-goreng*, *bahmi*, *sate*, *lumpia*, and *rendang* became commonplace on many island menus.

## A Glossary of Local Dishes

Dishes which you are likely to find at restaurants featuring local *krioyo* cuisine include some of the following.

**Stoba di cabrito** – goat stew

**Sopi di yuana** – iguana soup

**Morro** – rice and beans

**Banana hasa** – fried plantains

**Sopi piska** – fish soup.

**Keshi yena** – stuffed edam cheese

**Zarzuela** – seafood stew

**Quesilla** – baked custard with a caramel sauce

**Kadushi** – a hearty soup made from the cactus of the same name; the inner meat is prepared with fish, meat, vegetables and herbs.

Fish dishes feature *mula* (kingfish), *mero* (sea bass), and *dradu* (king dolphin), served with a squeeze of *lamunchi* (lime) or *salsa pika* (hot sauce).

Antillean-style fast foods are usually served at road-side stalls known as *truk'i pan*, or take-out restaurants. They often serve *pastechi*, a pastry

usually filled with meat, shrimp or fish, and
**empanas**, cornmeal crescents filled with meat.

 # Environment

## Flora

### Cacti

Though you will probably be expecting to see the
distinctive divi-divi tree, sculpted by the trade
winds with all its branches bent west, your first
impression of the ABC Islands will be the desert-
like landscape of cacti and dry brush along the
runway. With just over 20 inches of rainfall annually, the climate of the ABC Islands has more in
common with the American Southwest than with
other islands in the Caribbean. The palms gracing the beaches of Aruba and the Sea Aquarium
Beach on Curaçao are not native to these islands.

Over a dozen different types of cacti thrive in the
desert-like conditions common to all three islands. Most have lovely flowers, which add color
to the otherwise arid landscape. Several varieties
are prized by the locals for the healing qualities of
their flesh when used as a salve or compress for
an aching back. Others, such as the **prickly pear**
and ground-hugging **mountain melon**, or *melon
di seru*, offer a sweet, edible fruit.

Hardest to miss are the candlestick, or pillar,
cacti, of which the most common are the yatu (or

*datu*) and the **kadushi**. The taller of the two, the tree-like kadushi branches out a few feet above the ground, and its stem is often covered in white, pink and pale green flowers. It is treasured for its flesh, which is the main ingredient in a popular soup of the same name, and it is also used both for medicinal purposes and as a shampoo. The yatu grows straight up and down, branching out close to the ground, with white, pink or cream-colored flowers blooming at the tops of its stems. Quick to take root, yatus are often cut and replanted in rows to form fences designed to keep hungry goats from trampling the garden.

## Aloe

Also common to the islands are fields of aloe, which was once actively cultivated for export during the 18th and 19th centuries. Though no longer cultivated, the survival of the aloe is guaranteed by the bananaquits and the blue-tailed emerald and ruby topaz hummingbirds who, after drinking the nectar of its blossoms, scatter its seeds about the countryside.

## Trees & Flowering Plants

Despite their arid climate the islands do not lack for trees. In the northern reaches of Bonaire and Curaçao, you'll find dense wooded areas of low-lying **mesquite trees**, *palo de silla*, a local hardwood tree used to make kitchen utensils, and brazilwoods. In fact, it was the brilliant yellow flowers of the brazilwood that first attracted the Spanish to Bonaire. Also common to the islands is the kibra hasha. Considered one of the most beautiful trees in the Caribbean, its branches overflow with bright yellow blossoms after even the slightest rain.

Unfortunately, not all of the trees on the ABC islands are so benevolent. Beware of the ***manchineel***, or *manzanilla*, trees that grow along the beaches in several areas. Do not touch the tree or its green, apple-like fruit, and never sit underneath one during a rainstorm. Not only the fruit but the tree itself has such a high acidic content that a mere touch can cause a painful burn.

In gardens across the islands you'll find colorful **hibiscus** and the brilliant red blossoms of the expansive **flamboyant** tree. Just as popular is **bougainvillea**, named for the French sea adventurer who brought them to the Caribbean from Brazil in the 18th century. Locally, bougainvillea is called *trinitaria*, and it comes in shades of purple, white, red, and orange. **Oleander** graces many a garden. Goats, knowing it's poisonous, wisely stay away. **Orchids** are protected in Curaçao, and Christoffel Park is home to at least four types of wild orchids, including the lovely purple banana shimaron.

After a rain, tiny **wildflowers** will bloom along the roadside, lasting for only a few days. No matter how lovely they may look, don't get too close. Many wildflowers are protected by thorns or, like poison ivy in North America, may cause a painful rash when touched. You may see the tiny yellow blossoms of the ***anglo***, or angel plant, creeping along the ground. Not as well-intentioned as its name suggests, its blossoms die off and are replaced by painfully sharp thorns.

Don't be deceived by the equally innocent looking purple blossoms of the *palu di lechi*, or rubber-vine. In its quest for territory, it wraps its vines around other plants, thus strangling them to death. It was originally brought to Curaçao with hopes of producing rubber from the milky substance in its stem. Efforts failed and, to the chagrin of its keepers, the *palu di lechi* began growing out of control across the island.

After a heavy downpour, the *shimaruku*, or West Indian cherry, a small bush, practically explodes with orange-red flowers, which will ripen into a vermilion fruit as sweet as honey and rich in vitamin C.

Venturing out to the coast, you may see small white flowers blooming on the dunes. They are **seaside lavender**. The yellow blossoms are *suriana maritima*. Also common is *samphire*, which has blue, white and yellow flowers. **Sea grapes** grow wild on the dunes of Aruba's north coast.

## Fauna

### Birds

You don't have to be an avid bird watcher to enjoy the flamingo sanctuary at Pekelmeer. Sandpipers and black-winged stilts, along with several different types of ducks, and an occasional Bahamas pintail, often join the flamingos there and at other popular feeding grounds. Shore and water birds common to the ABC Islands include **pelicans**, **snowy egrets**, **red egrets**, **ospreys**, **cormorants**, **plovers**, **brown boobies** and various types of **herons**, including the yellow-crowned night heron.

Aruba proudly boasts one of only three breeding grounds for **terns** in the world. It is located beyond the beaches of San Nicolas. Aruba is also a rest stop for migratory birds flying between the Americas. They include **barn swallows**, **bobolinks**, **black skimmers** and **whistling ducks**. Following the example of those who came to vacation on the island and never left, the **quail** and **white-tailed hawk** are now common to Aruba. One of the island's most protected species is the rare **burrowing owl**.

Like Aruba, Bonaire has its share of less common birds. The **black-whiskered vireo**, the **pearly-eyed** thrasher and the **yellow oriole** are frequently sighted at Put Bronswinkel in Washington-Slagbaai National Park. **Scaly-naped pigeons**, **bare-eyed pigeons**, the **eared dove** and the **white-fronted dove** also nest on Bonaire. **Parakeets** and the **yellow-winged parrot**, or *lora*, which is found only on Bonaire, have been legally protected since 1931. Unfortunately, they frequently fall prey to smugglers, who take them to Aruba and Curaçao where they are sold as pets.

**Bananaquits**, **blue-tailed emeralds**, **ruby topaz hummingbirds**, **tropical mockingbirds**, **trupials**, **black-faced grassquits**, **yellow warblers** and several different varieties of **flycatch-**

**ers** are among the most common varieties found on all three islands.

## Lizards

If you venture out to the less traveled sections of the coastline you may come across **iguanas**, sometimes as large as three to four feet long, sunning themselves on the cliffs. Get too close and they'll disappear, possibly by jumping into the sea. And with good reason. Although protected by law, iguanas often fall victim to poachers. Their meat is considered a delicacy among the Antillean people, who believe it to be especially good for virility. The less timid **whiptail lizard** is found only on Bonaire. Males, with their blue head and greenish-blue hindfeet and tail root, are easily distinguished from the more sedately colored females and young whiptails.

## Mammals

Be on the lookout for **goats** and **donkeys** as you travel through the countryside, or *cunucu*, as it is referred to on the islands. Since goat meat is a staple of the island diet, the animals are certain to belong to someone. Donkeys have been running wild since 1925, when their exportation to Barbados and Trinidad was discontinued, though some are domestic. If visiting Christoffel Park in Curaçao, watch for the rare **Curaçao white-tailed deer**.

## Marine Life

If there is a separate heaven for divers and snorkelers, the reefs and wrecks off the ABC Islands must be "heaven on earth." Bonaire and Curaçao share the most pristine reef system in the Caribbean, home to over 200 different species of fish, 30 varieties of soft corals, and 50 species of hard corals. Both islands have designated all or much of their surrounding waters as national parks. Wreck divers will be in their element on Aruba, where several noteworthy wrecks are to be found just minutes from shore, including the *Antilla*, the largest wreck in the Caribbean.

*See individual islands for detailed descriptions of diving conditions and dive sites.*

Visibility ranges from 60 to 150 feet, revealing a fascinating landscape of **corals**, **sponges**, **sea fans**, and **gorgonians**, populated by colorful **tropical fish**, **sea turtles**, **crabs**, **anemones** and other sea creatures. The better part of many dives is within 75 feet of the surface, making this undersea world just as accessible to novice divers and snorkelers as it is to experienced divers.

Elkhorn and staghorn corals dominate the shallow plateaus before the drop-off, often followed by sloping walls covered with purple tube sponges, anemones, giant elephant ear sponges and iridescent vase sponges. While lizardfish, flamingo tongue snails and fingerprint cowries feed on the soft corals and gorgonians, moray eels, squirrel fish and blackbar soldierfish glide in and out of the crevices, often resting on the ledges, which serve as cleaning stations manned by banded coral shrimp and arrowhead crabs. French and queen angelfish, parrotfish, rock beauties, horse-eye jacks, yellow snappers and countless other tropical fish in all shapes, sizes and colors swim amidst labyrinths of soft coral, gorgonians, enormous brain corals, mustard hill corals, finger corals and mountainous star corals.

## Watch Out!

While the marine world is beautiful, it is not without hazards. Following the basic rule of "Look, but never touch" should keep you out of harm's way.

While in the shallow waters, be on the alert for **fire coral**. It causes painful and often infectious welts on contact. In fact, all contact with coral is to be avoided. Not only will you damage it, but skin abrasions caused by coral run a high risk of infection due to the many micro-organisms that live on it.

Heed the warning of the **do-not-touch-me sponge**. The benign appearance of this brown sponge is deceiving. It is covered with millions of tiny, razor-sharp needles. They will cause a burning itch that can last for several days.

The **scorpionfish** sports dangerous poisonous spines on its lateral fins. Since it spends much of its time resting on the sandy bottom, it is easily mistaken for a piece of algae-covered coral. However, a close look may reveal a fin or its eyes on the top of its head.

Don't be deceived by the delicate appearance of the **damselfish**. Many of the 12 varieties of this dainty-looking fish are extremely territorial. They feed on algae and have their own algae patches, of which they are very protective, literally chasing other, even larger, fish away. Damsels have even been known to nip at intruding divers.

## ⊚ RECOMMENDED DIVE GUIDES

Lonely Planet publishes *Diving and Snorkeling in Bonaire* and *Diving & Snorkeling in Curaçao*. Each sells for $14.95. Both can be ordered from The Complete Traveller Bookstore, ☎ 212-685-9007 or write to: The Complete Traveller Bookstore, 199 Madison Ave., New York, NY 10016.

# Nuts & Bolts

## Getting Here

Carriers generally recognize two high seasons for travel to the ABC Islands. The first runs from late June through mid-August when vacationing families are taking advantage of reduced rates at many hotels. The second coincides with the winter months, and runs from mid-December to mid-April. During these periods airfare will be higher than it is at other times throughout the year. Fares may also be higher for weekend travel during the low season, though they remain constant throughout the high season.

Several carriers offer regular nonstop service to Aruba and Curaçao out of New York (JFK International), Newark, Miami, Baltimore, Tampa, Amsterdam, and Caracas. Travelers to Bonaire usually have to change planes in Curaçao or Aruba. Carriers with frequent service to the islands are **American Airlines** (☎ 800-433-7300); and **KLM** (☎ 800-374-7747), which flies out of Amsterdam.

**ALM**, Antillean Airlines (☎ 800-327-7230) offers frequent service between the three islands, as well as two flights daily to Curaçao out of Miami. ALM flies to Aruba out of Miami on Thursdays,

Saturdays and Sundays, and to Bonaire on Wednesdays and Saturdays. Through its code-share program with **United Airlines**, passengers flying on United from other US cities connect with ALM in Miami. The codeshare fare is valid on direct flights only and reservations must be made through United (☎ 800-241-6522). **Delta** and **Continental** also offer service from the US.

## Via Cruise Ship

Terrific shopping, Dutch Caribbean charm and casinos have placed Willemstad and Oranjestad among the most popular ports of call. Kralendijk is increasingly being included in many itineraries as well. Lines calling on one or more of the ABCs include **Celebrity Cruises**, **Crystal Cruises**, **Costa Cruise Lines**, **Norwegian Cruise Line**, and **Cunard Line**. For more information, contact your cruise travel agent.

## Inter-Island Travel

A vacation on one island can easily be combined with a day-trip or overnight to at least one of the others. Though several tour operators offer day-trips between the islands, you should be able to do it on your own with some advance planning. ALM offers several daily flights among the three islands. Airline reservations will generally have to be made in advance, with the amount of notice dependent on the time of year you're visiting. Car rentals should be arranged prior to your arrival.

An attractive alternative to flying is to travel with one of the regularly organized sailboat trips, or to get together with a group of friends and charter your own. See the sections on sailing in each chapter for details.

# Getting Ready

## Entry Requirements

To pass through customs, visitors to Aruba, Bonaire or Curaçao must present proof of identity and a return or continuing ticket. Residents of the United States or Canada may present either a valid passport, an official birth certificate with a raised seal, along with a photo ID, or a certificate of naturalization. Non-US or Canadian citizens who are legal residents of either country must present a re-entry permit, a valid non-quota immigration visa or an Alien Registration Card.

## Money Matters

The currency on Bonaire and Curaçao is the **Netherlands Antilles Florin** (NAFL), which is also referred to as a **guilder**. The currency on Aruba is the **Aruban Florin**. Both the Aruban and Netherlands Antilles florins are extremely stable, backed by gold and foreign exchange, and they fluctuate with the dollar on the world market. At press time the exchange rate was 1.77 florins (NAFL or AFL) to US $1, as it has been for some time. US dollars are widely accepted on all three islands, as are travelers checks and all major credit cards. Personal checks, however, are not.

The exchange rate with the Canadian dollar is 1. 51 NAFL to $1 Canadian. Banks will exchange other currencies for a fee. Note that banks may also charge a fee to cash travelers checks, while restaurants, shops and hotels do not.

## *Alive Price Scale*

### *Accommodations*

You'll find a fine assortment of hotels on the ABC Islands, with modern, luxury resorts most prevalent on Aruba. On Curaçao there are many older resorts built in the 1950s and 1960s, some of which have been refurbished, along with newer accommodations and small inns in the countryside. Accommodations on Bonaire cater to divers, and they feature multi-bedroom apartment-style suites with fully equipped kitchens.

Our price scale is designed to give you a ballpark figure for planning. It is based on the price of a double room during high season, which generally runs from mid-December to mid-April, though exact dates will vary by hotel. The greatest fluctuation between low and high season rates is on Aruba. Overall, accommodations on Aruba are more expensive than those on Curaçao and Bonaire, with far more hotels falling into the expensive range.

Considerable savings may be had by taking advantage of special packages, such as those for honeymooners, divers and families. You may also do better by reserving with the hotel directly rather than through a reservation service or travel agent, especially if you're planning to visit during low season.

Breakfast and meals are generally not included in the rate, though most hotels do offer separate meal plans. A government tax, which varies by island, is levied on the room rate and a 10 to 15% service charge will be added to the rate as well.

All hotels described take major credit cards unless specifically noted. Prices are in US dollars.

### Accommodations Price Scale

Deluxe. . . . . . . . . . . . . . . more than $250
Expensive . . . . . . . . . . . . . . . $151-$250
Moderate . . . . . . . . . . . . . . . . $100-$150
Inexpensive . . . . . . . . . . . . . under $100

## Dining

Our price scale is based on a three-course dinner (per person) including appetizer or soup, main dish, dessert and coffee. Cocktails and wine are extra. Please keep in mind that these are ballpark figures. Prices among different appetizers and main courses obviously vary considerably. The final cost of your meal is dependent on your selections.

A 10-15% service charge will be added to your bill. If not, a 10-20% tip, according to the quality of the service you received, is appropriate. Keep in mind that the service charge does not go directly to your waitperson but is also used to cover restaurant costs. Whether or not to give an additional tip is at your discretion.

Though most restaurants accept major credit cards, many of the smaller, local restaurants may not. If that's a concern, phone ahead or ask when making your reservation.

**Nuts & Bolts**

---

### Dining Price Scale

Expensive . . . . . . . . . . . . . more than $35
Moderate . . . . . . . . . . . . . . . . $25-$35
Inexpensive . . . . . . . . . . . . . . under $25

---

## Customs Regulations

Since you may be planning to take advantage of the great shopping on Aruba and/or Curaçao, a review of customs regulations may be helpful.

US Customs regulations provide a $600 exemption for articles based on their retail value in the place of acquisition. A flat 10% rate of duty is assessed on the next $400 worth of merchandise, provided it is not intended for retail sale. This provision may be used once every 30 days, commencing the day after your last arrival. A traveler is permitted to mail an unlimited number of gifts valued at $25 or less to friends and relatives in the United States, as long as no person receives more than one gift per day. Members of a family traveling together can combine their purchases and exemptions.

The duty-free allowance for liquor, if you are over 21 years of age, is a 750ml-bottle plus a second bottle of locally produced liquor. Original works of art, including gold and silver jewelry made in the Netherlands Antilles, and local handicrafts and souvenirs, can be brought home duty-free.

## Packing

What you pack depends on the type of vacationing you have in mind. Dive equipment, tennis racquets and golf clubs can be rented if you prefer not to lug your equipment with you. Dress is casual, especially on Bonaire where shorts and T-shirts are standard during the day. Casual resort wear is best for evenings, though, especially if you plan on dining in town.

If you've made dinner plans at one of the finer restaurants on Aruba or Curaçao, men should wear trousers, a collared shirt and enclosed footwear. Men might also pack a sports jacket, just in case. Women can wear anything casually chic. Nightclubs usually require that men wear trousers and may refuse to admit you if you're wearing shorts.

## Packing Tips

&#x25CE; To prevent suits and dresses from wrinkling in your suitcase, place tissue paper between garments.

◎ Transparent zippered plastic bags, sold at five-and-dime stores, are ideal for carrying lingerie, cosmetics and shoes.

◎ Carry all liquids, shampoos, lotions and the like in plastic bottles. In case of leakage, it's often a good idea to put them in plastic bags as well.

◎ Don't feel you have to pack an entirely new outfit for every day of your vacation. Hotel laundry service is usually fast and efficient.

◎ Over-the-counter drugs and sundries are readily available. Even if they cost a little more, lighter luggage may be worth it. Do bring enough prescription drugs, in original bottles, to last your entire trip.

◎ Airlines have updated security rules about carry-on luggage. Call your airline to check for the latest information.

**Nuts & Bolts**

## Climate

Thankfully located below the hurricane belt, the ABC Islands are year-round destinations. Temperatures are in the low 80s all year long, with a constant breeze provided by the trade winds. The average rainfall is less than 24 inches a year, falling mostly in brief showers. November and December are the rainiest months.

## Electric Current

The electric current on Aruba, Bonaire and Curaçao is compatible with small appliances such as electric razors and hair dryers intended for use in the United States. You may need adapters in some cases. If this is a concern, call ahead of time.

## Language

The ABC islanders' amazing aptitude for language is sure to astonish you. Though the official language is Dutch, the native language is **Papiamento**, which is spoken nowhere else. Most residents also speak Spanish and English. Virtually all persons employed in hotels, restaurants and shops speak English and Dutch flawlessly, as well as Spanish. You'll be amazed at how effortlessly they alternate among the four languages. It's not unusual for a busy shopkeeper to speak to four different patrons in four different languages, simultaneously!

Papiamento first came into being as the language used among the slaves during the passage from West Africa to the Antilles; then it became the everyday language spoken among the different racial and national groups living in Otrobanda, a district of Curaçao's capital, Willemstad. It's not surprising that many words in Papiamento are strikingly similar to Spanish, Dutch, Portuguese, English and French, with some African influences as well. Until recently it had been more of a spoken than a written language, with Dutch the language of instruction in schools. An official spelling has been developed and Papiamento is now taught in schools along with Spanish and English.

---

### A Few Words in Papiamento

Bon Bini. . . . . . . . . . . . . . . . . . Welcome
Con ta bai. . . . . . . . . . . . How do you do
Mi ta bon, danki. . . I am fine, thank you
Pasa un bon dia . . . . . . . Have a nice day
Bon dia . . . . . . . . . . . . . . Good morning
Bon tardi . . . . . . . . . . . . Good afternoon
Bon nochi . . . . . . . . . . . . Good evening
Ajo. . . . . . . . . . . . . . . . . . . . . . Goodbye
Hopi Bon . . . . . . . . . . . . . . . Very good
Dushi . . . . . . . . . . . . . . . . . Dear/Sweet

---

As you become familiar with the language you will notice that several words have multiple spellings, with "c" and "k" used interchangeably (*cunucu* and *kunuku*). The same is true of "ñ" and "nj" (*saliña* and *salinja*).

## Time Zone

Atlantic Standard Time, which is one hour ahead of Eastern Standard Time, is in effect all year long.

## Newspapers/Broadcast Media

Both Curaçao and Aruba have English language dailies that feature international and local news. These are also available on Bonaire. Select stores and larger hotels carry *The New York Times*, *USA Today* and *The Wall Street Journal*, although they may be a couple of days old. There are radio broadcasts of the news in English and Dutch on all three islands. Hotels on Aruba and Curaçao, and several hotels on Bonaire have satellite television and carry CNN and other English-language programming.

## Telephones

Direct dialing to the United States and Europe is possible from all major hotels. AT&T's USA Direct Service is available. If you are calling any of the islands from the US, you must first dial the international access code, 011, then the country code, then the city code if applicable, and then the number. All numbers given in this book are local.

### Calling from the US

Aruba: 011-297 plus the local number.

Bonaire: 011-599 plus the local number.

Curaçao: 011-599-9 plus the local number.

# Aruba

If the thought of Aruba conjures up images of the palm-lined, sandy white beaches featured in Caribbean travel brochures, glitzy casinos and great shopping, you're not alone. Most first-time visitors to Aruba are attracted to the island for just those reasons. Sunny skies, cool breezes, and water temperatures averaging a fabulous 80° are ideal for the beach. They're just as ideal for diving, snorkeling, and windsurfing, all of which can be done from that very same beach.

Whether you stay at one of Aruba's in-town hotels or along the beach, you will be within easy walking distance of world-class dining, casinos and Las Vegas-style entertainment, along with great dance clubs, pubs and outdoor cafés. Travel between the lovely capital, Oranjestad, home to many of the finest shops in the Caribbean, and the beachfront hotels is just a short cab or bus ride away. Those who venture farther afield will be rewarded with championship golf at a course designed by Robert Trent Jones Jr., mysterious Indian caves, terrific diving, including the largest wreck in the Caribbean, and panoramic vistas of the island's rugged north coast.

Best of all, despite the fact that Aruba is one of the fastest growing destinations in the Caribbean, her Dutch-Caribbean charm promises to remain intact.

# Culture & Customs

## History

Although no written account exists, most assume that **Alonso de Ojeda** discovered Aruba in 1499 after leaving Curaçao in August and landing on Cape San Roman in Venezuela. It was from the shores of San Roman that he first set eyes on the then unknown island. Ojeda claimed Aruba for Spain, possibly without ever landing there.

## The First Inhabitants

At the time of its discovery, Aruba was inhabited by the peaceful **Caquetio Indians** of the **Arawak** tribe, who had been living there since the Stone Age. It is believed that the Caquetios, tired of living under the constant threat of attack by the more belligerent Carib Indians, immigrated to Aruba from the peninsula of Paragon in Venezuela. Today many of Aruba's towns, hills, coves, and caves still bear the names of the earliest Indian chiefs and warrior settlers, including Turibana, Guadirikiri, Camacuri, Andicuri, and Bushiri. Remnants of the Caquetio's fine craftsmanship and artistry still exist in cave paintings on Aruba's north coast and in the decorative motifs on shards of clay pottery which have been collected around the island. Unfortunately, with the arrival of the Spanish came the end of the Caquetio's quiet existence on Aruba. The conquistadors shipped them to Hispaniola to work in the gold mines as replacements for the island's native population, which had been exterminated by the Spanish.

Eleven years after its discovery, the Spanish turned Aruba into a large horse and cattle ranch. Some of the Indians who had been shipped to Hispaniola were brought back to work the ranch. The ranch never prospered.

## The 17th & 18th Centuries

In the mid-1630s, Peter Stuyvesant, director of the Rotterdam-based Dutch West India Company, conquered Aruba. As part of the spoils, he collected horses to use in raids against the Spanish on the Venezuelan coast and as payment for the damages caused by the Spanish in Bonaire during the 80 Year War for control of the three islands.

However, due to difficulties in maintaining regular communications with Curaçao, Aruba was left to her own devices, as was nearby Bonaire. Dutch military personnel maintained order on the island, but the Indians remained free. The Dutch West India Company began granting permission to a carefully selected few to settle and engage in commerce on Aruba. Oranjestad, named after Holland's reigning Royal House of Oranje, was founded during this period. With the weakening authority of the Dutch West India Company in the late 1700s, Europeans began immigrating to Aruba to settle permanently. Most were merchants from Curaçao. They were joined in the next century by Venezuelans fleeing the revolutions and counter-revolutions in that country.

*Another theory suggests that the Indians were brought back to Aruba by Juan de Ampues to help protect the Spanish Main along the Venezuelan coast.*

Aruba

*The first foreign settler in Aruba was Moses Van Salomon Levi Maduro.*

There was a short period of English rule lasting from 1805 to 1816.

## The 19th Century

While commerce on Curaçao was booming, Aruba's economy was quiet. For several years Aruba's main export was horses, primarily to Cuba and Jamaica. In 1824, the discovery of alluvial gold at Rooi Fluit on the northern coast marked the beginning of Aruba's gold rush years. Smelting works were set up in Bushiribana and Balashi. Though the amount of gold mined on Aruba would pale in comparison to other mines around the world, and the smelting works were eventually abandoned, gold's discovery provided the needed spark to the island's economy. For the next 100 years, gold, phosphate, cochineal, aloe, and the pods of the divi-divi used to make tannin for leather tanning, would be major exports. Thankfully, once the supply of gold dried up, aloe was there to replace it.

*Remains of the smelting works can be visited during a tour of the island. See page 107 for directions.*

★ **DID YOU KNOW?**

In the 1920s, Aruban aloe represented 70% of the world's aloe production and produced an annual income of $1 million, an enormous sum in the 1920s. Most of Aruba's aloe was shipped to England.

## The Oil Industry

Real prosperity came to Aruba in 1924, when the Standard Oil Company of New Jersey (Exxon) ended its search for a good seaport and stable government at the then sleepy village of San Nicolas, where it established a refinery to process oil from the Lake Maracaibo oil fields of Venezuela. Its Lago Refinery quickly became the world's largest and the island's primary source of livelihood. San Nicolas was transformed into a booming oil town. So dependent was the island on the refinery that its main thoroughfare, L.G. Smith Boulevard, was named for Lago's general manager. English gained prominence as a second language due to the large numbers of Americans who came to Aruba with the refinery.

*The large refinery had an output of 440,000 barrels a day.*

Aruba

The proverbial bottom fell out of Aruba's economy on March 31, 1985 when, due to reduced demand worldwide and refining overcapacity, the refinery was closed. Unemployment skyrocketed and Aruba's economy faced a downward spiral.

*In 1991, the refinery was reopened by the Coastal Oil Refining Company out of Texas.*

## Tourism Takes Over

Rather than give up, Aruba focused on its then secondary industry, tourism. Aruba's first tourists arrived aboard the *Tradewind* in 1957, the first cruise ship to dock in Oranjestad. It was soon followed by the Aruba Caribbean Hotel and Casino, which opened in 1959 and is now the Radisson. Tourism really began to develop in the mid-60s. To prevent the haphazard development that can spoil the beauty of an island as small as

Aruba, turning it into little more than a beach with a string of high-rise hotels, the government has implemented a carefully planned development program that emphasizes the preservation of Aruba's beautiful beaches and waters.

*The Spanish obviously did not look hard or long enough because gold was found on Aruba in 1834.*

> ★ **DID YOU KNOW?**
>
> Scholars have traced the origins of the word Aruba to the language of the Carib Indians, finding its roots in the words oruba or "well-placed," and in ora and oubao, which mean "shell." Another theory attributes the name to the Spanish conquistadors who, finding gold, referred to the island as oro hubo or "there was gold." This last option seems the least likely. When they first discovered Aruba, the Spanish had considered it, along with Bonaire and Curaçao, as one of the islas inutiles, or "worthless islands," since it appeared to lack the precious metals they were searching for.

## The People

Aruba's national anthem captures the friendly nature of the island's more than 93,000 inhabitants with the line, *"Grandeza di bo pueblo ta su gran cordialidad"* – "The greatness of our people is their great cordiality." Arubans are most often described as pleasant-natured, hardworking and well-educated. Their natural warmth and hospitality have even been recognized as national traits.

Forty nationalities live peacefully on this small island within an area of only 70 square miles. The truly native Aruban is of mixed Dutch, Spanish and Arawak Indian ancestry. While Dutch is the official language, its usage is eclipsed by Papiamento, which is spoken in the home, among friends and often in business. English and Spanish are taught in school.

## The Government

On January 1, 1986 Aruba seceded from the Netherlands Antilles to become a separate entity within the Kingdom of the Netherlands, now comprised of the Netherlands Antilles, Holland and Aruba. This was a surprise, as Aruba's separate status had been unanimously agreed to in March 1983 at a Round Table Conference of the partners within the Dutch Kingdom.

No longer managed by the Central Government of the Netherlands Antilles, Aruba enjoys direct contact with Holland and manages those internal affairs formerly managed by the Central Government. This includes aviation, customs, immigration, communications and other internal matters. Aruba's governor is appointed by the Queen of Holland for a six-year term to act as her representative. The role of the governor is entirely independent of the local governing body. Aruba's

Aruba

government is modeled after the central government of the Netherlands Antilles.

Though independent of Bonaire and Curaçao, Aruba's political status within the Netherlands is that of a commonwealth. Free to determine domestic policy, her cultural, political and defensive links to Holland and her sister islands are still strong.

## Festivals & Holidays

There are so many special events, tournaments and festivals on Aruba that your stay is almost guaranteed to coincide with something. Music and dance festivals, theater festivals, cultural expositions and sporting competitions are held at various times throughout the year.

## Annual & Special Events

**Bon Bini Festival:** Fort Zoutman hosts this weekly festival of Aruban arts and crafts, folkloric music and dance, and local foods on Tuesday evenings from 6:30 to 8:30 pm.

**Carnival:** Arubans spend the year preparing for this week of nonstop merrymaking, which comes to a close at midnight just before Ash Wednesday. See the following page for details.

**One Cool Summer:** From May through October, Aruba is filled with weekly street festivals, cultural events, outdoor concerts and friendly sporting competitions.

**Aruba Hi-Winds Windsurfing Pro-Am Grand Prix World Cup Event:** Every June windsurfers from around the world converge on Aruba to compete in this week-long competition.

**Deep-Sea Fishing Tournaments:** Throughout the month of October boats from Aruba, Curaçao, Florida and Venezuela compete in a series of tournaments hosted by the Aruba Nautical Club. For further information, contact Arend van Unen or Jossy Hunt of the Nautical Club, Barcadera Z/N (☎ 853022).

**Catamaran Regatta:** Every November since 1991 catamarans from Europe, Venezuela and the United States have been competing in this colorful week-long event held on Palm Beach.

For more information concerning these and other events held on Aruba, contact the Aruba Tourism Authority, ☎ 800-TO-ARUBA; or visit their website at www.arubatourism.com.

## Carnival

If you're hoping to be in Aruba for Carnival you'd better make your reservations well in advance, since Carnival season is one of the most popular times of year to visit.

Aruba's first Carnival was held in 1954, the year that Curaçao canceled its annual celebration in a show of empathy with Holland, which was suffering from the worst floods in its history. Just as they do now, many Curaçaoans spent the year following one Carnival season preparing for and looking forward to the next. Unable to face a year without a Carnival, several of Curaçao's carnivalists organized a celebration on Aruba. The rest, as they say, is history. What was originally reserved for a few social clubs is now an island-wide event.

Carnival unofficially gets underway in January with impromptu **Jump-ups** (nocturnal dancing free-for-alls) dotting the streets and countryside. Carnival spirits rise almost uncontrollably as residents put the finishing touches on their extravagant costumes and colorful floats. Just as in Curaçao, competitions for the official theme music, musicians and singers, and the election of the Carnival Queen precede the Grand Parade.

The **Lighting Parade**, organized by Aruba's oldest social club, the Tivoli Club, marks the beginning of Carnival. This is a week in which the tedium and worries of the rest of the year are replaced with merrymaking and dancing in streets filled with the joyous sounds of calypso, steel bands, Antillean tumba, Latin salsa and merengue.

*The Mummer King's ashes are distributed on Ash Wednesday.*

Children's parades and newer parades such as the **Roller Blade Parade**, **J'Ouvert** and the **4 am Pajama Parade**, lead up to the main event, the **Grand Parade**, through the streets of Oranjestad on the Sunday before Ash Wednesday. Revelers rest on Monday to prepare for Tuesday's **Old Mask Parade** and the traditional Burning of the Rey Momo, the Mummer King, which marks the end of Carnival and the beginning of Lent.

## National Holidays

Banks, the post office and government offices are closed on these days. Many shops and restaurants may also close.

New Year's Day . . . . . . . . . . . . . January 1
G.F. Betico Croes Day . . . . . . . January 25
Carnival Monday . . Mon. before Ash Wed.
National Anthem/Flag Day . . . . . March 18
Good Friday . . . . . . . . . . variable, as in US
Easter Monday . . . . . . . . variable, as in US
Queen's Day . . . . . . . . . . . . . . . . . April 30
Labor Day . . . . . . . . . . . . . . . . . . . May 1
Ascension Day . . . . . . . . . . . . May (varies)
Christmas Day . . . . . . . . . . . December 25
Boxing Day . . . . . . . . . . . . . . December 26

# Getting Here

Aruba is situated in the southern Caribbean, just 15 miles from the Peninsula of Paragon off the coast of Venezuela and 2,090 miles from New York. At 12° 30′ north and 70° west longitude, Aruba is the westernmost of the ABC Islands.

## By Air

Flights to Aruba land at the **Queen Beatrix International Airport** located on the island's southeast coast, five minutes south of the capital, Oranjestad. Several carriers offer regular non-stop service to Aruba out of New York (JFK International), Newark, Miami, Baltimore, Tampa, Amsterdam, Caracas, Puerto Rico, Sint Martin, Bonaire, Brazil and Colombia.

**American Airlines** (☎ 800-433-7300; www.aa. com) has daily nonstop service from JFK (10:45 am departure/3:10 pm arrival) and Miami (11:30 am departure/2 pm arrival), as well as flights out of Newark and LaGuardia with connections in Miami and Puerto Rico.

**ALM** (800-374-7747; www.airalm.com) flies to Aruba out of Miami on Thursdays, Saturdays and Sundays. Through its codeshare program with United Airlines, passengers flying on United from other US cities connect in Miami with the ALM flights. The codeshare fare is valid on direct flights only; reservations must be made through **United** (☎ 800-241-6522; www.ual.com). **Continental** and **Delta** also offer service to Aruba.

European can fly directly to Aruba via Holland aboard **KLM** (☎ 800-374-7747; www.klm.com) on Sunday, Monday, Thursday and Saturday.

In addition to the above, several charter flights are available from New York, Boston, Newark, Chicago, Washington DC, Houston, Philadelphia, Baltimore, Detroit and Canada.

## Via Cruise Ship

Aruba is among the most popular ports of call for cruise ships serving the Caribbean. The most exciting and luxurious trip is a transcanal cruise aboard Celebrity Cruise's ships. Aruba is also a featured destination on Celebrity's 10- and seven-

day southern Caribbean itineraries aboard the ul-
tra-elegant *Zenith*. Service and facilities aboard a
Celebrity liner are first-rate, and their cuisine
has received rave reviews. Cruise ships calling on
Aruba dock at the passenger terminal in
Oranjestad, steps away from shopping and restaurants.

# Orientation

Aruba is the smallest of the ABC Islands, covering an area of only 70 square miles. Not quite 20
miles long and extending six miles across at its
widest point, the entire island can easily be explored in a day or even a morning.

In-town hotels include the Sonesta Resort Hotel
and Sonesta Suites at Seaport Village, the island's largest shopping/entertainment complex.

Most of Aruba's hotels are located north of the
capital on the perfect strip of palm-lined, sandy
white beaches that extends for seven miles along
Aruba's southwest coast. Low-rise hotels dominate the section of beach closest to Oranjestad
known as **Eagle Beach**, while high-rise resorts,
most with casinos and nightclubs, are farther up
the coast on the section known as **Palm Beach**.
Many popular night spots and restaurants are in
this area as well.

**L.G. Smith Boulevard**, the main coastal road,
travels the coast north connecting Oranjestad
with the hotels and continuing all the way to the
island's northwest point, is known both as

**Kudarebe** and **California Point**. A recent arrival in this area is the Tierra del Sol Golf Course, a par 71 championship course designed by Robert Trent Jones. The calm waters of the south coast below the point offer excellent conditions for windsurfing and snorkeling. Offshore in the area known as Malmok is the German freighter *Antilla*, the largest wreck in the Caribbean.

Twelve miles below Oranjestad on the southeast coast, Aruba's "sunrise side," is **San Nicolas**, the second largest town on the island. Approaching the southeast tip, known as **Colorado Point**, or *Punta Basora*, are some lovely smaller beaches including **Baby Beach** and **Rodger's Beach**. Some of the island's best reef dives are located just north of San Nicolas at Savaneta and the area around the Spanish Lagoon. **Bachelor's Beach** on the windward side of the point is a mecca for windsurfers.

> ◎ **TIP**
>
> For a panoramic view of the island and nearby Venezuela head center island to Hooiberg or Yamanota Hill – at 617 feet – the highest point on Aruba.

In rugged contrast to the southern, or leeward coast, Aruba's windward coast is characterized by rocky shores and pounding surf, by-products of the trade winds blowing in from Africa. Dirt roads traverse the coast, known for its dramatic coral formations and wild beaches, where the crashing surf is best admired from afar. Just inland from

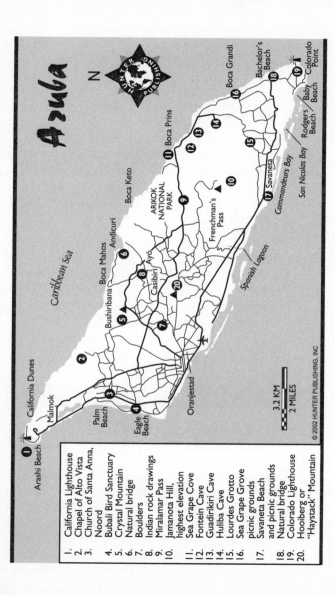

Aruba

1. California Lighthouse
2. Chapel of Alto Vista
3. Church of Santa Anna, Noord
4. Bubali Bird Sanctuary
5. Crystal Mountain
6. Natural bridge
7. Boulders
8. Indian rock drawings
9. Miralamar Pass
10. Jamanota Hill, highest elevation
11. Sea Grape Cove
12. Fontein Cave
13. Guadirikiri Cave
14. Huliba Cave
15. Lourdes Grotto
16. Sea Grape Grove picnic grounds
17. Savaneta Beach and picnic grounds
18. Natural bridge
19. Colorado Lighthouse
20. Hooiberg or "Haystack" Mountain

© 2002 HUNTER PUBLISHING, INC

the coast you'll find fascinating caves at Fontein, Guadirikiri and Huliba, where traces of Indian petroglyphs, centuries old, are still visible.

# Getting Around

## Finding Your Hotel

You should have no trouble finding your way through Aruba's Queen Beatrix International Airport. After passing through customs, you can hop a cab at the taxi stand just outside. Fares are calculated based on distance and are charged per cab, not per person. Fares to the Sonesta Resorts or Talk of the Town Hotel in Oranjestad should be under $10, while those to the hotels on Eagle Beach should be no more than $15. To the high-rise hotels on Palm Beach, it should be no more than $20.

## Car Rentals

Since rentals are popular on Aruba, if you're planning to rent a car for the duration of your stay, it is advisable to make arrangements for a car prior to your arrival. You may also get a better rate by doing so. When making hotel reservations ask if there is a car rental agency on the property. If so, you may be able to rent a car at the same time. Jeeps are especially popular and are a good idea if you'll be carrying dive equipment or plan on exploring the north coast. Though rates are more expensive, we prefer to rent from the larger international agencies since their cars tend to be newer and better maintained.

The following agencies have branches at the airport and/or offer free pick-up and delivery.

**AVIS:** Queen Beatrix International Airport, ☎ 825496; Kolibristraat 14, ☎ 828787 or 828617; Americana Aruba Hotel.

**BUDGET:** Queen Beatrix International Airport, ☎ 825423; Kolibristraat 1, ☎ 828600, fax 827212; Divi Tamarijn Beach Hotel and Divi Beach Resort.

**DOLLAR:** Queen Beatrix International Airport, ☎ 825651; Grenadaweg 15, ☎ 822783, fax 831237; Manchebo Beach Resort, ☎ 831237 or 826696.

**HERTZ:** Queen Beatrix International Airport, ☎ 824886; L.G. Smith Blvd. 142, ☎ 824545, fax 23012; De Palm Tours, Activity Desk, Holiday Inn, Americana Hotel, Manchebo Beach Resort, Divi-Divi Beach Resort, Divi Tamarijn Beach Hotel, Bushiri Beach Resort, Talk of the Town Hotel.

**NATIONAL:** Queen Beatrix International Airport, ☎ 825451, fax 838747; Tanki Leendert 170, ☎ 821967 or 824641; Holiday Inn.

**THRIFTY:** Queen Beatrix International Airport, ☎ 835335. Balashi 65, ☎ 855300/fax 850011.

In order to rent a car you must have a valid driver's license that has been held for at least 24 months. The minimum age requirement varies by agency and the type of vehicle you wish to rent, and can be anywhere from 21 to 26 years of age. Maximum age is 65-70 years of age. Payment can

Aruba

be made in cash or by credit card. However, if you pay by cash you may need to leave a $500 deposit. Most agencies offer unlimited mileage. Insurance is recommended, but will not cover you if you have been driving while intoxicated and get involved in an accident.

## Driving Hints

Driving on Aruba is on the right. Right-hand turns at a red light are not permitted. When driving in Oranjestad, pay careful attention to street signs since many streets are one way. The speed limit in town is 25 mph, and usually 35 mph in the countryside. When driving in the *cunucu,* or countryside, as well as in some residential areas, keep a lookout for goats and wild donkeys. Arubans are extremely friendly and outgoing, and Aruban drivers are no exception. As a result, they have a tendency to stop unexpectedly to say hello and chat with a friend.

If it does happen to rain while you're in Aruba, exercise caution when driving. Since rainfall is rare, grease, oil and dust tend to accumulate on the roads, making them extremely slippery when wet.

## Buses

Buses run between Oranjestad and the hotels on Eagle and Palm Beach all day long, including Sundays and holidays. The bus station in Oranjestad is located behind the government building on Zoutmanstraat. At only US $1.25, the fare is hard to beat. Ask at your hotel activity desk for schedule information or call **Arubus** at ☎ 827089.

## Motorcycles, Scooters & Bicycles

Two-wheelers are a great way to get around the island and are available at several agencies not far from the hotels. Avid mountain bikers will enjoy exploring the back roads of Aruba and the north coast. Your hotel activity desk should be able to make a recommendation or help you with arrangements.

Always check the brakes and tires, lights, etc., before riding away. And remember, just because you're on vacation doesn't mean you can throw caution to the winds. To rent a motorcycle or scooter you must be at least 18 years of age and have a valid driver's license.

Aruba

## Taxis

To call a cab, contact the central dispatch office at ☎ 822116 or 821604. Cabs do not have meters. Instead, fares have been fixed by the government. Ask the driver what the fare will be before getting into his cab. If you need transportation back to your hotel after dinner, you may request that a cab be called for you.

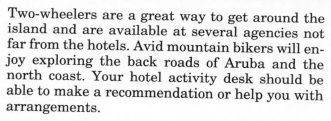

# Best Places to Stay

Happily, on Aruba you don't need to worry about paying a premium for a beachfront hotel since, no matter where you stay, you'll never be more than a few steps away from the beach. Most of Aruba's hotels are along the seven-mile strip of beach on the leeward (southern) coast above Oranjestad. Since 1986 the number of hotel rooms on the island has more than tripled, with options ranging from ultra-luxurious five-star resorts that will cater to your every whim, to all-suite accommodations with kitchenettes, or more traditional beach resorts and basic hotels.

*Lodging on Aruba is more expensive than on Bonaire & Curaçao.*

If you prefer a hotel with a laid-back atmosphere, try one of the low-rise hotels or all-suite resorts on Eagle Beach, the portion of the strip closest to town. But if it's glitz and glamour you're after, check into one of the high-rise resort hotels on Palm Beach, with their multiple restaurants, dazzling nightclubs and casinos, upscale boutiques and dramatic landscaping.

Regardless of where you vacation, an air-conditioned room is standard, as is a pool and, of course, watersports on the beach. Many hotels also have tennis courts and fitness centers. Mom and Dad will be happy to know that more and more hotels on Aruba are offering children's programs.

## Alive Price Scale

Our price scale is designed to give you a ballpark figure to plan with. It is based solely on the price of a double room during high season, which generally runs from mid-December to mid-April, though exact dates will vary by hotel. Keep in mind that rates fall sharply at other times, with significant variations from hotel to hotel.

Considerable savings may be had by taking advantage of special packages, such as those for honeymooners, divers and families. If you're planning on visiting during the off-season, you may do better by reserving with the hotel directly rather than through a reservation service or travel agent.

Breakfast and meals are generally not included in the rate, though most hotels do offer separate meal plans. A 17.6% service and room tax will be added to your room bill. All hotels described take major credit cards unless specifically noted.

Since we prefer to stay on the beach, we'll start with the hotels on Palm Beach and work our way to town.

### Accommodations Price Scale

Deluxe. . . . . . . . . . . . . . more than $250
Expensive . . . . . . . . . . . . . . $151-$250
Moderate . . . . . . . . . . . . . . . $100-$150
Inexpensive . . . . . . . . . . . . . under $100

Aruba

## Palm Beach

# HYATT REGENCY RESORT & CASINO
Palm Beach
J.E. Irasquin Blvd.
360 rooms
☎ 861234; fax 861682
In the US and Canada, ☎ 800-233-1234
www.hyatt.com
Deluxe

As you've come to expect from virtually any Hyatt, the Hyatt Regency is a showplace. Breathtaking both inside and out, 8,000 square feet of multi-level pools and lagoons wind through 12 beautifully landscaped beachfront acres on the island's northwest coast. The richness and colorful embellishments of traditional Caribbean architecture surround guests in an atmosphere of casual elegance. Soft trade winds gently blow through archways and terraces and magnificent vistas of the Caribbean are around every corner.

Dining is a pleasure at the Hyatt, which is vever short on ambience. Fashioned out of native island rock and overlooking the lagoon, the haunting splendor of Ruinas del Mar is a visual reminder of Aruba's gold mining past. For an evening of romance you'll long remember, dine at sunset aboard the Hyatt's catamaran. More casual dining is available all day long at the terraces, cafés or lounges, with their swim-up convenience and beachside ambience.

Rooms are flawlessly appointed. Recreational facilities include a modern health spa with tennis courts, and watersports available through Red

Sail Sports, a children's program. The Casino Copacabana offers gambling.

## ARUBA MARRIOTT RESORT & STELLARIS CASINO
Palm Beach
L.G. Smith Blvd., #101
413 rooms
☎ 869000; fax 860649
In the US & Canada, ☎ 800-223-6388
www.marriotthotels.com
Deluxe

Oversized guest rooms and spacious balconies overlooking the Caribbean are among the many pleasures awaiting guests at the Marriott. Five-star features include a lovely free-form swimming pool with waterfalls and swim-up bar, a spectacular beach, a fitness center, nearby golf and tennis, informal outdoor dining at the Seaview and fine Italian cuisine at the Tuscany restaurant. And Lady Luck is always around to tempt guests at the opulent Stellaris Casino. Next door is the Aruba Ocean Club, a Marriott Vacation Club timeshare, which has some apartments available for hotel use. They consist of one- and two-bedroom suites and are ideal for families.

*The Marriott is the newest five-star resort on the island.*

## RADISSON ARUBA RESORT & CASINO
Palm Beach
J.E. Irausquin Blvd. 81
386 rooms
☎ 866555; fax 863260
In the US & Canada, ☎ 800-333-3333
www.radisson.com
Expensive

Aruba's original resort, the Radisson, offers its guests unlimited opportunities for fun in the sun on and off its 1,500 feet along Palm Beach. Recre-

**Aruba**

ational offerings include swimming in the Caribbean or the Radisson's Olympic-size pool, water skiing, parasailing, catamaran sailing, snorkeling trips, sunset cruises, certified scuba instruction and dive trips, beach volleyball, bocci ball, and four lighted tennis courts, with professional instruction available. Professional massage therapy can be arranged at the Health and Fitness Center.

Dining options are just as plentiful. Caribbean-inspired French cuisine is served in elegant surroundings at **Bistro 81**. The **Laguna** features more casual dining, indoors or out, with a creative menu of Aruban, Caribbean and American-inspired specialties. The **Sunset Grill** is a favorite at lunch time as well as at sunset. Tropical refreshments, quick snacks and great conversation are always available at in the open-air lobby, while tropical drinks are tops at the **Beach Bar and Restaurant**. As if that weren't enough, ice cream and frozen yogurt served poolside at **Temptations** are nearly impossible to resist.

After-dark hours can be spent at the casino or enjoying one of the Radisson's nightly dinner shows. The guest relations department will be more than happy to recommend island attractions as well.

## HOLIDAY INN ARUBA BEACH RESORT & CASINO
Palm Beach
J.E. Irausquin Blvd. 230
600 rooms/8 floors
☎ 863600; fax 865165
In the US & Canada, ☎ 800-HOLIDAY
www.holiday-inn.com
Expensive

Taking advantage of its waterfront location on Palm Beach, the Holiday Inn offers its guests watersports galore, including parasailing, windsurfing, PADI certified diving, snorkeling and, of course, floats. Back on dry land, there's tennis, a modern fitness center, and hammocks that have been strategically placed throughout the beautifully landscaped gardens. A sports bar, nightclub and casino round out the entertainment. Dining options include American, Latin, Oriental and island cuisine. Rooms are comfortable and feature the standard amenities, including pay-per-view movies.

*Holiday Inn has many all-inclusive & honeymoon packages.*

## ALLEGRO ARUBA BEACH RESORT & CASINO

Palm Beach
J.E. Irausquin Blvd. 83
400 rooms
☎ 864500; fax 863191
In the US and Canada, ☎ 800-203-4475
www.allegroresorts.com
Deluxe

**Aruba**

Located on the strip at Palm Beach, the Allegro is a terrific value for young, active families. Kids between the ages of four and 13 can sign up for the Kid's Club, which will keep them happily entertained from 9:30 am to 5 pm, with a break for lunch. Meanwhile, mom and dad can sign up for snorkeling, scuba, windsurfing, sailing, water skiing or fishing with Red Sail Sports. The Allegro also has its own lighted tennis courts, volleyball beach pit, a modern exercise facility and as its centerpiece, a free-form fantasy pool with cascading waterfalls, built-in current, whirlpool spas and swim-up bar.

*Red Sail offers special sunset & moonight sails.*

Restaurants offer both casual and more formal dining. The Allegro has a small casino featuring roulette, craps, blackjack and slots, and a night-club.

## WYNDHAM ARUBA BEACH RESORT & CASINO

Palm Beach
J.E. Irausquin Blvd. 77
444 rooms
☎ 864466; fax 868217
In the US and Canada, ☎ 800-996-3426
www.wyndham.com
Deluxe

Formerly the Hilton, the Wyndham features a spacious beach area, a large free-form freshwater swimming pool, a shopping arcade, fitness center, three restaurants, and a casino. All rooms have a patio with an ocean view. However, not all directly overlook the Caribbean. To avoid disappointment, specify the type of view you want when making reservations.

## ARUBA GRAND BEACH RESORT & CASINO

Palm Beach
J.E. Irausquin Blvd. 79
186 Rooms; 35 rooms are one- or two-bedroom suites
☎ 863900
In the US, ☎ 800-345-2782
www.arubagrand.com
Expensive

Most of the rooms in this eight-story hotel are large with ocean views. There is an on-site PADI certified dive center that supplies all your needs. Golf arrangements can be made at the Tierra del Sol Golf course.

## Eagle Beach

### LA CABANA ALL-SUITE BEACH RESORT & CASINO
Eagle Beach
J.E. Irausquin Blvd. 250, PO Box 1012
441 suites
☎ 879000; fax 875474
In the US & Canada, ☎ 800-835-7193; in Holland,
☎ 31-47582409; fax 31-47582635
www.lacabana.com
Expensive

La Cabana is a terrific choice for families and fitness enthusiasts. Suites range from studios for one to two people all the way up to three bedrooms that will sleep six to 10. Parents can spend some carefree time on their own, leaving kids between the ages of five and 12 in the hands of the trained staff of Club Cabana Nana, where they'll play games on the beach, at the playground or in the pool, do arts and crafts, or listen to stories. Teens can join up with the Cabana Teen Club and hang out with their own crowd while windsurfing, playing billiards, snorkeling and participating in other supervised activities.

Of course, families can enjoy La Cabana's facilities together as well. Eagle Beach is a great place to start, with water skiing, diving, snorkeling, sailing, windsurfing, glass-bottom boat rides and catamaran cruises arranged through the watersports center. The oversized free-form swimming pool features a children's area with a slide and poolside whirlpools for the older folk.

*All La Cabana rooms feature TV, direct dial telephone, whirlpool, hairdryer, private patio or balcony, & in-room safe.*

Aruba

The Health and Racquet Club Center features advanced exercise equipment, including Lifecycle and Lifestep machines, free weights and circuit weight training equipment, as well as aerobics classes. Two racquetball courts, two squash courts, five lighted tennis courts, and men's and women's saunas round out the list of facilities.

La Cabana's long list of dining options – seven different places to get food – should satisfy even the most finicky kids. Or, if nothing but mom's cooking will do, all suites feature a fully equipped kitchenette. There's a mini-market conveniently located right on the premises.

## COSTA LINDA BEACH RESORT
Eagle Beach
J.E. Irausquin Blvd. 59
PO Box 1345
155 suites
☎ 838000; fax 836040
In the US & Canada, ☎ 800-992-2015
From Europe: InterConnect (Germany)
☎ 49-89-555-335; fax 49-89-523-2212
www.costalinda-aruba.com
Expensive

*Prices at Costa Linda are in the deluxe range, but we've categorized it as expensive since rooms are usually shared.*

Best for families and small groups, accommodations at the Costa Linda are limited to two- and three-bedroom suites. Each suite has a private balcony along with a fully equipped kitchen, baths with Roman tubs and separate showers, two televisions, and two direct dial telephones. In keeping with its name (which means "Beautiful Coast"), the Costa Linda is located on a 600-foot-stretch of the widest beach on the island, and also features a beautifully landscaped free-form tropical pool complete with whirlpools and even a small island at its center. Other facilities include lighted tennis courts, a fitness center and three restaurants offering snacks, casual and formal dining.

## BEST WESTERN MANCHEBO BEACH RESORT

Manchebo Beach
J.E. Irausquin Blvd. 55
POBox 4185
71 rooms
☎ 823444; fax 833667
In the US, Canada and Europe, Best Western at
☎ 800-5281234 or 800-223-1108
www.aruba-manchebo.com
Expensive

Rooms are spacious and overlook the beach or the resort's garden areas. The on-site dive shop features certified instruction and equipment rental for snorkeling, diving and underwater photography. Tennis is available next door and the Alhambra Bazaar and Casino are just across the street.

The outdoor, beachside Pega Pega Bar & Grill features festive entertainment nights, sumptuous buffets and island shows. A gourmet menu is featured at The French Steakhouse (see page 80).

## TAMARIJN ARUBA BEACH RESORT

Eagle Beach
J.E. Irausquin Blvd. 41
236 rooms
☎ 824150; fax 834002
In the US, Canada and Europe, ☎ 800-554-2008
www.tamarijnaruba.com
Expensive (all-inclusive)

The Tamarijn is adjacent to the Alhambra Bazaar and Casino. Guests enjoy unlimited watersports (applies to non-motorized equipment only), including snorkeling, windsurfing, Sunfish sailing, and float mattresses, with instruction for beginners. There's also tennis, beach volleyball, mountain bikes, a fitness area, and unlimited food and drink. Nightly entertainment, including special theme nights, add to the fun.

## BUCUTI BEACH RESORT
Eagle Beach
63 rooms
PO Box 1299
☎ 831100, fax 825272
In the US, ☎ 800-223-1108
www.bucuti.com
Moderate to Expensive

The Bucuti Beach Resort offers its guests four acres of powder-white sand. Virtually all rooms overlook the beach and are well-equipped, with a microwave oven, refrigerator, mini-bar, cable television, in-room safe and a king- or queen-size bed. Complimentary coffee and tea service provided.

The Pirate's Nest Restaurant offers romantic dining inside a 17th-century Dutch galleon that has seemingly washed up on the beach. A live steel band makes sunset happy hour extra special and helps put you in the mood to limbo under the stars.

## Close to the Beach

## THE MILL CONDOMINIUM RESORT
330 J.E. Irausquin Blvd.
PO Box 1012
200 rooms
☎ 867700; fax 86727; in US, ☎ 800-992-2015
www.millresort.com
Moderate to Expensive

The Mill offers you a choice of hot tub, kitchenette or both. This two-story condominium resort features adjoining suites that can be rented separately or grouped together to create your ideal accommodation.

Variations include the Royal Den, which features a mirrored bath area with hot tub and a king-size bed; junior suite with kitchenette, sitting area, patio and full-size bed; and a studio, which has a full kitchen and dining area, a bath with a shower and a sofa bed. You can combine a studio with a Royal Den to create a one-bedroom suite or go all the way and put three rooms together to create a two-bedroom suite that can comfortably accommodate six people.

The Mill is just steps away from Palm Beach as well as nightlife and restaurants. Rooms are in low-rise buildings set amidst tropical gardens and there are two free-form swimming pools with swim-up bar. Tennis and an exercise room and sauna are also on the premises.

### STAUFFER HOTEL
J.E. Irausquin Blvd.
370 rooms
PO Box 4185
☎ 860855; fax 860856
Moderate

You'll find a solid value at the Stauffer Hotel, which offers clean, comfortable rooms in a convenient location not far from casinos, nightlife and shopping. Excursions, car rentals and watersports can be arranged through the reception desk.

**Aruba**

## AMSTERDAM MANOR BEACH RESORT
J.E. Irausquin Boulevard 252
PO Box 1302
73 rooms
☎ 835600; fax 823820
In the US, ☎ 800-766-6016
www.amsterdammanor.com
Moderate

Europeans dominate the guest list at the Amsterdam Beach Resort. Located across from Eagle Beach, this 72-room low-rise resort features Dutch hospitality and colonial charm. Studio, one- and two-bedroom suites are available. Each has a terrace or balcony and a fully equipped kitchen or kitchenette, cable television, direct dial telephone and an in-room safe. Facilities include a restaurant and bar, swimming pool with waterfall, a laundry room, and a mini-market. Baby sitting services can be arranged. Hotel activities include a manager's cocktail party with bikini and carnival show, BBQ Night, Aruba Night and sunset happy hour. Two afternoon sessions of poolside diving instruction are included in the room rate.

## Oranjestad

## SONESTA RESORTS
## AT SEAPORT VILLAGE
Oranjestad
L.G. Smith Blvd. 82
300 rooms/250 suites
☎ 836000; fax 825317
In the US and Canada, ☎ 800-SONESTA
www.arubasonesta.com
Deluxe

The Sonesta Resorts at Seaport Village offer the best of all that is possible on Aruba. Guests have fabulous shopping, terrific dining, a marina and the island's most spectacular casino right at their doorstep. A unique downtown location puts many of the island's historic and cultural attractions within walking distance.

*Free water taxi service departs from the lobbies of the Sonesta Suites and Sonesta Resort every 20 minutes from 8 am to 8 pm.*

Best of all, Sonesta guests have their own private paradise, Sonesta Island. A mere eight minutes away by launch, this 40-acre tropical retreat of beaches, quiet coves and mangroves is reserved exclusively for Sonesta guests.

The island's six beaches are considered by many to be among Aruba's finest, and include a remote strand for naturalists and the very special Honeymoon Beach (with a masseuse available). Snorkeling couldn't be any better; there are crystal clear waters and coral reefs all around. A branch of Red Sail Sports right on the island caters to divers and watersports enthusiasts, providing equipment rental, boat dives and PADI certified dive instruction, along with windsurfing (with instruction), kayaking, banana boats, Sunfish, and water skiing. Of course there's always the option of a float bed or a lounge chair strategically placed under a palm.

**Aruba**

Activities aren't limited to sand and sea. There's a hiking trail around the island for nature lovers, as well as a fitness center and tennis court. As for refreshments, the **Seabreeze Bar** serves cool tropical drinks all day long and will even deliver them to your lounge chair. The **Seabreeze Restaurant** offers snacks, ice cream and lunch from 11 am to 4 pm. If you run out of suntan lotion or need some good beach reading, not to worry. The island even has its own sundries shop.

*Sonesta Resort & Casino was named a Superior 1st Class Hotel by the Official Hotel Guide. Sonesta Suites received the Interval International's Superior Service Award.*

Back on the mainland, guests have the option of staying at either the Sonesta Resort or Sonesta Suites. Both feature luxurious accommodations, decorated in soft Caribbean colors with all the amenities of a five-star resort. They have landscaped outdoor swimming pools with swim-up bars and poolside restaurants. Sonesta's Just Us Kids Program of supervised activities for children, daytime and evening, is available at both. Sonesta Suites offers the added benefit of an ultra-modern, fully furnished kitchenette, ideal for families or travelers who want more freedom. Those who prefer to avoid the kitchen altogether can dine elegantly at **L'Escale**, one of Aruba's finest restaurants; enjoy international cuisine in a more casual setting at **The Brasserie**; or head for the restaurants and sidewalk cafés at the **Seaport Marketplace**.

In between trips to Sonesta Island and shopping at Seaport Village, casino-goers can try their luck at the Crystal or Seaport Casinos. Deep-sea fishing charters and sailing trips can be arranged at the marina. There's music and dancing every night except Sunday at the Desires Nightclub, located off the main lobby at the Sonesta Resort.

## CARIBBEAN TOWN RESORT HOTEL
Oranjestad
L.G. Smith Blvd. 2
63 rooms
☎ 823380; fax 832446
In the US, Canada and Europe, Best Western at
☎ 800-528-1234 or 800-223-1108
Moderate

A casual international atmosphere and highly personalized service are among the many reasons to opt for this low-key resort, a 15-minute stroll from downtown Oranjestad. Rooms surround a lovely palm-fringed courtyard with a swimming pool, hot tub, and the poolside **Moonlight Bar and Grill**, a popular meeting place among guests and residents alike.

The more formal **Talk of the Town Restaurant**, a member of the Chaîne des Rôtisseurs, is open for dinner only and serves superb continental cuisine. Across the street is Talk of the Town's private Surfside Beach Club. It features a freshwater pool and two hot tubs, as well as diving, snorkeling, fishing and equipment rental from Aruba Aqua Sport.

**Aruba**

## More Resorts

Other resorts include the **Divi Aruba Beach Resort**, J.E. Irausquin Blvd. 45, on Eagle Beach (US, ☎ 800-554-2008; www.diviaruba.com) and **Casa del Mar Beach Resort** next door (☎ 827000; fax 829044; www.casadelmar-aruba.com).

### ⊚ APARTMENTS

If you prefer to economize on accommodations and splurge in other areas, consider renting an apartment. Call the **Marriott Vacation Club**, ☎ 800-VILLAS-9, for details.

# Best Places to Eat

As lovely as the island is, it's not surprising that many talented chefs have settled in Aruba. Falling in with the island's relaxed atmosphere, they've tempered their classical training with local ingredients to create a wealth of innovative new dishes.

With nearly limitless fine dining options available, it's no wonder that many consider Aruba the gastronomic center of the Caribbean. Restaurants range from casually elegant to island casual, and they offer an eclectic selection of cuisines from around the world. To help you experience the best the island has to offer, we've put together a list of those restaurants we believe best represent Aruba's culinary prowess.

Dinner reservations are advisable and even required at most restaurants, especially during high season. If you're planning to dine at one of the more elegant restaurants, you should dress appropriately – a sports jacket for men and a dress or pants suit for women. Ties are optional and rarely necessary. Otherwise, casual resort wear will be fine.

A 10-15% service charge will usually be added to your bill. If not, a 10-20% tip, according to the quality of the service you received, is appropriate. Keep in mind that the service charge does not go directly to your waitperson but is also used to cover restaurant costs. Tipping is at your discretion.

## Dining Price Scale

Expensive . . . . . . . . . . . . more than $35
Moderate . . . . . . . . . . . . . . . . $25-$35
Inexpensive . . . . . . . . . . . . . . under $25

## Fine Dining

### CHEZ MATILDE
Havenstraat 23
☎ 834968
French cuisine
Noon-2:30 pm; 6-11 pm
Expensive
Proper attire (jacket & slacks; no beachwear)

A member of the Chaîne des Rôtisseurs since 1989, Chez Matilde enjoys a well-earned reputation as one of the finest restaurants in the Caribbean. It is located in an immaculately restored and luxuriously decorated 19th-century townhouse, offering guests an evening of fine dining in a relaxed setting. Guests may dine indoors in one of two intimate dining rooms separated by restored stone walls, or in the glass-enclosed Pavilion amidst tropical gardens and fountains.

The menu features classic French cuisine with an emphasis on seafood and imported cultured beef, accompanied by a carefully selected wine list. The luncheon menu offers a lighter selection of Cuisine Naturelle. As an introduction to the dining experience that awaits them, guests are invited to savor a welcoming glass of Kir Matilde, a delightful blend of champagne, strawberry liqueur,

Aruba

crème de banane and fresh strawberries at the brass-lined bar. Exemplary service.

## L'ESCALE
Aruba Sonesta Resort & Casino
☎ 836000 (reservations advised)
Contemporary tropical cuisine
6:30-11 pm
Expensive
Proper attire is required

The innovative menu at L'Escale artfully introduces the culinary flair of the Caribbean into classic and progressive continental cuisines to create a dining experience unlike any other. You'll find dishes such as pan-roasted jerk quail with a papaya-tamarind glaze and funchi fleurons; filet of salmon served on a bed of spinach with a light curry-spiced citrus and avocado salsa; baked Caribbean grouper crusted with plantains and served with a poblano pepper medley, sweet onion and a touch of Madame Jeannette; châteaubriand for two served with Caribbean vegetables; and calypso chicken, boneless chicken breast stuffed with king crab meat, wild rice, corn and chives and served with a morel mushroom sauce. These are among the many offerings guaranteed to dazzle your taste buds.

L'Escale features an elegant setting above the Crystal Casino, overlooking the waterfront at Oranjestad. Music is provided by a Hungarian string orchestra. L'Escale also features a delightful Sunday brunch. Diners actually go into the kitchen to place their omelette order with the chef.

## GASPARITO
Gasparito 3
☎ 867044
Aruban cuisine
5:30-11 pm; closed Sunday
Expensive

Gasparito features award-winning local cuisine served in an authentic *cunucu*, a countryside home just minutes from the high-rise hotels along Palm Beach. When they opened their restaurant, gracious hosts Joyce Barsels-Daal and Gladys Croses hoped to create an atmosphere in which island guests could appreciate the local cuisine and culture.

The dining room doubles as an art gallery, displaying works by talented local artists. Many of the pieces on display are for sale. Don't hesitate to ask if you see something you're interested in.

The menu features steak, seafood and local specialties, including *keshi yena*, *stoba di bestia* (goat stew) and the Aruban Combo – a platter of fish cakes, *kari kari* and chicken stew. Be sure to try the *pan bati*, Aruban pancakes made with salt, sugar, corn and flour.

## VENTANAS DEL MAR
Tierra del Sol Golf Course
☎ 860879
International cuisine
11:30-3 pm; 6-10:30 pm.
Expensive

Golfers and non-golfers alike should plan a meal at Ventanas del Mar in the clubhouse at the Tierra del Sol Golf Club. Lunch is best, or arrive before sunset so you will see the spectacular golf course and Caribbean views. Managed by Hyatt

**Aruba**

Aruba, NV, who refuse to be outdone by the scenery. The dining room is lovely and the menu features superbly prepared international dishes.

## VALENTINO'S
Caribbean Palm Village Resort
☎ 862700 (reservations recommended)
Italian cuisine
6-11 pm; closed Sunday
Expensive

Dining at Valentino's is an occasion, so be sure to dress appropriately. It's in a separate building at the Caribbean Palm Village Resort, and features different dining areas, including one reserved especially for honeymooners. Pastas are homemade in the downstairs kitchen and you can watch the chef at work upstairs. The Italian region where each dish originated is noted on the menu.

## Local Cuisine

## OLD CUNUCU HOUSE
Palm Beach 150
☎ 861666
Continental cuisine
6-11 pm; closed Sunday
Moderate

Dining is a pleasure in this restored Aruban homestead built more than 80 years ago. Executive Chef Ligia Maria has created a menu featuring an inspired combination of international and local cuisine. Seafood lovers should try the seafood Palm Beach – lobster, fish, shrimp, scallops and squid – served in a delightful cream sauce flavored with wine and flamed with Pernod. The filet of beef fondue for two features small cuts of beef that diners prepare themselves in sizzling hot oil with a variety of sauces. The Old Cunucu's specialty coffees are a terrific ending to a meal in this lovely traditional setting.

## MI CUSHINA
Noord Cura Cabai 24
(just off the main road to San Nicolas)
☎ 848335 or 845871 (reservations advised)
Noon-2 pm; 6-10 pm; closed Thursday
Inexpensive to moderate

You just may get the chance to try iguana soup at Mi Cushina ("My Kitchen"). Home-style Aruban cooking features local favorites such as *stoba di bestia chiquito* – stewed goat or lamb with *pan bati* (pancake-like bread) and fried fish with *funchi* (cornmeal prepared like polenta), as well as other traditional seafood, meat and chicken dishes. The museum-like setting is a delight, with its coffee bag ceiling, wagon wheel light fixtures, antique photographs and assorted tools and kitchen utensils. Among the paraphernalia is a display of equipment used to produce aloe vera up until the 1930s.

## BRISAS DEL MAR
Savaneta 222
☎ 847718
Seafood
Noon-2:30 pm; 6:30-9:30 pm; closed Monday
Inexpensive

Located in the fishing village of the same name, Brisas del Mar has been a local favorite for years. The restaurant itself was once a fisherman's hut. Not surprisingly, fish prepared island-style dominates the menu. *Keri keri*, fish sautéed with vegetables and fresh herbs, is a personal favorite. The

**Aruba**

*sopi di pisca*, fish soup, is equally delicious. You'll dine in a lovely, open-air setting by the Caribbean.

## Extra Special

**CHARLIE'S BAR**
Zeppenfeldstraat, 56
San Nicolas
☎ 845086
Seafood
Noon-9:30 pm; closed Sunday
Bar is open 10 am-midnight
Inexpensive, credit cards not accepted

*Charlie's Bar is a must!*

An island institution, Charlie's is the watering hole in San Nicolas, the second largest town on the island. Its former owner is legendary, gone but never forgotten, and now his son carries on in his spirit. Hollanders Charlie and Marie Brouns founded Charlie's Bar in 1941.

*In keeping with tradition, staple your business card to the wall at Charlie's Bar. Mine is there!*

When the Second World War made San Nicolas a boom town, Charlie's became a favorite hangout for seamen, contractors, and refinery and harbor workers. Needless to say, they were a pretty rough crowd. Nowadays, artists, musicians, writers and island visitors have replaced the old crowd, but the bar is full of memorabilia from the old days. Charlie's is famous for its special atmosphere and known for its creole cooking, shrimp, squid, overstuffed sandwiches and cold beer.

**BOONOONOONOOS**
Wilhelminastraat 18a
☎ 831888
French and Caribbean cuisine
6-10:30 pm
Moderate

Boonoonoonoos is a self-proclaimed "Caribbean Bistroquet." They must be referring to their hybrid French/Caribbean cuisine. Innovative dishes from islands across the Caribbean are served in a warm and friendly atmosphere. House specialties include Jamaican jerk ribs made from a 300-year-old recipe, curried chicken Trinidad, *keshi yena*, *carne con papas Domenique* (sliced tenderloin served in a creole sauce), roast chicken Barbados (prepared with coconut and plantain), and mountain chicken (frog legs). The historic mansion that houses this bistroquet was the first to export aloe oil extract to England.

## THE PIRATE'S NEST
Bucuti Beach Resort
L.G. Smith 55-B
☎ 831100
Steaks and seafood
7 am-11:30 pm
Moderate

Will the real Henry Morgan please stand up? It's hard to imagine a more delightfully Caribbean setting than aboard this 17th-century Dutch galleon washed ashore on Eagle Beach. Come for the Sunset Happy Hour, with entertainment provided by a steel band, followed by dinner under the stars and a stroll along the beach.

*There's no air conditioning inside at the Pirate's Nest, so a table on deck is best.*

## THE MILL
J.E. Irausquin Blvd. 330
☎ 862060
International cuisine
6-11 pm; closed Sunday
Moderate

Another favorite among repeat visitors, The Mill has a well-deserved reputation for excellence. Entreés are expertly prepared using only the fin-

Aruba

est quality US steaks, chicken and veal, along with fresh fish and seafood from the Caribbean. If you choose the hearty Dutch-style pea soup, a house specialty, as an appetizer, order something light as a main course so you'll have room for one of The Mill's outrageous chocolate desserts.

The Mill is an authentic Dutch windmill imported from Holland and reconstructed on Aruba. The Dutch theme is artfully carried over into the dining room, with beautiful Dutch antiques, decorative tiles and paintings.

## LE PETIT CAFE
Emmastraat 1
☎ 826577
International cuisine
11 am-11 pm; closed Sunday from noon-3 pm
Moderate

*There is another Le Petit Café in Playa Linda next to the Holiday Inn.*

As charming as its name, this lovely restaurant offers shady outdoor dining or you can eat indoors in an air-conditioned dining room. Steak and chicken dishes are served on heated rocks as part of the last stage of cooking. Known as "Romancing the Stone," it keeps the meat warm while allowing diners to make sure that their meal is cooked to taste. In addition to a variety of steaks, the menu features local specialties and plenty of seafood.

## PAVAROTTI
Palm Beach 17A
☎ 860644
Italian and Argentinean grill
6-10 pm
Moderate

*Pavarotti and the Old Cunucu House are run by the same people.*

Everyone in your dinner party should find something to their liking at Pavarotti. The generous menu offers delicious Italian cuisine along with steaks and chops grilled Argentinean-style. There's a hot and cold antipasto bar for starters, or you can make it a meal.

## EL GAUCHO
Wilhelminastraat 80
☎ 823677
Argentinean steaks and seafood
11 am-2:30 pm; 5:30-11 pm; closed Sunday
Moderate

Though the pampas of Argentina and the Caribbean are thousands of miles apart, El Gaucho has managed to bring them a little closer. Reminiscent of La Cabaña, one of the best steakhouses in Buenos Aires, El Gaucho serves authentic Argentine parrillada prepared exclusively with beef imported from Argentina. You'll also find a selection of seafood dishes. Clever renovations have transformed this Aruban townhouse into an Argentine *estancia*.

## WATERFRONT CRABHOUSE
Seaport Marketplace
☎ 835858
Seafood
Noon-4 pm; 5:30-10:30 pm
Moderate

If you enjoy vacationing in the Caribbean but prefer the cooler waters of the Atlantic when it comes to seafood, the Waterfront Crabhouse will be just right. Atlantic swordfish, sea scallops, tiger shrimp, mahi mahi, sole and yellow tuna are flown in in direct from the Boston Fish Market every morning. Live Maine lobsters are shipped in three times a week. Seasonal specialties such as Maryland soft shell crabs have not been overlooked, or have locally caught red snapper and grouper been left off the menu.

## THE FLAME
Noord 19A
☎ 864688
Steaks and International cuisine
6-10:30 pm; closed Wednesday
Expensive

European-born owner Dieter Fischer brings a world of culinary experience to your table. After graduating from culinary school he toured the kitchens of the great hotels and restaurants of Europe, the world's most luxurious cruise lines, and even spent some time at the Four Seasons in New York, all the while picking up recipes and dreaming of opening his own restaurant. Now his guests at The Flame share in the dream and reap the benefit of his experience, enjoying succulent tournedos forestière, châteaubriand, flaming steak Diane and other house specialties. Reserve ahead and request a window table in the garden.

## KOWLOON
Emmastraat 11
☎ 824950
Chinese cuisine
11 am-10 pm
Moderate

Since 1972, Kowloon has been serving Aruba's best Chinese cuisine, featuring the regional specialties of Shanghai, Hunan, Canton, Szechwan and Peking. The selection of seafood platters seems endless, as do the various fish, fowl, pork and beef dishes prepared in an infinite array of sauces. The regular and seafood rice tables are equally appealing. Kowloon is located downtown just two blocks from Seaport Village.

## OKURA DYNASTY
Havenstraat 25, downtown
☎ 821349
Japanese and Thai cuisine
Noon-2:30 pm; 6-11 pm; closed Sunday
Moderate

The Okura Dynasty is best known for the Japanese steaks and seafood which the teppanyaki chef artfully prepares at your tableside hibachi. Also not to be missed are the sushi, the Okura steamed fish and other Thai specialties.

## DON CARLOS
L.G. Smith Blvd. 83
☎ 836246
Italian cuisine
Noon-11:30 pm
Inexpensive

Located across the street from the Seaport Village Mall, Don Carlos offers live music daily. The menu features pizza and other Italian specialties, as well as salads, seafood, chicken and steak.

## CAFE THE PADDOCK
L.G. Smith Blvd. 13
☎ 829021
Dutch café cuisine
11 am-11 pm; bar is open until 2 am
Inexpensive

This true-to-life Dutch café is located next to the fruit market on the waterfront in Oranjestad. Offerings include burgers, grilled sandwiches, omelettes, salads, and full dinners, including a pita bread with beef platter, a shrimp platter, the catch of the day, and a mixed grill platter. An all-you-can-eat spare rib special is featured on Wednesday evenings. There are two-for-one happy hours Tuesday night from 11 pm to midnight and Sunday afternoons at 5 pm.

## THE FRENCH STEAKHOUSE
Best Western Manchebo Beach Resort
☎ 823444
Daily, 6-11 pm
Expensive

Consistent quality has made The French Steakhouse a favorite of repeat guests to Aruba. The menu features churrasco steak, filet mignon and beef stroganoff; red snapper and chicken dishes are also available. Flaming desserts are a special finale to a delightful meal.

## LA PALOMA
Noord 39
☎ 874611
Italian seafood
6-11 pm; closed Tuesday
Inexpensive
Proper attire is required.

Hearty eaters will meet their match at La Paloma. If you like your pasta piled high, this is the place for you. Otherwise, consider sharing. House specialties include fried fish stuffed with shrimp and mushrooms, veal Marsala, chicken cacciatore, and a 12 oz. lobster fra diavolo.

## PAPARAZZI
J.E. Irausquin Blvd. 368
☎ 863659
Open daily, noon-midnight
Moderate

Located in front of Stauffer Hotel, this new Italian restaurant hosts an open kitchen where you can view your pizza or pasta dish being prepared. You can dine indoors or alfresco with live music. There is no AC but fans seen to do the trick. Next door is **Salt & Pepper**, a Dutch pub serving tapas and sangria. Both Paparazzi and Salt & Pepper stay open late.

Two familiar chain restaurant names are **Hooters** and **Benihana,** and both have branches on the main stretch of Eagle Beach. Their popularity is tested by the usual crowds of regulars.

## Fast Food

**Dushi Bagels** serves fresh authentic New York bagels with cream cheese spreads, no less. It's located in the Playa Linda Beach Resort between the Hyatt and Holiday Inn hotels.

Also scattered around town, you'll find branches of **Subway**, **Nathan's**, **Dunkin' Donuts**, **Mc-Donalds** and **KFC**.

# Sunup to Sundown

Many are those who come to Aruba planning to spend their days lazing on the beach or catching up on their reading. But, with so many other attractions vying for their attention, they're likely to return home with that bestseller still unread. Not far from every beach chair the crystal clear waters of the Caribbean beckon, offering ideal conditions for swimming, diving, windsurfing, sailing and a myriad of watersports.

Moving off the beach, championship golf is just a few miles away. Rare is the hotel that's without a tennis court. And if it's time for a break from Aruba's constant sunshine, you can experience the island's past in the museums of Oranjestad, explore Indian caves, or run amok in casinos and some of the finest shopping in the Caribbean.

## Beaches

The divi-divi tree, on a beautiful white sandy beach against a clear blue sky and turquoise sea, is Aruba's signature. Of course, those ever-present trade winds are just as hard to forget. While the divi-divi is quirky and fun to look at, the beach is what you'll long for after you've returned home. You'll have no problem finding the seven-mile strip of Palm Beach, Eagle Beach, et al. – a wide, palm-lined, sandy white stretch of beach that's in more Caribbean brochures than you could ever hope to count. Chances are your hotel is on this stretch. But you shouldn't let perfection keep you from discovering the many smaller beaches scattered along the leeward (southern) coast or from admiring Aruba's rugged windward side.

*Don't forget the sunblock. Those cooling trade winds make it easy to forget just how strong the sun really is.*

## Along the Strip

There's no lack of creature comforts on the seven-mile strip of virtually perfect beach with gentle surf and fine white sand that starts at **Punta Brabo**, just north of Oranjestad. All of Aruba's hotels and watersports outfitters are located here.

Most hotel facilities on the beach, including bars, restaurants and restrooms, are available to non-guests.

**Manchebo Beach:** Gentle surf and a broad expanse of powder white sand characterize this portion of the strip, starting at Punta Brabo and stretching between Druif Bay and Eagle Beach. The Manchebo Beach Resort is here. Topless bathing is permitted.

**Eagle Beach:** Gentle surf and endless miles of powdery white sand make this one of the most beautiful beaches of the Caribbean. Ideal for watersports; several outfitters are located here.

**Palm Beach:** As a symbol of the purity of their marriage, newlyweds sprinkle sand from Palm Beach on their threshold. Calm waters create ideal conditions for swimming.

**Arashi Beach:** The northernmost beach on the leeward coast, Arashi is located between the village of Malmok and the California Point. Calm, clear waters and gentle currents are optimal for snorkeling and diving. They make for great underwater visibility. This is an ideal shore dive for novices. Obviously, conditions are excellent for swimming too.

## South of Oranjestad

**De Palm Island:** As a consolation for those who aren't staying at the Sonesta, De Palm Tours operates its own island just off the coast, not far from the Spanish Lagoon. Coral formations and abundant marine life just offshore offer fine opportunities for snorkeling and diving. Guests can

*Special theme nights with music & dancing under the stars are also featured on De Palm.*

also explore the fascinating depths of the Caribbean aboard the *Atlantis* submarine. Also on the island are four restaurant/snack bars and plenty of beach-side hammocks. Transportation to and from your hotel is included. For more information, ☎ 24400.

Most of the following beaches have a refreshment stand, but no comfort facilities.

**Spanish Lagoon**, **Savaneta Beach** and **Commandeurs Baai:** The waters here are among the best on the island for diving and snorkeling. The beaches provide a lovely setting for a seaside picnic.

**Bachelor's Beach:** Also known as **Boca Tabla**, this, along with nearby **Boca Grandi**, is the favored hangout for experienced windsurfers. The shallow lagoon nearby is ideal for swimming and snorkeling. It is known as the "Grapefield" because of the grape trees growing on the sand dunes there.

**Baby Beach:** Aptly named, Baby Beach is a favorite of families with young children. The calm, shallow waters (no more than four to five feet deep) and powder-white sand are ideal for tots. Older kids will enjoy snorkeling in the small channel, which is loaded with beautiful coral heads. There is a refreshment stand but no facilities. Baby Beach is located on the southern point in the area known as Seroe Colorado.

**Rodgers Beach:** Popularly known as **Salina**, Rodgers Beach is west of the lagoon at Baby's Beach. The surf is slightly rougher, but conditions are still fine for swimming. Rodgers Beach also has a snack bar, but no changing facilities.

The dramatic beaches along the northern or windward coast, with their pounding surf and often rocky shores, are beautiful. However, even when the water seems relatively calm, discretion and the powerful undertow dictate that swimming be reserved for the southern coast. But you can still enjoy Aruba's northern beaches.

Sand dune surfing is a favorite pastime at **Boca Prins**. Surfing is best done sans board in jeans and sneakers.

**Dos Playa** nearby offers beautiful vistas. Andicuri Beach, a black stone beach, set on a deep cove just below the Natural Bridge and not far from Rancho Daimari, is considered Aruba's most beautiful secluded beach. It, and Boca Grandi, in the area known as Grapefield, are the only beaches on the north coast that are safe for swimming.

## Diving

Though overshadowed by Aruba's other attractions, namely beaches and casinos, diving and snorkeling are certainly worthwhile here. The waters off Aruba are home to thousands of tropical fish in all the colors of the rainbow, including stingrays, eagle rays, yellowtail snappers, parrotfish, queen angelfish, groupers, horse-eye jacks and a host of others. Aruba's reefs feature an endless variety of coral in all shapes and sizes, such as tube sponges, seafans, anemones and gorgonians. Wrecks make up a good portion of Aruba's dive sites. Included among them is the

German freighter **Antilla**, the largest wreck in the Caribbean.

With water temperatures in the 80s and visibility averaging 100 feet, or sometimes even 150 feet, the calm waters off the south or leeward coast are ideal for beginners. And since many dives are at depths of only 30-60 feet, novice divers won't feel cheated. Dives include the reef at **Mangel Alto**, located between Oranjestad and San Nicolas, known for its unusual coral formations and an abundance of colorful tropical fish; the waters off **Baby Beach** on the eastern part of island; **Spanish Lagoon, Commandeurs Baai**; and **Malmok** near the north coast. Only the most advanced divers should attempt the rough waters of the north coast.

## Dive Operators

One of Aruba's most reputable dive operators is **Red Sail Sports**. They offer Discover Scuba Dive Courses, a full curriculum of PADI certification courses and specialty courses. One- and two-tank boat dives and night dives are offered aboard the 38-foot **Vista Mar**, which features a freshwater shower and spacious dive platform. Prices include tanks, weights, fruit and juices. Rental equipment is available. Red Sail Sports centers are located at many of the major hotels, including Sonesta Island, the Americana, the Marriott and the Hyatt and downtown in the Seaport Marketplace. Advance reservations can be made through your travel agent or with Red Sail Sports (☎ 861-603; in the US 800-255-6425; www.redsail.com).

In addition to Aruba, Red Sail Sports Centers are located in the Bahamas, Grand Cayman, and Hawaii.

## Dive Sites

We've selected dive sites that are suitable for novice to intermediate divers as well as snorkelers and that are relatively easy to get to, either as shore or boat dives. It goes without saying that it is best to dive with an experienced dive operator. Traveling down the leeward coast starting at California Point, the following are among Aruba's most noteworthy dive sites.

### *CALIFORNIA* WRECK
Boat dive
Advanced

The rough waters off the northwest point make this dive suitable for advanced divers only. Located at depth from 30-45 feet, large coral formations surround the wreck and there is no shortage of colorful fish.

### ARASHI REEF
Shore dive
Beginners
Snorkeling

Located just below California Point, the calm waters and great visibility make the Arashi Reef an ideal shore dive for first-timers and a great refresher for more experienced divers who haven't been out in a while. This garden of brain coral, large star corals, and sea fans is one of Aruba's loveliest.

### *ANTILLA* WRECK
Boat dive
Beginner/advanced
Snorkelers
Excellent night dive

Locally referred to as the "ghost ship," this German freighter is the largest wreck in the Caribbean and Aruba's most popular attraction. Partially exposed, it reaches a maximum depth of 54 feet and is thickly covered with sponges and coral. Giant tube sponges also grow here. Large compartments make it a fairly uncomplicated wreck dive and safe for beginners. Residents include snappers, angelfish, groupers, grunt fish, clams and lobsters.

### MALMOK REEF
Shore/boat dive
Beginner/advanced
Snorkelers

Malmok Reef descends to a maximum depth of 70 feet. It's covered with colorful barrel sponges and brain and leaf corals. You'll spot plenty of stingrays and huge lobsters, too.

### *TUGBOAT* WRECK
Boat dive
Intermediate/advanced

The *Tugboat* is a favorite of underwater photographers. The drop-off starts at 40 feet and is covered with brain, star and sheet coral. The boat is on the bottom at 90 feet. Green moray eels and sting rays are its known inhabitants. Eagle rays pass through from time to time.

### KANTIL REEF
Boat dive
Intermediate/advanced

Another much-photographed dive, the Kantil Reef shelf starts at 40 feet and drops steeply to 110 feet. The shelf is covered with giant-sized brain corals as well as star, leaf and sheet coral.

Plant life includes seafans and gorgonians. Yellowtail snappers, tiger groupers, moray eels, and manta rays make their home here. Eagle rays are occasionally seen in the area.

## DANTCHI'S DELIGHT
Boat dive
Beginners

The slope, which ends at 100 feet, is covered with elkhorn coral in the shallower water and sponges as it descends. It is home to a diverse and fascinating population of moray eels, snappers, and schools of horse-eye jacks. If you're lucky, you may spot a sea turtle. This is another dive favored by underwater photographers.

## PLONCO REEF
Boat dive
Intermediate/advanced

Just below Dantchi's Delight, the reef crests at 20 feet and descends to 100 feet. Giant corals predominate. This reef is home to a large population of green moray eels. Large lobsters may be seen here as well.

## SKALAHEIN
Boat/drift dive
Advanced

The best drift dive site on Aruba, Skalahein slopes to a depth of 120 feet. Brain, star, fire and black coral cover the slope. Barracudas and manta rays are frequently seen in the area.

Aruba

## MANGEL HALTO REEF
Boat dive
Advanced

The reef slopes to 110 feet, ending in a magical garden of deep water gorgonians, sea anemones, and tube and vase sponges, tended by octopi, seahorses and yellow tails.

## BARCADERA REEF
Boat dive
Intermediate/advanced

Sea fans and corals sway in the current at this lovely dive located off De Palm Island. The reef crests at 20 feet and drops to 80 feet.

## PUERTO CHIQUITO
Boat dive
Intermediate/advanced

Nicknamed "snapper city." Manta rays also frequent this area, along with the occasional turtle. An incredible seascape of star, pillar, flower, fingerleaf and sheet corals make this one of Aruba's most memorable dives. It starts at 20 feet and reaches bottom at 80 feet.

## COMMANDEURS REEF
Boat/shore/drift dive
Intermediate/advanced

A colorful assortment of fish, including French and queen angelfish, groupers, grunts and snappers gliding through the sheet and leaf corals on the slope, make this a beautiful dive. The reef is home to crab, lobster and squid. Runners and barracuda pass through occasionally.

## *PEDERNALES* WRECK
Boat dive
Beginner/advanced/snorkelers

After being torpedoed by a German U-boat, this US oil tanker managed to limp home to the refinery. There, the center piece was cut out and the remaining fore and aft portions sealed together. The tanker went on to the Normandy Invasion. Groupers and angelfish now swim around the center piece, which includes the remains of entire cabins. You'll find interesting coral formations here as well.

## BABY BEACH REEF
Shore dive
Beginners
Snorkelers

An easy dive for beginners, the reef starts at 20 feet and gradually slopes to 60 feet. Elkhorn and sheet coral cover the slope, which is populated by crab, lobsters and squid.

## Dive Sites on the Northern Coast

Aruba's northern coast offers spectacular diving, which is best attempted only by the most advanced divers. Even then you should not attempt these dives on your own but go with an experienced dive master who is familiar with the site. Divers who brave the rough seas and strong currents to reach **Cabez Reef** will dive amidst numerous schools of barracudas, amberjacks, rainbow runners, sting rays and a host of other tropical fish. The dive at the **Natural Bridge** features fantastic black and soft corals and giant barrel sponges. Both dives are accessible from shore only.

## Other Underwater Delights

Non-divers need not miss out on the wonders hidden beneath the Caribbean. They can experience the beauty of Aruba's marine life in air-conditioned comfort aboard the *Atlantis* submarine or the *Seaworld Explorer*.

### ATLANTIS SUBMARINE
Seaport Village Marina
☎ 886881
www.atlantissubmarines.com

*The* Atlantis *has received Aruba's Artousa Award for the most outstanding tourist attraction & the International Incentive Quality Award four years in a row (1992-1995).*

Passengers aboard the coast-guard-approved *Atlantis* submarine descend to depths seen only by the most advanced divers. Approved to 150 feet, the *Atlantis* explores the fascinating sponge gardens and coral formations of the Barcadera Reef, including sights found only in deeper waters. There are 26 large viewports, each two feet in diameter, and an oversized 52-inch picture window in the front of the vessel. Expert narration identifying marine life and explaining the functioning of a living reef is provided throughout the hour-long voyage. The cabin is pressurized and air conditioned.

During the two-hour experience passengers will learn about Aruba from above and below the water. The trip starts at the Seaport Marina, on board the catamaran *Dorado* and travels 30 minutes along the southeast coast to where the *Atlantis* is docked. All participants receive a certificate after completion of the dive. Reservations must be made in advance. Tickets are $74 for adults and $37 for children.

## SEAWORLD EXPLORER
The Holiday Inn Pier
☎ 862807
See your hotel activities desk for reservations.

If you're still not ready to don mask and fins and aren't comfortable with the idea of being totally submerged, the *Seaworld Explorer* is a wonderful alternative. More than just a glass-bottom boat, this 49-foot semi-submarine was developed in Australia to investigate the Great Barrier Reef. Unlike a submarine, it does not submerge. Instead, passengers descend to the window-lined observatory in the vessel's hull, five feet below the surface. There, in air-conditioned comfort, explore the fascinating coral formations and exotic marine life of the Arashi Reef and the German freighter *Antilla*, Aruba's most famous wreck. Tickets are $29.

*Great for kids!*

**Aruba**

## Sailing

Aruba's constant trade winds provide near-perfect conditions for sailing, both for beginners and experts. It goes without saying that the less experienced should stick to the leeward side, (west and south coasts of the island) while experts will want to venture windward.

## Parasailing

Parasailing is an exhilarating way to get a bird's eye view of Aruba. Several operators offer it, including **Pelican Tours** (☎ 831228; www.pelican-aruba.com) and **Red Sail Sports** (☎ 861603; www.redsail.com). Both are on Palm Beach.

## Windsurfing

One week out of every summer the waters off Aruba are awash in brightly colored sails as hundreds of board sailors from around the world compete in the annual **Hi Winds Pro-Am Windsurfing Tournament**. Part of the Professional Boardsailing Association's Grand Prix World Cup Tour since 1988, this week-long tournament features several different events, including the Jibe Slalom, the Speed Slalom, a Moonlight Race, and the killer 64-kilometer "Round the Isle" race, made all the more grueling by the rough wind and wave conditions on the windward side of the island. Since it is scheduled to coincide with optimal conditions as determined by a careful study of the moon, wind and tides, tournament dates vary every year. If you'd like to visit Aruba during the event, contact the Aruba Tourism Authority for schedule information, ☎ 800-TO-ARUBA; or visit their website at www.arubatourism.com.

Aruba has become a mecca for serious (and not so serious) windsurfers, who are attracted by the constant trade winds, that average between 18 and 27 knots, and the wide variety of locations and wave changes found throughout the island. Experienced sailors enjoy the challenging conditions at Bachelor's Beach and the slalom board area on Manchebo Beach. Fisherman's Hut Beach, with its shallow water and calm winds, provides the perfect environment for beginners.

Outfitters that specialize in windsurfing equipment rentals and instruction include: **Divi Winds Windsurfing & Watersports Center**, J. E. Irausquin Blvd. 47 on Eagle Beach, between the Divi and Tamarijn Resorts (☎ 824150, ext. 623); **Roger's Windsurf Place**, L.G. Smith Blvd. 472 in Malmok (☎ 861918); and **Sailboard Vacations,** Windsurf Village, L.G. Smith Blvd. 462 (☎ 861072). Most major watersports centers offer rentals and instruction.

## Sailing Trips

There is no shortage of sailing trips and you can choose from a variety of vessels. Except for dinner and sunset cruises, most include stops at favorite snorkeling sites, such as the wreck of the *Antilla*. Snorkel equipment as well as refreshments and/or buffet or barbecue lunches are provided. Sites visited and departure times usually vary by day. Most operators require that you reserve a day in advance.

You and no more than 14 other guests will enjoy a day of luxury aboard the **S.Y.** *Wyvern II*, a 54-foot sailing yacht with teak decking and a beautiful interior. Substantially more expensive than other cruises, their day-cruise includes open bar service, gourmet lunch, and the use of snorkel, scuba and fishing equipment. Private day- and week-long charters to Bonaire and Curaçao are available. The *Wyvern II* docks at the Seaport Marina, where you can meet Captain Gerard Van Erp and his crew evenings from 6 pm to 8 pm. For more information and reservations, ☎ 930032.

Aruba

## Weddings at Sea Aboard the Wyvern II

Captain Gerard van Erp will perform a civil wedding in the waters outside Aruban territory. Both bride and groom must have a valid passport and be over 18 years of age. Following the ceremony Captain van Erp will provide the couple with a wedding certificate and a copy of the ship's registration. Upon returning home, the couple must register the certificate with the proper authorities. Since requirements concerning the legalization of wedding documents issued by the captain of a seagoing vessel in international waters vary by jurisdiction, you should check on such regulations prior to making arrangements with Captain van Erp. For more information, contact Aruba Marine Services N.V., Seaport Marketplace #204, PO Box 4104 Aruba, attention Captain Gerard van Erp; ☎ 839190; fax 839197.

*Civil weddings will only be performed in Aruba itself if one of the partners is a resident of Aruba.*

**Red Sail Sports** (☎ 861603) offers a variety of different cruises, ranging from a Morning Snorkel Buffet Sail to a Starlight Sail aboard ***Balia***, a 53-foot racing catamaran. Most mornings at 10 am, the 78-foot classic sailing yacht ***Mi Dushi*** (☎ 828919/823513) departs from the Aruba Palm Beach Resort Pier headed for the wreck of the *Antilla*. *Mi Dushi* also offers a Sundown Snorkel Safari featuring snorkeling, calypso music and an open bar a few nights a week.

*Balia means "to dance" in Papiamento.*

*For fun evening party cruises, see the* After Dark *section.*

Morning departures aboard the **Octopus** start with beverages and homemade baked goods, followed by two snorkeling stops and a buffet lunch. The *Octopus* also offers daily afternoon sails and two sunset sails a week. Reservations can be made by calling ☎ 833081 between 8 am and 9 pm. On a Snorkeling Sail aboard the 42-foot trimaran **Sea Venture**, you'll experience three different types of sites with stops at the Arashi elkhorn reef, Boca Catalina sponge reef and the wreck of the *Antilla*. Contact **De Palm Tours** for reservations (☎ 824400; www.depalm.com).

## *Aruba Catamaran Regatta*

Aruba's Catamaran Regatta is the largest race of light sailcraft in the Caribbean. Every November since 1991 Aruba has hosted this colorful, week-long event in which over 50 avid sailors from Europe, primarily Holland, followed by Belgium, Germany and Austria, compete in Hobie Cats, Prindles, Nacras, Darts and Olympic Torpedoes. Ruud Reij, a former catamaran racer from Holland, started the event after he recognized that Aruba offered optimal conditions for racing. The constant winds and smooth waters off the leeward coast are ideal for catamarans, and Aruba's fine sandy beaches offer easy launching and soft landing.

Since races take place close to shore on Palm Beach, there's no need for binoculars. Lucky spectators can board the VIP boat for an even closer view.

You don't have to be a participant, or even know one, to enjoy the regatta. For some, the best part of each day's events is the daily happy hour on Palm Beach where the Regatta is held. Do a good job mingling and you should find yourself with invitations to many of the parties held during the week.

## Deep-Sea Fishing

An extensive list of fish, including Atlantic gamefish, populate the waters just eight to 10 miles offshore heading toward Venezuela. While you're almost guaranteed a catch, you will definitely have a good fight. It's been said that fish off the coast of Aruba are fatter and stronger than most since they're able to feed better. You'll find blue marlin in the deep waters off the north coast. Heading toward Venezuela, you'll fish for barracuda, bonito, mahi mahi (known locally as dorado), kingfish, sailfish, shark, tarpon, tuna, wahoo and red snapper.

*The clean water & no overfishing produce an abundant food supply.*

A number of captains offer full- and half-day charters, with tackle, bait, food and refreshments usually included in their rate. Your hotel activities desk should be able to make arrangements for you, or contact **Pelican Tours** (☎ 831228/824739 or fax 832655).

## Watersports Galore

The calm waters off Eagle and Palm Beach are ideal for all types of watersports. Outfitters along the beach offer everything from Hobie Cats and

Sunfish to kayaks and paddleboats, tube and banana boat rides, or the basic water mattress. Most beachfront hotels have their own watersports center. If not, try **Red Sail Sports** (☎ 861603) on Palm Beach or the **Pelican Watersports Center** on the beach at the Holiday Inn Hotel.

## Golf

As any true golfer will tell you, it never rains on the golf course. That's practically guaranteed on Aruba.

With temperatures in the low 80s and very few, if any, rainy days, conditions could not be any better for golf than they are on Aruba, though some may object to the constant trade winds. The opening of the **Tierra del Sol Golf Course** in 1995 has made Aruba an ideal destination for those planning a golf vacation.

The 18-hole, par-71 championship course was conceived by Robert Trent Jones Jr., whose skillful design is equaled only by his commitment to land preservation and enhancement. The course is bordered by water on two sides with spectacular Caribbean views and desert vistas at every hole. The highest green is 98 feet above sea level. With multiple tees to accommodate varying levels of play, the course will challenge even the most accomplished golfer without completely frustrating determined beginners.

Ingeniously designed to maximize the unusual topography of Aruba's northwest tip, giant native cacti, divi-divi trees, rock formations, clusters of natural grasses and flora have been carefully incorporated into the landscape. In the planning stages, environmentalists were consulted to ensure the preservation of natural wildlife. An irrigation system was constructed so as not to disturb a bird sanctuary. The irrigation system functions independently from the island's water supply. Surprisingly lush fairways are juxtaposed against a desert landscape. At one point, the course was redesigned so as not to disturb the habitat of the rare burrowing owl, which lives in ancient caves in the coral rock not far from the sixth green. The fifth fairway runs alongside a saltwater marsh inhabited by wild egrets.

The course is the centerpiece of a luxurious country club-style community featuring low-rise residential estates, a health club, two swimming pools, eight tennis courts, and a clubhouse that is home to the pro shop and the spectacular Ventanas del Mar restaurant. Facilities also include a driving range, putting green, and a separate chipping area with sand traps. Tee times can be arranged through your hotel activities desk, or call the pro shop directly at ☎ 867800. Equipment rentals are available. Greens fees are $115 before 3 pm and $75 after.

A less pricey option is the nine-hole course at the **Aruba Golf Club** in San Nicolas. The uniquely designed course includes 20 sand traps, five water hazards, and 10 greens, to allow for 18-hole play. Greens are oiled sand, and goats are among the hazards you'll encounter. Facilities include men's and women's locker rooms with showers and lockers, a clubhouse with a bar, and a practice green and driving range. Equipment is available for rent. Greens fees, including caddie, are under $30 for 18 holes. For starting times and further information, contact the Aruba Golf Club in San Nicolas (☎ 842006).

Located behind La Cabana Beach Resort & Casino is **Joe Mendez Miniature Adventure Golf** (Sasakiweg, ☎ 876625), an elevated 18-hole miniature golf course surrounded by water. Paddleboats and bumper boats are also available for rent. Open 4 to 11 pm.

## Tennis

To avoid the blazing midday sun, tennis is best played in the early morning or late afternoon and evening. Most hotels have their own courts and often offer equipment rentals and instruction as well. Non-hotel guests are usually permitted use of the courts for a fee, though hotel guests have priority.

Aruba also boasts its own world-class tennis center. Designed by Stan Smith Design International and Aruba's SHS Design, the **Aruba Racquet Club** has eight lighted courts, an exhibition center court, pro-shop, swimming pool, fitness center offering aerobics classes, and a bar/restaurant. Open from 8 am to 9 pm, the Racquet Club is located in the Palm Beach area at Rooi Santo 21. Call ahead for reservations (☎ 860215).

## Horseback Riding

A fitting way to experience Aruba's desert landscape is on horseback, especially when your ride takes you through Arikok National Park for a refreshing swim in the natural pool. **Rancho Del Campo** (☎ 820290) and **Rancho Daimari** (☎ 860239) offer just that. Beginning and experienced riders are welcome. **Rancho El Paso** offers comfortable country and beach rides on paso fino horses, which are known for their smooth gait (☎ 873310). All three ranches provide transportation to and from your hotel. The cost is reasonable, approximately $25 an hour.

## Bowling

Bowling is popular and quite competitive on Aruba. In fact, local teams are often invited to compete internationally.

The **Eagle Bowling Palace** on Pos Abou (☎ 835038) has 12 lanes, all of which are completely computerized.

## Suggested Island Tour

Like many of your fellow guests, when you arrive on Aruba you'll check into your hotel, drop your luggage in your room, and step out onto the beach, thinking to yourself, "When you've found paradise, why leave?" That seven-mile strip of perfect beach makes it all too easy to forget that there's more to see in Aruba. You owe it to yourself to slip away for at least a morning and explore the rest, much of which is nothing like the beach you're standing on.

More akin to the American Southwest, Aruba's desert-like landscape has little in common with the lush tropical foliage and rain forests you'll find on the islands of the northern Caribbean. Instead, its countryside, known as the *cunucu*, is a fascinating world of aloe fields, abandoned gold mines, grotesque rock formations and mysterious Indian caves.

You'll drive past lovely cottages in the countryside, painted with colorful decorations. Those patterns are not mere ornamentation, but hex designs with ancient superstitious meanings. Just like the hex designs of the Pennsylvania Dutch, they are carryovers from the earliest settlers who used them to protect their homes from misfortune. Be sure to keep a lookout for wild donkeys or goats; they often venture out into the road, oblivious to the oncoming traffic.

Aruba

## HIGHLIGHTS

◎ Snorkeling at **Arashi Beach**.

◎ A seaside picnic at **Andicuri**.

◎ A refreshing swim in the **Natural Pool** at Boca Keitu.

◎ The view from the top of **Jamanota Hill**.

◎ A cold Amstel at **Charlie's Bar**.

The drive can easily be completed in a morning, but you may want to pack a picnic lunch and make a day of it. Snorkelers and divers should pack their gear since several of the best shore dives are along this route. You may be doing a lot of walking and possibly some hiking in the national park, so sneakers or sturdy sandals are a good idea. As always, be sure to bring plenty of water and sunscreen, as well as a hat.

Heading north out of Oranjestad on the coastal road, you'll travel along Aruba's seven-mile strip of wide white beach, the first portion of which is Punta Brabo on Druif Bay, before coming to the resorts on Eagle Beach.

Across from the Wyndham Hotel is the **Bubali Bird Sanctuary**, where hundreds of migrating birds stop to rest during their annual trek be-

---

### Aruba Driving Tour

*Leeward Coast Heading North*
1. Oranjestad
2. Eagle Beach
3. Bubali Bird Sanctuary
4. Palm Beach
5. Fisherman's Hut (windsurfing)
6. Malmok
7. Arashi Beach (great snorkeling)
8. Cudarebe Point
9. California Lighthouse & Dunes; Tierra del Sol Golf Course

*Heading South from the Point*
10. Church of Santa Ana
11. Chapel of Alto Vista
12. Seroe Plat (Crystal Mountain)
13. Bushiribana
14. Boca Mahos
15. Natural bridge
16. Andicuri Beach
17. Ayo (rock formation)
18. Casibari (rock formation)
19. Hooiberg (Haystack Mountain/ scenic viewpoint)
20. Arikok Nat'l Park/Boca Keitu
21. Jamanota Hill (highest point)
22. Boca Prins/sand dunes
23. Fontein (Indian caves)
24. Guadirikiri (Indian caves)
25. Huliba Cave & the Tunnel of Love Cave
26. Boca Grandi
27. Bachelor's Beach
28. Punta Basora/Colorado Point Lighthouse (SE point of island)

*Heading Up the Southern Coast toward Oranjestad*
29. Baby Beach
30. Rodgers Beach
31. San Nicolas
32. Commanders Bay
33. Savaneta
34. Spanish Lagoon
35. Frenchman's Pass

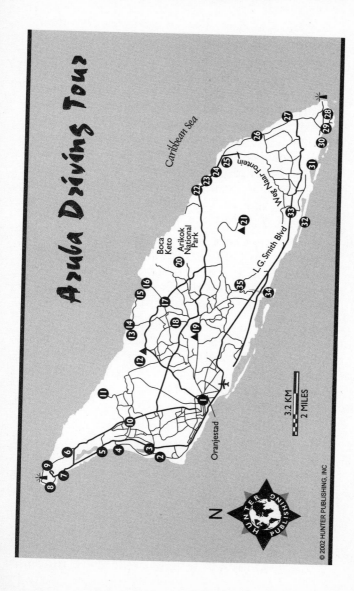

Aruba

© 2002 HUNTER PUBLISHING, INC

tween the Americas. The sanctuary has a working windmill.

Back on the coastal road, you'll continue along the sandy expanse, which underwent a second name change at the Wyndham Hotel, and is now **Palm Beach.** Just beyond Palm Beach is the area known as **Fisherman's Hut**, or *Hadikurari*. Shallow waters make this one of the world's most popular places for windsurfing. The next section of beach is **Malmok**, where several years ago an archaeological dig unearthed a fascinating assortment of ancient Indian artifacts – artwork, burial jars, pottery and utensils.

*Malmok is also the name of the village across from the beach.*

In the distance across the Caribbean you may see part of the hull of the German freighter *Antilla*. Scuttled at the outbreak of the Second World War, it is the largest wreck in the Caribbean and one of Aruba's most popular dive sites.

*Warning: Only advanced divers should attempt the* Antilla *dive due to the strong currents and choppy waters.*

Snorkelers and divers should set aside an hour or two for **Arashi Beach**. Gentle currents, fantastic visibility and a spectacular assortment of colorful corals and tropical fish have made it a favorite of snorkelers and novice divers.

As you near the turnoff to the northern coast, it should become readily apparent that rocky shores and wild surf have replaced the wide beaches and gentle seas of the southern coast. A lovely vista of high sand dunes set against the green fairways of the Tierra del Sol Golf Course and a distant lighthouse announce your arrival at the northwest point of the island, **Cudarebe Point**. The dunes and lighthouse are named California after the SS *California*, which sank offshore here in 15-30 feet of water. Many would agree that the *California*

*Fairly distant from shore, the California is accessible by a boat only. Caveat: Do not attempt to swim out to the wreck.*

deserved its fate, since it received and apparently never responded to the SS *Titanic*'s distress signal nine years prior to its own demise. The wreck of the *California* remains in its final resting place.

The par-71 18-hole championship **Tierra del Sol** golf course (see page 99 for more details) is the centerpiece of Aruba's first master-planned community. It features low-rise residential estates, a health club, two swimming pools and eight tennis courts. The **Ventanas del Mar** restaurant in the clubhouse offers panoramic views of the back nine and Caribbean.

*Ventanas del Mar is a lovely place to stop for lunch or a drink. Appropriate dress required. See page 71 for more information.*

Follow the inland road through the scrubby *cunucu,* or countryside, to the **Church of Santa Ana** (in Noord). Its elaborately carved oak altar, dating back to 1850, is the work of the Dutch artist Van Geld. It is an excellent example of neo-gothic design and won an award in Rome in 1870. Another small road climbs to the **Chapel of Alto Vista**, a popular destination for those seeking peace and contemplation. Located on the rocks that tower above the windward coast, it was built by Aruba's first Spanish missionary, Domingo Antonio Silvestre, in 1750. It is a pilgrimage church and is popularly referred to simply as the Pilgrim's Church. The stations of the cross are marked on the winding road that leads to it.

Heading east toward the windward coast, you'll reach **Seroe Plat, Crystal Mountain**, or Kristal Berg, in Dutch, which offers yet another scenic view. Abandoned gold mines are also in this area. Continuing to the coast, you'll reach the ruins of the gold smelter at Bushiribana which, as most visitors agree, looks very much like a pirate's fort.

**Aruba**

Travel the rugged north shore to the **Natural Bridge**, the largest of eight such coral formations on the island where the sea has battered the rocky cliff to form a bridge. It measures 100 feet long and is 23 feet above sea level, making it the highest coral formation in the Caribbean. The Natural Bridge is between Boca Mahos and Andicuri Beach, a black stone beach on a deep sandy cove. **Andicuri** is a fine setting for a seaside picnic and one of the few places on the north coast which is safe enough for swimming. Not far from here is **Rancho Daimari**. Dating back to the 17th century, it was one of the earliest coconut plantations in the Caribbean. The ranch's current owners raise international champion paso fino horses. They offer trail rides through Arikok National Park with a stop at the Natural Pool. They also operate a small bed and breakfast.

*Some compare Casibari to a mythical giant's playground.*

Double back to the inland road and then continue along it to the grotesque-looking diorite rock formations at **Ayo** and then **Casibari**. The remains of Indian rock drawings are still visible at both. Climb the stone steps at Casibari for a panoramic view of the island. The Casibari Snack Shack features live Aruban folkloric music Sunday afternoons from 11 am to 3:30 pm.

*Hooiberg means "haystack mountain."*

Just beyond Casibari is the **Hooiberg**, a cone-shaped, 541-foot volcanic rock formation located at the center of the island. On a clear day you can see the Venezuelan coast from the top. After a rainfall, the Hooiberg will be suddenly covered with the brilliant yellow flowers of the *kibra hasha*. Also at the Hooiberg, you'll find an Indian rock garden, tropical birds and a small island museum.

From the Hooiberg, head to the **Arikok National Park**. Hikers and naturalists will want to spend time in this 2,350-acre national park, which was founded by the Netherlands Antilles National Park Foundation, or STINAPA, in 1972. Marked hiking trails and scattered winding paths lead to Indian caves complete with hieroglyphics and a typical island cottage, or *cunucu*, as it is called in Papiamento. If you prefer riding to hiking, arrange for a horseback tour of the park at Rancho del Campo or Rancho Daimari. A must while you're in the park is a drive or hike through the lunar landscape en route to a refreshing swim in the natural pool at **Boca Keitu**.

After leaving the park, get on the road leading back toward the windward coast. For the best view of the island, take a detour to **Jamanota Hill**. At 617 feet, it is the highest point on Aruba. Luckily, you can drive all the way to the top. The road to the coast leads to the small inlet known as **Boca Prins**, where the pounding surf has created the bridge formation known as "Dragon Mouth." Though the water is too rough for swimming, many come to this beach, known as Playa Prins, to slide down the dunes.

Just south of the park is a series of caves. The first, **Fontein,** contains ancient Indian drawings on its ceilings. Aruba's only freshwater well is at the Chinese garden nearby. This is one of the few places on the island where fresh vegetables are grown. Next en route is **Guadirikiri**, a large network of caves inhabited by bats. The sections closest to the entrance are illuminated by natural skylights. **Huliba Cave**and the underground passage known as the **"Tunnel of Love Cave"**

*Most fruits and vegetables are imported from Venezuela.*

Aruba

*Watch for wild donkeys as you drive along.*

should be your next stop. Continuing along the coast, you'll come to **Boca Grandi** and **Bachelor's Beach** just beyond it. This is the favored area of experienced windsurfers.

Before reaching the turnoff to the southern coast, you'll pass another natural bridge, where just a short distance away the waves have also beaten a cave out of the rocky coastline. Then at Punta Basora, the easternmost point of the island, the road turns onto the southern coast. Your landmark here is the **Colorado Point Lighthouse**. Before reaching San Nicolas, you'll pass **Baby Beach** and **Rodger's Beach**. Continue toward **San Nicolas** on the southeastern shore. Aruba's largest town, it grew up around the opening of the oil refinery in 1924. Workers from 56 countries came and many remained, giving the area its international flavor and decidedly Latin spirit. It is famous as the home of **Charlie's Bar**.

Heading back toward Oranjestad on the leeward coast, you'll pass the **Savaneta Beach** and picnic area. Most of Aruba's fishermen live and work in this area, leaving from the Savaneta Beach. Inland are the **Savaneta Wetlands**, an abandoned salt pan that now serves as a bird refuge. There are mangroves in this area as well. A little farther up you'll cross the **Spanish Lagoon** which, now home to the island's electricity and desalinization plant, was once a pirate hideout.

*Several of the island's finest dive sites are in the Spanish Lagoon area.*

On the northwest edge of the lagoon is **Frenchman's Pass**, a narrow canyon populated by parakeets and egrets. Here in 1700 the Arawak Indians successfully defended Aruba against a French invasion. Nearby are the ruins of the

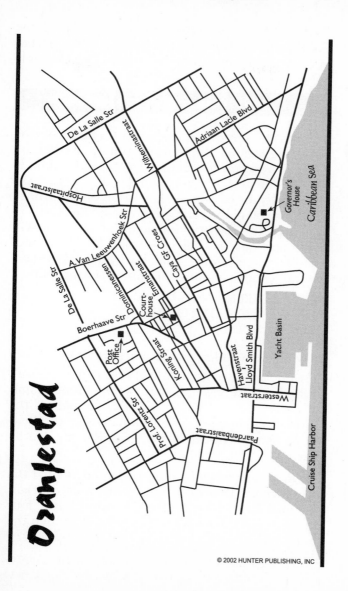

**Balashi Gold Smelter**, dating back to 1899. Continuing northward past the industrial harbor at Barcadera, you'll soon be back in Oranjestad.

## Sightseeing in Oranjestad

Though the terrific shopping on Caya Croes and in the malls along the waterfront may be what initially draws you to Oranjestad, take the time to explore the places in between. Be sure to visit the colorful fruit and vegetable market on the wharf. Then, as you make your way from the Seaport Village to Caya Croes (or vice versa), stroll down Wilhelminastraat, a showplace of colorful colonial architecture. En route, you may want to visit some of Oranjestad's historic buildings and museums.

### FORT ZOUTMAN & THE WILLEM III TOWER
Oranjestraat
☎ 826099
Museum hours: Mon.-Fri., 9 am-noon; 1:30-4:30 pm

Fort Zoutman, completed in 1796, is Aruba's oldest building. It was named in honor of Rear Admiral Johan Arnold Zoutman. A champion of the Dutch-English wars, he outmaneuvered the British on the North Sea during the Fourth British War.

The fort was originally built to defend against the pirates in the then booming Paardenbaai Harbor. In those days, the fort was equipped with four cannons and it was located on what was then the shoreline.

From 1816 until 1911, the fort was home to government offices, which are now across the street.

The Willem III tower was added to the Fort in 1868 to serve as Oranjestad's first public time keeper and lighthouse. Its kerosene lamp was first lit in 1869 on the occasion of King Willem's birthday. At other times, Fort Zoutman contained a police department and a prison.

Today it's home to the **Museo Arubano**. The museum's collection is made up of artifacts, furniture, clothing and assorted memorabilia from the island's past collected by volunteers who combed the island seeking donations from residents.

On Tuesday nights, Fort Zoutman hosts the Bon Bini Festival from 6:30 to 8:30, a celebration of local music, food, folkloric dance and crafts by Aruban artisans. Festival proceeds are donated to local charities.

## ARCHAEOLOGICAL MUSEUM
Zoutmanstraat 1
☎ 828979
Monday-Friday, 8 am to noon; 1:30 to 4:30 pm

The lifestyles of Aruba's early Indian settlers are explored in a permanent exhibit of artifacts and pottery collected at archaeological digs throughout the island. The collection even includes a mummified Indian in a burial urn.

## PROTESTANT CHURCH
Wilhelminastraat

Located behind the Archaeological Museum, this lovely church was built in 1846. Its successor has been built right alongside it. The church contains a small Bible museum, which is open during the week from 10 am to noon.

Aruba

## QUEEN WILHELMINA PARK
L.G. Smith Blvd.

This area of greenery alongside the Seaport Marketplace was just a patch of sand until the green-thumbed developers of the Seaport Village rehabilitated it. Now it is a lovely seaside park with a statue of the former Dutch Queen Wilhemina at its center.

## NUMISMATIC MUSEUM
Zuidstratt #27
☎ 828831
Monday-Friday, 9 am to noon; 2 pm to 4:30 pm

This small museum is located behind the police station one block east of Fort Zoutman. The museum houses a world-class collection of coin and paper currency items with more than 30,000 pieces from 100 countries.

## ADRIAN DE MAN SHELL COLLECTION
Morgenster 18
☎ 824246

Island visitors are invited to view this private shell collection, which fills an entire room in the rear of the De Man family's home. The collection includes a rare murex. Advance notice is requested.

## EQUESTRIAN STATUE OF SIMON BOLIVAR

This statue of Bólivar, presented to the people of Aruba by the government of Venezuela, stands in front of the Bólivar Center in Oranjestad behind the Talk of the Town Hotel.

# San Nicolas

Often referred to as Aruba's "Sunrise Side," San Nicolas is located near the southeastern point of the island, 12 miles from Oranjestad. Though it grew up around the Lago Oil refinery, the island's second-largest town is now dependent on tourism for its livelihood, just like the rest of the island.

*Noticeably absent in San Nicolas is the Dutch-style architecture that characterizes Oranjestad.*

A portion of its main street is a fine promenade with local handicrafts and art sold from kiosks, as well as drink and refreshment stands. In contrast to Oranjestad, San Nicolas is decidedly more Latin American than Dutch. **Charlie's Bar**, a holdover from the refinery days, is San Nicolas' and Aruba's most famous watering hole.

Nearby attractions include **Baby Beach** and **Rodger's Beach**; **Boca Grandi Beach** for windsurfing; the **Aruba Golf Course**; **Guadirikiri Cave** and **Fontein Cave**, with their Indian inscriptions; and the **Huliba** and **Tunnel of Love** caves.

On Friday evenings, from May through October, San Nicolas hosts the San Nifete, a Caribbean street festival celebrating the heritage of San Nicolas with colorful talent and fashion shows, expositions, live talk shows, basketball competitions, fairs and lots of local food to whet your appetite. The last Friday of the month the feature is a Street Art Gallery with Caribbean artists and musicians. The festival is held on Main Street from 6:30 to 10 pm.

Aruba

## Side-Trips

### Curaçao, Bonaire & Venezuela

Bonaire and Curaçao are just a day-trip away. Since **ALM** offers several daily flights to Bonaire and Curaçao, you can easily organize a day on either island by studying the relevant chapters in this guide.

Caracas, Venezuela is also less than an hour away via **Avensa Airlines**. However, if you'd like to spend just a day or two in Caracas we urge you to make the most of your time by taking advantage of an organized tour offered by **De Palm Tours**. For more information, see the De Palm activities desk in your hotel or contact the main office at ☎ 824400.

# Shop Till You Drop

After you've hung your bathing suit out to dry and before you dress for dinner and a night of gambling, you'll have time to head downtown to Oranjestad and explore the bargains available. Oranjestad is a picturesque town with pastel painted 19th century buildings that have been lovingly restored. There are four malls downtown we can recommend and fine shops scattered about. Featured items include perfumes, cosmetics, china, crystal, and watches. Handicrafts from Indonesia and Colombia are special items to consider. Popular too, are embroidered tablecloths. Stores are open from 9-6, Monday-Saturday, sometimes closing between noon and 2 pm. Some are open until 1 pm on Sunday. Credit cards are widely accepted as is the US dollar and travelers checks.

## Shopping Malls

The malls each include fine shops (many of which have hotel branches). It's fun to go there (preferably not during the midday's sun), sample the bargains and mingle with locals. The omnipresent harbor offers a scenic backdrop. Remember there are duty-free shops at the airport, so do not panic if you forgot someone back home when you are leaving. Liquor is duty free (and cheap) all over town and duty-free perfumes are sold almost everywhere.

### Royal Plaza Mall

This is Aruba's largest shopping mall and features shops such as **Little Switzerland**, a 40-year institution here that carries watches, crystal (Daum and Waterford) and porcelain. **Gandelman Jewelers** has similar items and fine porcelain Lladró figurines. Emeralds galore are available at **Colombian Emeralds** at prices similar to those in Colombia. **Tommy Hilfiger** and **Benetton** are among other shops in the mall.

### Seaport Village Market

This mall is located under the Crystal Casino and hosts an array of specialty stores. Our favorite is **Mopa Mopa**, where colorful, carved wooden figures are sure to be treasured. They are made by a natural process using the leaves of the Mopa Mopa tree. Powdered minerals are used for the color and the result is a unique handicraft that will make you the envy of your neighbors back home.

### Seaport Market & Port of Call

Next to the Sonesta Suites Hotel across the road from the harbor has a wide assortment of shops, as does is near the cruise landing. Our favorite is **Red Sails Sports**, featuring excellent resort-wear.

# After Dark

Unlike many Caribbean islands, when the sun goes down, Aruba does not go to sleep. The sandman has a tough time competing with the sounds of screams and money pouring out of slot machines. Restaurants are open late, nightclubs even later and the casinos hardly ever close.

## Casinos

There are about 11 casinos in Aruba. Some are world famous and draw gamblers by the junketful all year-round. The most popular games are blackjack, roulette, craps and poker. The **Crystal Casino** at Seaport Village also offers Race and Sports Book. This allows you to bet on horse races, basketball and football from 11 am till 2 am daily. The **Exelsior Casino** at the Holiday Inn has a similar facility. You can play stud poker at the

Royal Cabana Casino at the La Cabana All Suite Resort. The **Alhambra Casino** (☎ 835000), near Divi Divi Resort is popular and hosts the Alladin Theater. Perhaps the most luxurious, is the **Stellaris Casino** (☎ 836000) at the Marriott Hotel in Palm Beach.

Casinos are generally open seven days a week from 10 am till 4 am.

## Sports Bar

**Champions**, at the Marriott Ocean Club, lives up to its motto, "Good Food, Good Times, Good Sports." Satellite TV makes Monday night football, or any important sports event anywhere available live. There are pool tables, and each evening a DJ will keep you rocking. Ideal for the young at heart. Open 11 am-1 am.

## Discos

There are three clubs we can recommend. Two are in the Royal Plaza Mall. **Mambo Jambo,** one flight up, overlooks the dock and harbor. Musicians play Salsa and Latin beats on oil drums.

**Club 2000** is another flight up on the third floor. This disco is popular and crowded, especially Tuesdays (ladies' night), when ladies get free admission and two drinks on the house.

Finally, the **Havana Beach Club**, across from the Caribbean Town Resort on L.G. Smith Blvd. 1 offers mambo and merengue. The club is quite large. Wednesday is ladies' night here.

# Aruba A-Z

## Airlines

American Airlines, 822700; Continental, 880044; Delta, 886119; TWA, 826401.

## Airport Departure Tax

To US $34; to Curaçao $31.

## Credit Cards

Widely accepted everywhere.

## Currency

The Florin (aka Guilder). US $1=1.78 florins.

## Driving

Traffic moves on the right, as in the US.

## Electricity

110-120 volts, AC 60 cycles.

# Entry Requirements

US and Canadians citizens need a passport, original birth certificate, or certification of naturalization, along with a return ticket.

# Government

In 1986 Aruba let the Netherlands Antilles to become a separate entity within the Netherlands kingdom. Aruba has its own governor and Parliament.

# Language

Dutch is the official language of Aruba, while Papiamento is the native language. English and Spanish are understood by all.

# Shopping

Stores are open Monday-Saturday, 9 am-6 pm. Many are closed from noon-2 and some are open until 1 pm on Sunday.

# Taxis

There are no meters; rates are fixed by the government.

Aruba

## Telephones

The country code for Aruba is 297. All local numbers begin with the number 8.

## Time

Atlantic Standard Time (one hour later than Eastern Standard Time).

## Tourist Office

Aruba Tourism Authority can be found at J.E. Irausquin Blvd. #172, Oranjestad; ☎ 823777.

# Bonaire

**D**iving is, and always will be, what attracts most visitors to Bonaire. As a result, the casinos, nightclubs and shopping complexes of Aruba and Curaçao are noticeably absent. Though you won't find swank nightclubs, you will find several fine restaurants, friendly people and great diving. The atmosphere is definitely laid-back and, since everyone is on the island for the same thing, the camaraderie is instant. By sunset happy hour you'll be swapping stories and making plans for the next day's dive with the people you met on the boat just a few hours earlier.

But don't plan on spending all your time underwater. Bonaire ranks among the top bird watching islands in the Caribbean, both on dry land and in mangroves, which you can explore via sea kayak. Conditions for windsurfing couldn't be better, and you'll want to explore the Washington-Slagbaai National Park, and bike to Pekelmeer, home to one of the largest flamingo sanctuaries in the Western Hemisphere.

## Culture & Customs

### History

When Italian navigator **Amerigo Vespucci** discovered Bonaire in 1499, the island was inhabited by Arawak Indians. In fact, the word "Bonaire" is rooted in the Arawak word *bojnaj*, which means low country. Twenty-eight years later, in 1527, the **Spaniards** began their attempt to colonize the island. A century later, having abandoned any hopes for success, the Spanish left Bonaire, taking with them Arawak Indians to sell into slavery on Hispaniola.

In 1664, a year after the departure of the Spanish, the **Dutch** invaded Curaçao, using the island as a naval base in their war against Spain. They subsequently occupied Bonaire and the neighboring islands as well. Two years later, in 1636, Bonaire officially became a Dutch colony.

Shortly thereafter, in 1639, the Dutch West India Company drew up a plan for the economic development of Bonaire, focusing primarily on salt production, the cultivation of corn and stock breeding. Salt production became the island's primary source of revenue and slaves were brought in from Africa and nearby islands to work in the salt pans.

## The 19th Century

Though the 18th century passed quietly, between 1800 and 1816 Bonaire was frequently attacked by French and British pirates. Sometime during this period the **British** occupied the island but, not knowing what to do with it, leased it to a New York merchant for $2,400 a year. Finally, in 1816, the **Dutch** regained control of Bonaire and, in addition to working the salt pans, established a system of government plantations to cultivate brazilwood and aloe, and to manufacture cochineal. However, once slavery was abolished in 1863, the plantations were no longer profitable.

## The 20th Century

The island was parceled out and sold. Bonaire's economy fell into a deep recession until 1926, when the **oil industry** began to boom on Aruba and Curaçao. Thousands of Bonairean men migrated to the sister islands to work in the oil refineries, mailing money home to their families, who remained on Bonaire. This period, which would become known as the "era of the money order economy," lasted until the late 1950s, when the automation of the oil industry eliminated many of the jobs the Bonaireans had left home for.

Luckily, just as automation had done away with jobs in the oil industry, the arrival of **tourism** created new ones. Bonaire's first hotel, the Flamingo Beach Club, opened in 1951. Then, when the Netherlands Antilles were granted autonomy by the Dutch government in 1954, Bonaire was granted funds to improve its economy. The salt pans were modernized to use solar energy, making the saltworks one of the most environmentally conscious plants in the world. An enlarged power plant and new airport were built in order to accommodate building contracts from outside Bonaire.

The **Bonaire Petroleum Corporation**, or BOPEC, was founded in 1975. It constructed, not a refinery, but a terminal that would receive oil for transfer from giant tankers to smaller ones for

Bonaire

transportation to Venezuela and other countries. Hence, the risk that the oil industry might affect marine life or the environment is not as great on Bonaire as it is elsewhere. In fact, Bonaire was the first of the Antilles to enact legislation governing both land and sea to create a national park. To preserve Bonaire's cultural heritage, a non-profit foundation, the "Fundashon Arte Bonairiano," was established to train young people in traditional crafts.

## Diving

However, Bonaire's number one industry is tourism, and **diving** is its top attraction. This brings us to the pivotal event in the island's history, the arrival of **Captain Don Steward** in 1962 aboard the *Valerie Queen*, a 70-foot schooner out of San Francisco. Sailing into Kralendijk, Captain Don took one look at Bonaire's crystalline waters and coral shores and recognized its potential as a haven for divers. With one eye on promoting Bonaire as a diver's island and the other on conservation, Captain Don stayed on Bonaire and became actively involved in the island's development.

First, he took over the operation of Bonaire's sole hotel, where he would eventually found the island's first resort dive shop. Together, the hotel and dive shop eventually blossomed into **Captain Don's Habitat**, one of the foremost dive resorts in the Caribbean. Then Captain Don set an example for the world to follow, spearheading efforts to protect the marine life surrounding Bonaire by developing community and visitor educational programs designed to increase awareness of the reefs and the fragility of their ecosystems. Among his many contributions are Bonaire's first YMCA diving school, its first sport diving station, its first PADI five-star training facility, its first PADI Diving Instructor Institute and the foundation of the Council of Underwater Resort Operators, with a training center.

Thanks to Captain Don's efforts, Bonaire is not only one of the world's finest diving destinations but a world leader in underwater conservation. Though Captain Don has since taken a step back from diving and has moved on to the landscape business, the sea will always be his first love. You can join him on Tuesday nights at Captain Don's Habitat for a slide show and storytelling.

## The People

Bonaire's 15,000 residents are exceedingly warm and hospitable. Descendants of the African slaves, Arawak and other native Caribbean peoples, as well as Dutch and Spanish settlers, their mixed ancestry is a reflection of the island's history.

## The Government

As part of the Netherlands Antilles, which is administered by a parliamentary democracy, most of Bonaire's affairs fall under the jurisdiction of its governing bodies, while defense and foreign affairs are handled by the Dutch government in the Hague. Bonaire's internal affairs are adminis-

Bonaire

tered by the popularly elected Island Council, which carries out both executive and legislative functions. Bonaire's Lieutenant Governor is appointed by the Queen of the Netherlands and resides in Kralendijk.

## Festivals & Holidays

Special events and festivals on Bonaire center around the sea and island folklore. When competition is involved, jovial camaraderie comes before rivalry, with friendship and fun always in the lead.

## Annual Events

**Mascarade:** During the week between New Year's Day and Twelfth Night, costumed residents parade through the streets accompanied by a musical group.

**Carnival:** Glittering costumes, gaily decorated floats, and music and dance fill the streets of Kralendijk and Rincon during Carnival Week. A week of nonstop merrymaking held in February or March, Bonaire's Carnival is modeled after those of Curaçao and Aruba, with children's parades, and Grand Parades over the weekend. The Burning of the Rey Momo Tuesday at midnight before Ash Wednesday signals the start of Lent. And, so no one misses a moment of fun, events in Rincon and Kralendijk are scheduled a day apart.

**International Fishing Tournament:** Held every March, this popular event draws boats from neighboring islands, Venezuela and beyond.

**Simadan:** Those visiting Bonaire during Simadan experience an integral part of Bonaire's heritage. Traditionally, Bonaire's harvest season lasted from February through the end of April, during which time the entire community would pitch in to help the local *kunucu*, or plantation owners, harvest their sorghum crops. The completion of each harvest would be celebrated with a feast. Unique to the harvest was the music and dance of Simadan, including *wapa*, a dance symbolizing the coming together of the community at harvest time.

Once all the harvests were finished, the *kunuku* owners would parade to Rincon. They would bring baskets of sorghum seeds to be deposited in the Magasina di Rey, the storehouse for the community. Finally, on Easter Sunday, the *kunuku* owners would bring sorghum seeds to the priest, who would then bless the harvest. Simadan festivals are still held in Rincon and Nikiboko.

**Family Month:** Throughout the entire month of August, special family packages and activities are offered by island resorts, restaurants and tour operators.

**Bonaire Regatta:** Who would have thought that an impromptu race between Captain Don Steward's fishing sloop *Sislin* and Hubert Domacasse's *Vella* for a bounty of 27 cases of beer would give rise to one of the biggest events on Bonaire?

Every October, sailing vessels ranging from yachts and catamarans to windsurfers, Sunfish and Bonaire fishing sloops compete in this festive five-day event, which attracts participants from

**Bonaire**

neighboring islands, the United States, Venezuela and Holland.

For more information concerning these and other events held on Bonaire, contact the Bonaire Tourism Authority, ☎ 800-826-6247.

## National Holidays

Banks, the post office and government offices will be closed on these days. Many shops and restaurants may also close.

New Year's Day . . . . . . . . . . . . . January 1
Carnival Monday . . . Mon before Ash Wed
Good Friday . . . . . . . . . . variable, as in US
Easter Monday. . . . . . . variable, as in US
Queen's Birthday/Rincon Day. . . . April 30
Labor Day . . . . . . . . . . . . . . . . . . . May 1
Ascension Day. . . . . . . . . . . . May (varies)
National Anthem/Flag Day . . September 6
Christmas Day. . . . . . . . . . . December 25
Boxing Day. . . . . . . . . . . . . . December 26

# Getting Here

Bonaire is in the southern Caribbean, 50 miles north of Venezuela, 30 miles east of Curaçao, 86 miles east of Aruba and is 1,720 miles from New York. At 12°5′ north and 68°25′ west longitude, Bonaire is the easternmost of the ABC Islands.

# By Air

Flights to Bonaire land at the Flamingo Airport five minutes south of the capital, Kralendijk, on the island's southeast coast. Flying time between New York/Newark and Bonaire is just under five hours; from Miami, it's two hours and 45 minutes. Neighboring Curaçao is a mere 15 minutes away, while the flight from Aruba takes 30 minutes. Since there are only a limited number of direct flights to Bonaire, you will probably fly first to Curaçao and then pick up a connecting flight on **ALM** (☎ 800-327-7230), which offers several daily flights between Curaçao and Bonaire. ALM does offer nonstop service from Miami to Bonaire Wednesdays and Saturdays.

Through its codeshare program with United Airlines, passengers flying on United from other US cities connect in Miami with the ALM flight to Bonaire. The codeshare fare is valid on direct flights only and reservations must be made through **United** (☎ 800-241-6522). Other days, travelers in the United States and Canada will have to fly to Curaçao out of Miami, and then continue on to Bonaire.

**American Airlines** (☎ 800-433-7300) offers daily nonstop service out of Miami (11 am departure) to Curaçao.

**KLM** (☎ 800-374-7747) offers direct service from Holland a few times a week. Otherwise, travelers can fly to Curaçao and connect with one of the ALM flights.

Bonaire

A few days in Bonaire can easily be combined with a trip to Venezuela. **Avensa** (☎ 800-428-3672) offers regularly scheduled service between Caracas and Bonaire.

# Orientation

Covering an area of 112 square miles, Bonaire is the second largest of the ABC Islands. Shaped like a boomerang with its inner edge facing west, it is 24 miles long and three to seven miles wide. Rough seas driven by the constant trade winds that blow in from Africa batter Bonaire's north windward coast, while the waters on its protected leeward side are calm and well-suited for swimming, diving and other watersports.

Just outside the airport are Port Bonaire and the Plaza Resort, one of the island's two five-star resorts on the island. Most other island accommodations are located within the concave section of the leeward coast, and no more than 10 minutes from Kralendijk by car. The semi-arid landscape of Bonaire's central region is reminiscent of the American Southwest.

Several of the hotels north of Kralendijk are within easy walking distance of each other. **Playa Lechi**, one of the few beaches on the island, is at the Sunset Beach Hotel. Directly opposite the hotels, just half a mile offshore, lies **Klein Bonaire**. The white sandy beaches of this uninhabited 1,500-acre islet are popular for picnics and snorkeling. Many popular dive sites are in the waters surrounding the island.

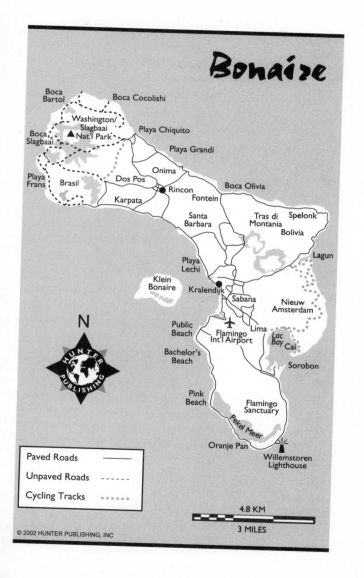

Bonaire

Boca Bartol
Boca Cocolishi
Washington/ Slagbaai Nat'l Park
Boca Slagbaai
Playa Chiquito
Playa Grandi
Playa Frans
Brasil
Dos Pos
Onima
Karpata
Rincon
Fontein
Boca Olivia
Santa Barbara
Tras di Montania
Spelonk
Bolivia
Lagun
Klein Bonaire
Playa Lechi
Kralendijk
Sabana
Nieuw Amsterdam
N
Public Beach
Flamingo Int'l Airport
Lima
Lac Bay
Cai
Bachelor's Beach
Sorobon
Pink Beach
Flamingo Sanctuary
Pekel Meer
Oranje Pan
Willemstoren Lighthouse

Paved Roads
Unpaved Roads
Cycling Tracks

4.8 KM
3 MILES

Thousands of years ago Bonaire was a steep coral mountain that rose out of the sea when volcanic eruptions caused sea levels to decline. This is most evident in the island's hilly northern region, where steep coral cliffs run along the coast.

Greener and more fertile than the rest of the island, much of Bonaire's northern section is occupied by **Washington-Slagbaai National Park**, a 13,500-acre nature preserve home to 189 species of birds, innumerable lizards, cacti, the divi-divi tree and Bonaire's best snorkeling. Also in the park is **Mt. Brandaris**, at 714 feet, the highest point on the island. **Gotomeer**, a beautiful inland lake and favorite feeding ground of flamingos, **Rincon**, the oldest village on Bonaire; and the **Indian caves** at Boca Onima are also nearby.

The flat open landscape of the southern region, covered with sand dunes, salt flats and mangroves, provides a sharp contrast with the north. **Pink Beach**, the longest expanse of beach on the island, and the **Azko Nobel Salt Works** are on the leeward side.

**Pekelmeer**, the world's largest flamingo sanctuary, occupies the salt pans inland of the southern tip. **Lac Bay**, a sheltered cove bordered by mangroves on the windward side, is a favorite destination of windsurfers, bird watchers and naturalists, who swim and sun on **Sorobon Beach**. **Cai**, a village on the northern edge of the bay, hosts a popular Sunday afternoon beach party, which is always a lot of fun.

# Getting Around

## Arrival

You should have no trouble finding your way through Bonaire's Flamingo Airport. After going through Customs, you can hop in a cab at the taxi stand just outside. Fares are calculated based on distance and are charged per cab, not per person. Cab fare to your hotel should be no more than $15.

Major car rental agencies, including Avis, Budget, Dollar and Hertz, are right outside. They should provide you with directions to your hotel as well as an island map.

When not diving, Bonaire's active visitors set off to explore the island on their own, primarily by Jeep, mountain bike or scooter. You will want to do the same.

**Bonaire**

## Car Rentals

Since rentals are popular on Bonaire, if you're planning on renting a car for the duration of your stay, it is advisable to make arrangements prior to your arrival. You may also get a better rate by doing so. When making hotel reservations, ask if there is a car rental agency on the property. If so, you may be able to rent a car at the same time.

Jeeps are especially popular and are a good idea if you'll be carrying dive equipment or plan on exploring the north coast. Although the larger international agencies are more expensive, we prefer to rent from them, since their cars tend to be newer and better maintained. To accommodate divers, most agencies offer minivan pick-ups and Jeeps.

The following agencies have branches at the airport and/or offer airport pick-up.

**AB CAR RENTAL:** Flamingo Airport, ☎ 717-8667, fax 717-5034. Open: 7:30 am-noon, 1 pm-5 pm.

**AVIS:** Flamingo Airport, ☎ 717-5795; J.A. Abraham Blvd. 4, ☎ 717-5795. Open: 7 am to 8 pm. Pick-up time: 9:30 am to 4:30 pm.

**BUDGET:** Flamingo Airport, ☎ 717-8315. Open: 6:30 am until last flight. Kaya L.D. Gerharts 22, ☎ 717-8300. Open: 8 am-noon and 1:30 pm-5:30 pm. Weekends: 8 am-noon and 1 pm-5 pm.

**DOLLAR:** Flamingo Airport, ☎ 717-5588. Kaya Grandi 86, ☎ 717-8888. Open: 7:30 am-noon, and 1:30-5 pm.

**HERTZ:** Flamingo Airport, ☎ 717-6020. Open: 7 am-6 pm.

**TOTAL:** Flamingo Airport, ☎ 717-8313. Open: 7 am until last flight.

In order to rent a car you must have a valid driving license, which has been held for at least 24 months. The minimum age requirement varies by agency and the type of vehicle you wish to rent, and can be anywhere from 21 to 26 years of age. Payment can be made in cash or by credit card. However, if you pay by cash you may need to leave a fairly substantial deposit. Most agencies offer unlimited mileage.

Driving is on the right side of the road and there are no traffic signals at intersections, so proceed with caution. While roads in town and major residential areas are paved, dirt roads predominate throughout much of the island. The speed limit is 25 mph in towns and villages and between 35 and 50 mph in the countryside. When driving in the countryside, and even in Rincon and the villages, watch for goats and donkeys.

## Motorcycles, Scooters & Bicycles

Two-wheelers are a great way to get around the island and are available at several agencies not far from the hotels. Avid mountain bikers will enjoy exploring the back roads, and our island tours can be done just as easily by bicycle or motorbike as by car. Your hotel activity desk should be able to make a recommendation or help you make arrangements. Always check the brakes, tires and other equipment before riding away. And remember, just because you're on vacation doesn't mean you can throw caution to the winds.

To rent a motorcycle or scooter you must be at least 18 years of age and have a valid driver's license. Scooters and bikes can be rented at **Hot Shop** ☎ 717-7100.

Bonaire

## Taxis

At last count there were 14 cabbies on Bonaire. To get in touch with one, contact the central dispatch office at ☎ 717-5330. Cabs do not have meters. Instead, fares have been fixed by the government. Ask the driver what the fare will be before getting into his cab. If you need transportation back to your hotel after dinner, you may request that a cab be called for you.

# Best Places to Stay

Accommodations on Bonaire range from a homey bed and breakfast in town to a luxurious five-star resort, with most falling somewhere in-between. Unlike Aruba, Bonaire has no strip of high-rise beachfront hotels – there is no such beach and Bonaire doesn't attract that type of tourist anyway.

What you will find are a few standard hotel rooms and a lot of one- , two- , and sometimes three-bedroom apartments or suites with fully equipped kitchenettes. Almost all are on the water, though only a few have sizeable beaches. Practically all of Bonaire's hotels cater to divers and dive groups. Most have dive shops on the premises. Some even have their own fleet of rental cars. Most offer dive packages, which may include a meal plan and even car rental, in addition to diving and accommodations.

# Alive Price Scale

Our price scale is designed to give you a ballpark figure to plan with. Since many accommodations are multi-bedroom suites, where appropriate, our price classifications are based on a one-bedroom suite, which usually sleeps four. Rates are given for high season, which runs from mid-December to mid-April. Keep in mind that Bonaire is rapidly becoming a year-round destination, so variations between winter and summer rates are gradually diminishing.

For some hotels it may be necessary to reserve far in advance, even during the summer months. If you're planning on visiting during the off-season, you may also do better by reserving with the hotel directly, rather than through a reservation service or travel agent.

Breakfast and meals are generally not included in the rate, though most hotels do offer separate meal plans. A $5 government tax is levied on the room rate and a 10-15% service charge will be added to the rate as well. All hotels described take major credit cards unless specifically noted.

### Accommodations Price Scale

Deluxe. . . . . . . . . . . . . . more than $250
Expensive . . . . . . . . . . . . . . . . $151-$250
Moderate . . . . . . . . . . . . . . . . $100-$150
Inexpensive. . . . . . . . . . . . . Under $100

Bonaire

## Resorts & Villas

## CAPTAIN DON'S HABITAT

Kaya Gob. N. Debrot
PO Box 88
Oceanfront villas, cottages and deluxe rooms
☎ 717-8290; fax 717-8240
US representative: Habitat North American Office
☎ 800-327-6709; fax 305-438-4220
www.habitatresorts.com
Moderate/expensive

*Captain Don is the Captain Don Steward, founder of Bonaire's dive industy.*

"Total Diving Freedom" is more than just a concept at Captain Don's Habitat. It's a commitment. Certified divers can dive 24 hours a day, 365 days a year, along pristine reefs not more than 90 feet beyond Captain Don's half-mile of shoreline (conditions permitting). Dive packages feature unlimited shore and boat diving, and cater to beginning as well as experienced divers, with over 20 diving specialty courses ranging from Open Water Certification to Master Scuba Diver. And there are special interest classes such as Photo Certification, Night Diver and many others.

*Morning & afternoon boat dives visit many different sites every day.*

The setting is hard to beat. Habitat's villa-style accommodations extend along the coral bluffs overlooking the Caribbean. Featured are deluxe studio and one-bedroom suites with a kitchen and outdoor patio and dining area, as well as superior rooms with private balcony or patio. In addition to fantastic diving, Captain Don's guests enjoy great oceanfront dining at Rum Runner's Restaurant (see description in the dining section), their own sandy beach, as well as a sweetwater pool with a sundeck and, of course, an oceanside seat for those fabulous Bonairean sunsets. The atmo-

*Rooms at Captain Don's are arranged to give guests a great deal of privacy. All are air-conditioned & have a private outdoor entrance.*

sphere is casual and definitely laid-back. Day and evening activities are highlighted in a daily bulletin available at the reception desk. Tuesday evenings feature an Antillean Buffet and folkloric dancing as well as a slide show and storytelling by Captain Don himself.

*Trade stories with fellow divers at Captain Don's Sunset Happy Hour at the Deco Stop Terrace Bar.*

## CARIB INN

J.A. Abraham Boulevard 46
PO Box 68
9 rooms (including apartments with full kitchens)
☎ 717-8819; fax 717-5295
www.caribinn.com
Inexpensive/moderate

If you picked Bonaire because you want to focus 100% on diving without distractions, go to your phone or fax machine right now and make a reservation at Bruce Bowker's Carib Inn. By purposely staying small and focusing on diving (the Carib has only nine rooms and no bar or restaurant), Bruce and his staff of PADI-certified instructors are able to provide personalized attention to all their guests, both in and out of the water. The dive shop is one of the most reputable on the island and features a full range of instruction, from a one-day resort course to specialty classes. An added advantage of the inn's small size is that friendships are formed quickly among both guests and staff, creating a family-type atmosphere. In fact, groups that meet at the hotel one year often plan to return together the next. The Carib Inn is a small, dedicated dive resort in the truest sense.

**Bonaire**

*We're not kidding. The Carib Inn has the highest return guest percentage on Bonaire. The average occupancy on a yearly basis is well over 90%.*

Though the inn does not have a restaurant, most rooms do have kitchens. Richard's Waterfront Restaurant is just a few steps away and town is also within walking distance.

## SAND DOLLAR
## CONDOMINIUMS & BEACH CLUB

Kaya Gob. N. Debrot 79
85 oceanfront apartments
☎ 599-717-8738; fax 599-717-8760
www.sanddollarbonaire.com
Moderate/expensive

*Sand Dollar is an especially fine choice for families with young children.*

Feature articles in *Skin Diver Magazine* have identified the Sand Dollar Condominiums & Beach Club as one of the foremost dive resorts in the Caribbean, and rightfully so. In addition to a full curriculum of dive certification and specialty courses, the Sand Dollar Dive and Photo Center features one of the most advanced underwater photography facilities in the Caribbean, in both expertise and equipment. Experienced as well as beginning underwater photographers and video buffs will benefit from the Sand Dollar's personalized instruction. On-site film processing plus a slide viewing room (open 24 hours) allow for immediate critiques, creating the potential for fast improvement.

*The photo center is great for budding underwater photographers. First-quality cameras and equipment can be rented at reasonable rates.*

Parents and kids love the Sand Penny Club. Mom and Dad get time off to dive or just do their own thing while kids 15 and under make new friends and participate in supervised activities, including arts and crafts, pool games, slide shows and supervised snorkel outings. All receive a coupon book featuring a free snorkel lesson and boat trip, among other "freebies," while children 12 to 15 receive a discount on resort dive courses and Junior Open Water certifications.

In addition to the dive center, the Sand Dollar also features a large freshwater swimming pool, two lighted outdoor tennis courts and oceanside terraces with easy access to the water – great for snorkeling, barbecues and sunbathing. The waterside Green Parrot Restaurant is best known for its giant Green Parrot hamburgers, and will gladly put together a picnic lunch. Accommodations include studio, one- , two- , and three-bedroom apartments. All boast fully equipped kitchens, air-conditioned bedrooms and large terraces or balconies. Since each unit is privately owned, décor varies by apartment, with wicker furnishings standard. A small grocery store is conveniently located in the shopping mall at the entrance, along with a car rental, an ice cream parlor and a bank.

## BUDDY BEACH & DIVE RESORT

Kaya Gob. N. Debrot 85
PO Box 231
Apartments
☎ 717-5080; fax 717-8647
In Europe, ☎ 0031-541-533-177
In the US, ☎ 800-934-DIVE
Rothschild Travel, ☎ 800-359-0747
www.buddydive.com
Moderate

Located between the Coral Regency Resort and Sand Dollar, this resort offers similar accommodations at a slightly lower price. Though "beach" may be misleading, the Buddy Beach and Dive Resort, like most accommodations on the island, does cater to divers. It features one- , two- , and three-bedroom privately owned condominiums, which the resort's management maintains and rents out when they are not in use by their owners. All come with fully equipped kitchens, including dishwasher and microwave, and they are tastefully furnished in rattan. One-bedroom units

*Most of the condo owners at Buddy Beach are Dutch, as are the majority of the guests.*

**Bonaire**

are located on the ground floor and have an out-door patio with a dining table off the living room, while the two- and three-bedroom units are duplexes and feature terraces off the living room and master bedroom. Although on the small side, all bedrooms are air conditioned and have private baths. Living rooms are not air conditioned but have ceiling fans.

Dive packages, including PADI, NAUI and CMAS certifications, as well as both boat and shore diving, can be arranged through the on-premises dive shop. Buddy Dive also has its own fleet of rental cars, featuring double cabin pick-ups, Jeeps and mini-vans. All-inclusive packages (accommodations, diving and rental car) can be arranged. Après diving hours can be spent at the waterfront Buddy's Dive Bar and Restaurant.

## CORAL REGENCY RESORT
Kaya Gob. N. Debrot 90
PO Box 380
32 apartments
☎ 717-5580; fax 717-5680
US Representative:
Neal Watson's Undersea Adventures
☎ 800-327-8150; fax 305-359-0071
Expensive

On the strip between the Buddy Beach and Dive Resort and Captain Don's Habitat, the Coral Regency has studio, one- and two-bedroom apartments in beautifully landscaped surroundings. All first-floor units (studios and some one-bedrooms) have a private patio, while those on the second floor (one and two bedrooms) have a balcony. The Dutch Caribbean-style buildings are arranged around the pool in a horseshoe open to the

Caribbean; all apartments have ocean views. There are ceiling fans in the living rooms and bedrooms. The bedrooms, all with private bath, are also air conditioned. Apartments are tastefully furnished in wicker and pastels. The **Oceanfront Restaurant** and **Bon Bini Dive Shop** are on the premises.

*The Oceanfront Restaurant known for i authentic "J maican jer cooking and Fr day night Re gae Jerk Bo gie Festival.*

## CLUB NAUTICO BONAIRE
Kaya Jan N.E. Craane 24
Kralendijk
☎ 717-5800; fax 717-5850
Deluxe

At Club Nautico Bonaire you will settle in to five stars of European-style comfort in a one-bedroom luxury suite or two-bedroom penthouse overlooking the waterfront promenade, just steps away from downtown Kralendijk. "Quietly refined" best describes these spacious apartments. All feature balconies off the living room and bedrooms; remote control air conditioners and ceiling fans in both the bedroom and living areas; large baths with hot tub and bidet; large closets; independent water heater and washer and dryer; cable television in the living room and master bedroom; and a fully equipped kitchen. Dark wood trim against white walls plus solid wooden doors and shutters, and understated yet obviously first-quality furnishings attest to the fact that no expense was spared.

**Bonaire**

*The penthouses at Club Nautico feature private rooftop terraces & walk-in closets in the master bedrooms.*

Just as you would expect, the centerpiece at Club Nautico is its private pier, home of Triad Boat Rentals, Inc. Experienced boaters can captain their own 24-foot Questand, explore the intimate bays and reefs along Bonaire's leeward coast, fish the reef beyond pink beach, or just laze off the coast of Klein Bonaire. You must have a valid boating license or proof of boat-handling ability and knowledge in order to rent a 24-foot Quest. Otherwise, you must arrange for a captain. Triad Boat Rentals are also available to non-guests. ☎ 717-5800 and ask for the piermaster.

If you'd rather let someone else do the work, charters can be arranged aboard a 46-foot Bertram or 46-foot Chris Craft. When not at sea, Club Nautico guests are just steps away from shopping and fine dining in town. Or, you can relax pierside with cocktails and informal dining at Club Nautico's Terrace Bar, prepare your own poolside barbecue, or just spend a quiet evening at home.

## Bed & Breakfasts

### THE BLUE IGUANA
Kaya Prinses Marie 6
7 rooms
☎ 717-6855; fax 717-6855
Inexpensive

Nestled in a quiet corner of downtown Kralendijk, the Blue Iguana is a historic Bonairean mansion with laid-back, funky charm. Guests here are not renting a room or apartment but sharing an entire home. Furnishings include ceiling fans, authentic West Indian antiques, an alfresco breakfast patio, shared kitchen and bath, living room and den with a small library, games, TV with VCR, CD player, and a spacious backyard with a do-it-yourself barbecue.

*Diving can be arranged by the Bon Bini Divers.*

## THE GREAT ESCAPE
E.E.G. Boulevard 97
10 rooms
☎ 717-7488; fax 717-7480
Inexpensive/moderate

*The Great Escape is a luxurious small hotel in the traditional sense.*

Although just minutes away from Kralendijk, Pink Beach and other island attractions, you'll feel pleasantly secluded from the rest of the world as you lounge by the pool at the Great Escape. This lovely Spanish-style villa features beautifully decorated guest rooms with air conditioning, ceiling fans and private baths in a tranquil garden setting. Breakfast is served buffet-style in the outdoor restaurant, which, as indicated by the large barbecue pit, specializes in grilled meats. Lunch and dinner menus change daily. There is a small playground for young children as well as a reading room and table games for older guests.

## *Five-Star Resorts*

Bonaire

## PLAZA RESORT BONAIRE
J.A. Abraham Boulevard
174 rooms (including apartments)
☎ 717-2500; fax 717-7133
www.plazaresort.com
Handicapped-accessible
Deluxe

A turquoise lagoon winds its way through the Plaza Resort, the youngest member of the Van der Valk family of hotels and the newest property on Bonaire. Uniquely situated on a peninsula just minutes from the Flamingo Airport, the Plaza Resort takes full advantage of its location to provide guests with a complete vacation, both on land and sea.

The Plaza's aquatic facilities have been carefully designed and constructed so as not to disrupt Bonaire's marine environment. Guests can sail in on their own yacht and moor it at their doorstep or rent a Boston Whaler from the resort's marina. The Complete Dive and Sports Center features dive instruction in a 10-foot-deep seaquarium built into the lagoon, as well as many watersports.

Snorkelers enjoy easy access to a reef just a few yards from a sandy beach on the ocean side of the resort. Steps away from the beach is a spacious terrace featuring a large freshwater pool and an adjacent kiddie pool. Light meals and snacks are served poolside at the Banana Tree Restaurant.

On land there are three tennis courts, a conference facilities, a shopping arcade, and a lagoon-side bar and restaurant with indoor and outdoor dining. The sparkling and intimate casino is the best on the island. Blackjack, craps, roulette, slots, and more are offered. The somewhat relaxed atmosphere and low minimums make it ideal for casual gamblers. Car rentals, tours and other arrangements can be made at the tour desk. A half-basketball court, squash courts and a jogging track are fun to use.

Accommodations include spacious villas with high peaked wooden ceilings and luxury suites, which are only slightly smaller. All are air conditioned, feature two queen-size beds, large European-style bath with a double sink and separate water closet, cable television, generous closet space with a safe, and a mini-fridge.

Should you decide you'd like to return again and again (or never leave), the Plaza's self-contained condominium complex features modern one- and two-bedroom apartments, many of which are currently for sale.

*All accommodations at the Plaza offer a choice of ocean or lagoon view and are priced accordingly.*

## HARBOUR VILLAGE BEACH RESORT
Kaya Gob. N. Debrot 72
70 rooms
☎ 717-7500; fax 717-7515
www.harbourvillage.com
In the US, ☎ 305-567-9509; fax 305-567-9659
In Venezuela, ☎ 02-571-8724; fax 02-576-4418
Deluxe

Spread across 100 acres, Harbour Village is a world unto itself. Shaded courtyards, colorful gardens, and spectacular ocean views contribute to the marvelously low-key luxury you'll find here. Guest rooms are elegantly decorated and feature a terrace large enough to accommodate four for a meal.

Dining is one of the many pleasures Harbour Village has to offer. Breakfast and dinner are served on the tri-level Kasa Coral Gourmet Dining Terrace. Lunch and happy hour drinks are served beachside at the more casual La Balandra Bar and Grill.

Guests have a long list of recreational facilities to choose from, including a private beach, swimming pool with terrace, tennis courts, a health club with aerobics instruction, bike rentals, plus a full range of watersports, including scuba diving, snorkeling, sailing, windsurfing, and deep-sea fishing. Harbour Village has a full-service marina. Guests can sign up for island tours, bird watching excursions and day-trips to Klein

Bonaire

Bonaire. Harbour Village also has its own disco featuring island rhythms and a piano bar.

# Best Places to Eat

Dining will certainly rank high among the activities you'll enjoy while vacationing on Bonaire. Menus range from local Antillean fare or that North American staple, burgers and fries, to French, Italian, and Indonesian cuisines, with plenty of options in between. Seafood, of course, tops most menus, with imported US beef a close second. You can be sure that the "catch of the day" is just that. This is because much of the seafood on the menu will have been brought in by the fishermen who sailed into Sorobon Bay at four that afternoon.

We've put together a list of our favorite restaurants, both in the hotels and around Kralendijk. Hotel restaurants are comparable to those in town. Those we've selected are right at the water's edge, the perfect vantage point for taking in Bonaire's fabulous sunsets. Dress is always casual and the atmosphere low-key and friendly. Whenever possible it's best to reserve ahead and plan on dining before 10 pm, since most kitchens close at that time.

### Dining Price Scale

Expensive . . . . . . . . . . . . . more than $35
Moderate . . . . . . . . . . . . . . . . $25-$35
Inexpensive . . . . . . . . . . . . . . under $25

## CAPRICCIO RESTAURANT
Kaya Isla Riba 1
☎ 717-7230
Italian and continental cuisine
Inexpensive to expensive

It started as a whim. Vacationing Italian restaurateurs fell in love with Bonaire, so they decided to join forces and open a restaurant. The chef is from Milan. His associates are from Padua, Piacenza and Torino.

*Ask for a table in the front for a view of the bay.*

Subdued lighting and tables elegantly laid with crystal stemware and china set the tone in the downstairs dining room, where fine Italian cuisine is served, highlighted by pastas imported from Italy and local seafood. Be sure to request the wine list, which features a carefully chosen selection of vintage Italian wines as well as selections from France and California. All are stored in Capriccio's custom-built wine cellar.

*Capriccio has assumed the task of educating the public on the pleasures of fine wine.*

For less formal dining, head upstairs to the open-air trattoria. Whether you dine upstairs or down, all guests are invited to enjoy a complimentary mimosa, spumante or orange juice. Take-out pizza is also available.

**Bonaire**

## RICHARD'S WATERFRONT
J.A. Abraham Blvd. 60
☎ 717-5263
Seafood & steak
Happy hour, 5-6:30 pm; dinner, 6:30-10:30 pm
Closed Mondays
Reservations for groups of six or more only
Moderate

If we were asked to name the one thing that makes dinner at Richard's Waterfront so unforgettable, we would be hard pressed for an answer.

*If you dine at Richard's on your first night on Bonaire you may never go anywhere else.*

It could be that pleasant feeling that washes over you as you step through the indoor foyer to the outdoor dining room. There, other than the stars, the only light comes from the candles on the tables and the strands of tiny white lights twinkling on the palms. Background music is provided by the gentle rhythm of the Caribbean lapping against the shore. Then again, there are those fanciful drink specials mixed up by Robby, who is behind the gleaming mahogany-topped coral bar with stools that were custom-made in Santo Domingo.

*Richard's was a hunting lodge in the 1970s.*

We have to mention Chef Benito's chalkboard menu, which changes daily depending on what was freshest at the market that very day. The emphasis is on seafood from the Caribbean basin, along with US sirloin, filet mignon, chicken and pasta. Benito's cooking is nothing short of magic, with subtle seasoning to enhance the fresh flavor of the ingredients.

*Richard, Robby and Mario are co-owners.*

It would be unfair if we didn't mention the waitresses, who come to your table with a smile and plenty of Bonairean charm, or Richard, your host, who brings it all together.

## MI PORON RESTAURANT KRIJOJO
Kaya Caracas 1
☎ 717-5199
Typical Bonairean cuisine
Lunch, noon-2:30 pm; dinner, 6 pm-10:30
Museum, 11 am-11 pm
Closed Sunday
Inexpensive

For a real taste of Bonaire, Mi Poron is a must. With so many different dive sites to explore, not to mention Washington-Slagbaai National Park, the

Flamingo Sanctuary and Lac Baai, visitors to Bonaire can go home both happily exhausted and refreshed – but without ever experiencing anything of the inland's history or people. Guests at Mi Poron not only sample traditional Bonairean cooking but a bit of the inland's past as well. Dining is outdoors in the shady backyard patio of this 130-year-old Bonairean home, which has been furnished with period antiques just as it would have been at the turn of the century. The daily menu features local dishes such as *sópi piska* (fish soup), *kabrito stoba* (goat stew), and *moro* (rice and beans prepared Caribbean-style) and, of course, *funchi*, a traditional side dish made from cornmeal and similar to polenta. The small wooden tables are gaily decorated with handpainted fish, birds and corals.

*A poron is a traditional cooking pot.*

## BEEFEATER GARDEN RESTAURANT & BAR

Kaya Grandi 12
☎ 717-7776
Local/International
Monday-Friday, 9 am-11 pm; weekends, 3 pm-11 pm
Moderate

Beefeater is set in an attractive traditional Bonairean home, but the dining room is rarely used. Patrons prefer dining alfresco in the breezy tropical garden behind the house. However, do take a few moments to admire the local handicrafts and paintings, most of which are for sale, before wandering out to the garden. Fresh local fish is the specialty and varies according to that day's catch. Also on the menu is a delicious *stoba* (stew) made with *cabrito* (goat), chicken Indonesian, banana or lamb curry, vegetarian dishes, pasta and grilled steaks. Lighter international

*Sunday evenings are especially lovely at the Beefeater, when a band plays.*

Bonaire

fare is offered at lunch time. A small band performs local music in the garden on Sunday evenings.

## RENDEZ-VOUS RESTAURANT & ESPRESSO BAR

Kaya L.D. Gerharts 3
☎ 717-8454 or 717-8539
Continental
Dinner, 6 pm-10:30 pm; bar, 5 pm-2 am
Reservations requested
Moderate/expensive

*Rendez-vous owner / chef Marcel is from Holland.*

"Quietly elegant" best describes the ambience at Chef Marcel's intimate restaurant, where you'll dine by candlelight, inside or out. French bread fresh from the oven, along with the chef's specially prepared garlic butter, is a fitting introduction to Marcel's culinary skill.

The menu features homemade soups and appetizers, followed by international and local dishes, including gregrilde vis "Bonaire" (grilled fish prepared Creole-style in a tomato, onion and celery sauce), the seafood platter "Rendez-Vous" (assorted seafood served in a garlic sauce), and the lamb filet "Rendez-Vous" (lamb baked in a puff pastry and served with a mild garlic sauce).

Although not always on the menu, *keshi yena*, a local favorite made with chicken and raisins prepared in a tomato sauce, rolled in cheese and baked, is held in high regard by Marcel's staff and regular guests. For dessert try the *quesillo*, a local sweet which is similar to flan, accompanied by the special coffee of the house, café a la Rendez-Vous, or an espresso or cappuccino.

Set aside a little time to visit the bar, which is tucked away in a separate room in the back of the restaurant. The beautiful bar itself is made of highly polished mirante wood. Proudly displayed above it is Marcel's cigarette lighter collection, the largest on the island. Also worth a look are the photographs, both in the bar and in the dining room, of island land and seascapes, including an episodic depiction of the sinking of the *Hilma Hooker* and slave huts. They were taken by well-known photographer Rien von der Helm.

## MONA LISA BAR & RESTAURANT
Kaya Grandi 15
☎ 717-8718
Continental
Mon.-Fri., lunch, noon-2 pm; dinner, 6 pm-10 pm
Bar, noon-2 am
Daily prix fixe (served at the bar only) $10
Expensive

When you walk past Mona Lisa, you'll probably turn around to give it a second look. Its heavy, old-world décor, accented by dark wooden paneling against whitewashed walls hung with still life paintings and Dutch landscapes, seems out of place in the Caribbean, though the ever-present Hollanders at the bar are perfectly at home.

French-inspired continental cuisine dominates the menu, which changes weekly depending on what's available. There is a selection of wines from Chile, France and Spain. The bar is a popular gathering place, with the late night crowd, mostly Dutch and a few locals, spilling out onto the street.

*Bonaire*

*Mona Lisa's chef/manager Dohwe Dooper puts his creative talents to work designing the weekly menu based on what's available at the local market.*

## JARDIN TROPICAL
Shopping Center La Terraza
☎ 717-5718 (reservations requested)
French
Dinner, 6-10 pm; closed Mondays
Expensive

*Jardin Tropical is a local favorite for birthdays and anniversaries.*

Innovative French-inspired cuisine, served in a romantic garden setting overlooking Kralendijk and the bay, and friendly, personalized service, have earned Jardin Tropical a listing in the "Best of the Caribbean," an annual guide to the finest hotels and restaurants. Kralendijk's only elevator, glass-enclosed and located next door to the Mona Lisa Restaurant, opens to the restaurant on the third floor of La Terraza Shopping Center. Plants from floor to ceiling and plenty of space between tables and windows create a breezy tropical ambience. Arrive in time for sunset cocktails at the bar, set on the side of the restaurant facing the bay, and then enjoy dinner by candlelight.

*Jardin is the highest restaurant on the island. The elevator ride affords a panoramic view of the southern portion of the island.*

Husband and wife team Jacques and Lisa Meijers own the restaurant. Jacques oversees the preparation of house specialties in the kitchen, such as lobster thermidor and *jardin de mer tropical*, as well as the catch of the day, while Lisa greets guests and ensures that the evening will be among their pleasant memories of Bonaire.

## DEN LAMAN
Kaya Gob
☎ 717-8955
Seafood and continental
Dinner from 5-10 pm, closed on Tuesday
Moderate

Located between the Sunset Beach Hotel and the Sand Dollar Beach Club, this airy restaurant serves the island's best spiny lobster fresh from the live lobster tank. If you wish, you can have a pre-meal cocktail watching the gigantic lobsters up close. There's a Saturday night BBQ featuring live music from 6-10 pm, and "Lobster Night," usually on Mondays, with half-priced lobster.

## ZEEZICHT
Kaya Craane 12
☎ 717-8434
Dutch, Indonesian and local cuisines
8:30 am-10:30 pm
Moderate

With antique ship wheels, lanterns, turtle shells and assorted nautical odds and ends for décor, Zeezicht looks just as you would expect of a seafood restaurant dating back to 1929. A change of pace from the newer restaurants on the island, Zeezicht is best known for its front porch overlooking the sea and local seafood specialties, including *cari cari* (a stew of chopped fish and vegetables), *chipi chipi* (local snails prepared in a sauce), and ceviche. Another popular dish is the *nasi goring*, an Indonesian entrée of mixed fried rice, chicken leg, sate, and shrimp koepoeke. Chicken, pork and steak are also on the menu. Meals come with a choice of fries, rice or *funchi*. Afternoon coffee and cake on the terrace is quite popular.

## EDDY'S FIFTY'S
Intersection of Kaya Grande & Kaya L.D. Gerharts
International
Open daily, 9 am-11 pm
Inexpensive

What do tropical cocktails, banana splits, Dutch specialties, polished chrome and Elvis Presley

Bonaire

have in common? They may not all be holdovers from the 1950s but you'll find them at Eddy's Fifty's in downtown Kralendijk.

In true diner style, Eddy's recreates the 50s with a modern Caribbean twist on everything from the black and white checkerboard floor, to the pink walls covered with photos of Elvis, Marilyn Monroe, James Dean, Humphrey Bogart, Jerry Lewis and Rock Hudson, along with period ads for Coca Cola and hair cream.

So put a quarter in the jukebox, grab a booth or a stool at the counter, order a burger and a shake, a rum punch or an Amstel, and join the fun.

Eddie's is open for breakfast, lunch and dinner, and offers hamburgers, sandwiches, steaks and fish prepared Dutch-style.

### TOY'S GRAND CAFE
Abraham Blvd., across from the Plaza Resort
☎ 717-6666
Indonesian/French
4 pm onwards
Moderate

The location isn't the only thing that sets Toy's apart from the many other restaurants on Bonaire. Far more memorable are its unique French/Indonesian menu and lively décor featuring, among other things, photos of celebrities. The unique dining experience you'll enjoy at Toy's makes it worth the few extra minutes it will take you to get there.

## Hotel Restaurants

### RUM RUNNERS
### COCKTAIL BAR & RESTAURANT
Captain Don's Habitat
☎ 717-8290
International
7 am-10 pm
Moderate

While enjoying a late dinner at Rum Runner's on the seaside terrace at Captain Don's, we couldn't help but notice the lights – the faraway glow of Curaçao to the west, the stars above, and the occasional glow of an underwater spotlight from one of Captain Don's 24-hour divers.

*Rum Runners has a sister restaurant in Curaçao in the Otrobanda section of Willemstad.*

Our meal was no less delightful. Rum Runner's features a Caribbean-inspired menu of international favorites, including assorted pasta dishes, seafood, chicken and steaks, along with nightly specials. Red snapper in a light coconut sauce proved to be an excellent choice. Just as delicious was that day's catch – barracuda, grilled to perfection.

**Bonaire**

Come for the sunset happy hour at the Deco Stop Bar, Wednesday through Sunday from 5:30 to 6:30 pm. Sundays feature a Rum Punch Party during the happy hour, followed by an all-you-can-eat barbecue buffet. Tuesday is Antillean night, with local cuisine and a folkloric dance show. Great live music performed by the Kunuku Band, followed by a delicious Mexican buffet, have made Thursdays just as popular.

## OCEANFRONT RESTAURANT & BAR
The Coral Regency Resort
☎ 717-5644 or 717-5580, ext. 108/110
International and Jamaican
7:30 am to 11 pm daily
Happy hour, 5:30 pm-6:30 pm; Fri. is Reggae Night
Sunday Champagne Brunch, 11 am-3 pm
Moderate

*Oceanfront's owners Carol and Danny hail from New Jersey. But please, no turnpike jokes.*

The music and the food are slammin' Friday nights at the Oceanfront's Reggae Jerk Boogie Festival. Milton Koeks cooks up a nonstop reggae beat headlined by Oceanfront Master Chef Gibi's authentic Jamaican jerk buffet. Don't limit yourself to Fridays. Though the oceanside dining room is perhaps a little quieter the rest of the week, Chef Gibi's fresh seafood dishes and steaks are terrific every night with or without music, and his Sunday Champagne Brunch is a real treat. The dining room, an alfresco terrace built right into the seawall, is lovely.

## GREEN PARROT
Sand Dollar Beach Club
☎ 717-5454
Standard North American fare
8 am-10 pm; happy hour, 5 pm-7 pm
Inexpensive/moderate

*The Green Parrot offers casual outdoor dining.*

The Green Parrot's biggest claims to fame are its Parrot Burger, a whopping half-pound char-grilled burger of US ground beef and its colorful tropical drinks with names like Lora Berde, the Green Parrot Special (brandy, Kahlua and Ponche Cuba), Flamingo Fling (vodka, peach schnapps, pineapple juice and grenadine), and Twisted Turtle (Malibu rum, melon liqueur, and pineapple juice). It is located right over the water at the Sand Dollar Beach Club, and you couldn't ask for a better view of Klein Bonaire or the beautiful Bonairean sunset. Come for happy hour, have a tropical drink or two and we can practically guarantee you'll stay for dinner. The menu features char-grilled fish, US steaks and chicken, all prepared in a variety of ways.

## *Lighter Fare*

Practically all hotel restaurants are open continuously all day long, serving sandwiches and snacks between the lunch and dinner hour. Should hunger strike when you're shopping or exploring Kralendijk, you'll always be within walking distance of any of the downtown eateries. You can grab a quick burger, sandwich or hot dog at **Naomi's Place**, a kiosk on Wilhemina Plein at the south end of Kayi Grande. **Je-Man**, a small, informal eatery just a few steps away, is open for breakfast and lunch and specializes in pancakes and vegetarian dishes.

For more North American-type fare, head to the **Harbourside Mall** on Kaya J.N.E. Craane, where there's a mini-food court featuring ice cream and frozen yogurt, KFC and **Cozzoli's Pizza**. At Cozzoli's you can order pizza by the pie or by the slice with up to 13 toppings, as well as calzone, stromboli, roasted lamb gyros, subs and sandwiches.

*Cozzoli's delivers too. ☎ 5195.*

The **Go Banana's Terrace** on the second floor of the Shopping Center La Terraza on Kaya Grandi is a great lunch spot, especially if you need to put your feet up and get out of the sun after spending the morning sightseeing or wandering through downtown. The specialty of the house is "Jungle Juice," but they also offer a full menu of salads, sandwiches, tropical drinks, ice cream, espresso and cappuccino.

For a late night snack after an evening of merengue (a must!) at the Fantasy Disco or the discotheque E Wowo, follow the local crowd to **Borinque Snack** on Kaya Gen. M. Piar. This take-out-only snack spot is open from 9 pm until 2 am and features traditional Antillean fare such as Indonesian *sate ku pinda saus* (pork kebobs with peanut sauce), French fries with peanut sauce, and *pisca hasa* (fried fish).

# Sunup to Sundown

Great diving is the best reason to vacation on Bonaire, and many visitors happily spend a good part of the daylight hours underwater. However, Bonaire has lots more to offer the active vacationer.

The waters on the leeward side of the island, as well as Lac Bay on the windward, are ideal for windsurfing, kayaking and other watersports. On land you can experience some of the Caribbean's best bird watching, biking and eco-touring. Needless to say, you'll probably leave Bonaire wishing you could have stayed a little longer, and immediately plan a return visit.

# The Marine Park

"Bonaire – Diver's Paradise." This description is well-earned and a lot of effort is going into keeping it. Bonaire's reefs are well protected due to the inland's privileged location south of the hurricane belt and to the dedication and effort of the dive community. Some of the coral was damaged by a storm a few years ago, but the majority of the best dive locations are still in great shape. In fact, together with the government, an industry association enforces environmental policy and proposes new legislation. The island banned spearfishing in 1971 and, in 1975, the Bonairean government banned the breaking off of coral, dead or alive, as well as its sale. That ban continues in full force today; in fact, nothing may be taken from the water, dead or alive. It is no wonder that Bonaire was the recipient of *Islands Magazine*'s Ecotourism Award in 1994.

*Bonaire's dive industry is "environmentally conscious" and self-regulated.*

Those two bans were forerunners to the foundation of the Bonaire Marine Park in 1979. Made possible by a grant from the World Wildlife Fund, the park covers the entire coral reef ecosystem in the waters surrounding Bonaire and Klein Bonaire from the high water line to a depth of 200 feet. The Netherlands Antilles National Parks Foundation, STINAPA, manages the park. Both non-governmental and non-profit, STINAPA finances its activities through the collection of a $10 annual admission fee from divers. Those fees are used to maintain the moorings, pay the rangers and administrative staff and fund the educational programs offered across the island.

*Marine Park Headquarters is located 3 KM north of Kralendijk in the former aloe cookery at Barcadera.*

Bonaire

Of course, Captain Don Steward has played a major role in the preservation of Bonaire's reef. Together with a group of sponsors and with funding provided by concerned divers, the Captain founded the Sea Tether project in 1987, with the objective of creating 100 moored dive sites on Bonaire. In order to prevent anchor damage, they installed permanent moorings, which are the buoys you see at the offshore dive sites. Additionally, dive operations are required to report the number of divers on each dive in order for the association to monitor the number of visitors to each site. Once the number of visitors to a particular site becomes excessive, or if the site shows evidence of damage, it will be closed for a period of time.

Education is another important way in which the Park Service strives to protect Bonaire's reef. As part of the Reef Preservation Program, free photo workshops are offered to divers through all island dive shops. To heighten diver's respect and awareness of the pristine beauty of Bonaire's reef and the need to keep it that way, weekly Marine Park slide shows are held at dive shops and hotels across the island. The Park Service also produces brochures and leaflets for distribution by island dive shops concerning proper diving etiquette, boating and fishing regulations and information about its many activities.

Constant monitoring of the condition of the reef, including diver impact surveys, enables the Park Service to evaluate changes in the reef and trace their cause. Studies have even included a fish census.

# Life on the Reef

Bonaire's efforts at preservation have not gone unrewarded. Its reef is the healthiest and most densely populated ecosystem in the Caribbean. As you drive along the perimeter of the island, you'll notice that the reef starts right at the shoreline. In some places it will seem that the island and the reef are one. In fact, a shallow shelf covered with a wealth of hard and soft corals surrounds Bonaire and crests in just 20-40 feet of water.

The reef consists of that shallow plateau area followed by a drop-off. Occasional sandy patches break up the otherwise thick coral growth. Scorpionfish, lizardfish and peacock flounders prefer this portion of the reef along with flamingo tongue snails and fingerprint cowries, who feed on the soft corals and gorgonians that thrive here.

Look carefully for camouflaged trumpetfish. These unusual looking creatures hang vertically and then dart downwards to the sand to suck up their prey. Trumpetfish are very territorial and will even nip divers who are trespassing on their space.

As you approach the drop-off, the number of hard corals increases, with large formations of "mountainous" star coral, finger coral and brain coral. Moray eels, squirrel fish and blackbar soldierfish glide in and out of the crevices, often resting on the ledges that serve as cleaning stations manned by banded coral shrimp and arrowhead crabs.

Bonaire

Also growing within the crevices are sea anemones, home to cleaning shrimp and juvenile wrasses. An symbiotic relationship exists between the anemones and the shrimp and wrasses. Immune to the anemone's sting, the shrimp and wrasses attract small fish, which they clean and the anemones eat. Also common to this area are fire and staghorn coral.

Though the reef may seem idyllic to divers, competition for space among the corals and other marine life is fierce. All must establish their territories in order to survive. When an aged coral head breaks off, its space is virtually covered with new growth immediately. Tube, vase and encrusting sponges will fasten to any dead coral skeletons. Hiding among them are brittle starfish, frogfish, juvenile fish and cleaning gobies. Just like a fisherman, the well-camouflaged frogfish cleverly dangles its bait from a filament hanging in front of its mouth. When its unsuspecting prey approaches, the frogfish merely leaps forward on its pectoral fins with its mouth open.

Seahorses are plentiful along the reef, but you'll have to look carefully to see them. Like a chameleon, seahorses change their body coloring to blend into their surroundings. Look for bright yellows, oranges, pinks, browns and black. They grow up to six inches in size and are usually found in the soft corals. Unlike other fish, they grasp onto the coral with their finless tails and do not swim great distances, but instead slowly glide along the bottom. Their transparent dorsal fin beats as many as 60 times per second.

## Sea Turtles

It is also not unusual to spot sea turtles, such as the hawksbill, along the reef. Just as noteworthy as Azko Noble's efforts to protect Bonaire's flamingos are those of **Albert de Soet**, a Dutch resident of Bonaire and the founder of the Sea Turtle Club Bonaire. Mr. de Soet founded the club to protect Bonaire's sea turtle population from extinction through research and educational programs geared toward island residents and visitors. Incidentally, sea turtles are not only threatened in Bonaire and throughout the Caribbean, but all over the world and are considered an endangered species by the Convention on International Trade in Endangered Species (CITES).

Four species of sea turtles are found in Bonairean waters, though their numbers are decreasing. The **green turtle** is found in waters close to shore and is characterized by its medium broad head, smooth-edged shell and white underbelly. The **hawksbill** is easily identified by its narrow head,

Bonaire

hawk-like bill, ragged shell and yellowish color. The **loggerhead**, which tends to stay in open waters, is similar to the green turtle but larger, with a massive head. The **leatherback**, the least common of the four, is very large and will come to shore only to nest.

Although sea turtles are air-breathing reptiles, they can stay underwater for long periods of time and rarely come ashore except to lay their eggs. Their survival is threatened in several ways. The extensive development of the Caribbean is inhibiting the sea turtle's ability to reproduce since it will nest only on quiet beaches – which are increasingly hard to find. Not only is mankind encroaching on its territory, but also polluting its waters. Many sea turtles choke to death or are poisoned by floating debris, especially plastics. Finally, sea turtles are being over-hunted.

In order to protect the sea turtle from extinction, the Sea Turtle Club requests that visitors and residents of Bonaire follow these guidelines.

- 🐢 Don't buy turtle products, either as food or gifts. Not only do you risk a fine, since turtles are fully protected on Bonaire, but you also encourage their extinction. This is a good rule to follow no matter where you travel.

- 🐢 If you are on a beach when a sea turtle lays its eggs, leave it alone. Inform Mr. de Soet at the Sea Turtle Club (☎ 717-5074) or the Marine Park (☎ 717-8444) as soon as possible.

- 🐢 Report any sightings of sea turtles in Bonairean waters to your dive shop.

# Diving

Bonaire boasts over 80 different dive sites, most of which are on the leeward side of the island. While the northern and windward coasts of Bonaire are constantly battered by powerful waves, the calm leeward waters are ideal for diving, thanks to Klein Bonaire, which acts like a barrier reef. Dive sites are installed and maintained by the Council of Underwater Resort Operators of Bonaire (CURO) and moored with buoys supplied by the Sea Tether Project and Aggressor Fleet Ltd.

*Only the most experienced divers should attempt to dive on the windward side of the island and then only with great caution.*

All of the dives that follow are accessible to both snorkelers and divers. We've limited our selection to just a few of our favorites, which are suitable for novice to intermediate level divers. As defined by Jerry Schnabel and Susan L. Swygert in *The Diving and Snorkeling Guide to Bonaire*, a novice diver is someone who is in satisfactory physical condition but recently certified, or certified but an infrequent diver. An intermediate diver is a frequent diver in excellent physical condition certified for at least one year and who has recently been diving in similar waters.

Bonaire

## A Typical Dive

While no two of Bonaire's dive sites are exactly alike, most share common characteristics. The reef surrounding the island has a narrow sloping terrace that extends seaward from the shoreline with a drop-off at 33 feet, followed by a slope averaging around 30 feet to a vertical wall that descends sharply 100-200 feet to the ocean floor.

## Bonaire Dive Sites

1. Boca Bartol *
2. Playa Benge
3. Playa Funchi
4. Bise Morto **
5. Boca Slagbaai
6. Nukove
7. Karpata
8. La Dania's Leap **
9. Rappel **
10. Bloodlet **
11. Ol' Blue
12. Country Garden **
13. Bon Bini Na Cas **
14. 1000 Steps (Trapi)
15. Weber's Joy/Witches Hut
16. Jeff Davis Memorial
17. Oil Slick Leap **
18. Barcadera **
19. Andrea II (Pali Coco)
20. Andrea I
21. Petries Pillar *
22. Small Wall
23. Cliff **
24. La Machaca (Habitat) *
25. Reef Scientifico (Habitat) *
26. Buddy's Reef (Buddy Dive) *
27. Bari (Sand Dollar) *
28. Front Porch (Sunset Beach) *
29. Something Special (Pali Grandi)
30. Town Pier (Waf Di Playa)
31. Calabas Reef (Dive Bonaire) *
32. Eighteenth Palm
33. Windsock (Riba Ruina)
34. North Belnem
35. Bachelors Beach (Fondu Di Kalki)
36. Chez Hines
37. Lighthouse Point
38. Punt Vierkant
39. The Lake
40. Hilma Hooker
41. Angel City
42. Alice In Wonderland
43. Aquarius *
44. Larry's Lair
45. Jeannies Glory

46. Salt Pier (Waf Di Saliña)
47. Salt City
48. Invisibles
49. Tori's Reef
50. Pink Beach
51. White Slave *
52. Margate Bay
53. Red Beryl *
54. Atlantis *
55. Vista Blue *
56. Sweet Dreams *
57. Red Slave (Kas Di Katibu)
58. Willemstoren Lighthouse *
59. Blue Hole *
60. Cai *

A. No Name **
B. Ebo's Reef **
C. Jerry's Reef
D. Just A Nice Dive **
E. Nearest Point **
F. Keepsake – Closed **
G. Bonaventure **
H. Monte's Divi **
I. Rock Pile **
J. Joanne's Sunchi
K. Captain Don's Reef **
L. South Bay **
M. Hands Off **
N. Forest **
O. South West Corner **
P. Munk's Haven **
Q. Twixt – Closed **
R. Sharon's Serenity **
S. Valerie's hill – Closed **
T. Mi Dushi **
U. Carl's Hill Annex **
V. Carl's Hill **
W. Ebo's Special **
X. Leonora's Reef **
Y. Knife – Closed **
Z. Sampler **

**\* shore dive only**
**\*\* boat dive only**

Bonaire
Marine Park

Boca
Bartol

Washington-Slagbaai
National Park

RESERVE

Brasil        Rincon

Indian
Inscriptions

Boca Oliva

Fontein                    Spelonk

RESERVE                                    Bolivia

Barcadera
Caves

Klein
Bonaire                    Kralendijk

N

Punt Vierkant

Lac
Bay

Sorobon

Akzo
Salt Works

MARINE RESERVES: Areas
labeled "reserve" are used for
scientific research. Diving,
swimming and snorkeling are
prohibited in these areas.

Willemstoren
Lighthouse

3.2 KM

2 M

HUNTER
PUBLISHING

Bonaire

© 2002 HUNTER PUBLISHING, INC

## Marine Park Regulations

These rules have been adopted to ensure that Bonaire will be a divers' paradise for years to come.

- ◎ In order to SCUBA dive you need an admission badge to the Marine Park. Badges can be purchased from your dive operator or at Park Headquarters.

- ◎ Anchoring is forbidden in the Marine Park. Use the mooring buoys provided.

- ◎ Spearguns and spearfishing are prohibited. If you have a speargun, leave it in safekeeping with the Police/Customs.

- ◎ It is forbidden to remove anything living or dead from the Park (except garbage).

- ◎ Make sure you do not damage the reefs in any way. Don't touch the corals and avoid silting up the bottom.

- ◎ Handling animals and fish-feeding may be conducted under expert guidance only.

Large elkhorn coral grow along the fringing reefs closest to the shoreline, followed by staghorn coral. Nearing the reef crest, colorful tropical fish, including French and queen angelfish, parrotfish, rock beauties and trumpet fish, swim amidst soft coral gorgonians, large brain corals, mustard hill corals and mountainous star coral. The sloping wall is covered with tube sponges, anemones, giant elephant ear sponges and iridescent purple vase sponges.

# Popular Dive Sites

## PINK BEACH
Shore/boat dive
Intermediate
Snorkeling

Pink beach is one of the featured destinations of the southern tour of the island (starting on page 188). To reach the reef's crest or drop-off from shore you'll have to swim out about 100 yards across a sandy flat dotted with soft corals and staghorn formations. The drop-off is literally covered with gorgonians and ranges from 30 to 40 feet. If you look carefully, you should be able to spot at least a seahorse or two gliding along the sand or latched onto a gorgonian, along with anemones and arrow crabs. Turtles are occasionally spotted too.

*The coral formations on the sandy flats a short distance from shore make Pink Beach an especially fine location to snorkel.*

Purple and iridescent vase sponges cover the face of the wall and you'll undoubtedly be joined by peacock flounders, stingrays and schools of goatfish as you glide along. If you head deeper, you may come upon a school of horse-eye jacks. Beware of scorpionfish. They can be easily mistaken for a rock and, when touched, their sting is painful and can be toxic.

## CALABAS
Shore dive
Novice
Snorkeling

Located just offshore in front of the Carib Inn and the Divi Flamingo Beach Resort, Calabas is an especially fine choice for new divers, as well as a popular night dive. In the shallow area you'll see a

Bonaire

great deal of staghorn coral and single coral heads. The site also features a colorful variety of fish, including French angelfish, many types of parrotfish and Spanish hogfish, along with anemones and sponges. The crest of the reef is at a depth of 30 feet and the wall drops to 90 feet, with purple tube sponges, orange sponges and formations of mountainous star coral growing on its face.

## FRONT PORCH
Shore dive
Novice
Snorkeling

Front Porch is another fine choice for new divers, as well as a great place for learning how to dive. Accessible from the beach in front of the Sunset Beach Hotel, the drop-off begins underneath the dive pier at a depth of 15 feet. Landmarks include a ship's anchor and a tugboat wreck at 50-75 feet. Tubastrea coral, fire coral and Christmas tree worms appear to have laid claim to the wreck, as has a green moray eel and schools of horse-eye jacks and large groupers. The reef itself, known as "Front Porch," begins at 20 feet and drops down sharply to 100 feet. Goatfish, parrotfish and French angelfish tend to linger along the upper crest of the reef, while schools of grunts and goatfish are easily spotted under the pier.

## SMALL WALL
Shore or boat dive
Novice
Snorkeling

Small Wall is a protected reef that starts just 100 feet from shore across from the Black Durgon Inn. In fact, the boat moorings are in only 10 feet of water. Elkhorn coral, finger corals, brain corals and gorgonians abound in the shallow waters, making this an ideal site for snorkelers. The wall itself starts at a depth of 40 feet and descends to 70. The soft corals and small finger sponges growing along the upper crest of the reef are popular resting spots for seahorses, while green moray eels and nurse sharks are often sighted in and around the cave on the southern portion of the wall. Elephant ear sponges grow in this area as well.

## ALICE IN WONDERLAND/HILMA HOOKER
Boat dive
Intermediate.

Side by side across from the TransWorld Radio Towers just south of Kralendijk, these two sites are part of a double reef system that runs south from Punt Vierkant. The *Hilma Hooker* is actually within another site known as Angel City. When this 1,000-ton, 235-foot steel-hulled freighter docked at the Town Pier for emergency repairs, customs officials were rightfully suspicious. An impromptu inspection uncovered a cargo of marijuana. After the cargo was burned, dive operators requested that the *Hilma Hooker* become a permanent dive site. In August of 1984 it was towed to its present location and sunk. A colorful variety of fish frequent these sites, including French angelfish, parrotfish, rock beauties, banded butterfly fish, scrawled as well as whitespotted filefish, black margates and schoolmaster snappers. Stingrays, garden eels and green moray eels have also been sighted here. Closer to the wreck you should find French grunts, mahogany and yellowtail snappers, large groupers and barracudas.

*Photographs document the demise of the Hilma Hooker and are on display at the Rendezvous Restaurant.*

**Bonaire**

*Wreck diving can be dangerous if not conducted properly. Unless you are a very experienced wreck diver don't attempt Hilma Hooker without a guide.*

# Klein Bonaire.

This uninhabited island on the leeward side of Bonaire features 24 dive sites at depths ranging from 20 to 130 feet. Many are shallow enough for snorkelers. Snorkelers can travel to Klein Bonaire aboard the Seacow Water Taxi. For information, ☎ 717-2568.

## SHARON'S SERENITY
Boat dive
Intermediate
Snorkeling

*The drop-off is extremely steep at Sharon's Serenity. It is imperative for all divers to monitor their depth carefully.*

Although the drop-off is very steep, the shallow portion of this dive on the southwestern coast is expansive, making it just as worthwhile for snorkelers. Staghorn corals and fast growing soft corals are prolific in the shallow waters. The reef crests at 30 feet, with mountainous star coral marking the drop-off. Tiger groupers and enormous jewfish make their home here, as do basket starfish, which are especially beautiful at night.

## LEONORA'S REEF
Boat dive
Novice
Snorkeling

*Stay clear of the fire coral at Leonora's Reef. Contact causes painful welts & burns.*

Shallow water fish, including parrotfish, yellowtail snappers and four-eyed butterfly fish, are regulars at this site on the northwestern coast of Klein Bonaire. Corals include brain coral, mountainous star coral and fire coral, as well as a stand of black coral and pillar coral. Lizard fish often rest in the sand patches around the mooring, as do goatfish and school masters.

## Sites on the Northern Tour

These sites are accessible from shore and can be combined with the Northern Tour of the island.

**WEBER'S JOY/WITCH'S HUT**
Shore/boat dive
Novice divers
Snorkeling

In the shallow zone that extends out 100 feet from shore sloping to 30 feet, angelfish, rock beauties and butterfly fish swim among staghorn, finger and brain corals. Gorgonians, seawhips and mountainous star coral mark the drop-off. Yellowmouth and tiger groupers frequent the cleaning stations provided by the tubastrea coral, which are also at the drop-off. The wall descends abruptly to 130 feet and is covered with purple tube, orange, and finger sponges.

**1,000 STEPS**
Shore/boat dive
Novice divers
Snorkeling

If you're determined not to leave Bonaire without seeing a hawksbill turtle, don't pass up this dive, as they are often sighted here. There's a lot to see in the shallow waters of this large cove, including schools of mahogany snappers, goatfish and schoolmasters in the area west of the moorings. Mountainous star coral soar to heights of up to 12 feet in the area surrounding the mooring buoy, while staghorn coral, brain coral, mustard hill coral and gorgonians dominate. Watch for manta rays, whale sharks, dolphins and other large sea creatures as you approach the drop-off. Pilot

*Divers, if unsure whether you can carry your gear up and down this steep flight of steps at 1,000 Steps, consider a boat dive.*

Bonaire

whales occasionally pass through during the winter months.

## OL' BLUE
Shore/boat dive
Novice/intermediate
Snorkeling

*Dive booties are a must for shore dives.*

This long coral beach up the coast from 1,000 Steps is within another protected cove. Great for snorkeling. French and queen angelfish abound along the reef shelf which, in just 20 feet of water, is overgrown with staghorn coral, seafans and other soft corals. Hard corals and gorgonians mark the crest at 25 feet. The wall descends to 150 feet. Finger corals are along the top, followed by mountainous star coral from 40 to 70 feet, and then sheet corals and wire corals to the bottom. Large boulders have toppled into the water on the eastern side of the cove, forming shelters that are favorite hiding spots of horse-eye jacks, tiger groupers and mahogany snappers.

## Washington-Slagbaai National Park

Bonaire's best snorkeling sites are in Washington-Slagbaai National Park. However, in deeper waters the current is very strong, making diving here a challenge and is recommended only for experienced divers.

## BOCA SLAGBAAI
Boat/shore dive
Intermediate
Snorkeling

Iguanas sunning themselves on the rocks along the shoreline keep a watchful eye on snorkelers in this large protected cove. While coral heads grow close to shore, tropical fish glide through the maze of seafans, staghorn and soft corals that grows on the sandy bottom at 25 feet, only to be replaced by horse-eye jacks, tiger groupers and school masters when the reef drops off at 40 feet. Hawksbill turtles, moray eels and barracudas are frequently spotted in deeper waters.

## PLAYA FUNCHI
Shore dive
Advanced
Snorkeling

Playa Funchi is one of Bonaire's best snorkeling sites. Elkhorn and staghorn corals abound along the shallow shelf until it drops off at around 135 feet out from shore. Midnight parrotfish and stingrays are often sighted in this area. Venturing out into deeper waters closer to the reef you should encounter creole wrasses, as well as bar jacks and horse-eye jacks. The current becomes quite strong at the wall face, which is relatively flat and dotted with just a few sponges and black corals.

## Night Dive

## TOWN PIER
Shore dive
Novice

The night show is spectacular at the Town Pier. Moray eels swim past pilings covered with vivid bouquets formed by the polyps of orange tube coral that have extended to feed. Sponge crabs are commonly sighted here at night and there's always a chance of an octopus or lobster wandering through. Daytime regulars that will probably

*Bonaire*

*Whether you dive at Town Pier day or night, you must always check in with the harbor master first. For your safety, stay close to the bottom in order to avoid any unexpected boat traffic.*

stick around after dark include French grunts and angelfish, squirrelfish, rock beauties and trumpetfish, along with seahorses, frogfish, crabs and banded coral shrimp.

## Snorkeling

**BONAIRE GUIDED SNORKELING**

Thanks to the island's Guided Snorkeling Program, snorkelers too can experience Bonaire's fascinating underwater eco-system in-depth, without ever having to put on a tank and regulator! All major dive shops participate in this series of 12 guided tours of snorkeling sites around the island. Each tour begins with a half-hour slide show preparing snorkelers for the wonders awaiting them below the sea. Tour arrangements should be made in advance, and may even be made prior to your arrival on Bonaire. Your hotel dive shop is almost certain to be participating. Inquire when making reservations.

## Fishing

Five minutes beyond the reefs, Bonaire's waters offer excellent deep-sea and light tackle fishing. The catch varies by season, with marlin and sailfish most prevalent from November through February; dolphin from February to April; wahoo and amber jack from March to late June; and yellowfin and bonito from June through September. Bonaire is also rated among the world's top bonefishing destinations, and its Blue Marlin

Tournament has fast become one of the most popular fishing tournaments in the Caribbean.

There are several charter operations on the island, including Captain Bob's **It's About Time** (☎ 717-7070; fax 717-7071); **Club Nautico** (☎ 717-5800; fax 717-5850); and Captain Chris Morkos of **Piscatur Fishing** (☎ 717-8774; fax 717-4784).

## Sailing Trips

A sailing charter is another great way to take to the high seas. Constant winds and calm water are virtually guaranteed. Options range from snorkel trips to Klein Bonaire, beach barbecues and sunset sails, to customized charters with a certified divemaster.

**BonSail Charters** (☎ 791-7891, fax 717-5398) specializes in trips to the uninhabited islands off the coast of Venezuela which, in addition to offering great snorkeling, are home to the scarlet ibis and other wildlife. Trips aboard the *Woodwind* (☎ 09-560-7055), a 37-foot trimaran, feature guided snorkel tours of the reefs surrounding Bonaire complete with instruction and equipment, along with an open bar and snacks. Half-day snorkeling trips, as well as a full-day tour of the coast, are offered aboard the *Samur* (☎ 09-560-7449), an authentic Siamese junk.

Captain Robert (PADI divemaster) will plan a customized dive itinerary, including Bonaire and the Venezuelan islands, for you and three friends aboard the *Sea Witch* (☎ 717-5433), a 56-foot

*Bonaire*

*For more info on the* Samur, *see page 219.*

*For customized trips, contact Captain Robert before you arrive. Write to him at PO Box 348, Bonaire, N.A. or fax him at ☎ 717-7678.*

ketch. An air compressor, tanks and weightbelts are on board.

## Sea Kayaking

Because the waters on the leeward side of the island are so calm, kayaking is a relaxing and peaceful way to explore Bonaire's coast. Plus Klein Bonaire is close enough that you can even paddle there for a picnic (don't forget your snorkel). Kayaks can be rented at several dive shops on the leeward coast.

Even more interesting are the mangroves in Lac Bay on the windward side of the island. This fascinating labyrinth is an aquatic nursery and a great spot for bird watching. Half- and full-day kayak rentals are available at **Discover Bonaire Kayaking** (☎ 717-5252).

## Swimming

Though the long, uninterrupted white sandy beaches featured in Caribbean travel posters are noticeably absent on Bonaire, the island does have some lovely beaches on its leeward and southern coasts. The gradual slope from shallow to deep water, combined with the usually gentle currents and absence of an undertow, create relatively safe conditions for swimming, provided the appropriate precautions are taken. With everyone else off diving or exploring Washington-Slagbaai, you are likely to have the beach almost all to yourself.

*With the exception of Lac Bay, do not attempt to swim on the windward side of the island.*

Bonaire

> ☺ **TIP**
>
> Getting in and out of the water can be tricky due to the abundance of dead coral washed up on the shores of many beaches. Bring "aqua socks" if you have them.

Bonaire's finest beaches are **Pink Beach** (no amenities); **Playa Lechi** at the Sunset Hotel (toilets, a restaurant and water sport rentals); **Sorobon Beach**, which is owned by the Sorobon Beach Resort; a naturalist resort at **Lac Bay** ($15 admission, sunbathing "au naturel" toilets, a restaurant and equipment rentals at Jibe City Bonaire next door); and the beach at **Cai** on the northern tip of Lac Bay, where there is a lively, family-style beach party every Sunday afternoon.

## Windsurfing

Windsurfing conditions on Lac Bay are as close to perfect as you'll find anywhere. Constant trade winds blow in from the east at 20-25 knots from January to August and 15-20 knots from August through September. Daily temperatures are in the low 80s, both in the water and out. Beginners will appreciate the clear, shallow and smooth waters of the bay, while those in search of a challenge can venture outside the bay to ride the long waves of the open sea.

*Only experienced windsurfers should attempt the open waters outside the bay.*

Ernst van Vliet's **Windsurfing Bonaire/Jibe City** (☎ 717-5233; fax 717-4455; www.jibecity.

com) offers instruction for sailors of all levels, beginner to advanced, along with state-of-the-art equipment, including production and custom boards. Afterwards, you can trade stories with your fellow surfers at the **Hang Out Bar**. Mr. van Vliet will also provide transportation to and from your hotel. Advance reservations are requested and should be made before 8:30 am of the same day (☎/fax 011-599-7-5363/7363). For more information, call or fax Mr. van Vliet, or drop him a card at PO Box 301, Bonaire, N.A.

## Biking

*See the Northern and Southern tours for some suggested routes.*

With more than 180 miles of trails, including goat paths and unpaved roads, biking is a great way to experience Bonaire's natural beauty. Bring along your snorkel gear, a picnic lunch, and plenty of water and sunscreen, and make a day of it. Trek bicycles are available for rent at **Cycle Bonaire**, Kaya L.D. Gerharts 11D (☎ 717-7558; fax 717-7690). Guided tours can be arranged as well.

## Seru Largo

From the observation point at the top of Seru Largo, a hill in the center of the island opposite the water desalination plant, you can see south to the salt pans and west to Klein Bonaire. On a clear day you may even be able to make out Curaçao's Christoffelberg in the distance. Seru Largo is also a great place to be at sunset.

To get to Seru Largo, follow the main road north until you reach the turn-off for Seru Largo, which is opposite the plant. Hike, bike or drive your way up. You can either park your car at the base of the hill or keep driving. It's a steady, though fairly gradual, climb to the top along paved roads. Rugged walkers may find a few shortcuts.

## A Day at a Ranch

If you've come to Bonaire with the kids and would like a break from the water, **Kunuku Warahama, Bonaire Riding Academy and Club** is a terrific alternative.

A working ranch since the beginning of this century, Warahama Ranch is not only a riding school but a living museum dedicated to the preservation of Bonaire's agricultural traditions. There is a petting zoo, a playground and pony rides for young children, while older kids (adults too), can take an hour-long trail ride through the ranch and learn about the wild and domestic animals and indigenous foliage found on Bonaire. At last count, there were 300 goats, 24 cows and enough chickens to produce 25 dozen eggs a day on Warahama. Plans are in the works to cultivate the fields at the entrance. The ranch hopes to produce much of the food served in its restaurant before too long.

*"Kunuku" is Papiamento for ranch.*

**Bonaire**

*You must make reservations for the trail ride 24 hours in advance. ☎ 717-5558 or 09-607-217.*

The Warahama's outdoor restaurant is definitely unique. Barbecue-type fare and local favorites are served, with entertainment provided by Paso Fino horses from Colombia. From time to time throughout the evening, horses and riders will perform in a ring surrounding the dining area, while the Master of Ceremonies tells the audience

*Call ahead to make sure that the horses will be performing when you visit. Dinner shows with folkloric dancing are usually planned for Wed. & Sat. nights.*

about the horse and the movement being performed.

Kunuku Warahama is owned and managed by former Deputy of Tourism Ramoncito Booi, who inherited it from his grandparents. When we visited, Mr. Booi was restoring his grandparent's home to make it part of the museum.

## Nature Tour

**Klaas Bakker**, a Dutch biologist/dive instructor, who has lived in the Antilles since 1978, offers a weekly eco-excursion through Washington-Slagbaai National Park, with several snorkel stops and visits to several little known locations throughout the island. Specialized tours can be arranged. Group size is limited to seven persons and reservations must be made with Mr. Bakker in advance (☎ 717-7714). Lunch and admission to the park is included and the excursion lasts from approximately 9 am to 6 pm.

## Tennis

Tennis courts are available at the **Divi Flamingo Beach Resort and Casino**, the **Sand Dollar Beach Club** and the **Sunset Beach Hotel**. Courts at the Sand Dollar and Sunset Beach are lighted. Courts should be reserved ahead of time with the front desk. Given the strong midday sun, you should plan on playing either in the early morning or late afternoon.

# Flamingos

Bonaire is one of the few remaining nesting places in the world for pink flamingos. Over the last century the number of breeding grounds for the southern Caribbean flamingo have decreased from 30 to four. Man has driven these shy birds dangerously close to extinction, indirectly with the noise of boats and planes, and directly by hunting and collecting their eggs. At one point Bonaire's flamingo population had dwindled to 1,500.

Now, thanks to the efforts of **Azko Nobel Salt Antilles**, N.V., Bonaire's flamingo population is on the rise, with a recent estimate putting their number at 15,000. Shortly after their arrival, the folks at Azko Nobel became determined to save Bonaire's flamingos. Consulting with environmentalists and ornithologists and using their own funds to lease the land from the government, they established the 137.5-acre sanctuary in Pekelmeer.

*Other breeding grounds are on Great Inagua, Cuba and the Yucatan.*

Pekelmeer is one of the largest flamingo sanctuaries in the Western Hemisphere and the only nesting ground on Bonaire. In some years over 3,000 pairs of flamingos have nested in the marshes within the confines of the sanctuary. A flamingo nest measures two feet across the bottom. The sides are 12-15 inches high with concave tops, which the flamingos form by using their beaks to smooth the mud. Each nest holds just one egg. Because nesting flamingos are extremely sensitive to noise and other disturbances, access to the sanctuary is strictly forbidden. However, it

*The Southern Tour of the island will take you past Pekelmeer.*

*Field glasses or binoculars will come in handy. Remember to keep quiet and avoid sudden movements.*

bonaire

is usually possible to see them from the road outside the sanctuary.

While Bonaire's flamingos nest exclusively in Pekelmeer, they feed in the salt pans at Goto and Slagbaai. Even all three areas combined do not produce enough food to support an entire colony, so many of the flamingos fly to Venezuela, either to the peninsula of Paraguaná (96 miles away) or to Chichiriviche, which is closer – a mere 72 miles away. As for how they feed, their long necks certainly come in handy. While walking or swimming, a flamingo forages for food by running its bill upside down along the sandy bottom of the salt pan. Moving its head back and forth, the flamingo filters out the larvae of the brine flies and brine shrimp, along with algae, fungi and bacteria that it has stirred up.

*Goto & Slagbaii are included in the Northern Tour of the island.*

Not only do the algae and bacteria growing in the salt pans turn the water a reddish color, they are also responsible for the brilliant pink plumage of Bonaire's flamingos. The algae and bacteria produce carotenoids, pigments related to carotene, which the flamingos assimilate when they eat them. Thanks to their diet, the Caribbean flamingos have the brightest plumage of all six species of flamingos.

## Suggested Island Tours

## Southern Tour

The southern portion of the island can easily be toured by car in under two hours. However, we urge you to set aside an afternoon in order to enjoy all it has to offer – sightseeing, snorkeling and diving, windsurfing at Lac Bay, flamingo watching at the Azko Nobel Sanctuary, and just hanging out at the beach. Divers or snorkelers should incorporate the southern portion of the island into their diving agenda since most of Bonaire's shore dives are along the route.

This portion of the island is relatively flat and ideal for cycling. Just be sure to wear a hat, and bring plenty of sunscreen and water, since there is very little protection from the sun. Whether you're traveling by bike or by auto, the route will be the same.

## HIGHLIGHTS

◎ Flamingo watching outside the **Azko Nobel Sanctuary** in Pekelmeer.

◎ Snorkeling at **Bachelor's Beach** or exploring the *Hilma Hooker* (experienced wreck divers only!).

◎ Visiting the **Azko Nobel Salt Works**, including the slave huts at Witte Pan and Rode Pan.

◎ Windsurfing or sea kayaking on **Lac Bay**.

◎ Hanging out at **Pink Beach**.

Our tour starts at the Town Pier in Kralendijk. Before heading out, you may want to stop off at the **Cultimara** supermarket in town and pack a picnic lunch. Purchase fresh fruit from the Vene-

*Town Pier is a popular dive site, especially for night diving. Prior permission from the harbor master is required.*

Bonaire

zuelan vendors at the fish market just a few steps away from the pier. Laden with fresh fruits and vegetables, they sail in from Venezuela and stay for the week or until they're sold out, whichever comes first.

Heading southward along the coast on Kaya Charles E.B. Hellmund, you'll pass **Fort Orange**, located just on the edge of town. Although not large by any standards, and hidden among the other buildings that have sprung up around it, Fort Orange was surely quite impressive in its day. It dates back to the mid-17th century when, formidably armed with four cannons, it protected the island from hostile invaders (thankfully a non-occurrence). Simultaneously, it served as a government center and depot for incoming and outgoing goods, as well as a prison. It was also the residence of the commander of the island until 1837. The stone lighthouse that towers over the fort was built in 1932 to replace the original wooden tower built in 1868. Formerly the home of Bonaire's police force and fire brigade, Fort Orange is now exclusively home to the island's Haven Kantoor, Harbor Office.

*The Dutch government was working on a design for larger signs, taking care that they be as attractive and unobtrusive as possible. The yellow signs should have been replaced by the time you visit Bonaire.*

As you drive or bike along, keep a look out for the small **yellow boulders** along the side of the road. Easily missed, they serve as markers for dive sites. Each bears the name of the site it is marking in black letters.

Just outside town you'll come to **Bachelor's Beach**, an especially good site for snorkeling. You'll climb down a ladder about six feet to a small beach. Looking out upon the turquoise water, you can easily see the reef from shore. Highlights include brain coral and a great variety of colorful tropical fish, including blue fish, sand fish, parrot fish and tiger fish.

Divers will want to check out the ***Hilma Hooker***, just south of Bachelor's Beach. Easily accessible from shore, this is a popular wreck site, named for a boat that had been used to smuggle drugs onto the island and was confiscated by the government in August, 1984.

In the distance as you continue onwards, you'll see blinding white hills of what almost looks like snow. These are actually the stockpiles of solar salt produced by Azko Nobel, the Dutch company now operating the salt works after many years of abandonment.

*Azko Nobel Salt is the world's largest producer of solar salt, with annual production of over 400,000 tons.*

That large structure stretching across the road to the sea houses a U-shaped conveyor belt, along which the unprocessed salt is transported to an awaiting ship. In slave times there was a different system. Three obelisks – one red, one white and one blue – were placed along the shore in 1838 to guide the salt ships to their moorings. When a ship was expected, a colored flag would be raised to indicate which mooring the ship should head to. Once it was anchored, slaves would load the salt.

**Bonaire**

On the inland side as you drive along, take a look at what appear to be a series of shallow bogs varying in color from green to brown to near-pink. These are the salt pans that have been put back into operation by Azko Nobel Salt. Sea water is released into the pans through a series of channels running inland from the sea. The water evaporates, leaving salt behind. The different colors

*As you drive, you'll see the remains of walls from many of the original salt pans.*

represent the varying stages of evaporation, with the pinkish color being the final stage just before complete evaporation when only the white salt remains.

Just beyond the hills of salt you'll come upon a group of low-lying **white stucco huts**. Not more than five feet high, these are the slave huts of **Witte Pan**. After working in the pans all day long, the slaves would literally crawl inside on their hands and knees, since the doorway is not tall enough to enter otherwise, and sleep five or six slaves to a hut. Not surprisingly, the huts were used exclusively for sleeping. Most of the slaves had families in the village of Rincon and would walk 20 miles each way to spend the weekend there.

*Snorkeling & diving are possible here, although you do need to swim out a fair distance from the shore.*

Witte Pan marks the entrance to **Pink Beach**, the longest expanse of beach on the island. Although not very wide and requiring you to walk through coral rocks to reach the beach, it features fine white sand and is a popular spot for swimming and sunning. There is no shade and no facilities; bring an umbrella and plenty to drink, since the sun is quite strong. The beach is also popular with brown pelicans.

*Only experts should dive at the Red Slave site. Should you opt to dive, head out toward the buoy and keep watch for dive boats.*

Continuing southwards beyond Pink Beach you'll pass several small huts. Formerly fishermen's homes, these are now primarily used as weekend getaways by Bonaireans. You are now approaching the southernmost point on the island, which is marked by the **Willemstoren Lighthouse**. Just before reaching the lighthouse, you'll come upon a second series of slave huts, this time a faded red color. This area is known as ***Rode Pan*** (or Red

Pan) and is the site of the Red Slave dive site, which is accessible by shore or boat.

As the lighthouse comes into view, take note of the sea, which becomes progressively rougher. The sea tends to be wild on the northern side of the island and, with the exception of Lac Bay, is unsafe for swimming and diving. The rocky shores are almost foreboding, full of driftwood, coral and debris – including a surprising number of old sneakers – carried in by the pounding surf. The stone walls along the side of the road were built to prevent the surf from washing across the road. Also in this area is the inlet where the salt company lets the seawater in and then pumps it into the salt pans.

The 137½-acre **flamingo sanctuary** is within the salt works, just beyond the Willemstoren Lighthouse, in the area of saltflats known as Pekelmeer. It was created by Azko Nobel on land it leases from the Bonairean government in order to protect the flamingos and their eggs. The flamingos have made their nesting ground on the marshes within the salt works. Though the public is prohibited from entering the area, it is possible to see flamingos from the road. Just be quiet and avoid sudden movements, since these shy birds are easily frightened. Though predominantly pink, you can see their black underwings when they take flight. Just like an airplane, they need to get a running start.

*Pekelmeer is also one of the largest flamingo sanctuaries found in the Western Hemisphere.*

Continuing northwards, you'll come to **Sorobon Beach** at the southern edge of Lac Bay. Nature lovers and windsurfers should plan on spending time here. Beyond the sand beach is an area of mangroves and seagrass beds, which makes Lac a

**Bonaire**

popular breeding ground for many different marine animals and birds. Its secluded location also makes it an ideal location for the Sorobon Beach Resort, a naturalist getaway. Since the beach is clothing-optional, you may need extra sunscreen. Because of its sheltered location, the waters here are relatively calm and crystal clear, ideal for swimming, snorkeling and windsurfing, though too shallow for diving. Beyond the beach, mangroves cover the coast here, making it a popular spot for bird watching and just plain eco-touring (not to mention mosquitoes).

*Sorobon Beach is private. A $15 admission fee is charged. Facilities include the fine Red Pelican Restaurant at the Lac Bay Resort.*

Next door to the Sorobon is the very funky **Jibe City Windsurfing,** run by the amiable Dutchman Ernst van Vliet. He is capitalizing on the shallow waters and constant breeze that make Lac Bay ideal for windsurfing. Van Vliet offers classes for beginning as well as experienced windsurfers. He also rents out sea kayaks and offers tours through the mangroves.

*It's a good idea to call ahead to schedule a lesson or reserve equipment. ☎ 717-5233.*

Take note of the changing vegetation as you drive along. Inland, it is very dry, dominated by short scrubby trees and bushes and lots of cacti. There are two types. One is used to make soup and is called **kadushi**. The other, **yatu**, is used for fences, and if you look carefully you'll notice that many of the residents have done just that. All they do is cut the cactus off and replant it where they want a fence. The fences are used to keep out the goats you'll see wandering around here and throughout the island. The goats are joined by wild donkeys.

*Drivers should beware: Goats & donkeys have been the cause of more than a few accidents on Bonaire.*

Just beyond Sorobon and Jibe City you'll come to a large clearing along the water and a cluster of three circular buildings, only one of which is finished. Formerly the shell of an unfinished hotel that was started 30 years ago, the building was bought by a local entrepreneur, who has turned it into the **Fanatic Nightclub**. Check to see if it's open when you visit. This area also serves as a sort of makeshift boat yard and a landing point for some of the local fishermen. This clearing also marks the beginning of the mangroves.

Turn off at the dirt road Kaminda Cai (road to Cai), the last stop on our southern tour. **Cai** is a small fishing village on the northern point of the entrance to Lac Bay. En route, the landscape is almost marshy, with a great variety of vegetation and birds, including hummingbirds. Oddly enough, you'll also see cacti. A closer look will reveal that you're driving alongside mangroves. You'll also pass some abandoned salt pans. Keep a lookout for flamingos. The private homes you'll pass along the way all have their own generators for both water and electricity.

As you near Cai you'll see conch shells piled up alongside the road. A sandy beach and calm waters make Cai an especially good destination for families with small children. Sunday afternoon is a great time to visit. The weekly beach party kicks off at around 3 pm, with plenty of food and music provided by Magic Sound.

*It's illegal to pick conch in Bonaire.*

To get back to Kralendijk, take the dirt road to the main street and follow the signs.

*Cai's Sunday afternoon beach party is popular with tourists and locals!*

**Bonaire**

## Northern Tour

The northern part of the island can also be toured by bike or car. The great many paths that branch off the main road toward the sea and then back again to the caves on the inland side make biking the more interesting option. Should you opt to bike, keep in mind that this part of the island is not only greener and more densely forested than the south, but it is also hillier. The northern tour of the island is easily combined with a visit to Washington-Slagbaai National Park. Unfortunately, this option will rule out biking, since visitors may only tour the park by car.

*Bikers should ask for a trail map or some recommendations when they rent their bikes.*

## HIGHLIGHTS

◎ Seeing the flamingos at **Gotomeer** and **Playa Frans**.

◎ Snorkeling or diving at the **Thousand Steps** and **Nukove Beach**.

◎ **Arawak Indian inscriptions** at Boca Onima.

◎ Stopping for ice cream at **Prisca's** in Rincon.

Snorkelers and divers will want to pack their gear since several of the best shore dives are along this route. As always, be sure to bring plenty of water and sunscreen as well as a hat. A picnic lunch is not a bad idea either.

*If you're staying in one of the hotels on the main drag north of town, start the tour from your hotel.*

For convenience sake, we'll start off in downtown Kralendijk on **Kaya Grandi**, which runs in a northerly direction to become Kaya Gobernador Debrot as it heads out of town.

Just past Captain Don's Habitat is the **Water Desalination Plant**, which supplies much of the island with not only fresh water but electricity as well. Soon you'll come to a part of Bonaire that is strictly reserved for private residences. Well-to-do Bonaireans, many of whom are Dutch, are re-settling in the developments here. In fact, the main road, which originally ran along the coast, was shifted inland in order to create oceanfront properties.

The homes are nearly as lovely as the setting itself. Modern Caribbean-style villas have been wisely designed to maximize the views provided by the gently rolling hills. All are set within beautifully landscaped gardens cared for by none other than Captain Don, who has traded in his diving gear for landscaper's tools. Translating his philosophy to the soil, he has created gardens that are as natural as the marine life he has dedicated much of his life to protecting.

*Hotels are not permitted in this area.*

Continuing onward, the road cuts back toward the coast and you'll travel along a cliff overlooking the turquoise waters of the Caribbean. The water is so clear that in some places you'll be able to see the reef from above, as well as brightly colored parrotfish, angel fish and the other fish that inhabit Bonaire's reef. Looking down or inland from the cliff, you'll realize that you are actually driving alongside a coral ridge, attesting to the fact that much of Bonaire was originally underwater. Note too that much of the coral has been burned black by the sun. In fact, throughout the drive you will often see this burnt coral.

**Bonaire**

*We once drove this route the morning after a steady rain had fallen in the night. Water was running down the coral formations alongside the road. The vegetation was at its greenest & the flowers were starting to bloom.*

Shortly after leaving the coral ridge, you'll pass the ruins of a **scout's house** on the inland side of the road. In former times, this area was home to several large farms, and the goatherds lived in homes such as this one. Throughout the northern portion you will see the remains of the stone walls built by the farmers to separate their plantations. In addition to raising goats, they cultivated aloe and the divi-divi — its tannin-laden fruit was exported to Holland for use in the tanneries. Just a few yards away from here is the old dirt road that leads to the village of Rincon, our final destination before returning to Kralendijk. The hut is also the landmark for the dive site known as **Witches Hut** or **Weber's Joy**.

Farther on you'll soon come to the dive site popularly known as the **Thousand Steps**, although its proper name is Trapi. Located across from the towers of Radio Nederlande, this site gets its name from the steep stone staircase that leads down to the water. Although there are really fewer than 70 steps in all, they seem like 1,000 when you are carrying dive equipment.

*Divers can park their cars alongside the road while diving. Just be sure to lock the doors.*

Continuing, you'll pass the coral formation known as the **Devil's Mouth**, which is on the inland side of the road. During the colonial period the plantation owners would often threaten the slaves, telling them that they would be fed to the devil if they did not work hard enough. The Indians were much more romantic. They believed that if a young girl wanted to find her true love she had only to sit among the coral and he would come to her. Nowadays, if you look carefully you may see mountain goats there instead.

Moving on, you'll come to the BOPEC Oil Terminal. BOPEC, which was founded in 1975, is an affiliate of Petroleos de Venezuela S.A., a Venezuelan oil company. This terminal on Bonaire's northwestern coast is the company's only deep-

Take some time to stroll through the village and get a feel for the daily life of its people. Rincon has around 3,000 residents, many of whom work in Kralendijk. It also has its own post office and police station, both of which are open for a few hours every day, except Sunday. You'll probably pass the monument to Julio Abraham, a key figure in the village and the island's history. Before you leave, be sure to stop at **Prisca's** and sample what residents proudly proclaim to be the best ice cream in the Caribbean. There is a branch of **Cozzoli's Pizza** here if you'd like to stop for lunch.

After leaving Rincon, follow the road marked **Boca Onima**. Shortly you'll come to a small inlet where the waves come crashing in against the rocks. Opposite the inlet is the beginning of a trail (driving or walking) past a series of **Arawak Indian inscriptions** that were painted onto the coral overhangs several centuries ago. The original inhabitants of Bonaire, the Arawaks, quickly departed for Venezuela upon the arrival of the Dutch and Spanish, who tried to enslave them. Experts have been unable to determine the meaning of the inscriptions or much of their history. There are many brasilwood trees in this area, along with the local *palo de silla,* the wood of which is used to make kitchen utensils.

*Streets in Rincon are named after fruits & vegetables.*

**Bonaire**

Following the signs to return to Kralendijk, you'll pass through the villages of **Noord di Saliñas** and **Antriol**. Noord di Saliñas is located on the site of the original Indian village and the street names are Indian. Antriol, the largest village on the island, is divided into two sections: *Pa Ariba,*

Upper Part, and *Pa Abajo*, Lower Part. The streets here are named after fish.

## Washington-Slagbaai National Park

*Since it's imperative that all divers wait 24 hours after their last dive before flying, save a visit to Washington-Slagbaai for your last day in Bonaire. Luckily, most of Bonaire's best snorkelling spots are within the park.*

This 13,500-acre game preserve, covering nearly all of the northwestern portion of the island, was the first of its kind in the Netherlands Antilles. With landscape varying from fields of cacti and low-lying mesquite trees, divi-divis sculpted by the trade winds, abandoned aloe plantations and secluded bays, to an underwater wonderland of corals, sponges and colorful tropical fish, a day spent exploring this park is sure to be one of the highlights of your visit to Bonaire.

### History of the Park

Washington-Slagbaai owes its existence to the generosity and foresight of two of Bonaire's earliest residents. You may remember that in the introduction we mentioned that when the Dutch government took control of Bonaire in 1636, they operated the island as a large plantation. Since most of the labor was supplied by slaves brought over from Africa and the neighboring islands, when the Emancipation regulation was passed in 1862, it became too costly for the Dutch government to continue operating such a large tract of land. That part of the island now occupied by the park was divided into two tracts of land, Brasiel and Slagbaai, and was sold several times over.

In 1892, the land was sold to Jean Luis Cadieres and Jean Jacques Debrot. Debrot subdivided Slagbaai, the northern portion of the land, into two lots and sold the northernmost portion to the

Herrera brothers. The Herreras converted their land into a plantation and, along with raising goats, cultivated aloe and divi-divi trees, and produced charcoal. They eventually named the land "Washington" and prospered from the 1940s until 1967, when the last of the family, Julio Caesar Herrera, who had run the plantation since 1936, passed away.

*The Netherlands Antilles National Parks Foundation, or STINAPA, was established to acquire, preserve & protect natural areas both on land & sea and make them accessible to the public for educational & recreational use.*

Luckily, Julio had the foresight to prevent the exploitation of the land upon his death by negotiating its sale to the Netherlands Antilles government under the express condition that it remain in its natural state. The government fulfilled its end of the agreement. In 1969, Washington became the first wildlife sanctuary in the Netherlands Antilles.

Shortly thereafter the government began a campaign to purchase the Slagbaai Plantation. Finally, owner J.H.R. Beaujon agreed to the sale, also requiring that the land only be used as a national park. In 1976, following Beaujon's death, the sale of the Slagbaai Plantation to the Netherlands Antilles National Park Foundation (STINAPA) was consummated and the Washington/Slagbaai National Park was founded. In 1979, the government gave Brasiel Plantation, including the land surrounding Goto Lake, to STINAPA to run and protect as part of the park.

**Bonaire**

### Getting Ready

Since the only way to visit the park is by car, you'll have to rent one if you haven't already. Four-wheel-drive vehicles are best, although not a necessity. Before setting off, make sure you have a good spare tire, along with a working jack, since you will be traveling on dirt roads. While it is possible to see the park in half a day, we recommend that you set aside a full day to make the most of your visit. This will give you plenty of time for an oceanside picnic as well as snorkeling, bird watching and, for the most hardy among you, climbing Brandaris Hill. Admission is US $3 (NAFL 5) – less for kids under 15.

Be sure to bring plenty of water and sunscreen (a hat is always a good idea too), along with comfortable and sturdy footwear and your snorkeling gear. Bird watchers should not forget their field glasses and a fieldguide if they have one.

## HIGHLIGHTS

◎ Snorkeling at **Playa Bengé** and Playa **Funchi**.

◎ Bird watching at **Pos di Mangel** and **Put Bronswinkel**. Panoramic view from the top of **Brandaris Hill**.

◎ The three-foot iguanas found between **Playa Funchi** and **Boca Slagbaai**.

◎ A picnic lunch at **Boca Cocolishi**.

*Bonaire's only public phone is located outside the entrance to the park. It serves the families who live near there.*

## Getting There

Follow the road to Rincon and watch for the green signs directing you to the park. You'll soon reach Kaya Gilberto R.E. Herrera, an unpaved road on the lefthand side that leads to the park entrance.

## Touring the Park

The park service has laid out two routes for touring the park. The 21-mile (40-kilometer) **Yellow Route** is the longer of the two. It covers all of the highlights of the park, traveling along the northern coast, through much of the Washington section as well as Slagbaai and the Panorama Road in Brasiel, which is discussed in our Northern Tour. If your time is limited and you are especially interested in snorkeling, we suggest you follow the **Green Route**, which will take you west through the middle of the park past the Brandaris Hill to Playa Funchi and Boca Slagbaai where it overlaps the Yellow Route for a short distance before heading east back to the entrance.

To better introduce you to park sites, we will follow the Yellow Route. Directions for the Green Route are in the margins.

Just after entering the park you'll drive through a field of aloe, cacti and low shrub-like trees. If you look carefully, you should notice that there are a few different types of cacti, including the fruit-bearing prickly pear. The taller candle cacti are called **yatu** and **kadushi** by the locals and are easily distinguished from one another by their shape and the arrangement of their thorns. The kadushi, which is the main ingredient in a popular soup of the same name, is taller and branches out a few feet above the ground, much like a tree. The yatu grows straight up and down, branching out very close to the ground. The yatu's thorns are tightly spaced together while those of the kadushi grow in small star-shaped bunches. Because it takes root very quickly, the yatu is used to make

*If aloe is in bloom when you visit, watch for the many different types of birds that come to drink the nectar, including bananaquits, blue-tailed emeralds and ruby topaz hummingbirds.*

Bonaire

fences, which the Bonaireans have found to be quite effective in keeping goats off their property.

*Saliña means salt pan.*

Just beyond the entrance is **Saliñas Matijs**. When flooded, the salt pans come alive with waterfowl, including flamingos, sandpipers and black-winged stilts, along with several different types of ducks. You might even see an occasional Bahamas pintail. Otherwise, it is a vast arid plain dotted with divi-divi trees.

*Instead of turning toward the north coast, the Green Route continues west toward the Playa Funchi on the leeward side of the island Brandaris Hill and Put Bronswinkel (see below) are along this route.*

After turning to the north coast, you'll come to **Playa Chikitu**. Don't be deceived by the seemingly idyllic water; a strong undertow makes swimming here extremely dangerous and not recommended. Instead, busy yourself looking for fossil shells and coral formations in the limestones that form **Boca Chikitu**, the small inlet. Sand dunes have formed here thanks to the extensive root system of the creeping crab grass that holds the sand in place. The small white flowers you may see blooming on the dunes are seaside lavender, while the yellow ones are *Suriana maritima*.

Studying the limestone terraces of **Seru Grandi** will give you a general idea of how the island of Bonaire was formed. This series of three terraces of increasing height, the lowest of which you drive across, were formed during the Ice Age when the sea rose and fell as ice melted in the polar regions. The highest of the three, estimated to be one million years old, emerged when the sea level dropped from as much as 250 feet above its present level.

The middle terrace is somewhere between 340,000 and 510,000 years old. Geologists believe it was deposited during a rise in the sea level that coincided with the melting of the polar ice during an interglacial period. The lowest terrace is believed to have formed around 125,000 years ago.

Stand back from the large red boulder at the foot of Seru Grandi (on the opposite side) and study it carefully. Eventually you should be able to make out an Indian's face formed by the holes and indentations in the rock. Hence its name, **Cara Corrá**, which means "red face" in Papiamento. Between the boulders to the right of Cara Corrá are the remains of an old goat corral. This area of the park belonged to the Washington Plantation. Descendants of the goats raised back then graze here just as their ancestors did.

A footpath to the left of Cara Corrá leads to the top of Seru Grandi, where there is a lovely view of the Sabana and a small ranch in the distance. You'll need to wear more than sandals or light tennis shoes, since much of the limestone on the middle terrace is deeply pock-marked and quite jagged in places. The climb to the top of the third terrace can be tricky. You'll have to do some hand-over-hand rock-climbing.

If you are ready to get your feet wet or spend some quiet time relaxing, the secluded beach at **Boca Cocolishi**, the next destination along the Yellow Route, will provide a welcome break. Formed as a series of terraces just like Ceru Grandi, the beach and shallow bay are located on the middle terrace, which is hidden by the highest terrace. The lowest terrace is still under water. A ridge of calcareous algae between it and the middle terrace serves double duty, marking the step to the middle terrace as well as forming a barrier that prevents the

*Bonaire*

*Algae growing along the ridge creates a tough layer that not only protects the ridge from erosion caused by the constant pounding of the surf, but also turns it a lovely shade of pink.*

surf from spilling over onto its shallow basin and beach. No matter how rough the sea may be, the water in the pool is almost always calm; and, since it is no more than three feet deep, it's great for kids.

Since *cocolishi* means "shell" in Papiamento, it shouldn't surprise you that the black sand beach was formed by bits of coral, mollusks and other shells. Just as appropriately named is **Ceru Bentana**, which gets its name from the window-shaped rock formation at the top of the hill. With or without the window, the hill offers a fine view across the Sabana. There is also a lighthouse here. At this point the road turns inland and you'll soon notice that the vegetation becomes thicker, while the soil takes on a reddish color due to its high iron content.

As you approach the leeward side of the island you'll come to **Saliñas Bartol**. This is a popular feeding ground for flamingos, although you will only be able to see them at a distance. Bird watchers will want to follow the road marked **Pos di Mangel**, one of Bonaire's best bird watching sites and one of the only places in the park where water is available all year long. Bananaquits, tropical mockingbirds, black-faced grassquits and yellow warblers are commonly seen here, along with several different varieties of flycatchers. More timid, and therefore a little harder to spot, are the scaly-naped pigeons, bare-eyed pigeons, the eared dove and the white fronted dove.

As long as you don't visit during the breeding season, which lasts from April to July, you may be lucky enough to hear, if not actually spot, a *lora*, the yellow-winged parrot found only on Bonaire. The lora is easily recognized by its bright green and yellow head and high-pitched cry, which distinguishes it from the more numerous parakeets with their bright orange heads and harsher cries. Both birds have been legally protected on Bonaire since 1931. Unfortunately, they still frequently fall prey to smugglers, who take them to Aruba and Curaçao where they are sold as pets.

An equally serious threat to the lora and the parakeet, both of which are fruit eaters, are the droughts that occur on Bonaire every six or seven years. With their food supply in the wild diminished due to this lack of water, they often feed in the gardens of island residents, running the risk of being captured and sold as pets. Many simply die of starvation. Sadly, the lora is currently threatened with extinction.

After returning to the main road, you'll drive between Saliñas Bartol and the sea to **Boca Bartol**, another small inlet. If you look across the inlet from the northernmost edge of the Boca you may see a yellow-crowned night heron on the opposite side. Snowy egrets are also frequently sighted here, as are pelicans, cormorants and brown boobies.

Continuing onwards in a southerly direction, you'll soon reach the turn-off to **Playa Bengé**, widely held as one of the finest snorkeling spots on Bonaire and also a great place to stop for a picnic. The best snorkeling is along the northern side of the bay where there are a great many coral groves and spurs, and the average depth is seven meters. In addition to, or because of, the corals,

Bonaire

*Avid hikers & bird watchers might want to follow the Green Route inland to Subi Brandaris & Put Bronswinkel before or in lieu of going to Playa Funchi. Both will be discussed later.*

the bay boasts a wide variety of fish. Osprey are also known to frequent this area.

Just beyond Playa Bengé, the Green Route meets the Yellow. The two overlap, heading west toward the coast and **Playa Funchi**. En route to the beach you'll pass a field of yatu cacti, along with low-lying prickly pears and a group of divi-divi trees at the entrance to a private farm.

While sitting in the shade of a mesquite tree at Playa Funchi you may be joined by a **whiptail lizard**. Found only on Bonaire, these lizards are used to visitors and will even eat from your hand or boldly crawl across your feet. Males, with their blue head and greenish-blue hind feet and tail root, are easily distinguished from the more sedately colored females and young whiptails.

Playa Funchi served as the harbor to the Washington Plantation. The two rows of stones jutting out into the water were part of the foundation of the original pier. Since there is no current within the bay, this is a great spot for beginning snorkelers and young children. The water is so clear that those who choose not to venture in can see coral and parrot fish from the cliff overlooking the bay.

The mesquite trees are joined by the brasilwood, easily recognized from its deeply grooved trunk. It played such an important role in the island's history that on the oldest map of the Caribbean, the "Ptolemaic," dating back to 1513, Bonaire is identified as the *Ysla do Brassil* – "Island of the Brasilwood Tree." It is also known as the dyewood tree, and the Indians first used the bark, leaves and berries for fishing. They would throw them in the water to drug the fish, which would then float to the surface, making them an easy catch.

Additionally, a red dye used to stain fabrics was extracted from the bark of the brasilwood tree by rasping it. Since this was often done by the prisoners in the Amsterdam jail, it earned the name "rasphuis" or rasping house. Many believe that it was the bright yellow flowers of the brasilwood tree that first attracted the Dutch to Bonaire in 1636.

After leaving Playa Funchi, follow the sign that reads "**Slagbaai**." You'll pass through the fence that separates Washington from Slagbaai and then drive along the coast. It's not unusual to see iguanas as large as three or four feet sunning themselves on the cliffs along this route. They are completely harmless, but if you try to get too close they'll fast disappear over the cliff and may even jump into the sea.

*Iguana meat is considered a delicacy among Antillean people, who believe it to be especially good for virility. Though protected by law, iguanas often fall victim to poachers.*

You may also run into a donkey or two. Watch your speed and keep your eyes open. These donkeys have been running wild since 1925, when their exportation to Barbados and Trinidad was discontinued. You'll pass several small, secluded beaches before the road turns inland again at **Pos Nobo** (New Well), another good bird watching stop, and **Saliñas Wayacá** at the foot of Subi Brandaris (Brandaris Hill).

*Iguanas are excellent swimmers & are able to stay underwater for extended periods of time.*

Continuing forward, you'll travel down a steep decline to what was once one of Bonaire's most important harbors, **Boca Slagbaai**, Slaughter Bay. Nowadays it is a popular dive and snorkel site. If you're traveling with young children, this is an especially fine spot for a break. There is a sandy

**Bonaire**

beach and very little coral on the northern side of the bay.

Its history dates back to 1868, when the land was sold to private plantation owners. The cattle and goats that grazed on the northwestern portion of the island were slaughtered and processed here before being exported to Curaçao – hence the grisly name. Also introduced during this period was the salt industry, which had been operating in the south since 1635. The largest of the yellow colonial-style buildings was the warehouse, or *magasina*, where the salt was stored, while the northernmost building was the Customs Office. They date to 1868 and have been restored by STINAPA to house the park's administrative offices.

Growing alongside the warehouse are calabash trees. Their large fruit serve a multitude of purposes. When it is unripe and green in color, it can be made into an unbeatable flea shampoo. When fully ripe, it produces a soothing syrup for sore throats. When allowed to dry to a hard shell, the fruit is carefully opened, its insides removed and replaced with the seeds of the flamboyant tree, to make a *maracá*, a popular instrument.

Reddish egrets are occasionally sighted in **Saliñas Slagbaai**, located just across from the bay. Its name is misleading since the reddish egret is just as white as its cousin, the snowy egret, but it is easily distinguished by its stiff mannerisms and black-tipped, flesh-colored bill. You are almost certain to see flamingos here since the salt pans are another of their favorite feeding grounds. For a closer look, quietly follow the

Green Route along the eastern edge of the salt pan.

Just beyond Boca Slagbaai you'll drive through what was once an aloe plantation, even passing the remains of an aloe oven on the right side. The difference in vegetation between the Washington side of the park (the northern section) and where you are now should be readily apparent. While the soil in Washington is lime-based, the soil in this area, the Slagbaai section, is relatively fertile. Also, the hills in the north and northeast shelter Slagbaai from the constant trade winds. Those winds give a beating to all but the most wind-resistant trees in Washington.

Protection from the trade winds, combined with more fertile soil, has given rise to a greater variety of plant life in Slagbaai. Formerly, the goats wreaked havoc here. They nibbled away at virtually everything that grew, hastening the erosion of the topsoil by destroying the plants that held it in place. By erecting fences to limit the number of goats in Slagbaai, the park service hopes to slow the erosion process and keep the plant life and soil relatively intact.

**Bonaire**

The Green and Yellow Routes branch off again at **Ceru Sumpiña**. If you are out of time, continue along the Green Route, which will take you directly to the park exit. Otherwise, continue along the Yellow Route, also known as **Brasil Panorama Road** because of the wonderful views in the Brasil section of the park. This drive is described in the Northern Tour. Highlights include the flamingos at Playa Frans and the panoramic views of Lake Goto and Subi Brandaris from Gotomeer.

*There's a fine view of Slagbaai with Brandaris Hill deep in the background from the top of Ceru Sumpiña.*

## Detour Up Brandaris Hill (Subi Brandaris)

At 784 feet above sea level, Brandaris Hill is the highest point on Bonaire. The hike to the top and down again should take you around three hours. Combine that with the Caribbean sun and you've got a workout! Needless to say, sturdy footwear is a must, and be sure to bring plenty of water and a hat. Extra sunscreen is not a bad idea, either.

Follow the Green Route to the turn-off to Subi Brandaris, a heavily wooded road that you follow to the end. There you park your vehicle. You're on foot from here. Along the way you will pass through a gate that separates Washington from Slagbaai. Be sure to shut it behind you since the fence was built to prevent Washington goats from entering Slagbaai. Remember that goats eat young shoots and so are responsible for much of the soil erosion in Washington.

The footpath continues to the rocks at the base of the ridge. Then follow the yellow circles marked on the boulders along the ridge of the hill. En route you'll enjoy wonderful views of Boca and Saliña Slagbaai, Goto Lake, Playa Funchi and the north coast. Reaching the top, you'll be greeted by a spectacular panorama of the island.

## Bird Watching at Put Bronswinkel

Just before the turnoff to Brandaris Hill, you'll find the entrance to Put Bronswinkel, another freshwater hole that is popular with a variety of birds, ranging from the most common to the very rare. Some of the less common varieties known to frequent this area include the black-whiskered vireo, the pearly-eyed thrasher and the yellow oriole. You may need to be patient and spend some time here. As any experienced birder can tell you, your patience may be rewarded. In order not to scare the birds, it is best to park your car at the entrance and walk the short distance to the Put.

As is always true where there is a pool of stagnant water, mosquito repellent is a must! The months of October through February bring small fruit flies that can be extremely annoying as they tend to fly into eyes, nose and mouth.

# Shop Till You Drop

Though serious shoppers will fare better in Curaçao, or even Aruba, that doesn't mean you have to leave Bonaire empty-handed. You'll still be able to find gifts for the folks back home (or for yourself), including china, crystal and French perfumes at great duty-free prices. And since Kralendijk is so small, you should be able to finish your shopping in time for a sunset happy hour or afternoon dive!

Shops in Kralendijk are open from 8 am to noon and 2 pm to 6 pm, Monday through Saturdays. Most are on Kaya Grandi or in the Harbourside Mall on Kaya Crane. US dollars and Antillean guilders or florins are accepted everywhere, as are major credit cards. We have listed a few stores sure to please on the following pages.

Bonaire

## Around Town

**Fundashon Arte Bonaireano**, on Kaya Hellmund. This non-profit foundation is dedicated to preserving Bonaire's traditions by teaching young people popular handicrafts. Its downtown shop offers a lovely selection of locally made items, as well as some fine pieces by island artists.

The **Bonaire Gift Shop**, Kaya Grandi 13. In addition to more standard souvenirs, including T-shirts, postcards, and knickknacks, the Bonaire Gift Shop features handicrafts from India, Holland and South America. Its sister shop, **Best Buddies**, at Kaya Grandi 32, features funky resortwear, including Indonesian batiks.

**Littman Jewelers**, Kaya Grandi 33. For well over a decade the Littman Family has been selling its own handcrafted designs, along with high quality Swiss watches, 18 kt. Italian gold jewelry, and Swarovski crystal. This shop is located in a traditional Bonairean house. The Littmans have opened a second shop, **Littman Gifts**, in the Harbourside Mall, where you can pick up hand-painted T-shirts, costume jewelry and other moderately priced gifts.

**Zulay's Place**, Kaya L.D. Gerharts. Zulay's features one-of-a-kind gifts, including paintings and prints, as well as handmade jewelry from Bonaire and the Caribbean, along with unique T-shirts.

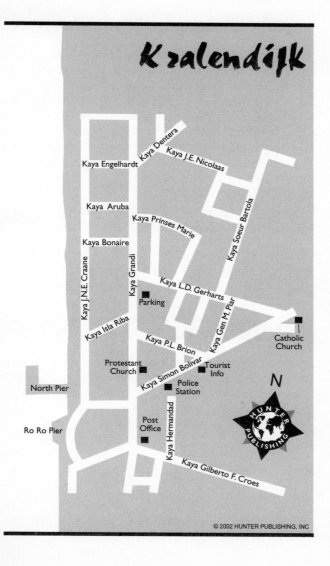

Kralendijk

Kaya Dentera
Kaya J.E. Nicolaas
Kaya Engelhardt
Kaya Aruba
Kaya Prinses Marie
Kaya Soeur Bartola
Kaya Bonaire
Kaya J.N.E. Craane
Kaya Grandi
Kaya L.D. Gerharts
Parking
Kaya Gen M. Piar
Kaya Isla Riba
Kaya P.L. Brion
Catholic Church
Protestant Church
Kaya Simon Bolivar
Tourist Info
North Pier
Police Station
N
Ro Ro Pier
Post Office
Kaya Hermandad
Kaya Gilberto F. Croes

HUNTER PUBLISHING

Bonaire

© 2002 HUNTER PUBLISHING, INC

## Harbourside Mall

You don't have to travel to Europe to find lovely Blue Delft porcelain or table linens from Holland. **Little Holland** also has a great selection of Cuban cigars kept fresh in a custom-made acclimatized cedar cigar room. Little Holland is part of a chain of shops found throughout the Netherlands Antilles. **Sparky's** offers a fine selection of perfumes and cosmetics at duty-free prices. Sister shops are found throughout the Caribbean.

## Bonaire Shopping Gallery

Located at Kaya Grandi, and far from run-of-the-mill, the **Bonaire Souvenir Shop** specializes in postcards, posters, maps, books and unusual gifts.

## At the Airport

You can do some last-minute shopping at the airport. Pick up postcards, T-shirts and assorted gifts at **Valerie's**. The **Duty Free Shop** offers the usual liquors and perfumes, as well as cheeses from Holland and fine chocolates.

# After Dark

"After Dark" is something of a misnomer since Bonaire's biggest post-daytime attraction is that magic moment when the sun meets the horizon, creating the legendary "green flash." Sunset happy hour, between 5 pm and 7 pm, is an institution on Bonaire. Virtually every bar on the leeward coast has one.

One of the most popular is at **Karel's Beach Bar** on the waterfront at Kaya Craane 12 in Kralendijk, where a lively crowd of locals and visitors starts to gather at around 4 pm and stays into the wee hours. If there is a major sporting event you need to see, Karel's will have it on their big-screen television via satellite. Live music often accompanies the sunset at **Rum Runners** at Captain Don's Habitat, while tropical drinks are featured at the **Green Parrot** in the Sand Dollar Condominium and Beach Club.

## Sunset Sails

The most memorable way to experience Bonaire's magnificent sunset is under the red sails of the *Samur*, the only authentic Siamese junk in the Caribbean. The *Samur*'s two-hour Green Flash Sail departs daily at 5 pm from November through February and at 5:30 pm from March to October. On Thursday evenings, sunset is followed by a seven-course Thai Feast.

The *Samur* also offers Full-Moon Sails (during the full moon only), with plenty of champagne to toast the Southern Cross. Both cruises include open bar. Reservations should be made in advance and a deposit may be required (☎ 717-5592 or 09-607307).

**Bonaire**

## Slide Shows for Divers

Once the sun sets, Bonaire quiets down considerably. If an outrageous nightlife is one of your prerequisites, then Bonaire probably won't be the island for you. However, this does not mean that you will be spending every night playing cards in your hotel room or going to bed at 9 pm. It does mean that it shouldn't be difficult for you to be on the 9 am dive boat. To get ready for the next day's dive, you may want to attend one of the underwater slide shows offered at hotels across the island.

*Call ahead in case of a schedule change.*

Sunday nights, you have a choice of **Bonaire Above & Below Water** from 8:45 to 9:30 pm at Captain Don's Habitat (☎ 717-8290) or **Reflections of Bari Reef** at the Sand Dollar Beach Club (☎ 717-8737) from 8 to 8:30 pm. On Tuesday evenings, the Sand Dollar offers the second part of Sunday's show with **Bari Reef – A Closer Look** at 8:45 pm. Then on Wednesdays, the Coral Regency Resort (☎ 717-5580) features **Bonaire Above & Below Water** at 9 pm. For an even closer look at Bonaire's marine life, join Dee Scarr for **Touch the Sea** Monday nights at 8:45 pm at Captain Don's Habitat. Movie buffs should find out whether there's anything playing in the small theater downtown.

## Live Music

Many of the hotel restaurants feature theme nights with live music. **Rum Runners** (☎ 717-7303) at Captain Don's Habitat offers a BBQ night with live music on Sunday evenings from 7 pm to 10 pm; a Bonairean night featuring island cuisine and a folkloric show on Tuesday evenings at 8 pm; and a Tex-Mex Night with Captain Don on Thursdays starting at Happy Hour, with live music provided by the Kunuku Band. Friday night's Reggae Jerk Boogie Festival at the **Oceanfront Restaurant** (☎ 717-5644), with Jamaican jerk cooking and live reggae, is a lot of fun.

## Casinos & Dancing

Choices are limited for casino and disco goers. There is a small "barefoot casino" at **Divi Flamingo Beach Resort**. Look for a larger casino at the Plaza Resort Bonaire on J.A. Abraham Boulevard 80, ☎ 717-2500, Bonaire's hottest night spot is the **Fantasy Disco** upstairs at the Stephany Shopping Mall on Kaya L.D. Gerharts. It features a large dance floor with ample seating areas in a tropical ambience (and a powerful AC). Latin and island rhythms are most popular, especially merengue and tumba, with some North American music added for good measure. Try to come on a Friday when "Magic Sound," one of the most popular bands on the island, performs. The Fantasy attracts a mature crowd, primarily locals and Dutch. The **E Wowo 2000 Disco**, the island's first disco, attracts a younger, local crowd.

*Bonaire*

*Wednesday is Ladies Night, with free admission for women at the Fantasy Disco. Otherwise, there is a cover charge.*

# ❓ Bonaire A-Z

## Airlines

Both **ALM** and **KLM** can be reached at ☎ 717-7400 or 717-7447; ☎ 717-8500 on Sundays and weekdays after 5:30 pm. The local number for **Servivensa** is ☎ 717-8361. Be sure to confirm your flight at least 24 hours in advance. The general number for the **Flamingo Airport** is ☎ 717-5600.

## Airport Departure Tax

If you are flying to Curaçao or any of the other islands of the Netherlands Antilles you must pay a departure tax of US $5.75 or NAFL 10. The departure tax for international flights, including Aruba, is US $10 or NAFL 17.50.

## Babysitting

Most hotels will arrange for a babysitter, often a member of the staff, if you request one. The **Sand Dollar Condominium and Beach Club** and the **Divi Flamingo** have children's programs.

## Banking

Banks are open Monday through Friday from 8 am to 3:30 pm. US dollars are accepted virtually everywhere on the island. The ATM machine at the **A.B.N. Bank** in Kralendijk at Kaya Grandi 2 dispenses US dollars, as well as Antillean guilders.

## Credit Cards

**American Express** and **Visa/MasterCard** are the most widely accepted. The American Express representative is Maduro Travel, Kaya Grandi 52 (☎ 717-8653). Services include personal and traveler's check cashing and the report of lost or stolen cards. Office hours are Monday through Friday, 8 am-noon and 1-5 pm; closed weekends and holidays.

**Maduro & Curiels Bank**, with branches at Kaya L.D. Gerharts 1 (☎ 717-5520; fax 717-5520) and the airport, is the island representative for Visa/MasterCard. Services include the report of lost or stolen credit cards and cash advances. Hours: Monday, Wednesday and Thursday, 8:30 am-3:30 pm; Tuesday and Friday, 8:30 am-noon and 1 pm to 6 pm; Saturdays from 10 am to 3 pm.

## Currency

The currency on Bonaire is the **Netherlands Antilles Florin** (NAFL), which is also referred to as a **guilder**. Florins are extremely stable, backed by gold and foreign exchange, and they fluctuate with the dollar on the world market. At press time the exchange rate was 1.77 florins (NAFL or AFL) to US $1, as it has been for some time. US dollars are widely accepted.

## Drinking Water

Tap water on Bonaire is purified, desalinated sea water and is safe to drink.

## Driving

Driving is on the right.

## Electricity

Bonaire operates on 127/120 V (50 cycles), and is compatible with US appliances. Adapters may be needed in some cases.

## Emergencies

To call an ambulance, the police or the fire department, ☎ 11. To contact the hospital, ☎ 14.

## Postage

Sending a postcard to anyone off the island will cost you NAFL 1.75 or US $1.

## Shopping Hours

Stores open from 8 am-noon and 2 pm-6 pm, Monday through Saturday. Some stores open on Sundays and holidays (except Christmas and Good Friday), when cruise ships are in port. For more information, ☎ 717-8322 or 717-8649.

# Taxis

To call the taxi stand at the airport ☎ 717-8100. Otherwise, ☎ 717-5330.

# Telephones

Bonaire's country code and area code is 599-717. For AT&T USA Direct Service, dial ☎ 001-800-872-2881. Bonaire's only public phone is at the entrance to the Washington-Slagbaai National Park. AT&T phone booths are located in the lobby of the Sunset Hotel and at the airport.

# Television & Radio

CNN and other cable channels from the US are available at some hotels. For the news in English, listen to **Transworld Radio** at 800 AM. You can get the news in Dutch on **Voz di Bonaire**, 94.7 FM every hour on the hour from 7 am to 6 pm.

# Tourist Office

The tourist office is at Kaya Libertador Simon Bolivar 12 in Kralendijk (☎ 717-8322). To reach the North American office, ☎ 800-826-6247 (in New York 212/956-5911); or write Tourism Corporation Bonaire, 10 Rockefeller Plaza, Suite 900, New York, NY 10020. Their website is www.infobonaire.com. To contact the European office in the Netherlands, ☎ 31-70-395-4444; or write Tourism Corporation Bonaire, Visseringlaan 24, 2288ER Rijswijk, The Netherlands.

Bonaire

# Happy Holiday Homes

**Y**ou'll find these delightful accommodations near the sea, and a visit here will make you feel as though you're coming home. Just step inside and make yourself comfortable.

Our charming bungalows are bright, sunny and always spotlessly clean. They come fully equipped with air conditioning, cable TV, and a kitchen with fridge and microwave. Your private garden sports a sun terrace (perfect to watch the sun go down and sip a cocktail) and is filled with colorful tropical flowers. Our attentive staff is always thoughtful and courteous and can assist with special requests.

These attractive accommodations offer seclusion and privacy, yet are located at Punt Vierkant, just minutes away from famous dive sites and windsurfing areas. Diving, windsurfing and car rental packages offered at competitive rates.

## www.happyholidayhomes.com

*Happy Holiday Homes*
*Post Office Box 216*
*Bonaire, Dutch Caribbean*
*General questions, info@happyholidayhomes.com*

*In Bonaire, call Louise or Kitty at*
☎ *599-717-8405; fax 599-717-8605*

*In the US, contact Garry at*
☎ *(610) 459-8100 ext. 204; fax (610) 459-3216*

*Opposite: Zeelandia, now an office building, is a fine example of Baroque architecture in Willemstad.*

*Above: Island crafts are often made by local women.*

*Below: Knip Beach is especially popular on weekends.*

*ve: The ABC islands are renowned for their spectacular underwater life.*

*low: Blinding white salt flats on Bonaire. (Tourism Corporation Bonaire)*

*Above: Windsurfers' sails make a colorful display.*

*Opposite: A diver plays peek-a-boo among coral.*

*Below: Handelskade ("Commerce Street") in Willemstad.*

*Above: Cyclists explore the Bonaire countryside.*

*...osite: Among island residents are eye-catching iguanas and other reptiles.*

*Below: Small, deserted beaches offer plenty of seclusion.*

*Above: Celebrations surround the arrival of a tall ship into Willemsta*
*Below: A shallow wreck off Curaçao's coast is accessible*
*to both divers and snorkelers.*

# Curaçao

**I**f the ABC Islands were a song, Curaçao would write the lyrics and compose the score. If they were a celebration, Curaçao would plan the party. And, if the ABC Islands were a feast, Curaçao would cater it. Much of what defines the islands and sets them apart from others in the Caribbean originated on Curaçao, birthplace of the local language, Papiamento; popular music and dance; and the biggest festival in the Netherlands Antilles – Carnival. Founded on commerce by the Dutch West India Company in the 17th century, Curaçao remains a major stop on the trade routes between the Americas and Europe.

Nowhere is the Dutch influence in the Antilles stronger than on Curaçao. The island's colonial past is preserved in the delightful architecture of downtown Willemstad and in country estates dating back to the 17th and 18th centuries. Pristine reefs promise spectacular diving while the more than 40 beaches gracing the shore are set against an unspoiled landscape of rolling hills and panoramic vistas. And, though Curaçao's colonial roots run deep, it has kept pace with the rest of the world to offer visitors modern pleasures.

# Culture & Customs

According to archaeological studies, Curaçao was among the earliest of the Caribbean islands, if not the first, to be inhabited. Human remains dating as far back as 2450 BC, the oldest in the Caribbean, have been discovered here. The island's earliest known inhabitants were the peace-loving **Arawak Indians**, who also lived on Aruba and Bonaire. The Arawaks were not warriors, but fishermen who traveled by dugout canoe to trade with their fellow tribes on neighboring islands. They documented much of their lifestyle with different cave drawings in the northwest corner of Curaçao.

*Make sure to visit the caves in Christoffel Park.*

## The Colonial Period

The first "modern man" known to have set eyes on Curaçao was **Alonso de Ojeda**, a lieutenant in the fleet of Christopher Columbus, who discovered Curaçao in 1499. Amazed by the size of the Indians living on all three ABC Islands, he nicknamed them *Islas de los Gigantes*, meaning the "Islands of Giants." Unfortunately, no gold or minerals were discovered on Curaçao, and the dry climate and lack of fresh water made it unsuitable for agriculture. Failing to recognize Curaçao's strategic value in the ongoing wars for control of the Caribbean, the Spanish included Curaçao among their list of *islas inutiles* (worthless islands). A little over a century later, however, the French, English and Dutch would recognize Curaçao's great value as a strategic port, thus beginning a series of skirmishes that would last until the 19th century.

In 1505, Curaçao was invaded by *indieros*, who made their living selling Indians as slaves. Approximately 2,000 of the island's able-bodied residents were shipped to Hispaniola to serve as slave laborers in the silver mines of Haiti. In fact, Curaçao was an important slave depot, with thousands of transactions a year until the beginning of the 18th century. At times, there were up to 14,000 slaves on the island at one time awaiting transport to the New Netherlands and the Spanish coast. The slave trade peaked in 1713.

Shortly after the Spanish government appointed **Juan de Ampués** a factor of Curaçao in 1526, he returned to the island with 200 slaves, along with sheep, goats, cows and horses from Europe. Throughout the next decades, he oversaw the operation of the island as a self-sufficient ranch supplying horses, hides and dye-wood. Marauding pirates were wreaking havoc throughout much of the Caribbean during this time, while English, French and Dutch forces fought for control, either among themselves or by joining together to wrest control from the Spanish.

## Dutch West India Company

This situation continued until July 29, 1634, when **Johann Van Walbeek** and a fleet of six ships with 225 soldiers arrived in Santa Ana Bay to claim Curaçao for the Dutch West India Company. Just prior to the attack, **Jan Jansz Otzen**, a dark-skinned Dutchman, had tipped off the West India Company that the island would be an easy target since it was inhabited by only a small group of Spaniards. Limited possibilities to land on the island would make it easy to defend against future attacks. Curaçao would also bene-

Curaçao

fit the company in several ways. Its natural harbor would be useful in the company's ongoing battles against the Spanish. It would also provide another stronghold in the Caribbean from which to police its trading routes and possessions in the New Netherlands and Brazil. In addition, the company believed that Curaçao could become an important agricultural colony.

*Fort Amsterdam is the seat of the government of the Netherlands Antilles today.*

The Spaniards surrendered Curaçao to the Dutch in exchange for safe passage to Europe for 32 Spaniards, including children, and 402 Indians. After their victory, the Dutch quickly set to work fortifying the entrance to the harbor, building Fort Amsterdam on the outcrop of land alongside the Santa Anna Bay.

## The Slave Trade

Though best known as the one-legged governor of New Amsterdam, later to become New York, Peter Stuyvesant was one of Curaçao's earliest directors. He was appointed governor in 1642 and was then named governor of the New Netherlands in 1646. Stuyvesant was based in New Amsterdam throughout his term as governor of Curaçao, which lasted until 1664. His most noteworthy achievement was the establishment of a slave depot on Curaçao where, following their capture, the slaves would rest and regain their strength before being sold and transported to their final destination. Until early in the 18th century, Curaçao's slave depot was the most important in the Caribbean, with about 40% of the slaves shipped via the Atlantic passing through Curaçao.

But Curaçao's maritime value went beyond serving as a slave depot. The island was also an important depot for South American and Caribbean products bound for Europe. In fact, French and English merchants were dependant on the trading expertise of the Dutch. Perhaps to an even greater extent, much of the island's commercial success was due to the Sephardic Jews who had fled to Curaçao after the fall of Brazil in 1654. This group quickly dominated the business community through their knowledge of local trading practices, trade routes and the Spanish language. Eventually Curaçaoan society was dominated by three ethnic groups: Western Europeans, the majority of whom were involved in government; Sephardic Jews who were primarily merchants; and black laborers, although their numbers were low since agriculture never flourished here because of the dry climate.

## The 18th Century

While Jan Otzen's vision of agricultural development would never come to fruition, his assessment of the harbor's importance was right on target. But he did err in his assessment of the island's defenses. Rather than attack the main harbor, Santa Anna Bay, the English and French would invade via the unprotected bays. Throughout the 18th century Curaçao's economy rose and fell with the whim of the warring Europeans. In 1713, the French pirate Cassard invaded the island, then pulled out in exchange for 115,000 pesos in money, goods and slaves. During the Seven Years War, which lasted from 1757 to 1763, sev-

Curaçao

eral West India vessels were seized by the English. Trade was resuscitated during the American War of Independence when Curaçao served as an important station on the supply route from Europe to America. It was also during this period that several Spanish colonies began trading with Europe. As many as 100 vessels would leave the Santa Anna Bay in a single day.

With the French occupation of the Netherlands in the later years of the 18th century, the exiled Prince of Orange wrote to the colonies advising them to seek the protection of the British. French forces, in an effort to prevent British interference, promptly attacked Curaçao. But the British intervened and controlled the island from 1800 to 1803.

Ironically, the British were driven out of Curaçao in 1804 by the Curaçaoan militia, led by Piar and Briar, who later became heroes in the Venezuelan Wars for Independence from Spain. The British regained control on January 1, 1807, by launching a surprise attack on Santa Anna Bay, taking advantage of the New Year's holiday to catch Fort Amsterdam unprepared. The British remained in control of the island until 1816, when the Dutch took over under the terms of the **Treaty of Paris**, signed in 1815.

## The Slave Revolt

Although it was not an agricultural colony, Curaçao did boast several large plantations. The most noteworthy were **Knip** and **Savoneta** on the western tip of the island. Maize, sugar (though not to the extent of other islands), peanuts, melons, and other fruit were cultivated, with as many as 50 slaves working in the fields. Goats and sheep were the primary livestock. While the plantation owners lived comfortably in lavish landhouses, the slaves lived in huts built partly with the remnants of maize stalks. Free slaves lived in the savannah area between plantations eking out a meager living fishing and doing manual work.

During good times, the plantations could produce enough food to be self-sufficient. However, those times were few and far between, given the island's arid climate, leaving island residents dependent on foods imported from Holland and the rest of Europe. Pirate blockades frequently prevented those imports from reaching Curaçao. One such blockade was a contributing factor to the slave revolt of 1765.

During this period, the ideals of liberty, equality and fraternity espoused during the French Revolution were echoing throughout the Caribbean. In 1794, the French General Rigaud helped the slaves of Haiti to free themselves. On August 17, 1795, the slaves of Knip Plantation rebelled. The revolt spread throughout Banda Bou, the western side of Curaçao. At Porto Marie, 1,000 slaves overcame the auxiliary forces that had been sent in to quash the revolt. But on August 26, the commander of the auxiliary forces seized control of the slaves' storehouses at Christoffel. The slave leaders Tula and Carpata were executed. The other slaves returned to work. Slavery would not be formally abolished on Curaçao until 1863.

## Emancipation

The emancipation of the slaves by King William III of the Netherlands was the biggest event of the 19th century. Sixty-seven government slaves and 6,684 private slaves gained their freedom, although their social standing remained low. In order to ensure the continued operation of the island's plantations, the "paga-tera" system was introduced. Under that system, former slaves could continue to work on the plantation; in exchange they were given a small piece of land for their own use as well as goods or a small salary.

Eventually, the little agriculture that there was on Curaçao, coupled with the production of Panama hats, was not enough to support the descendants of the freed slaves. Between the years of 1917 and 1920, nearly 2,500 men left for Cuba to work in the sugarcane fields.

## The 20th Century

Following the emancipation of the slaves in 1863, Curaçao's economy went into a fairly steady decline, forcing many laborers to seek employment on neighboring islands. This situation persisted until 1915, when the Royal Dutch Shell Group established a refinery on Curaçao. The refinery officially opened its doors on May 23, 1918. Although financially independent from Holland, the island's economy was now dependent on the Shell refinery. Shell became the largest employer. Many local industries disappeared as workers abandoned traditional jobs for the higher wages offered by the refinery. There was also a mass immigration of workers to Curaçao.

During World War II, Curaçao served as a refueling station for Allied jet fighters, making it a target for the enemy. Hence, the island was in a state of perpetual readiness against a German U-boat attack. Following the war, the oil business boomed, with nearly 18,500 residents employed by the refinery in 1952. In 1954, the Netherlands Antilles became an autonomous part of the Netherlands, and Curaçao was designated the seat of its government.

*In the 50s, the Netherlands Antilles were Aruba, Bonaire, Curaçao, Saba St. Maarten, & St. Eustatius. Aruba seceded in 1986.*

Curaçao prospered throughout the 1950s and 1960s. It became a popular tax haven for well-off Americans. Wealthy Venezuelans frequented the shops of Willemstad, which were well-stocked with European merchandise. Unfortunately, Curaçao's economy was not to remain strong forever. The island came upon tough times during the 1980s. Following the devaluation of the Bolívar in 1983, Venezuelans could no longer afford to shop in Willemstad. In 1984, a change in US tax laws made it possible for Americans to conduct business directly with the Eurodollar capital market, and they stopped investing in Curaçao. A declining oil market forced Shell to close the refinery in 1985.

**Curaçao**

## Curaçao Today

Curaçao worked hard to make a comeback in the 1990s. The government has taken over the oil refinery and is now leasing it to a Venezuelan company, PDVSA. Not only does this create revenue for the government, but it has also become a source of new jobs for island residents.

The island has regained its status as a major commercial center. Not only is Willemstad's **Shottegatt Harbor** the largest harbor in the Caribbean and the fourth largest port in the world, it is the biggest drydock in the Western Hemisphere and home to one of the world's major bunkering ports. Fifty cargo lines travel through Curaçao. On average, over 20 vessels a day come into port. It has become a major and indispensable port of call between the Americas, and is fast becoming a stopping point for trade between the United States, Europe, the Caribbean and Latin America.

Goods which pass through Curaçao have easy access to both the United States and European markets. Due to its political links with Holland, Curaçao is an Associate Member of the European Economic Community. As a participant in the Caribbean Basin Initiative, Curaçao receives preferential treatment from the United States.

The Curaçaoan government is also implementing incentive programs to promote private investment, one of which is the Free Trade Zone. Merchandise warehoused or processed with its final destination in the Free Zone is not taxed at the same rate as merchandise produced outside the country. Businesses that operate from within the Free Zone enjoy a 2% tax rate. This rate applies to as much as 25% of revenues generated by goods not produced or imported for domestic consumption. There are a growing number of industries on the island, including the Amstel Brewery, cigarette manufacturers, a paint factory, a battery factory and two soap factories. Curaçao is also home to one of the largest desalination plants in the world, producing 1.6 billion gallons of drinking water a year.

Yet Curaçao is not all business. Islanders are working hard to rejuvenate the tourism industry. New hotels are opening up, including the Lion's Dive and the Sonesta, and older ones are being refurbished. Since many of Curaçao's loveliest beaches and finest dive sites are on the western part of the island, far from the commercial center, it's easy to mix business with pleasure without having one interfere with the other. A recent tourist brochure aptly described Curaçao as "an island of business in a sea of pleasure."

## The People

Curaçao's population is remarkably diverse. Periods of growth in the Curaçaoan economy attracted laborers not only from the neighboring islands, but from other countries and Dutch colonies all around the world. Some 50 different nationalities are represented in Curaçao, which has a population of 165,000. Over 16% of island residents were born outside the Netherlands Antilles. It is also an island of great religious and racial tolerance. Catholics, Protestants, Jews and Muslims are all free to worship on the island.

Curaçao

## The Jews of Curaçao

Curaçao's Jewish Congregation, the oldest in the Americas, can trace its roots to the year 1492, when the Spanish Inquisition ordered the expul-

sion of all Jews who refused to be baptized by the
Catholic Church from Spain. Most fled to nearby
Portugal, where the long arm of the Inquisition
was still able to reach them. While many headed
to the Mediterranean, several stayed behind.
Known as *conversos* (secret Jews), they remained in hiding in Portugal for over a century
before eventually finding refuge in Amsterdam
under the tolerant reign of the Prince of Orange-
Nassau.

Amsterdam's newly arrived Sephardic community prospered. In 1651, appointed by the Dutch
West India Company to establish a Jewish agricultural settlement, **Joao d'Ilhan**, accompanied
by 10 Jewish families, traveled to Curaçao and established the New World's first Jewish congregation. They called it Mikvé Israel, The Hope of
Israel. In 1659, they were joined by 70 families
from Amsterdam. Many were Jewish settlers
from Dutch Brazil (Recife), who had returned to
Europe after the Portuguese conquered Brazil.
Immigration to Curaçao continued and, by 1732,
the Jewish Congregation had over 2,000 members.

In 1659, on what was originally agricultural property and is now the oil refinery, the settlers consecrated a cemetery, **Beth Hayim**, House of the
Living. Today it is the oldest Jewish burial
ground in the Americas. Some believe that a synagogue was also built there, which had to be replaced by a larger one in 1681.

It soon became apparent that neither Curaçao's
soil nor its climate were suited to agriculture. Fortunately the settlers recognized that the island's
location and harbor were ideal for shipping and

shipbuilding and quickly set out to develop those industries. Between the years 1670 and 1900, Jews owned over 1,200 ships. One shipping firm, owned by the Jesurun family, had over 100 ships sailing between the Caribbean islands, New York and Europe. Over 200 ship captains were Jews. Through their efforts, Curaçao became a major hub for trade among Europe, the Americas, and other island colonies, English and Spanish, in the Caribbean.

The Jews also played a major role in the development of related businesses, such as bunkering, off-shore banking and finance and the import/export trade. Prosperity followed and they went on to build many of the buildings in Punda, all of Scharloo, the mansions of Pietermaai and many *landhuisen* (landhouses) in the countryside. Their children and grandchildren became doctors, lawyers, civil servants and publishers.

*Jews formed a large part of the island's infrastructure.*

As they made the transition from agriculture to commerce, Curaçao's Jewish families began leaving their plantations and moving to Willemstad. The first city synagogue was built shortly thereafter. But, due to the rapid growth of the community, it soon proved too small and was torn down. A new one was built in its place in 1703, only to be torn down again. The final synagogue was built and consecrated in 1732 on the eve of Passover. It has been in constant use ever since, making it the oldest synagogue in the Western Hemisphere.

Curaçao

*For more details on the Synagogue, see* Museums, *page 332.*

Yet, it was not to remain the only synagogue on the island. In 1740, a second synagogue was consecrated on Breedestraat in Otrobanda. The Otrobanda Jews had been complaining that rowing across the harbor to attend services on

Shabbat violated the commandments. The new synagogue, a branch of Mikvé Israel called Neve Shalom, Peaceable Habitation, was built to appease them. But the new congregation, resenting the control exerted over it by the Parnassim of Mikvé Israel, wanted to secede. Relations between the two congregations deteriorated to such a degree that the economic and public life of the island was affected. The situation became so bad that in 1750 Prince Willem of Orange-Nassau in Holland issued a royal decree to end the dispute. Both congregations observed the decree. Eventually, the decline of Otrobanda's Jewish population forced Neve Shalom to close its doors in 1818.

Later, another schism in the Mikvé Israel congregation would have more enduring results. By 1864, the Reform Jewish Movement, which had been gaining support in the United States and Germany, had developed a following of around 100 families on Curaçao. They broke from the Congregation Mikvé Israel to establish their own congregation. The Reform Congregation consecrated its own temple, Emanuel, on Hendrikplein, in 1867. Though tense at first, relations between the two congregations gradually became friendly. They merged in 1964 to form Curaçao's present congregation: the United Netherlands Portuguese Congregation of Mikvé Israel-Emanuel, which is affiliated with the Jewish Reconstructionist Foundation and the World Union for Progressive Judaism.

*Now the Ashkenazim families are involved in the retail clothing, textile and jewelry industries.*

Today, Curaçao's Jewish population is made up of both Sephardic and Ashkenazim families who began arriving in 1926. Though economic recessions have forced members of both groups to emigrate, reducing their numbers substantially, their presence is still apparent in the religious, civic and commercial life of the island.

## The Government

As part of the Netherlands Antilles, which is administered by a parliamentary democracy, Curaçao's external affairs fall under the jurisdiction of its governing bodies based in Willemstad. The island's internal affairs are administered by the popularly elected Island Council, which carries out both executive and legislative functions. Curaçao's Lieutenant Governor serves as the Crown's representative in Curaçao and is appointed by the Queen of the Netherlands.

## Music

Curaçao's music is a reflection of the island's rich multi-ethnic heritage. Her African, Caribbean, European and Antillean ancestors have all played an important part in the development of Curaçao's folkloric music.

### Tambu

The music most essentially Curaçaoan is the *tambu*. It originated with the African slaves, who danced secretly to express their sorrow. Partners in the dance never touch. Their hips and feet sway to the rhythm while the rest of the body remains still. During the colonial period, slave owners forbade music and dancing, fearing they would lead to conspiracy and revolt. The ban was continued by the Catholic Church following the abolition of slavery in 1863. But the *tambu* eventually made its way into the drawing rooms and parties of the upper and middle classes, joining the danza, polka, mazurka and waltz.

The word *tambu* has three meanings. It describes the small drum on which the music is played; the dance performed to the accompaniment of the drum; or the social event where *tambu* is danced and played. In the modern *tambu*, the lyrics are usually in Papiamento and are accompanied by a *chapi*, or hoe, the small drum, and perhaps singers, while spectators clap to the rhythm. The *tambu* rhythm is a complicated one which, unwritten, is passed from generation to generation. It consists of two different beats – the *sla habri*, or open beat, and the *sla será*, or closed beat – which alternate to create a musical dialogue. Great skill is required to repeat the complicated rhythms. There are also two types of *tambu*. The *telele* is a long lilting melody sung slowly, while the *tambu* itself is faster paced and shorter in duration.

# Seu

Also of African origin is the *seu*, music and dance of the harvest of the *kassir* corn. To the music of the *tambu*, the *chapi*, *bastel,* (cowhorn) and the *kachu* or conch shell, men and women dance together, simulating the harvesting of corn. Men cut the stalks while women carrying baskets on their heads follow. With hips swaying, they walk forward and back, rhythmically dipping to pick up the cobs as they make their way to the storage bins.

## Tumba

Most popular of all is *tumba*, the music of Carnival. *Tumba*'s Afro-Caribbean beat is akin to the calypso of Trinidad, the merengue of Santo Domingo and the *cumbia* of Colombia. There are two related schools of thought as to its origin. One asserts that *tumba* has its roots in Latin America and was adapted by the people of the Netherlands Antilles; the other holds that it is a 20th-century version of the *tambu*.

There are seven different variations on the *tumba*, which can be broken down into two broad groups. There is ballroom *tumba*, which has a slow, uncomplicated and melodious rhythm and is relatively easy to dance to. Then there is the *tumba* of Carnival, which, although not nearly as melodious as its ballroom counterpart, is characterized by complicated rhythms. These, along with the lyrics, are repeated over and over, becoming progressively faster, until they reach a frenzied pace. Dancers hold each other and then part to do variations on the basic steps. A vibrant, lively and creative dance, the *tumba* is as much fun to watch as it is to dance.

## The Waltz

Curaçao's European colonists also played a role in the formation of the island's music. After watching their masters, the slaves eventually copied and adapted the waltz to their own rhythms. The first Curaçaoan waltzes were composed in the 19th century, and they are still danced today. The mazurka and the more complicated French quadrille were also popular.

If you're lucky enough to attend a local dance, you may discover that the music is not provided by a DJ or live band, but by the *ka'i orgel* organ. Imported from Italy and Spain at the turn of the century, the organ works like a player piano. Originally, the cylinders included only European music. Eventually local musicians began to compose their own. Nowadays, each organ has three cylinders, generally containing three waltzes, one mazurka, one polka, one horops, one *danza* and one *tumba*.

Rather than limit yourself to the hotel shows, find out if there are any dances or festivals you can attend. Check the local papers or ask around in restaurants, your hotel, a shop in town. It's a great way to experience Curaçao's wonderful music firsthand!

## Festivals & Holidays

Curaçao enjoys an active cultural life with music festivals held throughout the year, ranging from classical to salsa and jazz. Touring international theater and dance troupes, not to mention symphony orchestras, may offer a performance at the international trade center. Not to be overlooked are the cultural events held throughout the island, including the monthly festivals featuring folkloric music and dance, local foods and handicraft displays hosted by Landhouses Ascensión (first Sunday of the month) and Brievengat (last Sunday of the month). Willemstad celebrates the island's heritage and culture every month with the colorful Ban Topa Street Festival.

Sporting events are also popular. Curaçao's constant wind and placid seas are ideal for sailing, and regattas are a regular occurrence, frequently hosted by the yacht clubs at Spanish Waters.

## Annual Events

**Tumba Festival/Carnival.** Curaçao's Carnival is one of the biggest and flashiest in the Caribbean. See page 246 for details.

**International Blue Marlin Tournament.** This March event attracts sportsmen from Venezuela and across the Caribbean.

**Curaçao International Sailing Regatta.** Catamarans and Sunfish from Holland, the US, and the Caribbean compete in this week-long event hosted by the Sea Aquarium in April.

**Sami Sail Regatta.** A local favorite. Every April the fishing village of St. Michiel, just north of Piscadera Bay, hosts this one-day event.

**Curaçao Salsa Festival.** Top *salseros* from Latin America and the Caribbean perform at the Outdoor Festival Center in August.

**Curaçao Jazz Festival.** Warm weather and "cool jazz" have made this November event a favorite for at least a decade.

Curaçao

For more information concerning these and other events held on Curaçao, contact the Curaçao Tourist Board, ☎ 800-328-7222.

## National Holidays

Banks, the post office and government offices will be closed on these days. Many shops and restaurants may also close.

New Year's Day . . . . . . . . . . . . . January 1
Carnival Monday . . Mon. before Ash Wed.
Good Friday . . . . . . . . . . . . varies as in US
Easter Monday. . . . . . . . . varies as in US
Queen's Birthday . . . . . . . . . . . . . April 30
Labor Day . . . . . . . . . . . . . . . . . . . . May 1
Ascension Day. . . . . . . . . . . . May (varies)
Flag Day . . . . . . . . . . . . . . . . . . . . July 2
Christmas Day . . . . . . . . . . . December 25
Boxing Day. . . . . . . . . . . . . . December 26

## Carnival

If your dream is to be in Curaçao for Carnival, you'd better make your reservations far in advance. Carnival season is the most popular time of year to visit. Unlike the bawdy, bacchanalian free-for-all in Rio de Janeiro, Curaçao's Carnival is a family event, appropriate for children as well as adults.

It has its roots in the Dutch provinces of Brabandt and Limburg where the celebration of Carnival dates back to the Middle Ages. The Carnival tradition, as brought by the Dutch colonists, was one of small parties held in elite social clubs. The opening of the Royal Dutch Shell Oil Refinery in 1915 attracted workers from neighboring islands, who brought with them their lively carnival traditions. Carnival quickly spread to the popular classes and became an island-wide celebration until 1954. That year the government of Curaçao canceled the Carnival celebration as a gesture of sympathy and solidarity with the suffering people of Holland. The Motherland was in the midst of one of the worst disasters in history. During a violent storm the North Sea had broken through the dikes, flooding a large part of the country. Hundreds of lives were lost along with farmland and countless homes.

Despite repeated attempts over the next 18 years, the Carnival tradition was not revived until 1971, when Omalio Merien assembled the first Carnival Committee of Curaçao to organize a new Carnival. An addition to the celebration was the Tumba Festival. During this four-day event in the Curaçao Festival Center, hundreds of bands from across the island compete before an audience of thousands to have their *tumba* selected as the year's Carnival theme. The lead singer of the winning band is crowned Carnival King or Queen and the winning *tumba* is played by all the Carnival bands as they travel the route of the Grand March.

Carnival preparations begin long before the actual event. In fact, one year's Carnival will barely have ended before the groups convene to discuss the theme for the next year and to begin designing costumes and ordering fabric. The festivities get underway in January with the **Old Mask Parade**. As a final tribute to the previous year's cele-

Curaçao

bration, revelers don that year's costumes and dance through the streets to the old *tumba* before focusing on the upcoming Carnival. Elections are held for the Prince and Jester, who will be awarded keys to the city by the Lieutenant Governor, and a beauty pageant is held to select the Carnival Queen. Since children's parades are held in addition to the adult ones, both children and adult Princes, Jesters, and Carnival Queens are selected. Throughout the month of January, impromptu jump-ups (nocturnal dancing free-for-alls) dot the streets and the countryside as spirits start to rise.

*Some residents even camp out the night before to secure a good spot.*

Once the local authorities give the okay, about a week before the first parade, residents drag chairs, benches or whatever else they can think of, out to the street, to claim their spot along the parade route. Commotion ensues, with friendly disputes as to who got where first. When things settle down, chairs are chained in place and remain undisturbed throughout the week's festivities.

*Yards of fabric, sequins & feathers, and months of work go into every costume.*

The months of preparation culminate in the **Grand March**, which takes place on the Sunday before Ash Wednesday. All day long local groups in their colorfully elaborate costumes parade through the streets to the beat of that year's winning *tumba*. The merrymaking subsides a bit on Monday, only to rise to a feverish pitch on Shrove Tuesday. Following the torchlight Farewell March and the burning of the Mummer King (El Rey Momo), the dancing and partying will last well into the early morning hours.

# Getting Here

With Bonaire 30 miles to the east and Aruba 42 miles west, Curaçao is at the center of the ABC Islands. The island is at 12° north and 69° west longitude, 1,710 miles south of New York and 35 miles north of Venezuela.

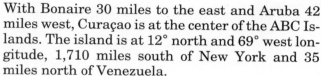

## By Air

Your arrival at the Curaçao International Airport should be relatively trouble-free. If you've arrived without a hotel reservation, there should be someone at the Tourist Information Booth to assist you. If you've made arrangements for a car, you can pick it up, along with directions to get you to your hotel. Otherwise, cabs are available right at the exit. Fares are calculated based on distance and are charged per cab for up to four persons. A 25% surcharge will apply for a fifth person. There is also an extra charge if luggage is so excessive that the trunk does not close. The fare to the hotels in and around Willemstad should be around $20. If you're staying at one of the more remote hotels, arrange for a hotel transfer when making reservations. Otherwise, you can expect to pay $30 to $50, depending on where you stay.

Nonstop service to Curaçao from the United States generally originates out of Miami. Flight time is two hours and 45 minutes. **American Airlines** (☎ 800-433-7300) offers daily nonstop service from Miami (11 am departure). **ALM** (☎ 800-327-7230) generally offers two flights

Curaçao

daily between Miami and Curaçao (1:30 pm and 6 pm). Through a codeshare program between the two airlines, passengers flying **United Airlines** from other US cities connect in Miami with the ALM flight to Curaçao. Reservations must be made through United (☎ 800-241-6522). ALM also flies to Curaçao out of Atlanta on Saturdays and Sundays at 1:30 pm. Flight time is four hours. **KLM** (☎ 800-374-7747) offers daily service between Holland and Curaçao.

A few days in Curaçao can easily be combined with a trip to Venezuela. **Servivensa** (☎ 800-428-3672) offers daily service between Caracas and Curaçao. ALM also offers several weekly flights between Curaçao and Venezuela.

## Via Cruise Ship

Willemstad is included in the itineraries of numerous cruise lines, including Crystal Cruises, Costa Cruise Lines, Norwegian Cruise Lines, and the Cunard Line. The passenger terminal is in Otrobanda alongside the Queen Emma Bridge. A Tourist Information Kiosk sponsored by the Curaçao Tourist Board is located in the terminal.

# Orientation

Thirty-eight miles long, with widths ranging from 7.2 to 2.5 miles at its narrow middle, Curaçao covers an area of more than 174 square miles and is the largest of the ABC islands.

Curaçao

© 2002 HUNTER PUBLISHING, INC

9.6 KM
6 MILES

North Point
Playa Kalki
Westpoint Bay
Westpoint
Boca Tabla
Indian Inscription Caves
Playa Grandi
Bartol Bay
Boca Ascencion
Boca San Pedro
Barber
Soto
San Willibrordo
Lagun Bay
Lagun
Boca Sta. Cruz
CHRISTOFFEL PARK

CURAÇAO

Boca Playa Canoa
St. Joris Bay
Santa Rosa
Brievengat
Hato Caves
Hato Int'l Airport
Bullen Bay
Bullenbaai
WILLEMSTAD AREA
Otrobanda
Punda
Schottegat
Nieuwpoort
Caracas Bay
Spanish Water
Curaçao Underwater Park
East Point

Caribbean Sea

N

HUNTER PUBLISHING

Like its sister islands, Aruba and Bonaire, Curaçao's rugged windward coast is constantly battered by pounding waves driven in by the trade winds, while its protected leeward side is known for its lovely tranquil bays and secluded beaches.

Flights to Curaçao land at the **Hato International Airport**, which is located not quite mid-island on the north coast. Southeast of the airport is Curaçao's capital, **Willemstad**, on the south coast, nestled between the Caribbean and the Schottegat Harbor. The city's two principal districts, **Punda** to the east and **Otrobanda** to the west, are separated by the Santa Anna Bay, which connects the Schottegat with the sea. Shopping, nightlife, most restaurants and hotels are in the area immediately in and around Willemstad.

Just southeast of Willemstad, in the area known as **Bapor Kibrá**, are the Curaçao Sea Aquarium and the Sea Aquarium Beach, two of the island's most popular attractions, along with the Lion's Dive Hotel & Marina. The Princess Beach Resort & Casino is in this area as well. Farther east is **Spanish Water**, a beautiful sheltered bay, home of the island's most exclusive residential areas and yacht clubs. The Marriott Beach Resort & Casino and the Curaçao Caribbean Hotel & Casino are located 10 minutes west of Willemstad on Piscadera Baai.

While the southeast, especially in the area around Willemstad, is more developed, Curaçao's northwestern region is more scenic, home to the island's loveliest beaches and most beautiful vistas. The Coral Cliff Resort and Casino is in this area, as is the Kadushi Cliffs Resort, a cluster of luxury villas dramatically perched atop a cliff overlooking **Playa Kalki**, one of Curaçao's most spectacular beaches. Nearby is the 4,500-acre **Christoffel National Park**, habitat of the rare Curaçao white-tailed deer and home of the island's highest peak. At 1,239 feet, the **Christoffelberg**, or Mount Christoffel, towers majestically above Curaçao. Those who manage the climb to the top are richly rewarded with magnificent views across the island, oftentimes reaching as far as Bonaire and Venezuela.

# Getting Around

Beach and dive enthusiasts will definitely want to rent a car, since the best beaches and shore dives are along the southwest coast and quite distant from hotels. Jeeps are preferable, both for carrying dive gear and for traveling the dirt roads that lead to the beaches.

## Car Rentals

Since rentals are popular on Curaçao, it is best to make arrangements for a vehicle prior to your arrival. When making hotel reservations, ask if there is a car rental agency on the property. If so you may be able to arrange for a car rental at that time. To accommodate divers, most agencies offer minivans, pick-ups and Jeeps.

Curaçao

The following agencies have branches at the airport and/or offer free pick-up and delivery. Most also have branches at several hotels.

**AVIS:** Curaçao International Airport, Anthony Veder Building, ☎ 4611255.

**BUDGET:** Curaçao International Airport and major hotels. ☎ 8683198.

**DOLLAR:** Curaçao International Airport, ☎ 690-262. Head Office, ☎ 613144.

**EMPRESS:** Curaçao International Airport, ☎ 691-280. Salinja, ☎ 4658808.

**HERTZ:** Dr. Hughenholzweg, ☎ 4658585.

**NATIONAL:** Curaçao International Airport. Branches at the Van der Valk Plaza, Lions Dive and Sonesta Hotels, and in Willemstad at Rooseveltweg, ☎ 8694433.

In order to rent a car you must have a valid driving license which has been held for at least 24 months. The minimum age requirement varies by agency and type of vehicle, and may be anywhere from 21 to 26 years of age. Payment can be made in cash or by credit card. However, if you pay by cash you may need to leave a fairly substantial deposit. Most agencies offer unlimited mileage. Curaçao has enacted seatbelt laws, so buckle up.

Driving is on the right side of the road. Heavy traffic at peak times, one-way streets and unfamiliar traffic patterns in the areas surrounding Willemstad will require that you pay a little extra attention. Watch out for goats and donkeys; they have been known to wander into the road in the countryside and also close to Willemstad. Finally, exercise caution if you're driving during or after a rainstorm when roads will be extra slippery due to built-up dust and oil occasioned by the island's infrequent rains. Remember to lock your doors when leaving the car unattended, and don't leave any valuables, such as a camera or dive equipment, in open view or in the trunk overnight.

## Buses

What you may lose in convenience and flexibility, you'll make up in savings when you travel by bus. Most beaches and sights are accessible by public transportation, including Christoffel Park, the Sea Aquarium, Knip Baai, Lagún, and Westpunt Beach. Several different routes criss-cross the island, with departures from the terminals in Punda and Otrobanda. To give you an idea of cost, the fare from Otrobanda to Westpunt, 90 minutes by bus, is under $1.50. For beach-bound buses, the average time between departures is two hours. For information, contact ABC at ☎ 684733 or 617182.

## Taxis

Taxi stands are located at all the major hotels. The rates should be posted in the cab and are valid between 6 am and 11 pm, after which time a 25% surcharge applies. Depending on the driver, you should be able to hire a cab for sightseeing at an hourly rate of around $30 for a minimum of one hour. Someone at your hotel may be able to help you arrange this.

Curaçao

If you need to call a cab, contact the **central dispatch office** at ☎ 690747 or 690752. The Punda branch is on the Plaza Piar (☎ 611187). The Otrobanda dispatcher is on the Plaza Brion (☎ 623621).

# Best Places to Stay

Accommodations on Curaçao run the gamut from small country inns and simple in-town hotels to five-star luxury resorts. Stay right in Willemstad at a continental-style hotel or in your own luxury villa atop a cliff overlooking the Caribbean. There are plenty of in-between options available as well, some more remotely located than others. All in all, you should be pleasantly surprised by hotel prices on Curaçao when comparing them to many other islands in the Caribbean.

The revival of tourism to Curaçao has spurred the renovation of a few of the island's older properties, though some still need a facelift. If your travel agent recommends an unfamiliar hotel, be sure to ask for a brochure. Also, find out how old it is and, if appropriate, if it has been renovated.

## Alive Price Scale

Our price scale is designed to give you a ballpark figure for planning. It is based on the price of a double room during high season, which generally runs from mid-December to mid-April, though exact dates will vary by hotel. Keep in mind that rates may be lower at other times, but the amount varies from hotel to hotel, and the difference may not be significant.

Considerable savings may be had by taking advantage of special packages, such as those for honeymooners, divers and families. You may do better by reserving with the hotel directly rather than through the main reservation office, a reservation service or travel agent.

Breakfast and meals are generally not included in the rate, but most hotels do offer separate meal plans. A 7% government tax is levied on the room rate and a 12% service charge will generally be added to the rate as well. All of the hotels described take major credit cards unless noted.

### *Accommodations Price Scale*

Deluxe. . . . . . . . . . . . . . more than $250
Expensive . . . . . . . . . . . . . . $151-$250
Moderate . . . . . . . . . . . . . . . $100-$150
Inexpensive. . . . . . . . . . . . . Under $100

## *Resorts & Hotels*

**Curaçao**

## MARRIOTT BEACH RESORT & EMERALD CASINO
Piscadera Bay
248 rooms, including studio & one-bedroom suites
☎ 7368800; www.marriotthotels.com
Deluxe

If the Marriott were your home, you would probably lock yourself in and throw away the key. As you step into the lobby and look beyond the fountains to the lush gardens surrounding the pool and then out to the azure waters of the Caribbean, you'll be swept away not only by the view but by the magnificent Dutch Caribbean setting and the friendly greetings you'll receive at the reception desk. One of the newest resorts on the island, the Marriott will pamper you with modern luxury. Guest rooms are spacious and beautifully appointed. The attentive staff will cater to your every whim, whether it be a massage at the health club, an exotic drink at the swim-up bar, or a special request at one of the Marriott's world-class restaurants. Several different types of accommodations are available, with island, garden or ocean view. Honeymooners should request a terrace suite, which has a large balcony with ocean view, Roman-style hot tub and private sunbathing terrace.

*The workout is optional.*

You can start your day with an invigorating workout at the Health Club, which features state-of-the-art exercise equipment, along with two steamrooms and saunas, whirlpools and a massage room. Follow that with a leisurely poolside breakfast at the Palm Café. As for the rest of the day, the Marriott has its own PADI dive shop featuring shore and boat diving; a watersports facility with windsurfing, Jet Ski rentals and snorkeling; and two lighted tennis courts (instruction available). Fishing or horseback riding can be arranged. Of course, there's always the option of a lounge chair under a palm on the poolside terrace or the Marriott's private beach. Baby-sitting can be arranged upon 24-hour notice. "Just Us Kids," a counselor-supervised children's program for children five-13, is also offered Wednesday through Sunday.

If you're looking for a little excitement, you can test your luck at the elegant **Emerald Casino** with its 5,000 square feet of slot machines, blackjack, roulette, craps, mini-baccarat and Caribbean stud poker. Minimum stakes at the tables are $5, with a $500 maximum. Jackpots go up to $20,000 at the slots. Complimentary drinks are served to players seated at the slots and tables. The fine shops in the Marriott Shopping Arcade, including Gandelman Jewelers and the Casa Amarilla, will gladly relieve you of your winnings.

*Remember: a dress code applies after 7 pm in the Emerald Casino.*

After a day in the sun and saltwater, the Marriott's full-service salon will get you ready for the evening. Guest relations keep you informed of special events and evening entertainment. Happy Hour is from 4:30 to 6:30 pm at the Seabreeze Pool Bar, followed by the dinner hour. Delicious Northern Italian specialties, including fantastic Italian desserts, are served in an airy Mediterranean atmosphere at the Portofino Restaurant. The Marriott's fine dining room, the Emerald Grille, features steaks and seafood, and made-to-order desserts, including fabulous soufflés. Casual outdoor dining is available at the Palm Café.

## PRINCESS BEACH RESORT & CASINO
Dr. Martin Luther King Blvd. 8
341 rooms and suites
☎ 7367888; fax 4614131
In US, ☎ 800-992-2015
Expensive

A lovely room with no surprises and attentive service is what you should expect from the Princess Beach, a Holiday Inn Crowne Plaza Resort. Spacious rooms feature modern décor, large modern bath, mini-fridge, in-room safe deposit box, cable

Curaçao

TV and direct dial telephone. Plus, there's lots to do. You can participate in any of the day's activities, go snorkeling off the beach or diving under the watchful supervision of the Peter Hughes Divers, play tennis, work out in the fitness center or just lounge on the beach or by the pool. Evening entertainment kicks off with Happy Hour, often with live music, at the poolside bar, followed by dinner at the Floating Market Restaurant, featuring a different theme every night. The casino is one of the island's largest, with hundreds of slots as well as roulette, craps, blackjack and Caribbean poker. For a more subdued evening, start with dinner at L'Orangerie; the rest is up to you.

## LION'S DIVE & BEACH RESORT
Bapor Kibrá
72 rooms
☎ 4348888; fax 4348889
In US, ☎ 866-LIONSDIVE
www.lionsdive.com
Moderate

*Lion's Dive is the #1 choice for divers!!* Whether you're a well-seasoned diver or an avid beginner, the Lion's Club of Curaçao had you in mind when they planned their hotel. The first new hotel to open on the island in 20 years, the Lion's Club built the Lion's Dive as the cornerstone of their campaign to revive tourism by promoting diving. Ocean Encounters, the hotel's five-star dive center is not only the island's largest, but features the largest air station in the Caribbean. It has two custom-designed 40-foot dive boats, and impeccably cared-for rental equipment (never more than two years old) and includes still and video cameras. Ocean Encounter's friendly staff of multilingual professionals offers all PADI certification courses as well as introductory dives.

Dive schedules are posted weekly and feature a variety of both shore and boat dives including one- and two-tank dives, night dives and wreck dives. Whenever feasible, snorkelers are welcome too. Divemasters will do their best to accommodate special requests for additional night dives, day-trips and special dive packages.

Lion's Dive has plenty to keep non-divers happy. With free admission to the Sea Aquarium for all Lion's Dive guests, non-divers too can experience Curaçao's underwater world. Fitness enthusiasts can take advantage of the state-of-the-art facilities and classes offered at the fitness center. Lion's Dive also offers sailboard rentals and instruction as well as Jet Skis and sea kayaks. A lounge chair under a palm on the Sea Aquarium Beach or at poolside is another possibility.

Guest rooms, most with ocean view and balcony, are set amid tropical gardens in a Dutch Caribbean ambience. An American-style breakfast buffet is served daily at Rumours, the oceanside terrace restaurant. Shuttlebus service is available between the hotel and the downtown shopping area. Babysitting service is also available.

**THE AVILA BEACH HOTEL**
Penstraat 130
Willemstad
90 rooms
☎ 4614377; fax 4611493
www.avilahotel.com
Moderate/expensive

Curaçao

Nestled behind a group of tall trees on the outskirts of Willemstad is a stately 18th-century building, originally the governor's residence, then a hospital and, for the past 40 years, the Avila

*The Avila Beach Hotel features modern luxury in a classic old-world style.*

Beach Hotel. Quietly refined, the Avila combines traditional Dutch Caribbean décor with modern comfort. One of the most traditional and lovely of Curaçao's hotels, the Avila does not have a casino, nor does it allow topless bathing. Accommodations, all tastefully furnished, range from standard rooms to two-bedroom suites with kitchenette and sitting areas. Practically all have an ocean view as well as a private balcony or terrace, and are air conditioned.

The Avila has its own beach, a tennis court and shady gardens, ideal for reading or just plain daydreaming. The Avila also offers its guests fine dining. Breakfast is served in a garden patio setting in the Avila Café. At the Belle Terrace, diners enjoy lunch and dinner under the shade of a giant royal poinciana on a terrace overlooking the Caribbean. Although a striking contrast with the rest of the hotel, the focal point is Blues, the Avila's jazz club/restaurant at the end of the pier overlooking the beach.

## SHERATON CURACAO
Piscadera Bay
181 rooms, 15 suites
☎ 4625000; fax 4625846
In the US, ☎ 800-223-9815, or Golden Tulip Hotels, 800-344-1212
www.starwood.com/sheraton
Expensive

*The Sheraton, built in 1967, was originally a Hilton.*

If swimming and watersports are your thing, then you should consider this hotel. Seascape Dive and Watersports offers a full curriculum of PADI dive instruction ranging from the introductory Discover Scuba and Resort Course to Advance Plus and Dive Master Certification courses, as well as specialty courses. Seascape also offers dive packages for certified divers, including equipment rentals, with dives scheduled at 9 am and 2 pm daily aboard their 38-foot Delta diving boat or their 22-foot offshore diving boat. Night and shore diving are also available.

In addition to diving, Seascape offers water-skiing, along with Jet Ski and Sunfish rentals, sea kayaking, snorkeling trips to Klein Curaçao, deep-sea fishing and a barbecue fun trip every Thursday. The *SeaWorld Explorer* semi-submarine, which offers daily tours of Curaçao's coral reefs, is also docked at the Curaçao Caribbean Marina.

If your idea of watersports is lying by the pool or on the beach with a piña colada, and diving in for a few laps every now and again, you can do that too. In addition to a freshwater swimming pool, the Sheraton boasts the largest natural beach of any hotel on the island, with a generous swimming area enclosed by a walk-around pier. The hotel has two tennis courts, available for day and night play, a playground, beach volleyball and a shuffleboard court. A shopping arcade is located just outside the hotel and complimentary shuttle service to downtown shopping is available.

Business travelers get special attention on the Executive Floor. It has a separate registration desk and offers full secretarial services as well as a daily continental breakfast in the lounge, an evening happy hour and laundry services. Banquet and convention facilities are available within the hotel, and the International Trade Center is just steps away.

Curaçao

Not only does the hotel offer guests a myriad of activities and services, but it has distinct dining experiences as well. American and continental cuisine are served at the outdoor Terrace Restaurant, while Pirates specializes in seafood. Guests can also choose Italian cuisine served in informal surroundings at La Piazzeta. A Champagne Brunch is served on Sundays, and special theme parties are held throughout the week, including the hotel's traditional Monday night barbecue with a Caribbean steel band, a Mexican Fiesta with live mariachi music on Wednesdays, and Saturday night's Caribbean Buffet and Folkloric Show. After dinner you can try your luck at the casino.

Guest rooms in this highrise hotel are well-maintained and comfortable, though the furnishings are dated. All come with individually controlled air conditioning, television, direct dial telephone and large, private balcony with either an ocean or garden view.

## VAN DER VALK PLAZA HOTEL
Plaza Piar, Willemstad
253 rooms
☎ 4612500
Moderate/expensive

*Sunset Happy Hour on the pool terrace is a must at the Plaza!*

A Van der Valk hotel, the Plaza caters primarily to a Dutch clientele. Its expansive lobby is a testimony to the days when Caribbean travel was reserved for the wealthy. Stroll through the lobby with its many seating areas, past the upscale boutiques and goldfish pond where the sounds of tropical birds join those of the waterfalls and fountains, and up the marble staircase to the Pool Terrace. From here you can take in the sweeping views of the Caribbean, the Santa Anna Bay and the Juliana Bridge. This is one of the best vantage points for watching cruise ships sail in and out of Willemstad.

Though the Plaza is not on the beach, it does have a dive school and rental shop, and provides guests with free transfer and discounted admission to the Sea Aquarium. Car rentals and island tours can be arranged at the tour desks in the lobby. Unlike the other five-star hotels on the island, the Plaza is within walking distance of the shops of Willemstad and fine restaurants of the Waterford Arches. The Plaza has an excellent restaurant.

The only area where you may consider the Plaza's age a drawback is in the rooms themselves. Though well-cared for, the furnishings are dated, the color scheme somewhat on the garish side, and many rooms are small. However, all are air conditioned and have a TV and direct dial telephone.

## OTROBANDA HOTEL
Plaza Brion
Willemstad
☎ 4627400; fax 4627299
www.otrobanda.com
42 Rooms
Moderate

The Otrobanda, located in the heart of Willemstad, is convenient to shops and historic sights. The bay terrace is a great place to come (even if not a guest) to view the bustle of the town particularly at sunset. There is a small swimming pool and a very busy casino, frequented by cruise ship passengers since the hotel is located near the cruise terminal.

Curaçao

## HOTEL & CASINO PORTO PASEO

de Rouvilleweg 47, Otrobanda
50 bungalow-style rooms
☎ 4627878; fax 627969
In the US, ☎ 800-328-7222
Inexpensive

*Curaçao's first hospital was at the Porto Paseo site.*

Don't be misled by the façade and lobby. The Porto Paseo is a garden oasis in Otrobanda. But if you're looking for five-star luxury and elegance, you won't find it here. Rooms are small and the furnishings are somewhat dated. However, if peace and quiet are what you're after, Porto Paseo may be right for you. The small, darkish lobby opens onto a beautiful oasis of winding garden paths replete with singing birds and tropical plants that bloom throughout the year. The 50 bungalow-style rooms, each with its own entrance and outdoor seating area, provide lots of privacy. All are air conditioned and come with a TV.

An artificial waterfall spills into the outdoor pool keeping the water fresh all day long. Diving is arranged through Dive Inn Curaçao. Porto Paseo's outdoor restaurant overlooks the Handelskade across the pontoon bridge in Punda. In keeping with most island hotels, the Porto Paseo has a casino. You'll find slot machines, blackjack and roulette. Shopping and dining are across the bridge.

## For Serious Divers

## HABITAT CURACAO

☎ 8648800
In the US, ☎ 800-327-6709
www.habitatdiveresorts.com
Deluxe

Located on Curaçao's southwest coast, this oasis is a PADI five-star training and instructor center. For beginning divers, you can do no better than here. Incredible coral formations and 400 species of fish are within your grasp. There are more than 30 dive sights within a short boat ride from the hotel's docks. Accommodations vary from junior suites for up to four people to two-bedroom cottages. All units have a kitchenette, balcony and air conditioning. Free shuttle service is available to town all day. Call for details and current rates. RumRunners Restaurant on the edge of a cliff is gorgeous and dramatic.

## HOLIDAY BEACH HOTEL & CASINO
Pater Euwensweg 31
☎ 4625400; fax 4624397
www.hol-beach.com
165 Rooms
Moderate

A mile-and-a-half from town, the 200-room hotel offers a pool, balconies, beach, tennis and dive center. The casino is popular, but the hotel could use a bit of sprucing up.

## *Get Away From It All*

Curaçao

## LANDHUIS CAS ABAO
Cas Abao
10 guestrooms
☎ 649688; ☎/fax 649460
Inexpensive

If you prefer quiet country inns or bed and breakfast accommodations in out-of-the-way locations, then the Landhuis Cas Abao is your alternative to Curaçao's resort hotels and casinos. This restored

18th-century landhouse is set amidst 1,400 acres of unspoiled countryside, and is within walking distance of the Cas Abao beach. Rooms and public areas are simply yet comfortably furnished, in keeping with the Curaçaoan countryside. The wooden ceilings are polished to a shine, and colorful pieces by local artists decorate the whitewashed walls.

The shady outdoor terrace is the perfect spot for reading or dozing when the sun is at its hottest, or for mingling with fellow guests during the late afternoon happy hour. The dining room is open from 8 am to 9:30 pm and features traditional Antillean fare.

All guestrooms are unique, especially room #4, which was formerly the kitchen. Slave huts are now suites with private baths. Friendly management creates a warm, family atmosphere.

## CORAL CLIFF RESORT & CASINO
Santa Martha Bay
PO Box 3782,
42 rooms; four suites
☎ 641610/641588; fax 9641781
In the US, toll free, ☎ 800-223-9815. (In NY, ☎ 212-545-8469 or fax 212-545-8467.)
Inexpensive

*Coral Cliff offers free transportation to and from the airport.*

The Coral Cliff Resort and Casino is nestled in the bluffs above one of Curaçao's best diving beaches, in an area of cliffs, mountains and secluded bays. It affords its guests a great deal of peace and quiet along with spectacular diving and snorkeling. Thirty years ago it was an exclusive resort with a country-club atmosphere. Nowadays it is a popular weekend retreat for wealthy islanders as well as a popular destination for dive groups. Coral

Cliff Diving offers PADI certified instruction and dive trips aboard the *Orca*, the shop's 40-foot custom dive boat.

Tennis, mini-golf, beach volleyball and a playground round out Coral Cliff's list of outdoor facilities. In addition, a portion of the beach has been set aside for naturalists.

All guest rooms offer spectacular views of the Caribbean. There is a casino and the open-air Cliffhanger Bar and Terrace Restaurant. Sunsets are beautiful and best viewed over cocktails at the Cliffhanger.

*On a budget? Request a room in the older pavilion at Coral Cliffs. At the time of our visit, those rooms had not yet been renovated and, though still comfortable, were cheaper.*

## Apartment Rentals

If you're planning an extended stay or prefer to do for yourself rather than be catered to at a hotel, you should consider renting an apartment. An apartment is also likely to be less expensive than a hotel. The **Curaçao Apartments and Small Hotel Association** (CASHA) ☎ 4616000, is a group of apartment and small hotel owners. You can obtain a brochure of current listings complete with photos. Write to: PO Box 8243 Curaçao, N.A.

**Tropic Resorts Marketing** represents a variety of apartments located throughout the island. Most are located in residential areas, though some are on the beach. For further information contact Tropic Resorts Marketing in Curaçao, ☎ 372328 or 609333, fax 371210; in Holland ☎ (31) 79-351-0025, fax (31) 79-352-1370.

Curaçao

# Best Places to Eat

Long after you've returned home, Curaçao's beautiful landmarks will remain in your memory. Though they may have impressed you with their history, your thoughts may linger more on wine and candlelight than the Seven Years War. Several of Curaçao's most noteworthy forts and landhouses are now home to the island's finest restaurants. You may find yourself dining in an 18th-century fortress far above the Santa Anna Bay one night, and having cocktails at sunset on the 300-year-old ramparts at the entrance to the bay the next. Lunch may be in a rustic setting on the water or on the terrace of a restored landhuis.

Dutch and South American influences are apparent in the local cuisine. Popular dishes include the Dutch influenced *keshi yena*, stuffed Edam cheese; the Spanish *zarzuela*, a tasty seafood stew; and *quesilla*, a light custard baked with a caramel sauce. International cuisines are also well represented on the island. When making dinner reservations, you can choose from French, Italian, Indonesian, Spanish and continental cuisines.

Since Curaçaoans enjoy dining out, dinner reservations are advisable and even required at most restaurants all year long, especially on weekends. If you're dining at one of the more elegant restaurants, you should dress appropriately – a jacket, and possibly a tie for men, and a dress or pants suit for women. Otherwise, casual resortwear will be fine. A 10-15% service charge will often be added to your bill. If not, a 10-20% tip, according to the quality of the service you received, is appropriate. Keep in mind that the service charge does not go directly to your waitperson but is also used to cover restaurant costs. Tipping is at your discretion.

---

### Dining Price Scale

Expensive . . . . . . . . . . . . more than $35
Moderate . . . . . . . . . . . . . . . . . $25-$35
Inexpensive . . . . . . . . . . . . . . under $25

---

## BISTRO LE CLOCHARD
French & Swiss gourmet cuisine
Rif Fort, Otrobanda
☎ 4625666
Reservations requested
Lunch, noon-2 pm, Mon.-Fri.; dinner, from 6:30 pm, Mon.-Sat.; closed Sunday.
Expensive

*The Bistro Le Clochard is a member of the famous Chaîne des Rôtisseurs.*

When native son Freddy Berends set out to open his restaurant in the ruins of the Rif Fort, he was met with more doubt than support. Today, not only has the Rif Fort become an internationally recognized historic landmark, Freddy's Bistro Le Clochard has earned a place among the world's finest restaurants as a member of the Chaîne des Rôtisseurs. Educated in the culinary arts at the Hotel School in Lucerne, Freddy has assembled a team of highly skilled Swiss chefs to create a unique menu of traditional French and Swiss haute cuisine with nouvelle flourishes.

As one might expect, butter and cream sauces top the ingredients on the menu, which features beef

Curaçao

and veal as well as seafood. You'll also find a vegetarian plate.

For a truly unique experience, try a dish called *La Potence*, named for a weapon used by medieval knights. Cubes of tenderloin are cooked on a small red hot steel ball with skewers fashioned after the knights' armament. The beef bakes on the ball, which dangles from a miniature gallows, while its juices drip onto a bed of rice. Once it's cooked to taste, diners carefully remove the cubes from the skewers and dip them into various sauces.

In keeping with the medieval theme, "Romancing the Stone" features a choice of beef tenderloin, US sirloin, porterhouse or a beef and shrimp brochette cooked tableside on a heated stone with absolutely no fat or oil.

*The cruise ships exiting the harbor appear close enough to touch.*

The setting is as unusual as the menu. Cocktails on the terrace at sunset is a terrific way to begin. Moving into the dining room, you may be seated in a beautifully furnished cell or even a rain cistern. Small kerosene lamps provide subtle lighting, while picture windows offer lovely views of the harbor lights and Punda.

## FORT NASSAU
Continental
☎ 4613086
Mon.-Fri., noon-2 pm; 6:30-11 pm (every night)
Sunset Happy Hour, Fridays, 6 pm-8 pm
Reservations required
Expensive

Curaçao's most spectacular dining is at Fort Nassau. Perched atop a hill overlooking Willemstad and the entire island, Fort Orange Nassau was built around 1796 to defend Willemstad and

Santa Anna Bay and was named for the Royal House of Orange.

Best at night, the view of the fort illuminated against the dark sky is spectacular. Just as beautiful is the view from the fort of the island, including the lights of the oil refinery. Faithfully preserved, the fort serves the harbor office as a signal and control tower to monitor the opening and closing of the pontoon bridge. It's best known as the home of the Fort Nassau Bar/Restaurant and the Infinity Night Club.

Crossing the tunnel-like archway into the fort, you'll feel you're stepping back into history. Yet the menu is definitely nouveau with its emphasis on originality, carefully selected ingredients and presentation. Among dishes featured on the menu the night we visited was a cold terrine of layered salmon and sole garnished with seaweed, served with Iranian caviar and a champagne dressing. There was also a carpaccio of fresh silver grouper, served with a pesto dressing and capers as an appetizer.

Main courses included fried sunfish breaded in pecan nuts, served with a coconut sauce and caramelized garlic, or prime tenderloin steak marinated in nut oil, grilled and served with potato pie and stir-fried vegetables. The dining room, with its starched white tablecloths, deeply polished wood and candlelit tables overlooking the lights of the island, is lovely. A must for a special occasion.

**Curaçao**

*Table #6 in the corner at Fort Nassau is a favorite of couples and often requested well in advance.*

## LA PERGOLA
Italian cuisine
Waterfort Arches
☎ 613482
Open daily lunch & dinner
Moderate

*La Pergola also operates an informal pizzeria next door with take-out.*

Though La Pergola has often been described as informal, the attentive service, exceptional selection of Italian wines, and the fine Northern Italian cuisine served here, including homemade pasta, is far from simple trattoria fare. Start your meal with an aperitif on the outdoor terrace alongside the Caribbean and finish with La Pergola's rightfully famous tiramisu. Tables in the front offer a view of the Caribbean, while the dining room in the rear is more intimate.

## RIJSTTAFEL
Indonesian cuisine
Mercuriusstraat 13
☎ 4612606
Noon-2 pm; 6 pm-9:30 pm; Sundays, dinner only
Reservations recommended
Moderate

*Unless you've rented a car, you'll need a cab to get to Rijsttafel. Get directions from the front desk of your hotel or ask when you make your reservation.*

A meal at Rijsttafel is feast for your eyes as well as your palate. Rijsttafel means "rice table" and refers to the traditional type of meal once served on the Dutch plantations in Indonesia and now known to Indonesian restaurants around the world. The earliest rice tables were actual tables with a hole in the center for the rice bowl, surrounded by six to eight smaller holes to hold the different dishes.

Today, rijsttafel refers to a selection of several dishes, including meat, fish and vegetarian, served buffet-style on copper warming trays. The

Rijsttafel restaurant offers a 16- , 20- , or 25-dish rijsttafel.

The thoroughly Indonesian décor features authentic batiks, copper pots and pans and wooden figurines. The owners are rightfully proud of their collection of over a hundred Wajang dolls displayed in the Holland Bar.

## TASCA RESTAURANTE DON QUIJOTE
Spanish
Gosieweg 148D
☎ 369835
Open 7 pm-11 pm
Reservations requested
Moderate

At the Tasca Don Quijote we treated ourselves to the best paella in the Caribbean, full of shellfish and lobster and seasoned with sherry. Though the emphasis is on Spanish cuisine, the menu features international dishes as well, with lots of seafood. There is no lack of meat dishes, with entrées ranging from chicken in orange sauce or grilled, several different tenderloin dishes and a mixed grill platter.

## *International*

## EMERALD GRILL
international
Marriott Hotel
☎ 7368800
Dinner, 7 pm-11 pm

Opposite the elegant casino, The Emerald Grill is a good choice for rack of lamb, steak, and carpaccio. There is live music in an intimate setting. Service can be leisurely unless you advise that you can't wait to head next door to the awaiting crap tables.

## DE TAVEERNE
Restaurant/Wine Cellar
Landhuis Groot Davelaar
International cuisine
☎ 370669
Lunch, Mon.-Fri., noon-2 pm;
Dinner, Mon.-Sat., 7-11 pm; reservations requested.
Moderate

De Taveerne, with its distinctive octagonal shape, bright red exterior and charming interior, stands out among Curaçao's finest restaurants. As you enter this restored landhuis, you'll feel as if you're back in old Europe. Burnished copper, highly polished woodwork, terra cotta tiles and stucco walls create a fitting backdrop for De Taveerne's Dutch and colonial antique furnishings.

The dramatic setting is outdone only by the superb international cuisine and tempting desserts. The à la carte menu is changed every five weeks.

## PLAYA PERLA CANOA
Boca Perla Canoa
Seafood
Linch, Monday-Friday, noon-2 pm; dinere Monday-Saturday, 7 pm-11 pm
Inexpensive

*See the Banda Riba tour, starting on page 357, for directions.*

For real local flavor, you won't do any better than this outdoor restaurant nestled alongside a natural limestone sea wall on the northern coast. Perfect for a lazy afternoon, you can sit at the water's edge, idly watching as the surfers ride the waves down the beach or the fishermen maneuver their skiffs into the rocky shore. There's a large thatched roof for shade, and bare feet are allowed, even recommended if you're seated at a table by the water's edge. Colorful aquatic motifs have been handpainted on the tables along with the menu. Fish, of course, is the staple, much of it caught by the fishermen who live nearby, and prepared island-style. The catches of the day will be announced by your waiter.

Though not needed otherwise, reservations are required for the Thursday night lobster feast. It's best to call early since there will only be as many lobsters as venture into their traps. If you want to let loose, dance and have a good time, come in the early evening or on a Saturday or Sunday afternoon when there's either a local DJ or a live band.

## JAANCHIE'S RESTAURANT
Westpoint 15
Local cuisine
☎ 640126
Inexpensive

Be sure to include lunch at this delightful family-owned restaurant in your itinerary. Jaanchie's father opened his restaurant in 1936, and it has been an island tradition ever since – one that will be passed on from generation to generation. With flowering trees and bushes for shade, cooling breezes and birdsongs drift through the open sides of the simple white stucco dining room.

The catch of the day determines the menu, which features *krioyo* (local) cooking and seafood, along with goat, chicken and steak. Jaanchie himself may take your order. You'll recognize him by his smile.

Curaçao

*Jaanchie's is the last restaurant on the west side of the island before the road turns north. It's a favorite lunch spot for tour groups.*

## THE LOCAL MARKET
Marshe Biu (Old Market)
Creole
Inexpensive

If you're in Punda at lunchtime and you notice that all the office workers and shop clerks seem to be heading in the same direction, join them. They're on their way to the Local Market, and you're in for a special treat, genuine creole cooking. Don't dawdle, but follow the regulars' lead as they jockey for position on line at their favorite kitchen. The best goes fast, so you've got to be there early.

Located on Handelskade behind the post office, this large open-air structure with a corrugated tin roof, kitchens lining the sides, and long banks of picnic tables in the center, is like the barbecue tent at a country fair. It's owned by the government, which leases the kitchens to local residents. Generally, the kitchens are family-run and passed down from generation to generation, along with the recipes. Each consists of a barbecue grill with a counter alongside it.

*This is the best place for local cooking. If you require A/C, tablecloths, linen napkins, and a waiter at your beck and call, the Local Market won't be for you.*

To be ready in time for the noon rush, the local chefs come in at around 7 am, light the charcoal, which is made from divi-divi and palu inju wood, and set about preparing that day's dishes, such as *cabrito stoba* (goat stew), *sopi piska* (fish soup), *guiambo* (okra soup with pork tails), *moro* (rice with beans and/or vegetables) and delicately fried fish, always accompanied by *funchi* and banana *hasa* (fried banana). Each kitchen has its own specialties and its own clientele. Special for Fridays is *toe toe*, a delicious dish made with corn meal, red beans, meat (usually ribs), brown sugar, butter, salt and melted cheese.

Many locals will order lunch to go, often bringing it home to feed the family.

**HARD ROCK SOCIETY**
Keuken Plein, Punda
International
☎ 656633
Mon.-Thurs., 9:30 am-1 am; Fri. & Sat., until 2 am;
Sunday, 3:30 pm-1 am.
Inexpensive

Name sound familiar? The menu and ambience may be too, though to a much lesser extent. After shopping in Punda, come by for lunch or cocktails. Enjoy snacks and appetizers such as nachos and sate, or a full meal. The menu features burgers, salads, oversized sandwiches, grilled fish, ribs, steaks and lamb. You can sit outdoors in the shade or indoors at the bar and listen to the rock music playing in the background. And, if you're in the mood for a little competition, head upstairs, where you can play darts, backgammon and pool. Drinks are half-price and snacks on the house at Happy Hour, Thursday, Friday and Sunday afternoons.

## Fast Food

**Pizza Hut** came to Curaçao over a dozen years ago and throughout that time has consistently distinguished itself among its fellow Pizza Huts, winning the Quality, Service and Cleanliness Awards from Pizza Hut International. In addition to the standards, the menu features the award-

**Curaçao**

winning "Curaçao Pizza." A spin-off of the local *keshi yena*, it is made with Dutch Gouda cheese, tuna fish, ham and raisins. There's also a 10-layer, three-cheese and meat lasagna, plus chocolate mousse for dessert. Branches are located downtown (☎ 656767), at Schottegatweg Oost 193 (☎ 616161) and Jan Noorduynweg (☎ 688278).

**McDonald's** and **KFC** both have outlets in Punda and Sta. Maria. There's another McDonald's in the Salina Shopping Gallery. Or, if you want more than a burger and fries, The **Green Mill** is there too. Choose from the varied menu of assorted pizzas, pastas, sandwiches and Indian dishes. There's a **Burger King** on Schottegatweg Oost and an Arby's at Ontarioweg 6.

 # Sunup to Sundown

On Curaçao you can close the deal of your life, meet with your accountants in the morning, then be on the 2 pm dive boat that afternoon. If only life could always be that good. Ready for a few days off? You've got many beaches to choose from, not to mention the pool and/or beach at your hotel. Why not sail to Klein Curaçao? Or, if you're feeling really ambitious, climb to the top of Mt. Christoffel. Did we mention the great shopping and beautiful Dutch Caribbean architecture in Willemstad, home of the oldest synagogue in the Western Hemisphere? And what about the casinos?

# Beaches

Although estimates vary, there are about 38 beaches on Curaçao. Noticeably absent are the seemingly endless expanses of white sandy beach found on Aruba and featured in posters and brochures hyping the Caribbean. Instead, what you will find on Curaçao are small secluded beaches in quiet coves; hotel beaches that have been helped along by man; and a few of the type of beaches the Caribbean is known for (albeit smaller). Some are sandy, while others are made up of coral stones or black volcanic sand. Most are easily accessible by car, while a few are best traveled to by four-wheel-drive vehicle. Curaçao's loveliest beaches are along the southwest coast.

*Each of Curaçao's beaches is unique.*

If you're looking for peace and quiet, visit the beaches during the week. It's more likely that you will have to share even the remote beaches during the weekends. Beach-going is a favorite pastime of island residents. The most popular are the **Seaquarium Beach**, **Jan Thiel**, **Porto Marie**, **Knip**, **Klein Knip**, **Cas Abao**, **Westpunt Baai** and **Daibooibaai**.

What follows is an abbreviated list of a few of our favorites. However, if you've got plenty of time, we urge you not to limit yourselves to these, but to speak to the locals, get yourself a map and explore on your own. You won't be disappointed.

## Beaches with Facilities

**The Seaquarium Beach:** Part of the Seaquarium complex, this long strip of man-made

Curaçao

beach fringed with palms attracts a largely Dutch crowd and is popular with young adults. Its quiet waters are well-suited to families with small children. Watersports enthusiasts can rent equipment. There is no shortage of palapas, large beach umbrellas made with palm leaves, which provide shade. Facilities include a beach bar with plenty of music, often live, and a restaurant.

*Topless bathing is quite common.*

The Seaquarium Beach is the closest beach to Willemstad and is within walking distance of the Princess Beach Hotel. The Lion's Dive Hotel is right on the beach, and guests receive free admission. Otherwise, admission is US $3.

**Playa Barbara:** Located at the mouth of the Spanish Waters Bay on Mining Company property, Barbara Beach is popular with local families because of its calm shallow waters and sandy beach. Broad, leafy trees offer plenty of shade. The beach is also a fine vantage point for watching the yachts and sailboats in the channel. There are toilet and changing facilities, and refreshments are provided by snack and drink vendors. Topless bathing, though not *de rigueur*, is tolerated. The beach is open from 8 am to 6 pm daily. There is an admission charge of US $5.75 per car on the weekends and US $3 during the week.

**Cas Abao:** Definitely poster material, Cas Abao, also known as Turtle Beach, is a beautiful white, sandy beach on a cove 25 miles west of Willemstad. Underwater visibility here is excellent, with the best snorkeling along the rock walls on either side of the cove. This pristine, delightful beach is maintained by the owners of Cas Abao, who intend on keeping it that way. The beach is cleaned several times a day and radios are forbidden.

Amenities include an outdoor bar and restaurant, and toilet and shower facilities. Twelve large palapas offer shelter from the sun and beach chairs can be rented for US $3 a day. Turn off at Cas Abao and follow the dirt road to the beach. There is an admission fee of US $3 per car.

**Varsenbaai:** If you're more of a sunbather than a swimmer, you're better off at one of our other selections. Other than a rocky shoreline, Varsenbaii offers very little in the way of beach. On the other hand, this deep bay is well-suited to serious swimming and snorkeling. Popular with families, there is a wading pool for young children as well as a small playground. Older kids, provided they are good swimmers, can jump off the pier and swim out to the raft. Services include a snack bar with an umbrella-shaded terrace overlooking the water.

*Dive booties are a good idea.*

Located just east of the center of the island, admission to this private beach is reserved for member residents and island visitors (you must show proof that you're visiting the island). There is no admission fee.

*Topless bathing is prohibited.*

Curaçao

### ⚠ WARNING

One word of advice. Beware of the *manchineel* **tree**, which provides much of the shade on the beaches. Not only is its small green fruit poisonous, but when it is wet or raining, the sap that runs off the trees causes a painful irritation upon contact.

## Public Beaches on the Southwest Coast

Admission to the following beaches is free. Most offer very little in the way of facilities, so bring plenty of water and refreshments. A beach umbrella is a good idea too. All are popular with locals during the weekends and quieter during the week, except during school vacations and holidays. Beaches are accessible from the main coastal road and are listed in order from Westpunt heading east.

**Playa Kalki:** The westernmost beach on the island, Playa Kalki boasts a lovely location and terrific snorkeling. This narrow beach of soft white sand is set against a backdrop of cliffs with natural terraces. Although the water can get pretty choppy when it's windy, calm days provide ideal conditions for snorkeling. You'll find a wealth of corals in the cove, especially mountainous star coral and fire coral. If you're here in the afternoon, be sure to stick around for the sunset.

*Watch out for the fire coral. It causes a painful and sometimes infectious irritation upon contact.*

**Westpuntbaai:** Cliff diving is a popular pastime among the more daring regulars at Westpuntbaai, popularly known as Playa Forti. So named for the remains of Fort Westpunt in the bluffs above, this black sandy beach is on a picturesque fishermen's cove surrounded by towering cliffs. That's not actually sand on the beach, but rather very fine volcanic pebbles. They become extremely hot, making dive booties or sandals a must for walking. Conditions are generally good for swimming. Just don't be caught off-guard by the drop-off. The water, though clear and calm, becomes extremely deep quite suddenly.

*Jaanchie's restaurant is just up the road heading toward Watamula and is highly recommended.*

With the exception of the morning hours, there is no shade on the beach. Facilities are limited to a restaurant located in the ruins of the fort and nearby snack bars, which are usually only open on the weekends. If you're here during the week, be sure to bring plenty of water and a beach umbrella.

In between Playa Forti and Playa Kalki, and not far from Landhouse Wacao, is **Playa Grandi**. This rocky beach offers sparse shade but is popular with the local fishermen, who spread their nets out to dry on the beach.

**Knipbaai:** Knipbaai boasts two of the island's most beautiful beaches, **Groot Knip** and **Klein Knip**. Set on neighboring coves, both have toilet facilities, snack bars (generally open weekends only), and a party-like atmosphere on the weekends. Groot Knip, also known as Knip Grandi, is the larger of the two and by far the favorite weekend destination of most Curaçaoan families. Beach chairs are available for rent, as are pedal boats. Shade is provided by the trees and by several large parasols on the beach.

*Take the turn-off at Landhouse Knip for facilities.*

*Groot Knip can be very crowded on Sundays.*

Klein Knip, or Knip Chikitu, as it is called in Papiamento, is a semi-secluded sandy beach. A fine diving beach, it features crystal clear waters and a sand bottom. It too is noisy and crowded during the weekends and considerably quieter during the week, when it is favored by couples.

**Playa Lagún:** Colorful tropical fish abound in this narrow inlet, which is, not surprisingly, one of Curaçao's best snorkeling locales. Fish tend to congregate along the cliff walls. Trees surround the beach, providing plenty of shade, while small

Curaçao

fishing skiffs moored in the inlet add a picturesque touch.

*Playa Jeremi is a popular shore dive.*

Just before you reach the village of Lagún as you travel east, you'll come to a turn-off on the right hand side of the road. It leads to **Playa Jeremi**, a rocky beach on a narrow bay. A nominal fee is charged for access to the beach.

**Boca Santa Cruz:** While the mangrove swamp surrounding this wide beach dotted with palm trees clouds the water, creating less than ideal conditions for snorkeling, it does attract a lot of birds. You can rent a sailboard, Jet Ski or small boat here during the day, then stick around at dusk – the best time for bird watching. Be sure to bring insect repellent, along with your field glasses. Local fishermen frequently have parties here in the evening.

To reach the beach, continue east on the main road after leaving Lagún, and bear right at the fork.

## Out-of-the-Way Beaches

Though these beaches are more remote than our other selections, they are not unknown. You need to travel down dirt roads to reach them and, since they are on private property, all charge an entrance fee per car. Most offer no facilities, so bring plenty of water, along with a picnic lunch and your dive or snorkel gear.

*Porto Marie is ideal for snorkeling & training dives.*

**Porto Marie:** There are far more beautiful beaches on Curaçao than Porto Marie. The beach itself is little more than a long expanse of coarse sand and pebbles backed up by a limestone wall.

Parking is right on the beach and there is really no shade at all. Facilities consist of a small restaurant, sans restroom, which is open only on weekends.

In this case, it's what's under the water that really counts. Just a short distance from shore is a fascinating double reef system. Though the main reef is fairly deep, the shallower areas are equally fascinating. Cavernous star coral, sheet coral, sponges, tube worms, flamingo tongues, plume worms, turtles, moray eels, scorpionfish, peacock flounders, slender filefish and schools of creole wrasses and schoolmaster snappers are among the many creatures that inhabit the reef.

To get there, head west on the main road along the southern coast and follow it toward San Willibordo. The dirt road to Porto Marie is almost opposite the Willibordus Church. The entrance fee is around US $4 per car.

Not far from Porto Marie is **Daaibooibaai**, another picturesque inlet featuring great snorkeling along rock cliffs. If you're here at dusk, you can watch as the fishermen pull their boats up to shore.

**Santu Pretu:** Just east of Boca Santa Cruz, Boca Santu Pretu is a small quiet cove with a smooth brown gravel beach. The setting is truly picturesque, with huge boulders jutting out from the water offshore, set against a backdrop of the neighboring hills. The beach is actually comprised of volcanic pebbles, which can really heat up. You'll need dive booties or sandals.

Santu Pretu is located in an area known as Pos Spañó. Look for the sign marking the dirt road to

Santu Pretu. It's off the main road just west of Santa Cruz. There's a US $3 admission fee at the gate, and then you'll drive through a forest of manchineel trees to reach the beach. It's best to park by the ruins just beyond the dry riverbed and then walk down to the beach. If you park too close to the beach, you run the risk of getting stuck should the tide come in while you're still on the beach.

If you continue down the dirt road past Santu Pretu, you'll come to two even more secluded beaches. A rugged access road leads to **Playa Hulu**, a relatively unspoiled beach characterized by rough seas and coral rubble. A concrete staircase leads to the small sandy beach. A little farther down the main road you'll come to **Boca Pos Spañó**, a narrow rocky beach in a lovely wooded setting. The sea tends to be fairly rough here, but it's a fine choice for couples seeking a quiet afternoon.

**Klein Curaçao:** Curaçao's longest and whitest beach is on Klein Curaçao, an uninhabited island eight miles off the southeast coast. There are no facilities on the island and very little shade. Daytrips to Klein Curaçao, including snorkeling and refreshments, usually a picnic or barbecue lunch, are offered by most sailboat charters.

*For more details on Klein Curaçao, see pages 303-305.*

## Diving

Over the past several years, Curaçao has been enthusiastically promoting itself as a dive destination, and with good reason. Visibility ranges from 60 to 150 feet, revealing an underwater landscape of pristine reefs covered with endless varieties of corals, sponges, colorful tropical fish, sea fans, gorgonians, sea turtles, crabs, anemones and other sea creatures. Though drop-offs are normally quite steep and better suited to established divers, much of Curaçao's most fascinating underwater scenery can be explored within 75 feet of the surface. In 1993, at least 9,000 divers visited Curaçao, making over 72,000 dives. However, compared to other Caribbean islands, much of Curaçao's reef is still essentially undiscovered. And, with over a hundred identified dive sites to choose from and experienced dive operations located at all the major hotels, novice as well as experienced divers can enjoy Curaçao's remarkable underwater world first-hand.

*Bonaire and Curaçao share the same reef system. For a more detailed description, see the section on diving in the Bonaire chapter, page 126.*

*Just as on Bonaire, diving is not recommended on the northern / windward side of the island.*

## History of Diving on Curaçao

Curaçao's marine life was first documented in pictures by an Austrian, Hans Hass. Unable to get a ship back to Europe, he spent 200 days on the island following the outbreak of World War II. With nothing but time on his hands, Hass studied the island's marine life, taking photographs with a primitive underwater camera. Those photographs were developed by Curaçao's well-known photographer Fred Fisher and published along with Hass's impressions of the marine life off the coast of Curaçao in *Three Years at the Bottom of the Sea* (*Drei Jäger auf dem Meeresgrund*).

Hass, however, was not a diver but a spearfisher, and during those 200 days he introduced the islanders to skin diving for fish. The popularity of the sport grew, peaking in the 1960s with the air-

Curaçao

ing of the television series *Sea Hunt*, starring Lloyd Bridges. At the same time, advances were being made in diving equipment, making diving more accessible to the public. Several scuba clubs were founded on Curaçao, including the Diving Club Curaçao and the Antillean Scuba Divers Association, both of which offered diving instruction, as well as the SATE Club, which still exists today. SATE is an acronym formed by the Dutch words for spearfishing, diving, snorkeling and recreation.

With the arrival of Captain Don Steward on Bonaire in the 1970s, recreational scuba diving really began to take off, eventually eclipsing spearfishing in popularity. Both Curaçao and Bonaire began to attract North American divers. PADI and NAUI were taught across the United States and divers who came to Curaçao brought with them a sense of environmental responsibility. Influenced by its visitors, in 1976 the Curaçaoan government banned spearfishing and implemented a reef ordinance prohibiting the breaking off of coral, dead or alive. Interest in diving was also growing among local residents, who began to take PADI and NAUI certification courses offered on the island.

*Two more underwater parks are awaiting approval.*

In 1983, the government founded the **Curaçao Underwater Park**, a 12½-mile expanse, stretching from the Princess Beach Hotel to the easternmost tip of the island, which is managed by STINAPA, the Netherlands Antilles National Parks Foundation. The 16 buoys within the park mark dive sites which are among the finest on the southeast coast. A self-guided snorkel trail, complete with markers describing the marine life, has been installed at buoy number three. This area was selected for the diversity of its marine life and for its unspoiled conditions. Diving sites on the western side of the island tend to be more popular, not only because the water is calmer, but also because they are more accessible. Since the land bordering much of the eastern shore is privately owned, dive sites can only be reached by boat. Plus most of the eastern beaches that are open to the public are not as attractive or comfortable as their western counterparts. Most visitors who want to dive from shore are more likely to spend their time exploring the western beaches and dive sites.

## ✎ JUST IN CASE

In case of a dive emergency, such as a collapsed lung or decompression sickness, commonly known as the bends, contact the St. Elizabeth Hospital (☎ 624900), which is located between J.H.J. Hamelberg Weg and Breedestraat and Pater Eeuwensweg in Punda. The hospital has a four-person recompression chamber staffed by a group of cardiac and pulmonary specialists.

**Curaçao**

In order to protect and preserve Curaçao's fragile reef system for generations of divers to come, dive centers, environmental protection groups, the tourism development bureau and the hotel association have joined forces with the **Curaçao Diving Operators Association** (CDOA). By choosing to dive with a center that is affiliated with CDOA, you will be diving in harmony with the environment. If you have questions about any of the dive sites or island dive schools, CDOA urges you to contact them at ☎ 658991.

# Popular Dive Sites

The coral and marine life of a typical dive site on Curaçao is fairly similar to that of Bonaire, although the slope may be less gradual. Elkhorn corals grow closest to shore, followed by staghorn coral hedges. Farther out, the variety of corals and sponges increases and is joined by Venus sea fans, gorgonians, and seemingly endless varieties of colorful tropical fish and other fascinating sea creatures.

The list of dive sites that follows is by no means exhaustive, nor does it purport to be a list of Curaçao's best. That decision is up to the individual diver. We've selected dive sites that are suitable for novice to intermediate divers as well as snorkelers, and that are relatively easy to get to, either as shore or boat dives.

For a more detailed survey of many of Curaçao's dive sites, pick up a copy of George Lewbel's *Diving and Snorkeling Guide to Curaçao*. Of course, the best way to experience Curaçao diving is with an experienced dive operator. One of the island's finest is **Ocean Encounters** (☎ 434-8888) at the Lion's Dive Hotel.

Curaçao Beaches & Dive Sites

North Point
Playa Kalki
Westpoint Bay
Playa Abao
Playa Jeremi
Playa Lagun
Boca Sta. Cruz
Boca Santa Marta
San Juan Baai
Playa Chikitu
CHRISTOFFEL PARK
Boca Tabla
Bartol Bay
Playa Grandi
Boca Ascencion
Boca San Pedro

Caribbean Sea

Rifbaai
Bullen-baai
St. Michielsbaai
Blauwbaai
Orrobanda

Hato Int'l Airport

WILLEMSTAD AREA

Punda
Seaquarium Beach
Caracas Boy
Barbara Beach
Fuikbaai
Spanish Water
St. Joris Bay
Boca Playa Canoa
East Point

N

9.6 KM
6 MILES

☀ Beach
◸ Dive Site

➤ Curaçao Water Park

© 2002 HUNTER PUBLISHING, INC.

Curaçao

## PLAYA KALKI
Shore or boat dive
Novice divers
Snorkelers

Calm waters are practically guaranteed in this well-sheltered cove. A gradual slope makes it a suitable shore dive for novices. And with its crystal clear waters and coral growth close to shore, it's equally ideal for snorkelers. Both beautiful and unique, Playa Kalki features a variety of corals, including star coral in the center, with sheet or plate corals in the deeper waters, starting at around 30 feet.

## KNIPBAAI
Boat dive (shore dive also possible)
Novice to advanced divers
Snorkelers

Conditions vary depending on where you are in Knipbaai, with some areas best for intermediate to advanced divers. Since the best diving is about a 15-minute swim away, those planning to dive here may want to consider a boat dive. Though the shallow portions of the dive, the areas closest to shore, are fine for less experienced divers, novices would be well advised to avoid the steep deep-water drop-off.

The area close to shore is not without interest. Divers and snorkelers should enter and exit the water at the south side of the beach, staying close to the wall. Small caverns are full of copper and glassy sweepers, while orange cup corals grow close to the water line. You'll also see conch and tall gorgonians, some reaching heights of more than 10 feet. In the center of the cove, in less than eight feet of water, there is a ledge under which you can usually find schools of sweepers, with fingerlings, moray eels and needlefish hovering nearby.

## PLAYA LAGUN
Shore dive
Novice divers
Snorkelers

Playa Lagún offers both excellent snorkeling and comfortable conditions for beginning divers. The drop-off, in 30-40 feet of water, is not far from shore and descends at a gentle 45° angle. Snorkeling is best along the cliffs lining this narrow inlet and in the caves that have formed within them. Coral formations are bigger than life with huge mountainous star coral and exceptionally large brain and barrel corals. You'll also spot shrimp, crabs and brittle starfish that have made their homes in tube, vase and barrel-shaped sponges, along with a plethora of gorgonians and plume worms.

## MUSHROOM FOREST
Boat dive
Novice to advanced divers

Though not accessible to snorkelers, Mushroom Forest can be enjoyed by novice as well as experienced divers. Located between Boca Santa Cruz and Boca Santu Pretu, it consists of a shallow shelf followed by a deeper slope and is one of the most diverse dive sites in the Caribbean. You'll find an awe-inspiring variety of coral and marine life, including innumerable anemones along with lobsters, spotted drums, spotted tupo, green and chain moray eels, and an endless assortment of tropical fish.

Curaçao

## WET SUIT CITY
Shore dive
Novice to advanced divers
Snorkelers

Fire corals dominate this shallow dive located off the beach at the Coral Cliff Resort & Casino. It's best to wear a wet suit, dive booties and gloves, and only attempt this one on calm days. Enter the water to the left of the breakwater on the left side of the beach, where you'll face out toward the open sea. Making sure you're always in a sandy area, walk out until the water is deep enough to swim; once you've hit water that's about 10 feet deep, head left and start snorkeling.

After about five minutes of swimming, you'll come to the Coral Cliff drop-off. A relatively strong current makes this portion of the dive better for intermediate and advanced divers. However, novices should not hesitate to dive the upper areas of the slope on calm days. Colonies of garden eels have settled into the terraces on the drop-off as well as at its base. You'll find several loggerhead and vase sponges, many up to two feet wide, large gorgonian fans and a few equally large basket sponges.

## VARSENBAAI
Shore dive
Novice divers
Snorkelers

An easy shore dive, Varsenbaai is perfect for beginning divers and snorkelers, and is also a popular night dive. The drop-off is just a short swim from shore across a sandy bottom with lots of corals. It crests at 30-40 feet and has a downward slope of 45°. Filefish are common to the area.

The dive is five miles west of Willemstad on the road to Bullenbaai and Meiber. Just watch for the sign to Varsenbaai.

This is a government-owned, weekend retreat for police officers and is well-maintained. It has a concrete parking lot, picnic facilities and a short pier, which provides easy entry into the water.

## BLAUWBAAI
Shore or boat dive
Novice divers
Snorkelers

This sheltered cove between Piscadera Bay and the village of Dorp Sint Michiel features a wide variety of corals, including sheet, wire and black corals on the drop-off. Snorkeling is best along the sides of the bay entrance. Rather than attempt to swim to the drop-off from the main beach, divers should drive over to the beach on the left side of the bay, where it will only be a five-minute swim. It is a good idea to dive with someone who is familiar with the site. The drop-off, which crests in 30 feet of water, plunges sharply in places, while in others it slopes at a 45° angle. Blauwbaai, one of the island's most popular beaches, is usually crowded on the weekends. There is a small entrance charge, often waived for tourists.

## JAN THIEL
Shore or boat dive
Novice/intermediate divers
Snorkelers

Park Buoy Number Four marks this dive site at the entrance to the Jan Thielbaai. Protected by a breakwater, the water inside the bay is calm, making it a fine training site for beginning divers and comfortable for snorkeling. However, cur-

*The buoy at Jan Thiel is located at the drop-off.*

Curaçao

rents can get rough near the drop-off, so a boat dive is preferable to a shore dive, and novices who venture out to the drop-off should stay on the inland side of the ledge.

The bay itself is relatively shallow and has a sandy bottom, which is almost covered with turtle grass. Snorkelers should explore the sides of the bay; they feature lovely coral growth, gorgonians and sea lilies. There is a coral-covered shelf on the inland side of the drop-off, located just at the entrance to the bay. The drop-off slopes gradually and is covered with star coral, gorgonians, sponges, especially barrel sponges, wire coral and anemones. The area is frequented by spotted moray eels, porcupine fish, trumpetfish, blackbar soldierfish and brittle starfish that love to lounge on tube sponges. There's a lovely coral bed not far from the buoy, and staghorn coral grows quite abundantly in the shallower waters of the bay.

## PIEDRA DI SOMBRE
Boat dive
Novice to advanced divers
Snorkelers

Between Caracasbaai and Jan Thielbaai at Park Buoy Number Five, this site offers three separate dives that can be done in one tank if you go with an experienced diver and plan the dive right. The first of the three is a vertical wall. Start at the mooring facing the sea and head toward the edge of the terrace. You'll come to the crest of a wall at 30-40 feet, which drops straight down to depths much deeper than you should dare to go. However, at about 70 feet there are several caves in the wall where squirrelfish tend to linger. Wire coral, black coral, large sponges and star coral grow on the face of the wall. As you move to the left, the wall gradually changes over from a vertical drop to a gentle slope, and is better suited to less experienced divers. The shallow terrace on the inland side of the buoy offers fantastic snorkeling highlighted by anemones and huge gorgonians.

## TOWBOAT
Boat dive
Novice divers
Snorkelers

Just north of Park Buoy Number Eight in 20 feet of water lies the wreck of a small tugboat. It has been there since 1970 and is becoming quite overgrown with orange tube coral, brain coral along the gunwales, and plants. It's also a favorite gathering place for a colorful assortment of fish. This is a rare treat for beginning divers and snorkelers. The wall to the left of the slope is also worth exploring.

*Towboat is located near the eastern side of Caracasbaai.*

## THE CURACAO SEA AQUARIUM
Bapor Kibrá
☎ 616666 (ext. 17 for the Animal Encounter)

Who would have suspected that hidden beneath a garbage dump and mangrove swamp lay a spectacular coral reef waiting to be discovered? Adriaan "Dutch" Schrier did. Either that or he was incredibly lucky in 1984, when he set out to build what is now one of Curaçao's top attractions and the biggest marine aquarium in the Caribbean, the Curaçao Sea Aquarium. When you visit Dutch's Sea Aquarium you can play with a stingray or go nose to nose with lemon sharks and loggerhead turtles while you feed them by hand at the Animal Encounters; explore a shipwreck over-

Curaçao

grown with 90 years worth of corals; enjoy a refreshing tropical drink and Caribbean sounds at the Mambo Beach Bar; have lunch or dinner at the Rodeo Ranch Saloon & Steakhouse; and even snooze on the beach.

Though others called him crazy, Dutch, a diver and adventurer by nature, convinced several of his friends to invest in his brainchild. He also ignored the area's ominous past. In 1906, it had been the site of a devastating shipwreck. Hence its name Bapor Kibrá, which means "shipwreck" in Papiamento. Despite several unexpected obstacles and without the help of an architect, the Sea Aquarium was built in record time. By the end of 1984, construction was complete, and Dutch, with the help of his friend and fellow underwater adventurer Rudy Cijintje, had stocked the 46 aquariums with nearly 400 species of Caribbean fish and marine life.

Now the Sea Aquarium's popularity is eclipsed only by the beautiful expanse of palm-lined sandy white beach, known as the Sea Aquarium Beach, and Mambo Beach Club, which Dutch built on the neglected shoreline. Also within the Sea Aquarium Complex is Underwater Curaçao, a five-star PADI dive facility, the largest dive operation on the island.

*Underwater Curaçao's staff & facilities can't be beat!*

To provide visitors with a true-to-life view of life on a coral reef, the Sea Aquarium's 46 aquaria have been modeled after the three depth zones of the waters surrounding Curaçao. Each tank is a living ecosystem, existing almost exactly as it would in open water. Representative of the shallow reef flat where depth levels range from zero to 30 feet, tanks one through 17 are characterized by stretches of sandy bottom dotted with gorgonian forests, patches of elkhorn coral, and expanses of rock covered with hard and soft corals, and sponges. The varying features of the drop-off have been re-created in tanks 19 through 31 with a series of caves, valleys and ledges highlighted by mountainous corals. Tanks 32 through 45 offer portraits of the reef slope, featuring fish that frequent only deeper waters.

*Many tanks are sponsored by local businesses.*

Mixed in among those 45 aquaria is an open touch tank as well as tanks with larger open water fish. One of them is home to a very special resident: Herbie the jewfish, the mascot of the Sea Aquarium. When he was captured in 1986, Herbie, a grouper, was a mere eight inches long. Today he measures over four feet and weighs in at a healthy 188 pounds.

*The sea lions are the only foreigners in the Sea Aquarium. The rest of the marine life is native to the Caribbean.*

The deep channel at the Sea Aquarium entrance has been divided into four pools, where you'll find a pair of sea lions from Uruguay and South Africa, hawksbill, loggerhead and green turtles, nurse sharks; and lemon sharks. Two on-staff marine biologists constantly monitor conditions and make sure everyone stays healthy.

Curaçao

Unlike aquariums in the United States, Europe or anywhere else in the world, the Sea Aquarium relies exclusively on natural seawater and sunlight, enabling it to display sponges, corals and other marine life that would not survive outside their natural habitat. All of its aquaria and tanks are virtually an extension of the living coral reef. Skylights provide natural sunlight, while an ingenious system of pumps brings water in from the Caribbean and then allows it to flow naturally back into the ocean. Not only does the water in the tanks and aquaria have the same salinity and temperature as the water outside but, as it flows into the tanks, so do plankton and other vital nutrients. And because the Sea Aquarium is located up-current from any polluting agencies, the water supply is relatively clean.

## Animal Encounters

*Thick Plexiglas barriers keep divers out of harm's way.*

A natural tidal pool at the edge of the coral reef allows visitors to the Sea Aquarium the unusual opportunity to swim alongside sharks, sea turtles and stingrays. While the more adventurous types don scuba gear, non-divers can climb down into the observatory, a once-functional semi-submarine. From here, you'll watch as divers and snorkelers mingle with the extra-friendly stingrays, tarpons, jacks and angelfish on one side of the pool and hand-feed fierce sharks and mammoth-sized turtles on the other. Each diver is supplied with a full tank which, when the encounter is over, they can finish with a dive at the wreck of the *Orange Nassau* just outside the pool.

Reservations for the Animal Encounter must be made 24 hours in advance. As a wonderful memory of your visit to the Sea Aquarium, professionally taken photo or video accounts of your encounter are available.

## Seaworld Explorer
☎ 628833
Curaçao Caribbean Hotel & Casino

*Great for kids!*

If a visit to the Sea Aquarium leaves you yearning to learn more about Curaçao's marine life, but you're still not ready to don mask and fins, the Seaworld Explorer is a wonderful alternative.

More than just a glass-bottom boat, this 66-foot semi-submarine was developed in Australia to investigate the Great Barrier Reef. Unlike a submarine, it does not submerge. Instead, passengers descend to the window-lined observatory in the vessel's hull, five feet below the surface. There, in air-conditioned comfort, they'll watch as hundreds of colorful tropical fish glide through intricate coral formations and even a shipwreck. Able to move about the vessel freely, passengers can go on deck for a bit of sun and a change of scenery. Narrated tours of the coast aboard the *Seaworld Explorer* depart daily from the pier at the Curaçao Caribbean. A ticket costs $29.

## Night Dives

Divers should keep an eye on the board at their dive shop and schedule at least one night dive while on Curaçao. Fascinating by day, the marine world becomes magical after dark. Night diving is an exhilarating, even other-worldly experience that should not be missed.

## Sailing Trips

The constant trade winds make the waters off Curaçao a veritable heaven for sailors. Beginning and novice sailors can take lessons and hone their skills in the shelter of Spanish Waters, while experienced sailors may want to head out to the high seas. Or, if you'd prefer to leave the sailing to someone else, take a day-trip and combine a day of sailing with snorkeling and an on-deck picnic,

or even a beach barbecue on Klein Curaçao. However, a day-trip pales in comparison to a weekend
sail to Bonaire or a mini-cruise to Trinidad or
Venezuela.

## SAIL CURACAO
Spanish Waters
☎ 676003

Ideally located on the bay in Spanish Waters, Sail
Curaçao offers sail boat rentals as well as instruction. The basic course consists of four two-hour
lessons. Its pride is the *Vira Cocha*, a two-masted
cutter that was custom-built in Norway and is designed to remain upright in all conditions. Day
sails to Caracasbaai aboard the *Vira Cocha* depart from the Sea Aquarium Marina. You can
stretch out on deck, snorkel the **Towboat** dive
site, and eat to your heart's content at the on-
board picnic. Owner Hank van Gert is a former
Olympic sailor for the Netherlands.

## THE *MERMAID*
☎ 375198

This 66-foot motorized yacht is available for private charters for divers and snorkelers, and also
offers day-trips. It specializes in day-trips to Klein
Curaçao, an uninhabited island with a beautiful
white sand beach, less than two hours away.

The trip includes a barbecue lunch, and snorkel
gear is available. Since there is plenty of cargo
room on board, windsurfers and certified divers
should feel free to bring their equipment (call the
captain ahead of time to ensure space). Sunset
Cruises in Spanish Waters are also available.

## THE *INSULINDE*
☎ 601340

Of Belgian origin, this 120-foot sailing ship was restored in Holland in 1987. Today it is owned by a pair of Canadians. Phil, an expert seaman, has sailed around the world more than once. Laara is a gourmet chef with experience in restaurants across Canada. Together they will ensure that you have a terrific time on board, whether you select a day-trip to snorkel the beautiful reefs of Porto Marie, a weekend sail to Bonaire, or a mini-cruise to Venezuela or Trinidad. Customized packages are also possible. The *Insulinde* boasts nine two-person cabins, including a honeymoon suite. If you opt for an overnight trip and the cabins are booked, you have the option of a hammock on deck or booking a room on shore.

## Windsurfing

Although the trade winds may prove too challenging for beginners, here are great conditions for boardsailing (aka windsurfing). Spanish Waters offers the best conditions for beginners. Lessons and rentals can be arranged at **Sail Curaçao** (☎ 766003). **Top Waterports** (☎ 617343) at the Sea Aquarium Beach offers a variety of sailboarding equipment for all levels.

## Deep-Sea Fishing

Blue marlin, wahoo, kingfish, dolphin and sailfish frequent the waters off Curaçao. Charters can be arranged through the **Princess Beach Resort &**

Curaçao

Casino (☎ 367888) or the **Curaçao Caribbean Hotel & Casino** (☎ 625000), as well as the *Mermaid* (see above).

## Running & Fitness

Runners are invited to join the local road runners club for their morning jog, usually 5 to 10K. Another option is the **Koredor**, the jogging track that runs along the waterfront between the Sonesta Hotel and the desalinization plant. For information, contact **SEDREKO**, the government sports department (☎ 614233).

Just steps from the track is the **Sundance Health & Fitness Center** (☎ 627740. Open: Monday-Saturday, 7 am-10 pm). It features outdoor aerobics, free weights, a cardiovascular room and a juice bar.

## Horseback Riding

**Asahari's Ranch** offers rides through the countryside as well as along the beach for beginning and advanced riders. For information, contact Alberto and Tica (☎ 690315). **Ranch Alegre** also offers trail rides (☎ 681181).

## Golf & Squash

Golfers may need to adjust their putting to allow for the sand greens on the nine-hole course at the **Curaçao Golf and Squash Club** ☎ 373590 in Emmastad. Apart from the trade winds, it should be business as usual. The club also has two squash courts and a bar. Phone ahead for a tee time or court time. Open 8 am-6 pm.

The **Blue Bay Golf and Beach Resort** (☎ 868-1755) is a 18-hole course designed by Rocky Roquemore. It is affiliated with Tierra del Sol in Aruba and opened in December 1999. It is an 18-hole, par 72 course at 6,815 yards.

## Tennis

Tennis is best played in the early morning or late afternoon and evening, before and after the sun hits its peak. Courts are available at the **Avila Beach, Coral Cliff, Curaçao Caribbean, Princess Beach** and **Sonesta** hotels. If you're staying somewhere else, phone ahead to find out about their guest policy.

## Day-Trips to Aruba & Bonaire

Aruba and Bonaire are just a day trip away. Since ALM offers several daily flights between Curaçao, Aruba and Bonaire, you can easily spend a day on either island on your own by studying those chapters in this guidebook.

## Willemstad Walking Tours

Predecessor to modern Punda, the township of Willemstad was established on *De Punt*, "The Point," a naval base on the Santa Anna Bay between the Waigat Lagoon and the Caribbean. The

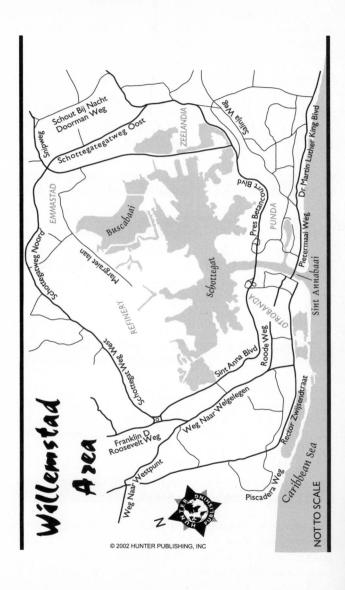

© 2002 HUNTER PUBLISHING, INC

settlement's streets had been planned on a grid pattern, and it was surrounded by an 18-foot-high city wall. Unfortunately, those early city planners had not anticipated the enormous growth experienced by the city. By 1861, the districts of Pietermaai, Scharloo and Otrobanda were already well entrenched outside the original city limits and the wall was removed.

*Were the wall still standing, Punda would fall right within its confines.*

Even with the removal of the wall, the township of Willemstad remains divided into the districts of Punda, **Otrobanda**, **Scharloo** and **Pietermaai**. The following walking tours have been designed to help you discover the individual charm and style of each of Willemstad's districts.

# Punda

The best way to appreciate Punda's rich architectural history is to look upward. While the ground floors of most of the buildings have been remodeled to accommodate the needs of modern-day shops, the upper floors have been maintained much as they were in the 17th, 18th and 19th centuries. It is only by studying the gables and upper floors that you'll be able to get the full flavor of Punda's architecture.

*Punda means "downtown" in Papiamento.*

**Curaçao**

## Distinctive Architecture

When the first Dutch settlers arrived on Curaçao, they were faced with the dual need of protecting themselves from the blazing Caribbean sun and allowing for the circulation of fresh air inside their houses. To meet those needs, they developed a Dutch-inspired, yet distinctly Curaçaoan style that would evolve over the years.

The basic style features the traditional Dutch **saddle roof**. The ground floor was usually used for storage and shops, and living quarters were on the second, with an outdoor balcony or gallery on the street side of the house. Prior to the middle of the 18th century, the gallery protruded out from the façade. Gradually, the open galleries were enclosed with wooden shutters. Fluid lines characterized the gable above the gallery. Also characteristic of the homes in Punda is the 18th-century northern European tradition of ornate rococo gables, dormer windows, and red roof tiles.

Willemstad's earliest settlers built their homes using bricks brought from Europe to balance the otherwise empty cargo vessels that had come to Curaçao to pick up sugar, salt and wood. Soon the supply of bricks could not keep up with the increasing demand, and coral stones replaced the brick. The stones were covered with stucco and painted bright colors, as required by an ordinance enacted in 1817 forbidding the use of white plaster. It seems the governor had been told by experts that the reflection of the sun's rays off the white walls would harm the eyesight of his populace.

### A Walk through Punda

We'll start at the **Waterfort Arches**, at the entrance to the Santa Anna Baai. Built in the early 17th century to store provisions and medical supplies, they're now home to some of Willemstad's finest boutiques, restaurants and cafés. The **Van der Valk Plaza Hotel** is also located here, which, although built in 1956, uses part of the 1634 Waterfort, as its foundation.

*The Plaza is one of the two hotels in the world that has marine collision insurance.*

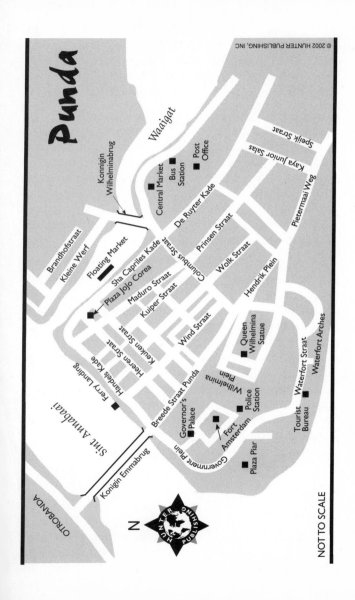

© 2002 HUNTER PUBLISHING, INC

Punda

Waaigat

Konnigin Wilhelminabrug

Post Office

Central Market

Bus Station

De Ruyter Kade

Speijk Straat

Kaya Junior Salas

Pietermaai Weg

Brandhofstraat

Kleine Werf

Floating Market

Sha Capriles Kade

Plaza JoJo Corea

Maduro Straat

Kuiper Straat

Columbus Straat

Prinsen Straat

Wolk Straat

Hendrik Plein

Wind Straat

Heeren Straat

Keuken Straat

Handels Kade

Ferry Landing

Breede Straat Punda

Queen Wilhelmina Statue

Wilhelmina Plein

Waterfort Straat

Waterfort Arches

Sint Annabaai

Governor's Palace

Fort Amsterdam

Government Plein

Police Station

Tourist Bureau

Plaza Piar

OTROBANDA

Konigin Emmabrug

N

HUNTER PUBLISHING

NOT TO SCALE

Curaçao

Walking along the Arches, you'll notice that there are still cannons on the battlements. The sea wall still has iron links from the heavy chain that once stretched from Waterfort to Rif Fort, on the opposite side, to prevent invaders from entering the bay.

*Be sure to take in the view of the Santa Anna Bay. You can imagine how well the entrance to the harbor was protected during wartime with Waterfort & Fort Rif Fort at the entrance, & Fort Nassau on the hill above.*

Just in front of the Arches is the **Plaza Piar**. The statue of Manuel Piar was a gift from the Venezuelan government to honor this famous Curaçaoan who served under Simón Bolívar during the wars for independence from Spain. Piar was the first foreigner to become a general in the Venezuelan army. Unfortunately, he was later accused of treason and executed – only to be acquitted posthumously and declared a hero.

The mustard-colored walls on the opposite side of the square belong to **Fort Amsterdam**. Once the most important of the eight forts on Curaçao, from 1648 to 1861 it was the center of Willemstad and is now the seat of the government of the Netherlands Antilles. The **Governor's Residence** is directly above the entrance to the fort, while the Ministry and several government offices are along the sides. The **Fortkerk**, or Fort Church, is across the courtyard. Built over a vaulted cellar, it has a monumental staircase at its entrance. The stark interior is in keeping with that of a Dutch Reformed seafarer's church. Decoration is provided by brass chandeliers, the mahogany pulpit and ornate governor's pew. The church houses a small museum that opened in 1991 following its renovation.

The church has an interesting history. When the Protestant West India Company first built Fort Amsterdam, they constructed a church inside. In

1763, Amsterdam granted the colonists permission to restore the church but not to build a new one. Contrary to those instructions, a new church was built. Throughout the colonial period the church was in a constant state of readiness in case of a siege. Its spacious cellar was stocked with provisions and it had its own cistern. Interestingly, merchant's sails were kept in the church loft, since it was considered the driest spot in the fort. Still embedded in the church's southwest wall is the cannonball fired by Captain Bligh in January 1804, when he laid siege to Punda for 26 days.

*The same Captain Bligh made famous in the* Mutiny on the Bounty.

At the entrance to the fort is the **Monument to World War II**, presented to the Netherlands Antilles by the Dutch Royal Family to commemorate the support the islands gave to the Netherlands during war. The monument, the work of Dutch sculptor A. Termote, is a statue of a woman with a rose in one hand and a horn of plenty in the other. From here you can see the **Queen Emma Pontoon Bridge**. Walk along the waterfront past the bridge to enter the Santa Anna Baai, which flows into the Schottegat Bay, the second busiest harbor in the world.

The buildings along the Handelskade were originally offices and warehouses. The red tile on their roofs came from Europe during those early days when Curaçao was first becoming a commercial center. The tiles would serve as the ship's ballast during the voyage from Europe and be replaced by large quantities of salt from the salt pans for the trip back. During this period, salt to be used in Holland's herring industry was the island's primary export. Running parallel to Handelskade,

**Curaçao**

one block inland, is **Heerenstraat**. This pedestrian promenade is one of Willemstad's principal shopping streets.

Continue to the end of Handelskade and along **Sha Caprileskade**, home of the **Floating Market**, a colorful array of small fishing boats shaded with tarps. Traditionally, merchants sailed in from Venezuela laden with fruits and vegetables, and headed home four or five days later, once they had sold all their produce. Nowadays, instead of making the frequent trips, vendors purchase their wares from the freighter that arrives every morning, and live on their boats for two to three months at a stretch before returning home. Also here are fishermen with the day's catch of snapper, grouper, yellow tail and other fish, fresh from the Caribbean basin. Opposite the market is the **Plaza Jojo Correa**, a favorite meeting place.

A little farther down on Waaigat Plein is the **Central Market Building**, a large semi-indoor market with stalls of meat, fish, fruits and vegetables, plants and handicrafts. Come early in the morning for the best selection. From here you can see the **Queen Wilhelmina Drawbridge**, which connects Punda with Scharloo, formerly a wealthy residential quarter where Jewish merchants built lavish homes. In the distance, atop Mt. Arrat, with the American flag flying over its black-tiled roof, is the **Roosevelt House**. A gift from the people of Curaçao to the United States government, it is the residence of the US Consul General and part of the US Consulate Complex. A block beyond the Market Building is the monument to the Antilleans who died while serving in World War II.

Continue walking until you reach the Queen Wilhelmina Bridge. Turn up Columbusstraat to the **Mikvé Emmanuel Synagogue**, the oldest synagogue in the Americas. The entrance is around the corner on Hanchi Snoa. There is a privately funded museum in the courtyard with memorabilia donated by the Jewish Community as well as replicas of the most noteworthy tombstones in the **Bet Chayim Cemetery**. The oldest Jewish cemetery in the Western Hemisphere, it dates back to 1659 and is located on Schottegatweg next to the Isla Refinery.

*For a detailed description of the synagogue, see* Museums, *page 332.*

Follow **Columbusstraat** toward **Wilhelmina Park**. Several impressive buildings are along this strip, including the **McLaughlin Bank**, which was originally built as a Masonic Temple in 1869. The **Temple Emmanuel Jewish Reformed Synagogue**, built in 1864 by a group of more liberal Jews who seceded from the original Dutch Portuguese Israelitic Community is nearby. It is painted in typical Curaçaoan fashion, with yellow walls and white trim. In front of the temple is a model of the city gate. Though designed in the 19th century, the gate was never built, since the wall surrounding the city was dismantled in 1861.

The most important building on Wilhelmina Park is the **Parliament of the Netherlands Antilles and the Court of Justice.** The Dutch coat of arms adorns the pediment above the main entrance. It was built from 1857 to 1858, at the same time as the Ministerial Council in Fort Amsterdam, and for many years was home to the Colonial Court of Justice and the Colonial Council. The building is made up of five pavilions, with the

**Curaçao**

principal rooms on the second floor and a prison on the first. Plans to construct a clock tower were thwarted by a lack of funds. A statue of Queen Wilhelmina is at the top of the park.

The **Department of Finance Building**, on the waterfront nearby, has been immaculately restored to its colonial splendor. Across the street is the **Curaçao Tourism Development Office**, housed in a Georgian-style building.

Backtrack to **Breedestraat** and then head toward the Queen Emma Bridge. Instead of window shopping, look up to admire the distinctive gables of the buildings, some with the year of construction on their façade. The best known of all is the **Penha Building** at the foot of the bridge, which was once a social club with a gallery from which members could look out over the bridge and the harbor. Other noteworthy buildings include the **1751 building**, now home to the Antraco Copycenter, **Diva** on the opposite side of the street, the small house next door to Cozzoli's Pizza, and the building that houses **Little Switzerland** and **Casa Amarilla**.

On **Heerenstraat**, you will find a diverse group of buildings, both modern and traditional. Make sure not to miss the Mother and Child façade of **David's**; the rosette that adorns the **Grand Bazaar**; and the pot-bellied columns on the **Weekender Shop**. Just after the intersection with Sommelsdijkstraat are four lovely and quite old façades, among the oldest in Curaçao. Truncated gables crowned by pediments characterize **L'Amiga**. The **Casa Blanca** and **Palais Hindu** both boast the oldest sinuous gables on the island, which go back to 1703 (the Jewish date 5466 is on the façade). Don't miss **Happy House**, just a little farther down. It is the oldest merchant's house in Willemstad and has living quarters on two floors instead of just one.

If you still have some time, you may want to wander along some of the side streets. There is always something else to discover. Just keep looking up at the gables.

## Otrobanda

If Punda is the brain of Willemstad, Otrobanda must be its heart and soul. As the constant influx of immigrants to Curaçao grew too numerous to be contained within the walls of Punda, Otrobanda became Curaçao's melting pot. From rich merchants who wanted to get away from the hustle and bustle of Punda, to slaves and free men, craftsmen and small businessmen, and refugees from the South American colonies and neighboring islands, a diverse blend of peoples from differing ethnic, religious and socio-economic backgrounds settled in Otrobanda.

*The translation of Otrobanda is "other side."*

This mix of cultures is best demonstrated by the island's universal language. Papiamento first came into being as the language used among slaves during the passage from West Africa to the Antilles, and then became the everyday language spoken among the different racial and national groups living in Otrobanda. It's not surprising that many words in Papiamento are strikingly similar to Spanish, Dutch, Portuguese, English and French.

Curaçao

Almost all of Curaçao's artists, poets, writers, composers, musicians, teachers, politicians and craftsmen were born, raised and lived much of their lives in Otrobanda.

### History of Otrobanda

While Punda grew as a typical, well-planned Dutch settlement, Otrobanda's development was more haphazard, resulting in a colorful labyrinth of twisting alleyways and narrow streets, filled with buildings and peoples of all shapes and sizes.

The district's first residents were criminals and lepers who had been banished there from Punda. Due to the ongoing threat of attack by British or French forces, pirates and otherwise, no other development was permitted in Otrobanda, so as not to obstruct the line of fire from Fort Amsterdam. However, in 1707, the governor gave out 14 lots, with the express condition that only one-story houses and warehouses be built on them.

By that time Punda was already overcrowded. The large open spaces in Otrobanda presented an attractive alternative, spurring illegal building. By 1752, there were as many houses in Otrobanda as there were in Punda. Taking advantage of the available land, the wealthy built large homes with galleries on several sides. Since there was no need to build more than one floor, many of these mansions resemble landhuisen, the plantation-style estates that dot the countryside.

Influenced by the landhuisen, the mansions were built on large yards known as *kurás*. Scattered along the edges of the yard were the ramshackle huts of the poor, who paid rent to the landowner.

No boundaries were drawn between the homes of the renters, whose goats, pigs, chickens, dogs and children roamed freely. Such a tight-knit community was formed that the renters had virtually no secrets from one another. In fact, it was the *kurás* of Otrobanda that gave raise to the Caribbean "yard culture."

When the Queen Emma Bridge was built in 1888, development in Otrobanda escalated. Lavish homes were built on the waterfront, which at that time started before Pater Euwensweg. The reef over which Pater Euwensweg would eventually be built had not yet been filled in. Rif Fort was on an island apart from the mainland.

Otrobanda's glory days would not last forever. The arrival of the automobile prompted an exodus of Willemstad's upper and middle class residents, who sought the peace and quiet of country villages such as Van Engelen, Damakor and Toni Kunchi. Mansions were deserted or were taken over by the lower classes. Never a business center, Otrobanda fell into neglect. The district, which boasted a population of 8,000 residents in the 1930s and 40s, saw that number drop to fewer than 1,500.

Happily, Otrobanda is now in the midst of a renaissance thanks to the efforts of **Plataforma Otrobanda**. This non-profit foundation has its roots in a movement founded in the late 1970s by the parish priests of Santa Famia and Santa Anna. Their mission was to counter the physical and moral decay that was then threatening the well-being of Willemstad. Now, Plataforma Otrobanda works in cooperation with the Merchants Association of Otrobanda.

Curaçao

*A World Heritage City is one in which the historic & social development of mankind is visible in existing monuments & buildings.*

The Curaçaoan government has also recognized the value of Otrobanda, both as a remedy for the recent housing shortage as well as for its historic significance. Home to over 500 of the 800 buildings in Willemstad that can be classified as historic, the district is vital to the government's success in its efforts to get Willemstad on the list of UNESCO's World Heritage Cities. Hence, much of the revitalization of Willemstad has been concentrated in Otrobanda. Entire neighborhoods have already been restored, including Sanchi and its many alleyways, Frederikstraat, Shon Toms and Hoogstrat. Residents are returning too, breathing new life into Otrobanda.

## Architecture of Otrobanda

The homes of Otrobanda are representative of the last stage of architecture on Curaçao. This blend of Dutch and Spanish styles was modified to suit the local climate and building materials, and crafted by local tradesmen schooled in the traditions that developed through the course of Curaçao's colonization; it has gained wide recognition. Ample space allowed residents to construct their homes so as to take maximum advantage of the trade winds. Windows generally opened to the northeast, with wooden shutters to block the sun while allowing the breeze to cool the interior. Large rooms with wide openings allowed the wind to blow freely through the house. Moorish arches, reminiscent of Andalusia, supported the roof and upper floors. Living quarters, which were typically on the ground floor, were set back so as to be sheltered from the heat of the sun.

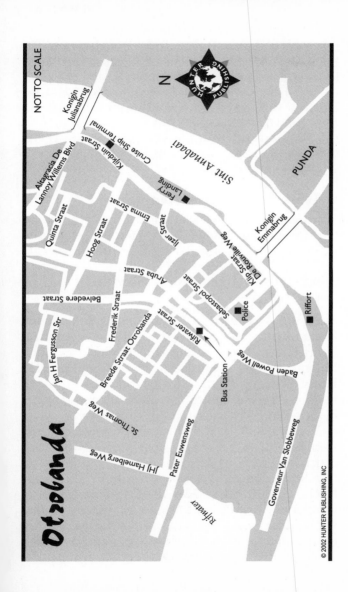

Otrobanda

NOT TO SCALE

N

HUNTER PUBLISHING

Konigin Julianabrug

Altagracia De Lannoy
Willems Blvd

Quinta Straat

Hoog Straat

Emma Straat

Ijzer Straat

Kriklulu Straat

Cruise Ship Terminal

Ferry Landing

Sint Annabaai

PUNDA

Konigin Emmabrug

De Rouville Weg

Kilp Straat

Aruba Straat

Sebastopol Straat

Belvedere Straat

Frederik Straat

Breede Straat Otrobanda

Rifwater Straat

Police

Riffort

Jan H Fergusson Str

St. Thomas Weg

Pater Euwensweg

Bus Station

Baden Powell Weg

JHJ Hamelberg Weg

Rifwater

Governeur Van Slobbeweg

Curaçao

© 2002 HUNTER PUBLISHING, INC

Among the noteworthy buildings in Otrobanda is the **Santa Anna Basilica** at Breedestraat 31. Built in 1734, it is the oldest church in the Antilles and one of the world's smallest. Other buildings to look for include the **Curaçao Museum**, built in 1853, originally a military hospital; the **Otrobanda Police Station** on Molenplein; and the **Sebastopol Mansion**, located close to the bus terminal. Watch for these buildings as you wander through Otrobanda.

## Walking Tour of Otrobanda

Since wandering aimlessly is a great way to see Otrobanda, the following are just suggestions to guide you as you walk along the winding streets and narrow alleyways. Otrobanda is small enough that you shouldn't worry about getting lost.

Start on **Brionplein**, adjacent to the Queen Emma Bridge. At its center is a statue of Admiral Pedro Luis Brion, a Curaçaoan aide to Simón Bolívar. Walk along the waterfront on **De Rouvilleweg**, heading away from Rif Fort and toward **Breedestraat**, the main shopping street in Otrobanda. Be sure to take a moment or two to admire the view of Handelskade across the bay in Punda. The 18th-century design of its buildings contrasts with the style of the buildings of Otrobanda, most of which were built 150 years later. You'll pass **Koral Agostini**, one of Otrobanda's renovated buildings; it now houses shops, bars and restaurants. A little farther down, just opposite the cruise ship terminal, you'll come to **Porto Paseo**, another group of restored buildings that includes the Porto Paseo Hotel & Casino.

Turn up Ijzerstraat or Hoogstraat to **Emmastraat**. You'll pass several impressive homes, many with well-tended gardens. Turn right onto **Frederikstraat**. Many houses in this area have been restored for use as government buildings. Wander a little along Willemstraat. Try to head in the direction of the open Caribbean in order to make your way over to Breedestraat. Turn down the hill and head back to the waterfront, taking time to browse in the quaint shops, with their displays of household goods and curiosities.

To explore the area behind Brionplein, stroll up **Consciëntiesteeg**, which runs parallel to Breedestraat. Turn toward the sea and wander along the narrow winding streets. Don't miss the **Sebastopol House** at 26/28 Sebastopolstraat, restored by its private owners. You may want to take a detour along **Hanch'i de Lannoy**, a narrow alley leading to Breedestraat. If you continue up Consciëntiesteeg, the street name will change to Hanch'i Lou de Windt after the overpass, to end in front of a lovely restored home dating back to 1788.

From there, turn left onto **Schrijnwerkersstraat** and wander along the narrow alleys. We recommend that you turn onto St. Martinsteeg, then go left onto Zaantijessteeg and right onto Gravenstraat, which backs up to the most stately homes in Otrobanda. These homes were built along the reef prior to the construction of the Pater Euwensweg.

Curaçao

Sabasteeg boasts two especially impressive homes. White with blue trim, **Stroomzigt** is owned by the artist/physician Chris Engels, whose work at restoring the mansion is depicted in a mural on the wall beside the entrance to the kitchen. The house was built in two stages. The main wing in the rear was built during the second half of the 18th century, while the imposing multi-story wing in front was added in the 19th century. The yellow building next door is the **Freemason's Lodge**.

Standing in stark contrast to its neighbors is **Batavia**. This house owes its bright red exterior to the color of a winning lottery ticket purchased by its owners. All of the other houses owned by this family are painted the same color. When in bloom, the poinciana in the backyard creates an entirely new palette of reds. Across the street, Otrobanda, the Caribbean and the sky are beautifully reflected in the glass walls of the **SVB Building**. Built a century after most of its neighbors, this modern building was carefully designed to blend into the neighborhood.

Make your way back to Gravenstraat, which eventually changes name to Bajonetstraat, and follow it to **Gasthuisstraat**, where there is a house with wooden shutters and the date 1857. Turn right onto Gasthuisstraat, whose tiny homes contrast sharply with the stately mansions you've seen so far. Gasthuisstraat runs into Zaantijessteeg, which takes you back to Breedestraat via Elleboogstraat. Finally walk along the waterfront to the **Rif Fort**. On Molenplein, you'll pass a restored merchant's house with graceful dormer windows, unusually shaped gables and a double staircase dating back to 1750.

Hopefully you've timed your walk to arrive at Fort Rif Fort around 5 pm, just in time for cocktails on the **Waterside Terrace**. If not, you should still take in the view of the floating bridge and harbor from the restored ramparts.

## Scharloo & Pietermaai

By the beginning of the 19th century, Punda was becoming quite crowded. Rich merchants, primarily members of Curaçao's Jewish community, began to build lavish homes on the north side of the Waigat Lagoon in Scharloo, a suburb of Punda. Influenced by European and North American Classicism, a new architectural style developed. Classic lines replaced the ornate rococo flourishes that were then the trademark of the gables in Punda. The floorplan was also unique. A variation on the landhuis plan, living quarters were still located upstairs. Front and back galleries were added, with additional wings on the sides to form the signature open patio in the center, which was decorated with ceramic tiles, fountains and classical pillars. In later years, the classic lines would be replaced by the more decorative South American Vermicelli style.

### A Walk through Scharloo into Pietermaai

Cross the Waigat Lagoon into Scharloo via the picturesque **Queen Wilhelmina Bridge** and walk up Wilhelmina Straat to **Scharloo Weg**, where you should turn right. Just off Scharloo is the **Simón Bolívar Plein**. At its center is a statue of Simón Bolívar presented to Curaçao by the Venezuelan government as a symbol of everlasting friendship. Also on the plaza is a bust of Luis Brion of Curaçao, who served as Commander in Chief of the Venezuelan Army during the Wars of Independence.

Several lovely buildings are on Scharloo Weg, including the **Ashkenazim Synagogue** at #39, built by the Eastern European Jews who settled in Curaçao in the 1930s, and the **Civil Registry Building** at #150-152, with its lovely gables and open gallery. The South American Vermicelli-style **Central Historic Archives** at #77, popularly known as the *Bolo di Bruid*, which means "wedding cake" in Papiamento, was built by the Da Costa Gomez family in 1918. Its design was inspired by the Spanish Embassy in Caracas.

Continue down Scharloo Weg until it changes name to Oranjestraat and then turn right onto **Helenastraat**. This will take you down to **Penstraat**, which runs along the sea. At the foot of Helenastraat at Penstraat #126-8 is the **Octagon**. Simón Bolívar's sisters lived in this building, as did the Liberator while in exile in 1811. It now houses a small museum featuring antiques and exhibits from the period of South America's Wars of Independence from Spain.

Next door to the Octagon is the **Avila Beach Hotel**. Once known as La Belle Alliance, its main building dates from the late 1700s and served as the governor's residence from 1812 through 1825, when the British occupied the island. It continued as such under Dutch rule until 1828.

To return to Punda, continue along Penstraat, which will become **Pietermaai Weg** when you enter the Pietermaai district, finally becoming **Breedestraat** in Punda. Marking the border between Pietermaai and Punda is a model of the 19th-century city gate, which was never actually constructed since the wall around the city was taken down in 1861.

## Willemstad Bridges

### Queen Emma Bridge

It's hard to think of anything more delightful than strolling across the Queen Emma Bridge at sunset. Especially if you're on your way to happy hour at the Plaza Hotel or Bistro Le Clochard's Harbourside Terrace. Resting atop 15 pontoons and powered by two motors attached to the last one, this pontoon swing-bridge stretches 551 feet across the Santa Anna Bay to link Punda and Otrobanda. It opens up to 30 times a day to let ships pass. When open, a ferry transports pedestrians to the other side for free. The opening of the bridge is announced by sirens and a blue flag raised outside the small shack by the bridge. Pedestrians hurry to cross the bridge before the barrier comes down.

The original bridge was built in 1888 under the direction of the United States Consul L.B. Smith, who held the concession to the bridge for the next 30 years. Until 1934, four years after the bridge was sold to the Curaçaoan government, users of the bridge had to pay a toll. An exception was made for those who were so poor that they hadn't enough money to buy shoes. Needless to say, the general population caught on and would take off their shoes and hide them in order to cross for free. The current bridge was built in 1939 and is the third one. With the opening of the Queen Juliana Bridge, it is now reserved for pedestrians only.

## Queen Wilhelmina Bridge

A small dock in the Waiagat, the inlet off the Santa Anna Bay, once necessitated the construction of the Queen Wilhelmina Bridge to link the commercial areas of Punda with Scharloo. Originally a drawbridge, when the dock was demolished the bridge was converted to a regular bridge. Now it serves more as a remnant of the past.

## Queen Juliana Bridge

The Queen Juliana Bridge towers 185 feet above Santa Anna Bay, offering motorists a panoramic view of Willemstad and a highway bypass of the Schottegatt. This four-lane, 3,400-ton bridge was constructed at a cost of $30 million and 14 lives. Use is reserved to motor vehicles only. Pedestrians and bicycles are prohibited.

## Willemstad Forts

### The Waterfort

When it was first built in 1634, the Waterfort was intended to serve as the primary outer defense of Punda. It was replaced in 1827 by an even larger structure that spanned the entire waterfront, with an additional 136 turrets and vaults for supplies, stables and a military hospital. Troops were housed there during World War II and coastal and anti-aircraft artillery were mounted on its walls. With the return to peaceful times, the key to the Waterfort was ceded to the local hotel corporation in 1957. A hotel was built, then operated by the Intercontinental Hotels, which is now the Curaçao Plaza. The eastern end of the fort has undergone a renovation and is now home to the Waterfort Arches, a complex of restaurants and shops.

## Rif Fort

Across the harbor entrance from Waterfort, the Rif Fort was built in 1828 to defend the outer section of Otrobanda and to form a dual defense with Waterfort. To prevent enemy ships, especially submarines from entering the harbor during World War II, a steel net was stretched across the bay between the two forts. Since the war, the Rif Fort has housed the Harbor Authority, Public Works, the police and the Boy Scouts. The fort is undergoing a complete restoration. The battery ramparts have been restored and are now home to the Bistro Le Clochard Restaurant and the Harbourside Terrace.

## Fort Nassau

Fort Nassau's history goes back to 1797, when it was built for the defense of the Santa Anna Bay and the City of Willemstad. It was named for the Royal House of Orange – Fort Oranje Nassau. Among the best preserved of the island's forts, it remains mostly intact and functions as a harbor office and signal and control tower to regulate the opening and closing of the Pontoon Bridge. A favorite panoramic viewpoint, it is home to the Fort

**Curaçao**

Nassau restaurant, which is one of the island's finest, and a small nightclub.

### Fort Waakzaamheid

Only ruins remain of this fort in the hills over-looking Otrobanda not far from the Juliana Bridge. It was victim to Captain Bligh (of *Mutiny on the Bounty* fame) in a 26-day siege in 1804. During World War II, the Americans mounted guns and established barracks and an observation post there. Today it is home to the Fort Waakzaamheid Restaurant.

### Fort Beekenburg

From 1701 to 1704, Director van Beek designed the plan for the defense of Willemstad. Recognizing that the outer bays were the weak points in Curaçao's defense, he ordered the construction of Fort Beekenburg at Caracas Bay in 1703 to protect the Spanish Waters. The fort served as a key defense point in battles waged against invading pirates, the English and the French throughout the 18th century. It is relatively well-preserved with its tower still intact.

### Fort Amsterdam

After the Dutch conquered Curaçao, their immediate concern was to secure the Schottegat. Construction of Fort Amsterdam was begun almost immediately. Though the original design called for five bastions placed equidistant from each other, the fifth at the seaside was never built. The fort is four sided, with a bastion at every corner.

Forced to substitute rock for their usual brick walls, the Dutch built Fort Amsterdam with coral stones found along the coast and rocks from the tops of the hills cemented together with a mixture of silt, sand and clay. To make the fort appear more imposing to attackers than it actually was, the limited quantity of bricks they were able to import from Holland were used to cover the wall facing the sea. A brick wall would have been much stronger than the wall as it was actually built. But the ships of that time could not have carried all the bricks needed to construct an entire fort. Fort Amsterdam is one of the few forts built in this fashion.

With its only cannons located on the corner bastions, the defense provided by Fort Amsterdam proved dangerously limited. Once the Waterfort was completed in 1827, Fort Amsterdam was no longer needed. From then on, it was used primarily as a residence for high-ranking government officials and officers, as well as for government offices, as it is today.

## Trolley Tours

A scenic interesting 1¼-hour ride in an open-sided trolley can give you a great perspective of Willemstad. The trolley takes you along the waterfront, the once wealthy Scharloo, and as far out as Fort Amsterdam. Your hotel can make all the necessary reservations for the trip, which operates only on Monday mornings and Wednesday afternoons. Ask them for details.

Curaçao

## Museums

# MIKVE ISRAEL EMANUEL SYNAGOGUE & JEWISH CULTURAL MUSEUM

Columbusstraat and Hanchi di Snoa

☎ 4611633

Monday-Friday, 9 am-11:45 am; 2:30-5 pm

Closed Jewish and public holidays

Small donation requested

Services: Friday, 6:30 pm; Saturday, 10 am

*Most Curaçao museums charge a nominal admission fee.*

Hidden behind the thick yellow walls at the corner of Columbusstraat and Hanchi di Snoa in Punda is the Mikvé Israel-Emanuel Synagogue, the oldest synagogue in the Americas and Willemstad's most priceless treasure. Built in 1732, its yellow façade and gabled roof are reminiscent of 17th-century Amsterdam. Not surprisingly, its design seems to have been based largely on that city's old Portuguese Synagogue. In the wall surrounding the synagogue are four large portals leading to the Spanish-tiled courtyard. Three are on Columbusstraat; the fourth and most frequently used portal is on Hanchi di Snoa.

*Hanchi di Snoa means "Synagogue alley." In the 17th century, this street was called Joodenrkstraat or Jewish Church Street, and later Kerkstraat. To mark the 250th anniversary of the Synagogue in 1982, it was renamed Hanchi di Snoa.*

Entering the courtyard, it's hard to miss the buttresses on the façade of the synagogue. Rather than provide support, they serve as drainage canals for rainwater. Along the courtyard walls are reproductions of tombstones from the Bet Chayim cemetery. As you pass through the heavy mahogany doors into the sanctuary, you'll be awestruck by its quiet splendor, just as worshippers have been for centuries.

The gentle white interior, with its richly carved mahogany fixtures, provides a welcome respite from the dazzling brightness of the Caribbean sun. Four magnificent brass chandeliers, each with 24 sconce candlesticks, are suspended from the lofty ceiling, while the floor is covered in a thick blanket of soft, white sand. The chandeliers are copies of those in the Portuguese Synagogue in Amsterdam. Two of them, dated 1707 and 1709, were brought over from Holland and used in the original synagogue built in 1703.

The sand is as functional as it is symbolic. Many believe it to represent the journey of the Israelites across the Sinai Desert to freedom. Others believe that the sand recalls the promise God made to Abraham in the Book of Genesis to multiply his descendants " ... as the sand which is on the seashore" (Gen. 22:17). From a more practical standpoint, during the time of the Inquisition it had been the custom of Jews in Spain and Portugal to hold services in secret, using sand to quiet their footsteps. Though long since replaced by cement, the original floor in the Synagogue was made of hollow wooden planks, which were then covered with sand in order to quiet the sounds of footsteps during services.

The synagogue's original pipe organ is located in the balcony above the entrance. Built in 1866 in Amsterdam, it is no longer functional and has been replaced by an electronic organ. Within the heavy, silver-trimmed, mahogany Hekhal (Holy Ark) on the east wall of the Sanctuary are 18 Torah Scrolls, several of which are older than the synagogue.

The Jewish Cultural Museum is located in the 18th-century residence of the first rabbis. It is one of the most beautiful of Willemstad's restored buildings. Its columned façade is richly adorned with jugs along the sides and flowers in its center. A shield on the outside wall facing the street contains the date 1728. The museum's second building was the bathhouse. The Mikvah, or Ritual Bath, is at the entrance to the museum.

The museum, established in 1970, is home to a collection of ceremonial and cultural objects representing nearly four centuries of Sephardic life on Curaçao. Much of the collection has been donated by members of the island's Jewish community and many objects are still used today, including a Torah scroll dating from 1492, circumcision chairs, Torah Crowns, Hanukkah lamps, a large collection of prayer books, a silver wedding tray, and Ketubot, which are hand-decorated marriage contracts.

*A guide to the synagogue can be purchased in the museum gift shop, as can mezuzahs, seder plates & other items.*

Upstairs, a table has been set for seder using 17th- and 18th-century silverware and ritual objects for the celebration of Passover. Replicas of tombstones from the Bet Hayim cemetery are in the courtyard.

**CURACAO MUSEUM**
Anthony v. Deeuwenhoek Straat
Otrobanda
☎ 4623873
Mon. to Fri., 9 am-noon; 2-5 pm; Sun., 10 am-4 pm

The Curaçao Museum offers a glimpse back in time, both to Curaçao's colonial and Indian past. Featured in the permanent collection are sculptures, art, architecture, antique furnishings, and even an old-fashioned Curaçaoan kitchen, authentic right down to the traditional white dot-on-red-wall motif designed to keep dizzy flies out. Archaeological artifacts found in sites formerly inhabited by Indians are also part of the collection. A museum showpiece is the stained-glass map of the Caribbean. Special exhibits are frequent.

The building that houses the museum was originally designed as a military hospital and built in 1853. The architect based his plan on the typical Curaçaoan *landhuis*. The dispensary storerooms and sickrooms were on the ground floor, which was purposely kept open to the trade winds to prevent bacteria from settling and spreading.

## FORT CHURCH MUSEUM
Fort Amsterdam
☎ 4611139
Monday-Friday, 8 am-noon; 2-5 pm

The Fort Church Museum, located in the oldest church on the island, appropriately features antique churchware and artifacts dating back to 1635, including copies and reprints of rare maps, silver chalices, offering plates, lace christening gowns from the last century and a silver and mahogany baptismal font that is still in use. A small museum shop features books and postcards. Private tours can be arranged in English or Dutch.

## BOLIVAR MUSEUM
Penstraat 126-8
Monday-Friday, 9 am-noon; 2 pm-4:30 pm

This two-story eight-sided building, popularly known as the Octagon, was home to exiled Venezuelan freedom fighter Simón Bolívar and his two sisters from 1811 to 1812. Their time on Curaçao is commemorated with period furniture, maps, etchings and documents relating to the liberation of the South American contingent.

Curaçao

## CURACAO POSTAL MUSEUM
Corner of Keukersenstraat and Kuiperstraat
☎ 658010
Monday-Friday, 9 am-5 pm; Sat., 10 am-3 pm

Curaçao's history is depicted in stamps, cancelled envelopes, and assorted postal artifacts. It's the only museum of its kind in the Caribbean and located in the oldest building in Punda (1693).

## NUMISMATIC MUSEUM
Central Bank of the Netherlands Antilles
Breedestraat
☎ 613600
Monday-Friday, 8:30-11:30 am; 2-4:30 pm

The Numismatic Museum has a fine collection of rare coins dating back to the early 19th century, along with cut and uncut gemstones.

## TELE MUSEUM
Wilhelmina Plein
Monday-Friday, 9 am-noon; 1:30-5 pm

Modeled after Stockholm's Tele Museum, Curaçao's newest museum traces the history of the telecommunications equipment used on the island, from inception to modern times. A replica of a century-old optic telegraph is prounded featured in the collection.

## GALLERY 86
Punda
☎ 613417
Mon.-Fri., 9:30-noon; 3-5:30 pm; Sat., 9:30-noon

Gallery 86 features a permanent exhibit of works by local and Caribbean artists along with monthly expositions.

## KURA HULANDA MUSEUM
Klipstraat 9, Willenstad (Near floating bridge)
462-1400
Monday-Friday, 10 am-5 pm

Kura Hulanda is a wonderful but sad way to experience the Dutch slave trade. Exhibits show the transatlantic trade of humans from the capture in Africa to the New World and "life" thereafter. Ships used, documents, restraining devices, art and much more is all there. This black holocaust museum is a must.

## KAS DI PAL'I MAISHI
Road to Westpunt
☎ 642742
Daily, 9 am-4 pm

This authentic *kunuku* house dates back to the middle of the last century. It's built from limbs of divi-divi trees woven together, packed with mud and dung, and then covered with lime and aloe. Tree limbs and cornstalks are intertwined to form the roof. Inside is a display of period tools, furniture and clothes. As was typical of the times, the kitchen is outside with a clay bread oven as its centerpiece. Refreshments are served daily, with live local music and an arts and crafts show held the first Sunday of the month.

Curaçao

## *Other Attractions*

## AMSTEL BREWERY TOURS
☎ 612944
Tuesday and Thursday mornings at 9:30 am

Desalinated sea water and ages of Dutch tradition and experience go into the local brew. Beer aficionados won't want to miss this one.

## BOTANICAL GARDEN & ZOO
Chuchubiweg
☎ 378500
Daily, 9 am-5:30 pm

Best visited with kids, the zoo features flamingos, bears, lions, monkeys and assorted creatures. There is also a small playground and souvenir shop.

## SENIOR CURACAO LIQUEUR DISTILLERY
Lanhuis Chobolobo, Salinja
☎ 378459
Monday-Friday, 8 am-noon; 2 pm-5 pm

Often imitated, but never duplicated, this authentic Curaçao liqueur is still made just as it was over a century ago with that special ingredient found only on Curaçao – the *laraha*. The result of a failed effort by the Spanish to grow Valencia oranges on Curaçao, this bitter, inedible fruit was abandoned until decades later when its secret was discovered. When dried in the sun, its rind contains a fragrant oil that is the essential ingredient of the Curaçao liqueur. For over a century the Senior family has been making this world-famous liqueur according to the family recipe. Their history and that of the factory is documented through pictures and artifacts in the distillery which is still operating just as it did in the 1800s.

## Landhuisen

Landhouses, *landhuisen*, played an important role in Curaçao's history. Many have been renovated and are now lovely restaurants, guesthouses and museums. Try to visit at least one or two as you explore the island.

Despite the fact that agriculture was not a viable industry, Curaçao's settlers wanted to live the dream of the Caribbean colonist – to be lord and master of an island plantation, complete with a spacious plantation house and large tract of land. Curaçao's earliest plantation houses, or *landhuisen,* as they were called by the Dutch settlers, were built during the latter part of the 17th century by the directors and officials of the Dutch West India Company. During this period the salt trade was the island's primary source of income. Demand for salt was great, especially by the Dutch herring industry. To meet the demand, salt pans were built on the western side of the island, forming a close-knit group of salt plantations, including Santa Cruz, Groot Santa Martha, Jan Kok, Knip, Savonet and Ascensión.

Since roads had not yet been built, the salt was transported in small boats along the coast to Santa Anna Bay, where it was transferred into larger ocean-going vessels. Supposedly the salt harvested at Ascensión, the landhouse closest to the north coast, was miraculously transported via the rough windward seas and around Oostpunt to Santa Anna. Over time, primitive roads were built, making it possible to transport salt via donkey as well. As roads improved, plantation owners began building coach houses and stables for their horses and donkeys.

Faced with lower-priced competition from other islands, Curaçao's salt trade began to dwindle in the early years of the 19th century. In the 1840s, many plantation owners crossed over into agricul-

Curaçao

*Plantations, such as Knip, which raised sheep & cattle, would also have corrals.*

ture, but met with little or no success after attempting to grow sugar, cotton, tobacco and silkworms for export. Those who cultivated aloe vera and made cochineal, which were better suited to the island's harsh, arid climate, were only marginally successful.

Luckily, most plantation owners were not dependent upon agriculture for their livelihood. By the 19th century, Curaçao had become a commercial center. Many plantations were owned by "absentee landlords," who lived in town and made their living as government officials, bankers or merchants while an overseer managed their country estate. The landhuis was more a status symbol than anything else.

Even greater was the prestige of not just owning a landhouse, but having slaves as well. But unlike other islands where plantations often had slaves by the hundreds, most of whom worked in the fields, few plantation owners on Curaçao owned more than 10 slaves. This was understandable given the small role agriculture played in the Curaçaoan economy. So it's not surprising that most owners were on familiar terms with their slaves. It was not unusual for the domestic or house slaves to be the mulatto descendants of the landowner himself. Most lived in small houses on their master's property and were often given a small plot of land for a garden. Even after their emancipation in 1863, many slaves chose to remain and work for their former masters in order to pay for the necessities their master had once provided.

## The Typical Landhouse

Landhouses were usually built on high ground, to provide the owner with a vantage point from which to watch over his domain and to take maximum advantage of the breeze provided by the trade winds. In the Banda Bao, the western side of the island, landhouses were built within sight of at least one other landhouse in order to form a communication network throughout the area. By signaling to each other from their roofs, either with flaming torches or mirrors, they could warn their neighbors of trouble or call for help.

Landhouses were built primarily of coral cement which was often mixed with rocks from the higher reaches of the island. Typically the design consisted of a central core with wings built on at least two sides and a gable above the center. Roofs were gabled or pitched in order to keep the sun from beating down on the house directly. Bedrooms were usually on the second floor, though it was not uncommon during a heatwave for the family to sleep in the open galleries on the ground floor, which were cooled by the constant trade winds.

Most landhouses had a *broodbakoven*, a bread oven, in the garden. It would be lined with bricks, which retained the heat of the wood fire. Once the bricks were hot, the fire would be removed and the bread inserted for baking. The kitchen itself was located on the west side of the house so that odors would be carried off by the trade winds. The same held true for the outhouse.

Whenever possible, estates were built over groundwater, with wells to provide water for plants and livestock. Rain, on the other hand, was the primary source of water for household use. It was collected via a series of coral cement aqueducts running from the roof to a large cistern. During times of drought, water was purchased from "water plantations" built over large natural water tables.

## Landhouses through the Years

Though many landhouses have dates inscribed under their gables, they don't necessarily represent the date of construction. Owners sometimes selected a date much earlier than the actual one to make it seem as if they had inherited an antique of great historic value. To ascertain the age of a landhouse, you must look instead to the design and shape of the gable itself. Given the fragility of the building materials, chiefly coral cement, which soon crumbles without proper attention, many of the earliest landhouses have collapsed. In addition, many were burnt down during the slave revolt in 1795. Thankfully, several landhouses have been renovated or entirely rebuilt.

*The western tour of the island will take you past Landhaus Ascención (☎ 641950).*

Curaçao's earliest landhouses were built during the later years of the 17th century and the early 18th century. With fluid lines and a triangle on top of a square motif, their gables resemble those that had been popular in Amsterdam a century earlier. Examples include **Landhaus Ascención**, one of the few landhouses remaining from the 17th century. It was built around 1672 and was restored in 1963. Today it is used as a recreation center for Dutch Marines stationed in the Antilles. It is open to the public on the first

Sunday of every month, when there is an open house featuring folkloric music, handicrafts and refreshments.

Though the present landhouse was built in the 18th century, **Landhuis Daniel** goes back as far as 1634. It was never used for agriculture. Instead, given its central location, it served as a rest stop for travelers and their horses who were traveling from east to west. Today it is a guest house featuring a restaurant, dive center and souvenir shop. Fresh-brewed coffee, homemade pastries, Dutch pancakes, and snacks are served on the terrace. Dinner is by reservation only.

*Landhuis Daniel is a delightful place to stop at the end of the western tour of the island. The terrace is open daily from 9 am to 6 pm, except Tues. & Thurs. (☎ 648400).*

**Groot Santa Martha** was built sometime before 1750 by Daniel Ellis who, as the story goes, was shipwrecked here on St. Daniel's Day. It was restored by the government in 1979 and is now used as a center for the physically and mentally handicapped, who make handicrafts and souvenirs.

*Visitors are welcome Monday-Thurs., 9 am-noon and from 1 pm to 3 pm, as well as Friday mornings and the first Sunday of the month (☎ 64-159).*

Otrobanda's **Landhuis Habai** dates back to the 17th century and is the only remaining landhouse in the Jewish Quarter that belonged to the early Sephardic settlers. Unique are its full second floor and cobblestone courtyard.

The more ornamental Baroque style, with its curlicues and fancifully carved gables, came into favor in Curaçao in the 18th century, a full century after its debut in Europe. **Landhuis Savonet** in Christoffel Park, originally built in the 17th century, was rebuilt in Baroque style after being destroyed by British invaders. A minaret-like pinnacle caps the fluid lines of its gable. Other fine examples include **Landhuis Jan Kok**, which dates back to the 18th century, and

Curaçao

**Zeelandia**, a restored office building in Willemstad. Private tours of **Landhuis Jan Kok** are offered weekdays by appointment only (☎ 648087). It is open to the public on Sundays and offers a menu of Dutch-style pancakes, and local cooking, along with chilling ghost stories by the owner, Jeanette.

*Plantation Knip is open weekdays 9 am to noon & 2 pm-4 pm; and Sundays 10 am to 5 pm. Closed on Saturdays. Call for guided tour reservations (☎ 640244).*

The early years of the 19th century were marked by a return to simplicity with a small square atop the gable replacing the more fanciful Baroque designs. **Plantation Knip**, first built in 1700, was the starting point of the slave uprising of 1795, led by Tula. The landhouse was destroyed completely and rebuilt in 1830 on a plan not unlike the original, although the gables are early 19th-century style. **Landhouse Knip** has been remodeled twice since then, first in the 1930s and again in the 1980s. It is not far from Knip Bay, which is home to two of the loveliest beaches on the island. The landhouse is open to the public and frequently hosts handicraft fairs.

**Landhuis Chobolobo** dates back to the 1800s. It was acquired by the Senior Family in 1948 and flourished as an elegant supper club for several years. Now it is home to the **Curaçao Liqueur Distillery**, which is open to the public weekdays from 8 am to noon and 2 pm to 5 pm. Tasting is included in the free visit (☎ 378459).

In the 18th century, **Landhuis Brievengat** was a prosperous cattle ranch with a domain of 1,200 acres. Unfortunately, it was devastated by the hurricane of 1877 and fell into ruin, despite its abundant ground water. In the early years of the 20th century it was sold to the Shell Oil Company for one guilder. In 1952, it was restored by the Ukrainian architect Serge Alexeenko. Nowadays it is a popular cultural and social center. By day it hosts antique and craft fair exhibits. Evenings are quite busy, with happy hours Wednesday and Friday, featuring rijsttafel, followed by live dance music on the terrace Friday evenings from 9 pm onwards. Dance lessons are offered Thursday evenings at 8:30, and there's another happy hour on Sunday from 5 pm to 7 pm with live music. Plus, there is a folkloric show on the last Sunday of the month. Though lovely during the day, Brievengat is especially beautiful at night.

*The Landhuis Brievengat is open weekdays from 9:15 am-12:15 pm and 3-6 pm. Happy Hour is 5-7 pm.*

The late 19th century marked an extreme departure from earlier *landhuis* styles, with the elimination of the decorative gable top. Many of the landhouses on the eastern side of the island are in this style, as is **Landhuis Papaya**. It is open to the public and features a display of early photographs. Hours are from 10 am to 6 pm weekdays, and weekends until 9 pm. There's a barbecue with mariachi music on Sundays (☎ 695850).

Private ownership of landhouses began to decline at the beginning of the 20th century. Many of the descendants of the former slaves who had remained on the plantations went to work for the newly opened Shell Refinery. Their source of labor gone, much of the land went uncultivated and the landhouses became nothing more than an economic burden to their owners. While some were sold to the government for public use, many were simply abandoned.

In recent years, Curaçao's landhouses have been rediscovered, both for the important role they played in the island's history as well as for their

**Curaçao**

charm. Many are enjoying second lives as museums, art galleries, restaurants, hotels and cultural centers. The Monument Bureau has plans for others, while some still serve as private homes.

## Island Tours

## Banda Bou (Western Tour)

*Banda Bou is Curaçao's better half.*

The western side of the island, or the Banda Bou as it is called by the locals, is the most scenic part of the island. Much of the landscape is unspoiled and many of Curaçao's loveliest and most secluded beaches are along the southwest coast. In fact, our tour will take you past several of them as well as many of Curaçao's historic plantation houses.

*If you're planning on climbing Christoffelberg, get to the park in the early morning hours before the sun gets too strong.*

*To better plan your day, review the sections on beaches & landhouses before setting out and decide what you want to see.*

### HIGHLIGHTS

◎ The breathtaking views from atop **Christoffelberg**.

◎ The spray of waves crashing into the Viewpoint Cave at **Boca Tabla**.

◎ Snorkeling at **Playa Lagún**.

◎ Picture-perfect vistas of **Santa Martha Baai**.

The drive that follows can be completed in one day, but that won't leave you much time for hiking in Christoffel Park or hanging out at the beach, not to mention snorkeling and diving.

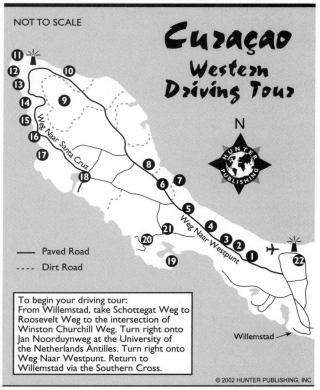

NOT TO SCALE

# Curaçao
## Western
## Driving Tour

N

—— Paved Road

---- Dirt Road

To begin your driving tour:
From Willemstad, take Schottegat Weg to
Roosevelt Weg to the intersection of
Winston Churchill Weg. Turn right onto
Jan Noorduynweg at the University of
the Netherlands Antilles. Turn right onto
Weg Naar Westpunt. Return to
Willemstad via the Southern Cross.

Willemstad →

© 2002 HUNTER PUBLISHING, INC

Curaçao

| | | | |
|---|---|---|---|
| 1. | Landhuis Papaya | 12. | Playa Kalki |
| 2. | Grote Berg | 13. | Westpuntbaai |
| 3. | Kleine Berg | 14. | Knipbaai (beautiful beaches) |
| 4. | Landhuis Daniel | 15 | Playa Jeremi |
| 5. | Tera Cora | 16. | Playa Lagún |
| 6. | Pos di San Pedro | 17. | Boca Santa Cruz |
| 7. | Boca San Pedro | 18. | Soto/Groot LandhuisSanta Marta |
| 8. | Landhuis Ascensión | 19. | Saliña Santa Marie (flamingos) |
| 9. | Christoffel Nat'l Park | 20. | Willibrordus (village) & |
| | & Christoffelberg | | Cathedral of St. William Brothers |
| 10. | Boca Tabla | 21. | Landhuis Jan Kok |
| 11. | Watamula | 22. | Hato Caves |
| | (western point of island) | | |

Keeping that in mind, read through the tour and plan your itinerary according to your own interests.

Water buffs should pack their snorkel and or dive gear, including dive booties. Don't forget good walking shoes if you plan on climbing Mt. Christoffel or hiking in the park. Regardless of your plans, bring sunscreen, a hat and water. Stop for lunch at Jaanchie's Restaurant in Watamula, or pack a picnic.

Leaving Willemstad, head northwest on the **Schottegat Weg**, the beltway around Willemstad and the Schottegat. At the intersection by the police station, turn west onto Roosevelt Weg and follow it until you reach the Winston Churchill Weg intersection, where you should make a right-hand turn followed by a quick left onto Jan Noorduynweg. You'll pass the **University of the Netherlands Antilles** on the left. Degrees are offered in law, industrial engineering and public administration. Students interested in other fields study abroad, usually in the Netherlands, Puerto Rico or the United States.

*Landhuis Papaya is often rented out for private parties.*

At the next traffic light, turn right onto the Weg Naar Westpunt, the road to Westpunt, and you'll be on your way. Among the landmarks you'll pass is the gaily painted **Landhuis Papaya**. The smallest of the landhouses on Curaçao, it was once a popular "resting point" for men traveling between Willemstad and the other plantations. After passing Landhuis Papaya, you'll climb 330 feet to the top of **Grote Berg** (Big Mountain) and then **Kleine Berg** (Small Mountain). From either of the two peaks you can see the **Christ-**

offelberg, which, at 1,230 feet, is Curaçao's highest mountain. This is the narrowest part of the island.

A little farther down the road on the left is a small chapel-like building that was built by artist/physician **Chris Engels** for his wife Lucille, a talented painter. One day, as Lucille was painting, Engels thought the canvas she was painting was too small. He promised her a wall to paint on and, in the end, wound up building a house to go with it. In addition to Lucille's mural, sculptures by the Dutch artist Charles Eyack are also here. If you'd like to have a look, stop by the house across the road and request the key.

Just beyond the road to San Willibrordo you'll pass **Landhuis Daniel** and then a cluster of homes in an area known as ***Tera Cora***, "Red Earth," due to the red color of the soil. The soil in this area is quite fertile, and you'll note that the vegetation growing along the roadside is greener and more dense than in other areas of the island. If you were to follow the road next to the house with the number TC24A painted on its wall, you would arrive at a beautiful view of the salt pans, the Landhuis Jan Kok, and the Church of Willibrordo just about a mile later. We'll pass through this area later on in the tour. On the left side of the road you may be able to spot the remains of a **stone wall**. This is one of the walls dating back to colonial days and known as "slave walls." When there was no other work to be done, the slaves would be ordered to build walls out of coral rocks rather than be idle.

Curaçao

## Scenic Detour: The Road to San Pedro

Take a right turn on the road marked San Pedro 1.6. You'll drive past a fertile area known as *Pos di San Pedro,* "San Pedro Well," as well as a field of cactus. Since you are driving across a high plateau, you'll have a wonderful view of the Caribbean. On a clear day you can even see Bonaire. Bear right at the bottom of the plateau and you'll come out at Boca San Pedro, or *Houtjes Baai*, as it is called by the islanders, due to the large amounts of driftwood that turn up on its shores. Also located at the end of the road is **Kodela's Wind Farm**, a series of windmills along the coast, and the **San Petro Plantation**, a small farm. After enjoying the views, turn around and head back to the main road.

*You're driving along the northern coast of the island.*

*The house museum is open Tues-Fri. from 9 am-4 pm and weekends from 9 am to 5 pm. There's a small admission fee. Closed Monday.*

Just after returning to the main road you'll pass a group of divi-divi trees. The **Landhuis Ascensión** is just down the road, followed by the **Kas di Palu di Maishi**. This house was built by a former slave over a hundred years ago and is now home to a small museum dedicated to country life. A museum piece itself, it has been maintained in the traditional style with a straw roof and walls made of branches and rocks covered with a mixture of clay and manure. Small farm animals wander about freely, and there is an outdoor restaurant in the back serving typical foods, primarily stews.

This part of Curaçao is fairly hilly and often densely forested, with cacti and tall manzanilla trees dominating the landscape. After passing through the village of **Barber**, the largest settlement on the western side of the island, and best known for its historic cemetery, you'll see **Christoffelberg**. Shortly thereafter you'll come to the **Landhuis Savonet** and the entrance to **Christoffel National Park**.

The park, which covers an area of 5,000 acres, was founded in 1978 on land owned by three former plantations – Savonet, Zorgvliet, and Zevenbergen – and is managed by STINAPA, the Netherlands Antilles National Parks Foundation. Park highlights include a natural history museum in the *landhuis*, which houses a collection of archaeological artifacts dating back to 2000 BC, Indian cave drawings on the north coast, a nature reserve and, of course, Christoffelberg.

*Christoffel National Park is open from 8 am to 4 pm, Monday-Saturday & Sundays from 6 am-3 pm. Admission to the park & museum is US $5. Guides can be hired for walking & driving tours. Make arrangements in advance (☎ 640-363).*

The park can be experienced by a combination of driving and hiking. The following overview should get you on your way. Maps are available at the entrance. If you can manage it, sunrise is a fabulous time to tour the park and climb Christoffelberg.

**Curaçao**

The **Savonet Route** (5½ miles, 45 minutes). Starting at the Landhuis Savonet, the Blue Route, as it is also called, takes you out to the north coast, where you can explore the Indian drawings and caves in the cliffs there.

The **Savonet Hiking Trail** (90 minutes) travels through a mahogany forest past wells, dams and a salt pan to the limestone terraces of Boca Grandi on the north coast.

*Sunrise atop Christoffelberg is spectacular.*

The **Zvorgvlied Route** (driving only, 7.6 miles, 90 minutes), also called the Green Route, heads west from Landhuis Savonet past the ruins of the Landhuis Zvorgvlied. If you stop to study the ruins, you will see that it was constructed using a combination of coral from the coast as well as rocks from the island's higher elevations. A path to the left of the ruins leads to the Slave Pillar. Traditionally, slaves would be chained to a pillar such as this one as a punishment. However, the absence of the iron links used to chain the slaves to the pillar indicates that it may have been used as a beacon for smugglers.

As the route continues onward past Boca Tabla and Landhuis Knip, you'll enjoy panoramic views of the coast and Christoffelberg. A little beyond the Landhuis, it links up with the hiking trail to Christoffelberg, which starts at Landhuis Savonet. There is a parking area here where you can leave your car. A shortcut from the Zvorgvlied ruins leads directly to the trail.

The hike up the mountain and back should take you about two hours (three if you start at Landhuis Savonet) and can be quite challenging, especially the last few minutes, when you literally have to climb up the steepest part of the hill. Upon reaching the top you'll be rewarded with spectacular views of the island and the Caribbean, even Bonaire on a clear day.

Returning to the road, you'll come to the ***Piedra de Monton***, the "Pile of Rocks" at the intersection with the Zevenbergen Route (the Yellow Route).

> ### ★ DID YOU KNOW?
>
> The slaves of the Caribbean be-
> lieved that by refraining from
> eating salt, one would be able to
> fly back to Africa. The slaves of
> Curaçao believed that *Piedra de
> Monton* was the launching pad
> for that flight.

The **Zevenbergen Route** (seven miles, 75 minutes driving, plus walking time) or Yellow Route
is the most beautiful of the driving routes. You'll
drive through rolling hills with wild orchids and
banana *shimaron* growing along the roadside.
The first highlight of this tour is the panoramic
view of Santa Martha Baai. A little farther on
you'll reach the hiking trail to **Seru Bientu**, Wind
Mountain, so named because it is one of the windi-
est spots on the entire island. It's a short hike to
the top. Looking west, you'll see Landhuis Knip
and the village of Westpunt in the distance. The
route continues past abandoned manganese
mines, eventually rejoining the Green Zvorgvlied
Route, which will take you back to the entrance of
the park.

Leave the park and continue on toward the **western tip** of the island. You'll soon come to the
**Parke Nacionale Shete Boca**. Countless years
of violent battering by the rough seas of the north
coast have formed these seven inlets, the most impressive and best known of which is **Boca Tabla**.
Follow the path to **Viewpoint Cave**. You'll climb
down to a low grotto with a seemingly quiet pool.

Curaçao

*The coral ter-
race at Boca
Tabla is quite
jagged. Sturdy
footwear is rec-
ommended.*

> ## ⚡ WATCH OUT!
>
> According to local legend, when a beautiful woman enters the grotto, the sea gets excited. Though perfectly dry when we climbed down into the cave, we were sopping wet when we left.

*Stop for lunch at Jaanchie's Restaurant.*

Back on the road, you'll drive past the other six bocas and then follow the curve of the island at **Watamula** to the southern coast. Several of our recommended beaches are in this area, including Playa Kalki, Westpuntbaai, Knipbaai, Playa Jeremi, Playa Lagún and Boca Santa Cruz.

Just beyond Santa Cruz, you'll come to the village of **Soto,** where you can visit the **Groot Landhuis Santa Marta**. Soto is also the starting point for one of Curaçao's loveliest drives, the road to the **Coral Cliff Resort and Casino**. Well worth a detour, it offers panoramic views of the village of Santa Martha and Santa Marthabaai set against a background of hills dominated by Christoffelberg. You'll also pass the **Saliña Santa Marie**, a popular feeding ground for flamingos. The beach at the Coral Cliff Resort is open to the public, though you will have to pay an admission fee at the reception desk. **Wet Suit City**, a popular snorkeling and dive site, is located in front of the resort.

Return to Soto via the same road and then continue east on the main road. About four miles outside Soto you'll arrive at the turn-off for Playa and Landhuis Cas Abao. Shortly thereafter, you'll come to a fork in the road. Bear right toward the village of **Willibrordus**, best known for its church, the **Cathedral of St. William Brothers**, which has been beautifully restored.

Heading back toward Willemstad, you'll come to the **Landhuis Jan Kok**. It dates back to 1650 and, according to the locals, is haunted by its original owner, the infamous Jan Kok, who had a well-deserved reputation for cruelty. Its current owner, Jeanette, is the first person to live in the house for more than 10 years. Belief in Jan Kok's ghost is so strong that she can go out, leaving the doors unlocked, without a care. Jeanette maintains the house in its original colonial style and offers guided tours by appointment (☎ 648087). Be sure to walk out to the terrace, which overlooks the Saliña Santa Marie.

*Jeanette tells terrific ghost stories.*

If time allows, stop at the **Hato Caves** before returning to Willemstad. The last tour is at 4 pm.

## HATO CAVES
F.D. Roosevelt Weg (across from the Hotel Holland)
☎ 680379
Tuesday-Sunday, 10 am-5 pm
Guided tours every hour; last tour at 4 pm
Admission: US $4 adults; $3 children

Nearly 200 million years ago, predating the formation of Curaçao and even the Caribbean basin by more than 100 million years, pounding waves and tidal movements were gradually wearing down a portion of a large underwater landmass. Another 100 million years later, volcanic eruptions, underwater earthquakes and other massive shifts would cause that mass to break apart, forming the two Americas and the Caribbean basin. Curaçao too would rise out of the sea, with the caves formed by the millions of years of pounding

Curaçao

seas still intact below the plateaus or *mesetas* of the north coast.

Fossilized sea creatures, corals, scallops and other crustaceans embedded in the walls and ceilings of the Hato Caves lend credence to the theory of the cave's underwater birth. Though no longer pounded by waves, the caves are still in a slow process of formation, with stalagmites and stalactites growing at a rate of one centimeter (just over a third of an inch) per century. As you may remember from your science classes, stalactites and stalagmites are formed by tiny deposits of calcium carbonate left by the beads of water that leach out of the limestone. If untouched, the stalactites and stalagmites will gradually join in the center, forming a thin pillar that will slowly thicken with the passage of time.

Evidence suggests that the caves may have been used for religious rituals by the Caquetío Indians in the 16th century. Modern-day tourists are not the first to visit the caves. Dutch plantation owners often offered their guests tours of the caves, conducted by their slaves.

Nowadays, tours are led by professional guides who offer a running commentary on the cave's formation, along with delightful anecdotes. You'll cover much of the cave's 52,000 square feet (over an acre), with its freshwater pools, waterfalls and interesting formations, including the remarkable Virgin Mary and the Sleeping Giant. Clever lighting adds to the enchantment.

In addition to the underground tour, the path just outside the entrance to the cave leads to Indian petroglyphs, which were created by the Caquetios about 1,500 years ago. They are among the only Caquetío drawings in the Caribbean outside their homeland along the Orinoco River in Venezuela. Discovered by an amateur geologist in 1950, they have since attracted the attention of the Smithsonian Institution. Also of interest is the large cage at the base of the staircase leading to the caves. Resident within are iguanas of all shapes and sizes, toucans, parrots and turtles from Venezuela, and Surinam parrots from the Amazon Basin.

*It is a 49-step climb to the Hato Caves. The entrance offers a fantastic view of the north coast.*

The Caves are run by a private company from Tennessee, under the watchful supervision of STINAPA. A souvenir shop and snackbar serving local fare are at the entrance.

## Banda Riba (Eastern Tour)

More a scenic drive than anything else, this tour can easily be completed in a couple of hours. You may want to stop at the Curaçao Liqueur Distillery and Landhuis Chobolobo or spend the afternoon at Barbara Beach, our final destination.

---

### HIGHLIGHTS

◎ Lunch at **Playa Perla Canoa**.

◎ Samples of liqueur at **Landhuis Chobolobo**.

◎ Watching the yachts go by at **Barbara Beach**.

---

Curaçao

Cross the Queen Juliana Bridge, heading east out of Willemstad on **Schottegat Weg**, popularly known as "the Ring." Six-tenths of a mile beyond the bridge you'll pass the **Autonomy Monument**. It was dedicated in 1955 to coincide with the eradication of the colonial status of the Netherlands Antilles. The six birds represent the six Antilles. The inscription reads: "Trusting in our own strength, but ready to support each other."

*The Curaçao Liqueur Distillery is open weekdays from 8 am to 12 pm and from 1 pm-5 pm for tours and tastings.*

Shortly after passing the Autonomy Monument, you'll come to the **Landhuis Chobolobo**, the original and present home of the Curaçao Liqueur Distillery, located just at the border of Salinja, Curaçao's newest shopping district and also home to many of the island's popular nightclubs.

*If you'd like to visit Landhuis Breievengat, described earlier on pages 344-345, turn left at the T.*

Not quite two miles beyond the distillery you'll come to a major intersection where there should be a sign for **Landhuis Brievengat**. Follow the signs past the Sentro Deportivo Korsou until you come to the T-intersection, where you should turn right. You'll soon come upon three windmills, the landmark for the **Hofi Pachi Sprockel**, a former plantation that now features an outdoor display of artifacts and dwellings dating back to the times of slavery. If you'd like to visit, you'll need to make an appointment ahead of time (☎ 369957).

Follow the signs to **Santa Rosa** and then, upon reaching Santa Rosa, watch for the sign to **Ronde Klip** and follow it. To your left you'll see two hills. The higher of the two is Ronde Klip, or "Round Cliff." Atop the other, which is accessible by car, is the transmitter for Radio Korsou. To reach the top, take the first road that runs in front of the hill and then the paved road to the left. From here you'll have a sweeping view of Schottegat Harbor as well as the eastern side of the island.

# Curaçao Eastern Driving Tour

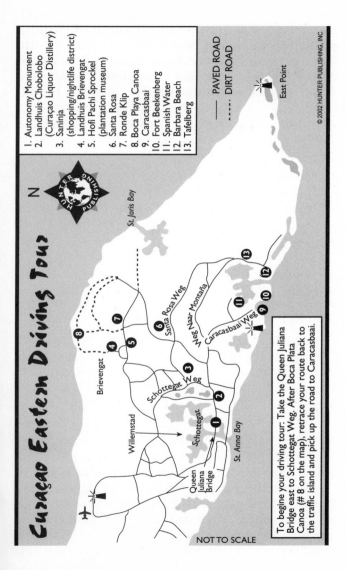

N

1. Autonomy Monument
2. Landhuis Chobolobo
   (Curaçao Liquor Distillery)
3. Saninja
   (shopping/nightlife district)
4. Landhuis Brievengat
5. Hofi Pachi Sprockel
   (plantation museum)
6. Santa Rosa
7. Ronde Klip
8. Boca Playa Canoa
9. Caracasbaai
10. Fort Beekenberg
11. Spanish Water
12. Barbara Beach
13. Tafelberg

——— PAVED ROAD
----- DIRT ROAD

© 2002 HUNTER PUBLISHING, INC

NOT TO SCALE

To begine your driving tour: Take the Queen Juliana Bridge east to Schottegat Weg. After Boca Plata Canoa (# 8 on the map), retrace your route back to the traffic island and pick up the road to Caracasbaai.

Curaçao

Get back on the main road, and continue until you reach the turn-off to **Boca Playa Canoa**, which will be on your right. You'll drive through an arid landscape of cactus and low vegetation to the island's rugged north coast. Upon reaching the coast, you'll come to the **Natural Bridge**. Standing alongside this natural limestone formation should give you an idea of the force with which the surf pounds the northern coast, as compared to the more tranquil waters of the southern coast.

Drive along the coast to **Boca Playa Canoa**, the only fishing inlet on the northern coast and a popular hang out for surfers. Thanks to a limestone wall that serves as a breakwater, this is the only spot on the north coast where it is possible to sail a small boat into land. However, it requires a great deal of skill and is attempted only by experienced fishermen. According to popular legend, pirates used to land here and hide their treasure in a hollow tree outside the Landhuis Brievengat.

A popular stop for lunch, or at least a drink, is the **Playa Perla Canoa**, an outdoor restaurant featuring great scenery, fresh, fresh fish and local cuisine. The restaurant has been built into the limestone wall and is right at the water's edge – so close that if you're lucky enough to get an ocean-side table, you may want to take off your shoes, just in case.

*For a description of Playa Perla Canoa, see page 276.*

Once you're ready to head out to the southern coast, retrace your steps back to Salinja and the traffic island, where you should pick up the road to Caracasbaai. Once the site of the Shell Oil Terminal, the tanks and other vestiges are being dismantled, and plans are in the works to turn this into a tourist area, with facilities that may include a hotel. **Towboat**, a popular dive and snorkel site, is located here and the area draws a crowd on the weekends. The remains of **Fort Beekenberg**, with its battle tower still intact, is also here and the **Fishermen's Wharf** and **Pisces Bar and Restaurant**. Also on the bay is a fishermen's harbor and marina, where a busy market is held in the mornings and evenings after the fishing boats come in. Many local restaurants purchase their fish here.

On the northern side of Caracas Bay is **Spanish Waters**. With its only entrance hidden from sight, during the colonial period this large inner harbor was a favorite hiding place for those in the know. No longer a secret, this is Curaçao's most exclusive residential area, home not only to the island's wealthiest residents, but also to four yacht clubs.

On the eastern side of Spanish Waters is **Barbara Beach**. This white sandy beach is the loveliest on the Banda Riba and a delightful vantage point from which to watch the yachts and sailboats as they leave the harbor and head for the open sea. The **Landhuis Santa Barbara** is nearby. Also in view is the **Tafelberg**, or "table mountain." Once a phosphate mine, now it is home to the only solar-powered radio transmitter in the world. From the top you have a panoramic view of the island; on a clear day you can see Bonaire and even Venezuela.

**Curaçao**

*There is a bus to the top of the Tafelberg Tuesdays & Fridays at 2 pm.*

# Shop Till You Drop

Commerce is nothing new to Curaçao. Long before the first Europeans arrived, the Caquetio Indians from Northwestern Venezuela had settled on the island and were trading with the mainland from dugout canoes. Centuries later, the Dutch, French and English fought for control, recognizing the strategic value of Curaçao's protected harbor and prime location on the trading routes between Europe and South America. The Dutch eventually won out, but that hasn't prevented fine French perfumes and cosmetics and English porcelain from penetrating the market, along with other goods from around the world.

Modern-day Curaçao is the shopping mecca of the Caribbean. Venezuelans used to flock here to shop during the oil boom years in the 1970s when their pocketbooks were full and the Bolívar was strong. Its **Free Zone**, the largest in the Caribbean, is patronized by retailers from throughout the region, who come to stock up on goods from all over the world. Goods purchased in the Free Zone must be shipped directly to your home or transferred to your ship or flight. You can pick them up when you arrive home. Some goods can only be purchased in bulk. But, as far as we're concerned, the real shopping is in **Willemstad**, where you'll find a wonderful selection of European clothing, Indonesian crafts and jewelry, French perfumes, Japanese electronics, Irish crystal, English china, pre-Columbian style jewelry, fine Italian and South American leathers, Chinese embroidered linen tablecloths, Indonesian batik clothing and accessories, Austrian crystal (Swarovski), Swiss watches... the list goes on and on.

## Where to Go

Starting at the Queen Emma Bridge, **Breede-straat**, the main shopping street in Punda, is lined with international shops featuring European perfumes and cosmetics, fine linens hand embroidered in China and Portugal, Dutch Delft porcelain, Bohemian cut crystal, Swiss watches, jewelry, electronics, and designer clothing. You'll find similar values on the pedestrian promenades, **Heerenstraat** and **Madurostraat**. Handicrafts and Haitian woodcarvings are displayed at the end of Heerenstraat on the Plaza Jo Jo Correa. From there you can turn onto Madurostraat, with its shops offering affordably priced designer apparel, sportswear and shoes.

*"Breedestraat" means Broadway in Dutch.*

Before crossing the floating bridge to Otrobanda, browse through the designer boutiques in the **Waterfort Arches**. They'll contrast sharply with the shops on **Breedestraat** in Otrobanda. The Orchard Street of Willemstad, Otrobanda is known for bargains, including imported fabrics and lace from Europe and the Far East.

No matter where you go, prices may be as much as 30% below what you would pay for the same or similar items at home and there's no sales tax. Credit cards, US dollars and Dutch guilders are accepted almost everywhere. Payment in cash may sometimes result in a discount. No matter where you shop, the salespeople are courteous and attentive. You'll be amazed at how effort-

Curaçao

lessly they switch between English, Spanish, Dutch and Papiamento, sometimes in the same conversation.

Since the downtown shopping district is small, it is possible to see all of it at a leisurely pace in a morning. However, if you're serious about shopping and your time on the island is limited, the following descriptions should be of some help.

## Sportswear & Cosmetics

### PENHA & SONS
Breedestraat, Punda

This store, located at the corner of Breedestraat and Heerenstraat alongside the Queen Emma Bridge, is nearly impossible to miss. Not only is the name prominently displayed along the façade of the building, so is the date of construction, 1708, making this the oldest building in Willemstad. Penha & Sons is the exclusive distributor of several lines of fine cosmetics and perfumes including Estée Lauder, Elizabeth Arden, Biotherm, Lancaster, Shiseido, Boucheron, Escada and Lalique.

Casual apparel by Liz Claiborne, Carole Little and Jones New York is featured in the Ladies Boutique. Sportswear by Tommy Hilfiger, Nautica, Botany 500, Ralph Lauren and Givenchy are upstairs in the Men's Boutique along with French and Italian ties and Sperry Topsider deckshoes. Penha & Sons' selection of Hummel figurines, Blue Delft porcelain, souvenirs and T-shirts make fine gifts.

## LA CASA AMARILLA (YELLOW HOUSE)
Breedestraat 46
Sonesta Beach Hotel

This fine perfumerie dates back to 1887. Of course, the cosmetics and perfumes are totally contemporary. It carries fragrances by Elizabeth Arden, Cartier, Dior, Guerlain, Givenchy, and Nina Ricci, and cosmetics by Stendhal, Swisscare, and Beauté, Lancaster and Svelte by Dior, along with a large selection of liquors and gift items.

## LITTLE HOLLAND
Gomez Plein 6
Breedestraat 37

Little Holland features Curaçao's largest selection of hand-embroidered linen tablecloths and placemats, along with Tommy Hilfiger and Nautica sportswear, Gotcha Beachwear, and Polo fashions. You'll also find terrific buys on Bally and Clark's men's and women's shoes. The Breedestraat branch has a special acclimatized cedar cigar room.

*Prices at Little Holland are unbelievable. We got four pairs of Bally shoes during our last visit.*

## NEW AMSTERDAM STORE
Gomezplein & Breedestraat

The New Amsterdam has been offering shoppers bargain prices since 1925. You'll find top quality hand-embroidered tablecloths, doilies and placemats, Nao (by Lladró) and Delft porcelain, and the most complete selection of Hummel figurines on the island. Both 14 kt. and 18 kt. gold jewelry are 20% off. Women can choose among fashions by Escada, Gottex, Steilman, Esprit, and Nicole Miller, and accessorize with Italian leather shoes, bags and belts by Isanti. Men's sportswear is by Carven, Tom Taylor, Nike and Reebok.

Curaçao

## LA PERLA BOUTIQUE
Gomezplein

This lovely boutique features its own line of prêt-à-porter fashions – Ritmo di Perla – along with an exclusive selection of fine lingerie and swimwear.

## Watches & Jewelry

## LITTLE SWITZERLAND
Breedestraat 44

If a Rolex has been on your wish list for years, this may be the time to make that wish come true. Little Switzerland carries the finest Swiss watches, 14 kt. and 18 kt. gemstone and diamond jewelry and a lovely selection of china, crystal figurines including Swarovski, leather goods and accessories. Prices are among the best in the Caribbean at this store.

## GANDELMAN JEWELERS
Breedestraat 35
Sonesta Beach Hotel

An old-timer in Curaçao, Gandelman Jewelers is best known for its exclusive selection of hand-crafted gold jewelry set with diamonds and colored gemstones, including emeralds, rubies and sapphires.

The store also has one of the largest selections of timepieces by Cartier, Piaget, Ebel, Movado, Tag Heuer and other well-known watchmakers. Crystal by Lalique, Baccarat, Daum and Swarovski, leather goods by Prima Classe, and Mont Blanc writing instruments round out the selection.

## KYRA
Cozy Point, Suite B
Corrieweg

Kyra features exquisitely reproduced pre-Colombian jewelry in pewter and 24 kt. gold. It also has a collection of beautiful 18 kt. gold jewelry from Germany, Italy and South America, set with diamonds and precious and semi-precious gemstones, as well as lovely gift items in silver, crystal and fine porcelain.

## *Electronics*

## BOOLCHAND'S
Breedestraat at Heerenstraat

Boolchand's offers a hard-to-beat selection of photographic and electronic equipment, including cameras by Nikon, Minolta, Olympus and Pentax, and electronics by Alpine, Bose, Braun, Hitachi, JVC, Kenwood, Nintendo, Sony and TDK. Citizen and Seiko watches, Ray-Ban sunglasses and Swarovski crystal are also sold here.

## *Shoes & Leather Goods*

## EXOTIQUE PLAZA
Waterfort Arches

You'll find a great selection of high-quality leather goods and gifts, such as briefcases, handbags, wallets, shoes and more. Additional locations are in the airport and the International Trade Center.

Curaçao

## ECCOLET
Breedestraat 39

Made in Denmark, these trendy shoes appeal to the young at heart. They are designed to provide maximum comfort using soft, flexible materials for a perfect fit.

## ARAWAK CRAFTS
Cruise Ship Terminal, Otrobanda

Works by local potters are featured at this combination workshop and showroom where you'll find both mass-produced and one-of-a-kind pieces by local artisans. On display in the showroom are miniature *landhuisen*, porcelain models of the famous Handelskade, ceramic windchimes and countless other gift ideas. A walkway around the workshop lets you observe the artisans at work. Placards describe each phase of the process and identify the artisans.

# Floating Market

*Shop at the Floating Market if you are planning a picnic or doing your own cooking. Brush up on your Spanish & be ready to bargain.*

Not to be missed, Willemstad's colorful Floating Market is reminiscent of those simpler times before Price Clubs and Super Stores. Located at the end of the Handelskade farthest from the Queen Emma Bridge, small fishing boats from Venezuela are lined up beneath a sea of colorful sailcloth canopies. Though many used to make the trip from Venezuela every day, nowadays vendors set up housekeeping on their boat and remain on Curaçao for two to three months, selling fresh tropical fruits and vegetables, fish, Caribbean spices and assorted odds and ends. Their mangoes, papayas, and other fresh fruits and vegetables are shipped in aboard a larger boat from

Venezuela in the wee hours of the morning. For a real slice of life, get here in the morning when the local housewives are buying for their families. Nearby on the Plaza Jo Jo Correa there is often a small artisans' market featuring local crafts.

## Shopping Centers

Most centers are located in Salinja and cater to well-heeled Curaçaoans. The **Douglas Shopping Gallery** features a full-service salon and upscale boutiques. **Salinja Galleries** are comprised of three large buildings painted in island colors of yellow, coral and green, which are home to clothing and gift boutiques selling high-quality Dutch and German clothing and pre-Colombian jewelry. The **Promenade Shopping Center** features unique boutiques, while the **Bloempot Shopping Center**, located on an 18th-century estate, is a charming complex with restaurants and boutiques. **Landhuis Zuikertuintje,** which means "sugar garden" in Dutch, is a modern supermarket selling European and North American goods. It has a snack bar in the back with a patio. Finally, the **'77 Shopping Center**, or *Siete Siete,* and the **Esperamos Shopping Center** across the street, offer a wide variety of shops.

## After Dark

Exhausted after a full day of shopping, snorkeling, sightseeing, golf, tennis and diving? Take a nap! Then after a quick shower, change and put your dancing shoes on, 'cause Curaçao is an island that knows how to party. There's no such thing as early to bed here. Not when you've got casinos, nightclubs and discos galore, and romantic outdoor cafés on the shores of the Caribbean.

Don't miss sunset happy hour. Have dinner at one of Curaçao's world-class restaurants. Then it's up to you. Culture buffs may want to check the local paper or the concierge or activities desk at their hotel to see if there are any performances scheduled. Dance troupes, musicians and theater groups often stop in Curaçao when traveling between Europe and the Americas. Performances are often held at the **International Trade Center**. Pub crawlers may want to check out the action at **Rum Runners** and **Carlito's Cantina**, next door to the Hotel Porto Paseo on De Rouvilleweg in Otrobanda.

If you'd be more content with a low-key evening, relax under the stars at an outdoor table along the Waterfort Arches or in a sidewalk café in Punda. **Hard Rock Society** on Keuken Plein and **El Patio** at Santa Rosaweg 155 near Salinja are open till 1 am. A chaise by the pool or on the beach at your hotel may not be a bad idea either. But don't make it a habit. Curaçao is an island to experience, both day and night!

## Sunset

How to construct the ideal Curaçao night? Start off with a Sunset Happy Hour. Rare is the hotel or restaurant that doesn't honor this island tradition with discounted drinks, snacks and maybe even live music. Hotel happy hours are usually out by the pool, a great way to meet other guests.

If you're in town at sunset, you're likely to find yourself mingling with the local business crowd. Among our favorite in-town sunset vantage points are the outdoor bars at the **Waterfort Arches**, **Bistro Le Clochard's Harbour Terrace**, and the poolside terrace at the **Van der Valk Plaza Hotel**, which features live music from 6 to 8 pm. A sunset sail is another delightful option. Remember, make reservations that morning.

For live jazz, don't miss the Thursday Night Happy Hour at the **Avila Beach Hotel's Blues Bar**. The Sunday Beach Party at the **Mambo Beach Bar** continues well past sunset with live music provided by one of Curaçao's hottest bands, the Mambo Kings.

For a taste of Indonesia, head to **Landhuis Brievengat**. On Wednesdays and Fridays, from 5- 7 pm, it hosts a happy hour featuring an Indonesian rice table, or rijsttafel. Live music is featured at the Landhuis' Sunday Happy Hour from 6 to 7 pm.

## Nightclubs & Discos

If it's after 10 pm and you're looking for a nightclub or disco where you can burn off those extra calories dancing to the best American and Latin music, hop in the car or grab a cab to **Salinja**, where you'll find the island's hottest clubs. Many offer live entertainment on Wednesday (Ladies Night), as well as on the weekends when they stay open till 3 am. Closing time during the week is

2 am. Cover charge and entertainment vary by night, so it's best to call ahead. Local bands to watch for include Doble R, Gibi y Su Orquesta, the Mambo Kings and ERA.

A young crowd gathers at **Havana** in Salinja (☎ 61290), which features a lot of North American music mixed in with fast-paced merengue and salsa. The more glitzy **Façade** (Lindergheng 32, ☎ 614640) and **Studio 99** (☎ 614353) – popularly called LA – both attract a slightly older, more up-scale clientele and play classic as well as contemporary Latin music with some North American dance music mixed in. The activity desk at your hotel should be able to provide you with a Tourist Courtesy Card for LA. Even if you've never attempted a salsa or merengue before coming to Curaçao, don't be shy. Just move your hips and you'll soon merengue with the best. For a special night under the stars, there's live music on the terrace at **Landhuis Brievengat**, on Friday nights starting at 9 pm and again on Sundays starting at 6 pm. As a warm-up to Friday's festivities, the Landhuis holds a dance class on Thursday evenings from 8:30 to 9:30 pm.

## Casinos

The casinos are another of Curaçao's most popular attractions. Most larger hotels have one, as do several of the smaller ones, including the out-of-the-way **Coral Cliffs Resort**. Though the slots dominate, Caribbean stud poker, blackjack, roulette and craps are also popular. The elegant **Emerald Casino** at the Marriott Hotel is one of the few casinos on the island to offer baccarat. There are wall-to-wall slots in the popular **Princess Beach Casino**, which even has one large room entirely devoted to those one-arm bandits. There's no lack of gaming tables either.

Most casinos open around midday, though the slots may open earlier, and don't close until 4 am. Appropriate attire is required, though you should be able to get away with shorts and T-shirts during the day.

If you opt for one of the casinos in town such as the **Van Der Valk Plaza** or **Porto Paseo** casinos, you can combine gambling with a moonlight stroll across the Emma Bridge and a nightcap at the Waterfort Arches.

# Curaçao A-Z ?

## Airlines

To call **American Airlines,** ☎ 8695707. **United Airlines** can be reached at ☎ 613033 or 695533. The local number for **British Airways** is ☎ 4617187. To reach **Lufthansa,** ☎ 657799. **ALM** can be reached at ☎ 8695533 and **KLM** at ☎ 4652747. The local number for **Servivensa** is ☎ 680500 or 680538. Be sure to confirm your flight at least 24 hours in advance. The general number for the **Curaçao International Airport** is ☎ 681719.

Curaçao

## Airport Departure Tax

There is a US $20 departure tax for international flights. The tax for inter-island flights is US $5.65. If you are flying to Curaçao or any of the other islands of the Netherlands Antilles you must pay a departure tax of US $5.75 or NAFL 10.

## Babysitting

Most hotels will arrange for a babysitter, often a member of the staff, if you request one. The Marriott and Princess Beach Hotels have children's programs.

## Banking

Banks are open Monday through Friday from 8 am to 3:30 pm. The bank at the airport is open from 8 am to 8 pm, Monday through Saturday, and from 9 am to 8 pm on Sunday. US dollars are accepted virtually everywhere on the island.

## Credit Cards

American Express, Visa/MasterCard and Diners Club are the most widely accepted. The American Express representative is **S.E.L. Maduro & Sons**, Breedesstraat 3B in Willemstad (☎ 616-212). Services include personal and travelers check cashing and reporting lost or stolen cards. **Maduro & Curiel's Bank N.V.**, with its head office on the Plaza Jojo Correa in Willemstad (☎ 661100/fax 661444) is the island's Visa⁄

MasterCard representative. They also have 12 ATM machines across the island where you can access your account at home using a Cirrus bankcard or get a cash advance with your Visa/MasterCard.

## Currency

The currency on Curaçao is the **Netherlands Antilles Florin** (NAFL), which is also referred to as a **guilder**. The Netherlands Antilles florins are extremely stable, backed by gold and At press time the exchange rate was 1.77 florins (NAFL or AFL) to US $1, as it has been for some time. US dollars are widely accepted.

## Drinking Water

Curaçao boasts that it has the best-tasting drinking water in the world. It's distilled sea water produced on Piscadera Baai in the world's largest desalination plant. Not only is it delicious plain, it's also used to produce Amstel, the beer of the Netherlands Antilles, and Curaçao Liqueur.

## Driving

Driving is on the right.

## Electricity

Curaçao operates on 110-130 volts (50 cycles), and is compatible with small appliances designed for use in the United States. Much of the island's electricity is generated by the desalination plant. Adapters may be necessary in some places.

# Emergencies

To call an ambulance, ☎ 112; police, ☎ 911; fire department, ☎ 114. To contact the hospital, ☎ 110.

# Island Tours

**Curaçao Sightseeing Tours**, a division of ShorEx International, offers wonderful tours of Willemstad and the countryside, including a tour of historic Willemstad by trolley. The activities desk at your hotel should be able to provide you with a schedule and additional information. For a less conventional perspective of the island, the non-profit **Unique Curaçao Foundation** will show you the other side of Curaçao. Attractions include Voodoo Caves, the Underground Lake of Shingot, the Watamula Crater and much more. Customized Jeep tours and helicopter rides can be arranged. For information, ☎ 628989.

# Newspapers & Broadcast Media

English language dailies include the *Dutch Caribbean Gazette* and *Curaçao Today*. Both cover international as well as local news. The news is given in English several times daily on **Transworld Radio** at 800 on the AM dial and on **Radio Paradise** 103.1 FM. **CNN** headlines are announced every half-hour from 10 pm to 2 pm the following day on **Semiya FM** at 98.7 FM.

Most hotels have satellite television and carry CNN and other English language programming, as well as stations from Venezuela.

## Shopping Hours

Stores are open from 8 am to noon and 2 pm to 6 pm, Monday through Saturday. Certain stores will open on Sundays and holidays (except Christmas and Good Friday), when cruise ships are in port.

## Telephones

Curaçao's area code and country code is 599-9. For AT&T USA Direct Service, ☎ 001-800-872-2881.

Curaçao has a modern phone system and you should have no problem making local or international calls. ☎ 125 for the international operator.

## Tourist Office

The main office of the **Tourist Board** is at Pietermaii #19 in Willemstad (☎ 4616000). There is also a kiosk by the exits in the airport and at the cruise ship terminal in Otrobanda. In the United States, ☎ 800-332-8266 (in New York, 212-683-7660) or write: Curaçao Tourist Board, 475 Park Avenue South, Suite 2000, New York, NY 10016 or 330 Biscayne Blvd., Miami, FL 33132 (☎ 305-374-5811). In the Netherlands, contact Mr. Guillermo Neef, Vasteland 82-84, 3011 BP, Rotterdam (☎ 31-10-4142639).

Curaçao

## Business & Investor Information

If you're interested in business and/or investment opportunities in Curaçao, contact any of the following.

**Chamber of Commerce:** Kaya Junior Salas 1, ☎ 611455/fax 615652.

**Curaçao Convention Bureau:** International Trade Center, ☎ 624433/fax 624408.

**Curaçao Industrial & International Trade Development Co. (CURINDE):** Emancipatie Boulevard #7, ☎ 376000.

**Curaçao Inc.:** International Trade Center, ☎ 636250/fax 636485.

**Foreign Investment Agency Curaçao (FIAC):** Scharlooweg #174, ☎ 657044/fax 615787.

**Trade & Industry Association:** Kaya Junior Salas, ☎ 611210.

# Index

3-

# Feng Shui

*The characters representing* feng shui.

# Feng Shui

## THE CHINESE ART OF PLACEMENT

## Sarah Rossbach

E. P. DUTTON NEW YORK

Published in the United States by
E.P. Dutton, a division of NAL Penguin Inc.,
2 Park Avenue, New York, N.Y. 10016

Library of Congress Cataloging in Publication Data
Rossbach, Sarah.
Feng shui: the Chinese art of placement.
1. Feng-shui.   I. Title.
BF1779.F4R67   1983      133.3'3      83-1609
ISBN: 0-525-48061-7

Calligraphy by Lin Yun.
Illustrations by David Acheson.

Published simultaneously in Canada by
Fitzhenry & Whiteside, Limited,
Toronto

10   9   8   7   6

_To those who were in the right place at the right time._

# CONTENTS

# CONTENTS

# PREFACE

In 1977, while living and working in Hong Kong, I began Chinese lessons with a man named Lin Yun. Vague stories circulated around the colony of his prowess in an ancient art called *feng shui*. I knew that feng shui translated literally is "wind" and "water," but beyond that I had only a sketchy idea that it had something to do with the ambience of a place. Lin Yun and I would begin our classes in the opulent, colonial-style lobby of the Peninsula Hotel, sipping orange juice and talking of the heroic exploits of Chairman Mao, but more often than not, our dialogues would get short shrift. A young bellhop would circulate through the massive lobby ringing a bell and parading a sign paging Lin Yun. On returning to the table, Professor Lin would say, "Don't pay me for this lesson. I have to look at a friend's mother's grave. Would you join me?"

So I'd shut my textbook and off we'd go on his feng shui rounds: the home of an American journalist whose marriage was rocky, the grave of the mother of an investment banker whose holdings were shaky, the office of a jeweler whose store had been robbed, even the home of a doctor who suffered from insomnia and migraines.

During those lessons, I gradually began to understand what this mysterious "feng shui" actually means. I saw that it combines mystical meaning, common sense, and, sometimes, good taste. I learned that it could involve everything from chairs to corners, from architecture to astrology—determining dates for weddings, festivals, funerals, parties, and even mundane chores such as chopping trees and mowing lawns. But it is more than that. It is an eco-art dealing with conservation, ecology, orientation, and spatial arrangement—basically how and where man should place himself or build his shelter in this vast world. It is a means to define one's position in the physical universe, and then improve on it. And I discovered that it held the promise of everything anyone could possibly want: happy family, good marriage, healthy and long life, successful career, wealth, good luck....In its full scope, feng shui tells us how to locate ourselves in the universe in a better way.

Most of the inspiration for this book belongs to Lin Yun. Though each feng shui practitioner has a different approach, good feng shui demands he act as philosopher, psychologist, doctor, father confessor, and interior designer all rolled into one. Lin Yun is one of the foremost living adepts of this complex art.

A Mandarin teacher by day and a feng shui man by night, Lin Yun began his training when he was six years old. Born in Peking in 1932, he used to play with friends on the grounds of a Tibetan Buddhist temple near his family's home. The temple housed several lamas trained in the Tantric Black Hat sect, a mystical sect of Tibetan Buddhism. One day, a monk approached the boys and offered them lessons in religion. While Lin Yun's friends ran away, he ventured closer to hear what the monk had to say. For the next nine years, Lin Yun was instructed in the writings and practices of the sect. These included both Tibetan Tantric mystical arts and traditional Chinese texts and teachings, such as the *I Ching* and feng shui. Since then, he has studied law, philosophy, and urban planning, and has lectured on feng shui in the United States.

The early chapters of this book give an overview of feng shui tradition, history, and method shared by all experts, and the later chapters are generally based on Lin Yun's treatment of feng shui—his practice, teachings, and experience.

I found feng shui appealing, though, frankly, I was skeptical at first. I don't know why or how it operates—I'm not a scientist—but I do know it has worked for many people for thousands of years. And, in the five years of studying it, I've seen marriages saved, careers made, and restaurants prosper. You may call it coincidence, but I can testify that it works.

I should like to thank the following people who were generous with their time, knowledge, and hospitality: Vivien Chang, Tong Yi-fang, Suzanne Green, Lynne Curry, Lucy Lo, Sylvia Edgar, Eric Cumine, Tao Ho, David Lung, Di-mon Lu, Veronica Hwang Li, Doris Wang, Mrs. Margery Topley, Mike Chinoy, Shao Fon-fon, John Warden, James Hayes, Robert Upton, John Chu, Barbara Butterfield, Rockwell Stensrud, Ching Cruz, George Lee, Dr. William Whitson, David Keh, Johnny Kao, George Hsu, The Hong Kong Tourist Association, the Ossabaw Island Project, Georgia, Ju Mu, Christine Douglas, Ernie Munch, Penny Coleman, two Hong Kong feng shui experts, Choi Pak-lai and Chen To-Sang; and a Singapore feng shui adept and exhumer, Tan Chat Lung.

## PREFACE

I should also like to express special thanks to Spencer Reiss for reading this manuscript in all its incarnations, to David Acheson for his architectural comments and drawings, to Glenn Cowley for his advice and encouragement, and to the late June Shaplen for her support in all stages of this book. Most important, I am especially grateful to Lin Yun for his time, knowledge, and patience with this project, and without whom it would never have been written.

SARAH ROSSBACH

*New York 1983*

# CHRONOLOGY

# CHRONOLOGY

| | |
|---|---|
| Sung | 960–1279 |
| Yüan (Mongols) | 1260–1368 |
| Ming | 1368–1644 |
| Ch'ing (Manchus) | 1644–1912 |
| Republic | 1912– |
| People's Republic | 1949– |

# GLOSSARY

*amah*  A Chinese nurse or servant.

*ba-gua*  An eight-sided symbol of the *I Ching*, with eight trigrams.

*ch'i*  Cosmic breath, human energy.

*chung-guo*  "The Middle Kingdom," China.

*chu-shr*  That which is outside our realm of experience, that is, illogical cures.

# GLOSSARY

*feng shui*   "Wind" and "water," the Chinese art of placement.

*jusha*   A red, non-edible, medicinal/mystical powder.

*karma*   The Buddhist concept which holds that one's destiny is determined by one's own good and bad deeds, performed in this and past lives.

*li*   A Chinese mile.

*ling*   Airborne particles of embryonic human ch'i.

*lo*   Cantonese for "priest."

*ru-shr*   That which is within our realm of experience, that is, logical cures.

*Tao, Taoism*   "The Way," a philosophical concept of unity. A religion and philosophy deriving from this concept.

*tsai*   "Food" and "money."

*Tun Fu* ceremony   A spirit-placating rite.

*tzu wei*   The North Star.

*yin-yang* theory   The Taoist concept that unifies all opposites.

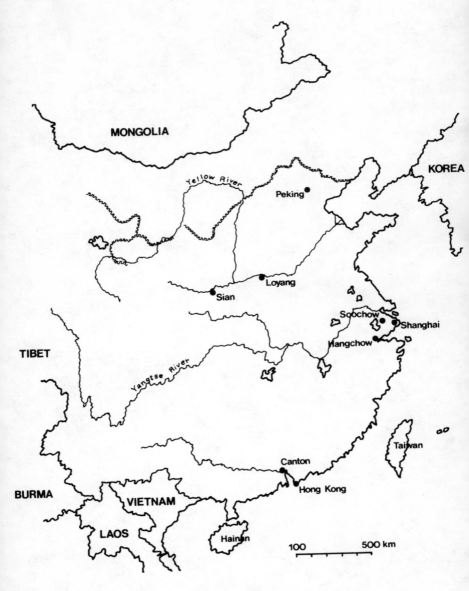

*Map of China.*

# Feng Shui

# One

# INTRODUCTION:
# EXPLAINING FENG SHUI

The Chinese often trace success or failure not so much to human actions, but to the workings of mysterious earth forces. Known as *feng shui*—literally "wind" and "water"—these forces are believed to be responsible for determining health, prosperity, and good luck. Ancient Chinese emperors consulted feng shui experts before building huge public works or waging war. Chiang Kai-shek's rise to power is traced to the especiallly good feng shui of his mother's grave; his downfall is blamed on the Communists later digging it up. Some say kung-fu king Bruce Lee's untimely demise occured because he lived in an unlucky house.

Though officially suppressed in the People's Republic of China, feng shui is today still widely but surreptitiously practiced, mostly in the countryside. It flourishes in Hong Kong, where it is also often used in one form or another by most Chinese and even some Westerners. It has begun to spread to the United States. One Hong Kong and Shanghai Bank officer said, "If my clients believe it, well, so do I."

For all the mystery that surrounds it, feng shui evolved from the simple observation that people are affected, for good or ill, by surroundings: the layout and orientation of workplaces and homes. In addition, the Chinese have long observed that some surroundings are better, luckier, or more blessed than others. Every hill, building, wall, window, and corner and the ways in which they face wind and water have an effect. They concluded that if you change surroundings, you can change your life. The aim of feng shui, then, is to change and harmonize the environment—cosmic currents known as *ch'i*—to improve fortunes.

Feng shui has broadly been applied from the smallest of spaces—say, a bedroom or even the location of a chair—to the largest, cosmic dimension. Its philosophical roots span a whole range of Chinese thought from Taoism and Buddhism to rural magic. It operates on many levels: superstitious and practical, sacred and profane, emotional and physical. There are even those who draw parallels to Western psychology and scientific thought, and believe that its metaphysics operates similarly to modern physics, linking all matter and all mind in one unified theory. Carl Jung wrote, 'The ancient Chinese mind contemplates the cosmos in a way comparable to that of the modern physicist, who cannot deny that his model of the world is a decidedly psychophysical structure."*

In practice, feng shui is something between a science and an

---

*Carl Jung, Foreword to *The I Ching or Book of Changes*, trans. Richard Wilhelm (Princeton, N.J.: Princeton University Press, 1950), p. xxiv.

art. Westerners often call it *geomancy** but the two are not really identical. Feng shui encompasses more than geomancy. Besides arranging living quarters with optimal comfort for mind and body, feng shui also includes astrological and other "psychic" aspects. Experts consider orientation (often with the aid of a cosmic compass), configurations, and juxtapositions. Lin Yun, a leading Hong Kong feng shui expert, explains, "I adapt homes to harmonize with the currents of ch'i," meaning man's nature and cosmic breath. "The shapes of beds, the forms and heights of buildings, and the directions of roads and corners all modify a person's destiny." With that in mind, an international design competition for a multimillion-dollar complex in Hong Kong stressed, along with the usual technical stipulations, feng shui as a crucial consideration.

Fees for feng shui advice vary widely. Choi Pak-lai, one of Hong Kong's most famous feng shui priests, commands roughly sixty cents a square foot for a consultation. Shau Fon-fon, who attended college in the United States, but is now an actress and businesswoman in Hong Kong, moved into a new, spacious apartment and spent $10,000 on interior design—$3,000 of it related to feng shui.

Feng shui is so extensive in Hong Kong that people joke that the practitioner must be in cahoots with building contractors or at least hold stock in a mirror factory (mirrors figure prominently as feng shui cures). Even the commodities exchange is not immune. A commodities reporter noted the marked improvement on the cotton exchange after its exit was changed from a simple door opening onto a small lobby to a revolving one leading to a spacious loading platform.

Although few feng shui practitioners in Hong Kong speak

*The Oxford English Dictionary* definition is "The art of divination by means of signs derived from the earth, as by the figure assumed by a handful of earth thrown down upon some surface—hence, usually, divination by means of lines or figures formed by jotting down on paper a number of dots at random."

English, the American Chamber of Commerce, the *Far Eastern Economic Review*, and N. M. Rothschild, the British merchant bank, have all used feng shui services. Ignatius Lau, a Hong Kong architect, says that before any officical building is constructed the British colonial government consults with local feng shui priests to see if the structures are ritually aligned with wind and water. Even *Newsweek*'s executive editor, Maynard Parker, says that though he didn't take much stock in feng shui, when he was warned that a Hong Kong apartment he was considering renting had bad feng shui, he searched elsewhere for suitable living quarters.

Feng shui has migrated to the United States. A New York woman, after living in a luxury apartment for ten years, happened to consult a feng shui man. The prognosis wasn't good. She must move, he said, if she was to survive. Within a week of the visit she did—and as far as I know she is still alive. Graphic artist Milton Glaser's office had been robbed six times, so he sent the layout and seating plan to a Hong Kong expert. Since he followed instructions—installing a tank with six black fish and hanging a red clock—the office has been secure. In Washington, D.C., in 1980, before Johnny Kau opened his restaurant House of Hunan on a site where two previous businesses had failed, he sought feng shui advice on his $800,000 worth of renovations. Today, he says, business is booming as a result of feng shui. "Things took off more than I expected," he comments, looking around at full tables and a long waiting line.

Despite its pragmatic aspect, feng shui is in a sense a rosetta stone linking man and his environment, ancient ways and modern life. It interprets the language articulated by natural forms and phenomena, by man-made buildings and symbols, and by the continual workings of the universe, including moon phases and star alignments. Feng shui is the key to understanding the silent dialogue between man and nature, whispered through a cosmic breath or spirit—ch'i. The Chinese term *ch'i* is a life force or energy that ripples water, creates mountains, breathes life into plants, trees, and humans, and propels man along a life course. If ch'i is misguided, man's life and luck might falter. Man feels and is affected by ch'i, though he may not know it.

Feng shui experts fill the need to intuit, decode, and interpret our environment. They watch for patterns in nature and for the human reaction to it. They listen to the symphony of interrelated occurrences and to the unseen cosmic powers governing the universe and affecting our bodies, minds, and, ultimately, our fates.

# *Two*

# ORIGINS

I climb the road to Cold Mountain,
the road to Cold Mountain that never ends.
The valleys are long and strewn with boulders,
the streams broad and banked with thick grass.
Moss is slippery though no rain has fallen;
pines sigh but it isn't wind.
Who can break from the snares of the world
and sit with me among the white clouds?...

# Origins

Among a thousand clouds and ten thousand streams
here lives an idle man,
in the daytime wandering over green mountains,
at night coming home to sleep by the cliff.
Swiftly the springs and autumns pass,
but my mind is at peace, free of dust and delusion.
How pleasant, to know I need nothing to lean on,
to be still as the waters of the autumn river!

—Han-Shan, "Cold Mountain"*

China has no shortage of awesome landscapes. For centuries the Chinese have drawn inspiration from snaking, craggy mountain ranges with peaks melting into misty sky to rivers weaving through fertile valleys and feeding a patchwork of yellow and green oddly shaped rice paddies. Eighth-century poets celebrated nature in verse, courting the moon, sky, mountains, and streams. T'ang dynasty (A.D. 618–906) painters glorified nature's vastness, power, and peace: on silk scrolls, they created miniature panoramas of jagged, towering peaks, razor-straight waterfalls cascading through clouds into terraces and gorges, tiny footbridges crossed by even smaller hermit sages. Taoist thinkers became disciples of nature: idealizing it, seeking a harmony with the natural "way," an identity with the cosmos. Poets, artists, and philosophers alike all yearned to fit into the grand scheme, the harmony and immortality of nature. From this reverence for nature sprang early Chinese religion (Taoism), science (astronomy, geology, magnetism, and alchemy), superstition (astrology, shamanism, fortune-telling), and lastly—a peculiar combination of all three—feng shui.

*Han-Shan, *Cold Mountain: 100 Poems by Han-Shan,* trans. Burton Watson (New York: Grove Press, 1962), pp. 58, 79.

# FENG SHUI

## MAN AND NATURE (Chinese-Style)

The Chinese saw a magical link between man and the landscape: Nature reacts to any change and that reaction resounds in man. They saw the world and themselves as part of a sacred metabolic system. Everything pulsed with life. Everything depended on everything else. The Chinese felt they shared a fate with the earth: When it was healthy and prospered, they thrived; when the balance was destroyed, they suffered. So it made sense, in feng shui terms, to enhance the environment rather than to harm or deplete it, thus hurting the chances for good luck and happiness.

The roots of feng shui grow out of a primitive agrarian way of life, when the fate of man was inextricably bound up with the whims and cycles of heaven and earth: with weather, fertility of the earth, floods, accessibility of water, and amount of sunlight. Man was vulnerable to nature, so he kept watch on it.

From the semidivine emperor—the go-between of heaven and earth—to the laboring peasant, a yearly concern was successful crops. Both ruler and subject looked to nature for signs of drought, flood, and famine. In agriculture, the farmer depended on nature for his life source. In government, the emperor looked to nature for reaffirmation of his right to rule, the mandate of heaven. Since the Chou dynasty (1122–256 B.C.), emperors made annual appeals to heaven on behalf of their kingdom for good crops, good health, and peace. A natural disaster signified that an emperor had lost the balance between heaven and earth, leaving him vulnerable to overthrow. So he relied on special advisers to look for and to interpret omens.

Control of nature's creative and destructive forces—harnessing wind and channeling water—was therefore crucial. "He who controls water, governs the empire,"* is an old Chinese saying. An

*Paul Sun, trans., "Feng Shui: An Ancient Theory of Village Siting," in *The Village as Solar Ecology* (East Falmouth, Mass.: The New Alchemy Institute, 1980), p. 22.

emperor's hold on power depended on controlling both floods, rivers, and canals.

In China—a nation slightly larger than the United States, including Alaska—natural conditions vary widely. In north China, where cold winds rip through houses, mountains and trees provide screens. In the south, where floods annually threaten crops, homes, and lives, mountains provide elevation and irrigation lessens damage. In flat, loessial soil regions, such as the Loyang area, where winds whip up sands, the Chinese dug a network of tunnel homes as shelter from the wind.

Thousands of years ago, as Chinese civilization sprang up along the fertile Yellow and Wei river valleys, feng shui's basic premises also developed from the topographical and geographical nature of the area, a mixture of rugged mountains, plateaus, rivers, valleys, and plains. Long before there were architects, natural phenomena such as wind and water were viewed as sacred signs mysteriously instructing shamans where the most auspicious place was for a house, an altar, or a grave.

The ancient Chinese found that a house sited halfway up a hill on the north side of the river facing south received optimal sun, was protected from harsh winds, avoided floods, and still had access to water for crops. In such surroundings, it was easiest to survive: rice, vegetables, and fruit-bearing trees grew under an unhindered sun, cattle grazed on lush grass, and a house stayed relatively warm in the winter. The environment proved comfortable and harmonious, and helped inhabitants to survive and to grow successful and even wealthy.

When that significant, auspicious, and ideal space was unattainable, the search for antidotes led to the study of feng shui. Soon thereafter, the pursuit and fabrication of a viable physical setting became a basic environmental science, with its goal the control of man's immediate surroundings.

Feng shui supports the modern idea of ecology and conservation. Its message is: Harmonize with, do not disrupt, nature.

Tampering with nature might disrupt its equilibrium. Costs of changing the environment range from pollution to overpopulation. Changes must therefore be planned and executed carefully. Indiscriminate altering of nature can set off a series of events leading to unpredictable results. (The Chinese did not always practice what they preached. Throughout the nineteenth and twentieth centuries, they lumbered extensively in the north for firewood and consequently drastically altered the ecological balance, changing dense forest into a dust bowl.)

## THE SACRED ART OF POSITIONING

The Chinese have always stressed position, be it within the landscape, the world, or the cosmos. And to locate the correct spot, they used mystical methods ranging from numerology and astrology to orientation and images. For example, they sought meaning through designating cities, buildings, and people with names implying and invoking central power. China itself, *Chung-guo,* means "Middle Kingdom"—the nation at the hub of the universe, the heart to which all power flows and from which even greater power emanates. In Peking, the emperor's domain, the "Purple Forbidden City," (*Tzu Chin Ch'eng*), alludes to the North Star, *Tzu Wei,* the constellation around which all stars revolve. There the emperor, the son of heaven, mediated the country's fate, keeping peace between heaven, earth, and man.

But power and good fortune came initially from the landscape. The Chinese invested their surroundings with sacred meanings derived from natural shapes, growth, and orientation. The earth had many guises ranging from dragon to disembodied god, all possessing a cosmic power that ruled man's destiny. The entire Chinese universe was imbued with sacred gods, spirits, and creatures, who lived in heaven and earth, moon and sun, sea and land.

The Chinese cosmos, however, was holistic, tying all natural features into one body. In one creation myth, the landscape itself was not just a chaotic and hostile mass of mountains, rivers, and forest, but a god figure transformed.

> The origin of the world lay in a primordial egg which hatched a god who lived 18,000 years. Then he died. His head split and became the sun and moon, his blood the rivers and seas, his hair the plants, his limbs the mountains, his voice the thunder, his perspiration the rain, his breath the wind—and his fleas the ancestors of man.*

So the Chinese were building not on an undefined, unknown wilderness but on the flesh of a god figure, who once had human form and spawned and fed human parasites. On a religious level, feng shui is an attempt to communicate with and to attain blessings and power from the primordial god/earth, tapping its resources and power.

## FENG SHUI EXPERTS

Feng shui experts are at once the priests and the doctors of environmental ills. They hold the sacred and profane knowledge of the fates of man and earth. As priests, they read and interpret both visible and invisible signs and positive forces in the cosmos. They define man's place in the universe. As doctors, they detect the earth's pulse, determining where man will live the most healthy, productive, prosperous, and happy life, and where buildings will least disturb the earth's circulation.

Being receptive to the environment, the feng shui expert can analyze physical settings such as mountains, trees, wind, water, and

*Maggie Keswick, *The Chinese Garden* (New York: Rizzoli, 1978), p. 29.

star alignments. Most likely, the early feng shui man was similar to a rainmaker. He gathered information from his surroundings, reading signs and forewarnings in breezes, leaf colors, moon rings, the smell of rain, insect and animal behavior, rock moisture, and stars. To stay in step with nature's best ch'i and to gain power from it requires special talents and special knowledge. As Lin Yun explains:

> We possess many senses, not just the five common senses—hearing, smelling, tasting, seeing and touching—but many more. We all have insights. We pick up feelings from people, places, dreams, atmospheric energy. Some people give us a sense of foreboding. Some places make us feel happy and comfortable. We pick up these yet-to-be-named feelings and intuit reality and destiny from that.

He claims people possess more than one hundred "senses," most of which are latent. Feng shui experts have developed their senses to be more keenly aware, more tuned into the environment—like a shortwave radio, they use psychic antennae to pick up messages, signals, and static from their surroundings.

Today feng shui is a complex system that some Chinese choose to handle themselves, while most call for professional advice. Advice varies because of the different theories practiced today. Around the third century A.D., feng shui divided into two principal schools. One, developed in Fukien province, stressed direction and depended on a cosmic compass, where the relationship of various elements in the Chinese universe—the stars, the *I Ching or Book of Changes,* and others—are charted in concentric circles around a compass. The other, originating in Kiangsi province, was concerned with shapes and directions of land and water masses. In the twelfth century, feng shui blossomed through the metaphysical theories of Chu Hsi, a respected scholar who stressed the "investigation of things (leading to) the extension of knowledge."

Historically, feng shui men ranged from semiliterates and

scholars to Buddhist and Taoist priests. Though there are several feng shui texts, much of the information has been passed down orally, often from father to son. (A feng shui woman did not exist, because Confucian custom prevented transmitting important and sacred knowledge to females: "Teach sons, not daughters.")

In the Chinese eye, feng shui experts, as in most vocations, run the gamut from wise man to charlatan. Some hold positions of respect in communities and use feng shui not only to divine sites, but also to settle local disputes. Others, however, are less public minded, milking residents of money and giving feng shui rhetoric in return. At the turn of the century, near Canton, for example, one geomancer charged a whopping $3,000 for choosing an auspicious burial site for a wealthy woman. Feng shui frauds are not infrequent: They assign bogus cures, leading some skeptics to use "feng shui professor" as another term for liar.

The Chinese are not beyond invoking the mystical to solve the mundane. While a few with a philosophical bent might see feng shui as a way to stay in step with the cosmos, the more ambitious see it as a necessary edge over others in life. Still, many view feng shui as a paradox: While some scorn it as superstition, most don't turn their backs on it completely, suspecting that feng shui experts possess an innate special wisdom, power, and knowledge.

Feng shui experts guard the secrets of their practice. This practice crops up in various incarnations in Korea, Japan, Laos, Thailand, the Philippines, Vietnam, Malaysia, and Singapore. Feng shui methods are tailored to a range of local needs; a village wise man in Malacca, Malaysia; a graveside exhumer in rapidly developing Singapore, where even the dead can't rest in peace; a publicity-conscious businessman turned feng shui expert; a professional feng shui man who became the most financially successful geomancer in Hong Kong.

Feng shui men today don't exactly fit the image of Mandarin sage—no long silk robes, no white wispy beards. When crew-cut Chen To-sang checks out a client's ancestor's grave, he dons bright yellow running shoes. Choi Pak-lai prefers well-cut three-piece suits. Although he occasionally sports a cotton mandarin jacket, Lin Yun generally garbs his portly shape in Hawaiian print shirts, black slacks, and slightly elevated shoes.

### Black Hat Feng Shui

Tibetan Tantric Black Hat feng shui is practiced by only a handful of experts, among them Lin Yun. Black Hat feng shui is a hybrid of many customs, thoughts, and practices. It arose from the long journey of Buddhism from India through Tibet and finally to China. Along the way, it incorporated religious and philosophical theories, rites, and disciplines from the countries it passed through. From India it carried the word of compassion, the concept of *karma,** the practice of yoga, and the structure of an organized church, replete with proselytizing monks and religious ritual. In Tibet, it picked up magical and mystical knowledge and ritual such as chants and charms. After arriving in China, it was influenced by indigenous culture—yin-yang theory and Taoism, ancestor worship and animism, divination and feng shui, and even folk cures for every imaginable problem ranging from stomachaches to malign spirits, scholarly aspirations to childbearing, from attaining wealth and power to manipulating the destruction of one's enemies.

One outcome—Black Hat feng shui—is a practical eclectic version of feng shui, mostly based on intuition and mystical knowledge. Its feng shui cures are both logical—*ru-shr,* translated as "within our experience or knowledge"—and illogical—*chu-shr,* translated as "outside our experience."

---

*Karma:* briefly, that one's destiny is determined by one's own good and bad deeds performed in this and past lives.

---

## DIVINATION

One of the origins of feng shui was Chinese divination. The early Chinese used omens to decide on cures for sickness, sacrifices, and the advisability of war; to check out the hunting, farming, and fishing prospects; and to determine the auspiciousness of time and space.

One form of divination that influenced feng shui was astrology, a celestial model of cosmic order on earth. The emperor's palace in Ch'ang-an, the first capital of Imperial China, built in the third century B.C., was constructed, some say, in the shape of and along the astrological path of the Big Dipper—a particularly lucky constellation revolving around and pointing to the ever-stable North Star. Thus the emperor sat at the center of earthly power.

Divination and rituals are not new to the West. Before building any city, Greeks and Romans determined a site's suitability by inspecting the livers of animals grazing there to see if they were healthy. They also employed astrologers to ensure that the city was oriented in line with the cosmos. And like most Chinese towns, Western counterparts generally were laid out along a north-south axis.

But, more than astrology, feng shui was influenced by the pre-Taoist text the *I Ching or Book of Changes*. Growing out of a divining process using "oracle bones"—tortoise shells and ox shoulder bones that, when placed over a fire, cracked in several "yes" or "no" directions—the *I Ching* is the mother of Chinese thought and practices. It stresses the connection between man's destiny and nature.

By tossing coins, wooden blocks, or yarrow stalks, the Chinese interpreted omens, instruction, and wisdom from the resulting trigrams. These trigrams symbolize nature: ☰ heaven, ☷ earth, ☳ thunder, ☶ mountain, ☲ fire, ☴ wind, ☱ lake, ☵ water. They became symbols of other concepts such as family relations ( ☷ mother, and ☰ father), cardinal directions, time, and, finally, various stages of change.

The *I Ching* stresses a fundamental Chinese approach: constant cyclical change. Philosophically, it provides an overview of the universe as an entity and all things in it in constant flux. In fortune-telling, the outlook is never static: If circumstances are good, danger lurks around the corner; if luck is bad, things will look up—eternal regenerative change. Man floats with the ebb and flow of nature's tides.

I Ching symbols conjure up cosmic power and energy and are used as good luck charms and hexes. Printed on a cosmic compass, its trigrams provide feng shui men with eight bearings to properly align desks, doors, and buildings, setting man along a correct course in life.

## TAOISM

Out of observation, identification, and dependency on nature came *Taoism* (pronounced "dowism"), a philosophy based on the patterns of nature. Influenced by the *I Ching,* it defined man's relationship to the universe. The Taoists believed man was influenced by the cosmos, its topographical permutations, and its passages of time. By studying nature, the Taoists made contributions in scientific fields: astronomy, mathematics, geology, cartography, mineralogy, and chemistry.

The Taoists glorified nature. Love of nature permeated their view of life. Things would not be correct until man could mirror within the harmony of nature without. They exalted it in their poetry. Taoism "seemed to answer the yearnings of men of feeling and imagination for a vision of the eternal in which they could forget the chaos of the present."*

*Michael Sullivan, *The Arts of China,* rev. ed. (Berkeley, Los Angeles, and London: University of California Press, 1979), p. 96.

High rises the Eastern Peak
Soaring up to the blue sky.
Among the rocks—an empty hollow,
Uncarved, and unhewn,
Screened by nature with a roof of clouds.
Bringing up my life ceaseless change?
I will lodge forever in this hollow
Where Springs and Autumns unheeded pass.*
—*Tao-yun,* A.D. 400

Man's place in nature's enormous expanse and eternal change seems insignificant, "a drop of water in a flowing stream." Yet, he is also an integral part of the universe, swept along and controlled by its flow. This was expressed in the traditional landscape paintings of monolithic mountains looming over streams crossed by tiny human figures. It was at once a transcendental solace and a humbling thought to know you were part of a huge eternal structure.

Taoists perceive man and his surroundings as microcosms of the universe, *Tao.* Ideally, man should reflect the balance of nature. A third-century sage, Liu Ling, underlined this identification with the cosmos. Prone to lounging naked in his room, even when receiving visitors, he remarked to shocked guests, "I take the whole universe as my house and my own room as my clothing, why then, do you enter here into my trousers?"† Some T'ang dynasty poets would drink themselves into dreamlike stupors to unite and commune with nature. One eighth-century poet is said to have drowned when he reached out for the moon in drunken ecstasy.

Although remaining a philosophy, Taoism also became a popular religion. Prompted by the influx of Buddhism to China,

*Arthur Waley, *Translations from the Chinese* (New York: Alfred A. Knopf, 1941), p. 79.
†Feng Yu-lan, *A Short History of Chinese Philosophy* (New York and London: The Macmillan Company, 1948), p. 235.

Taoism adopted the trappings of an organized church: priests, rituals, and temples. To popularize Taoism and to compete with the growing appeal of Buddhism, Taoist priests also integrated native Chinese customs and wisdom: folklore, filial piety, sacrifices, astrology, herbal medicines, and feng shui. Hence, popular forms of Taoism and Buddhism became interchangeable. Even Confucian elements crept into Taoism, as many devotees prayed for scholarly advancement, offspring, and blessings from ancestors.

Unlike Taoist philosophy, the religion is worldly, more pragmatic than the Taoist philosophy. It deals with daily dilemmas rather than esoteric thought. Taoist priests use rituals to help believers achieve earthly comforts—social position, money, good marriage—preoccupations Taoist thinkers sought to transcend.

Along with its large repertoire of folk cures, religious Taoism adopted *I Ching* and Tao symbols to work as sacred charms. These potent religious symbols, while infused with Taoism's original message of an ever-changing universe, functioned as a precaution against earthly ills. Circling a mirror or a Tao symbol, *I Ching* trigrams create an amulet with mystical powers purportedly strong enough to ward off demons, disease, and other destructive forces from homes, shops, and temples. These charms operate in a manner similar to a Christian cross against vampires and devils or a dashboard Jesus against car crashes.

Though the seeds of feng shui were sown thousands of years ago, feng shui, as practiced today, grew out of both esoteric and popular forms of Taoism. Man's place in nature was to be in harmony. The Chinese used feng shui as a way of linking man's destiny with that of nature by placing graves, buildings, and people in what they divined to be a cosmologically auspicious environment.

*Tao,* of Taoism, literally means way, principle, process, or road. Tao is the eternal rhythm of the universe and how the universe works. It is also the way of man: Both the universe and man obey the same natural law. From early times the Chinese saw the cosmos as a way, a moving pattern. And that way was Tao.

## Origins

Tao's roots spring from the Chinese people's witnessing the cyclical seasonal changes from summer to winter to summer again and the daily replacement of the sun and the moon—opposites continually spawning each other, constantly changing yet eternally recurring. Opposites seem to flow from one another rather than to conflict. Tao unites everything, exemplifying the need of nature and man to bring all opposing forces into a fluctuating harmony.

Tao connotes both a doctrine and a process. In the sixth century B.C., Confucius used Tao to preach the moral way or social order, emphasizing political and bureaucratic responsibilities. At roughly the same time, Taoist philosophers, such as Lao-tse, reacting to Confucius, used Tao to express the way of nature, urging people to return to the simple life and thus to return to the original harmony with nature.

Taoism offers a philosophical genesis. Lao-tse said, if opposites do indeed spawn each other, if summer gives way to winter, then reality must have sprung from nonreality: Before there was an *is,* there was an *is not:* a big void, a unity in nothingness, or a cup—maybe it is empty, maybe it is full, but it is undifferentiated. As Lao-tse wrote, "It was from the Nameless that Heaven and Earth sprang; the named is but the mother that rears the 10,000 creatures. . . ."*

To balance the environment, feng shui men must determine the patterns of Tao. Two Taoist concepts—*yin-yang* and *ch'i*—guide the Chinese in establishing cosmic harmony on earth.

### Yin and Yang

Yin and yang, the two primordial forces that govern the universe, symbolize harmony. They are opposites. Yin is dark, yang is light, yin is passive, yang is active. Yin is female, yang is

*Arthur Waley, *The Way and Its Power* (New York: The Macmillan Company, 1958), p. 141.

*Yin-yang symbol.*

male. In the *I Ching,* yin is —— , yang is —— . But, unlike Western ideas of conflicting extremes, yin and yang are complementary. They depend on each other. Without dark, there is no light. Without hot, there is no cold. Without life, there is no death. Like a magnet's positive and negative poles, yin and yang unite.

All things contain varying degress of yin and yang. Yin and yang continually interact, creating cyclical change. Some describe this ceaseless change as the swing of a pendulum: Winter gives way to spring, only to return in a matter of months; heat replaces cold, which gives way to heat; night follows day, which reemerges after some hours of darkness. There is a sense of wholeness in the movement of yin and yang. And the natural process that unites the two is Tao.

Lin Yun explains Tao's process:

> Yin and yang merge together into one—naturally and constantly creating Tao, the universal situation. The moon

(yin) comes out and as it recedes, the sun (yang) rises, then sets equaling one day, and this moon-sun interplay goes on natural-ly, creating the Tao of heaven and earth. The Tao of couples is when a woman and a man get married and become a family, giving and receiving with each day. Or luck can be rotten and then improve, becoming man's fate and fortune which is never constant, but fluctuates, sometimes good, sometimes bad. This is the Tao of man.

In Chinese traditional medicine, the body needs to maintain harmony. The Chinese say the inside is yin and the exterior is yang. When something goes wrong, the Chinese doctors say they can trace it to an imbalance of one of the principles. If you have an upset stomach (yin) and you feel nausea, your mouth will open (yang) and you will vomit—then you will feel better. This applies also to the emotions. If your heart or mind is upset or uneasy, you might cry; or if you are angry, you might yell. People's personalities must also have a complementary amount of yin and yang to get along har-moniously in marriage and in work.

In feng shui, the yin and yang of a house or a gravesite must be balanced, bringing residents into harmony with their environments.

## Ch'i

Ch'i is the most important component of feng shui. One feng shui expert wrote: "If a geomancer can recognize ch'i, that is all there is to feng shui." Ch'i is the vital force that breathes life into animals and vegetation, inflates the earth to form mountains, and carries water through the earth's ducts. Ch'i is a life essence, a motivating force. It animates all things. Ch'i determines the height of mountains, the quality of blooms, the extent of potential fulfill-ment. Without ch'i, trees will not blossom, rivers will not flow, man will not be. And while all things—hills, streams, trees, humans, stones—inhale ch'i, they also exhale it, thus affecting each other.

庚申元月時授課於
舊金山州立大學
林雲

*The character* ch'i.

Ch'i is a pervasive concept in Chinese traditional arts ranging from acupuncture and medicine to feng shui and gung fu (commonly known as "kung fu"). It can include such diverse phenomena as the energy that moves waves; the source of fertile earth; what martial artists channel when striking powerful blows; what acupuncturists seek to activate with their needles; and even man's aura. For thousands of years, the Chinese have hired feng shui experts to divine, like architectural dowsers, where the best ch'i flows in the landscape.

Mentioned as early as the *I Ching,* ch'i later blossomed as a neo-Confucian concept in the twelfth-century work of Chu Hsi. To the Chinese, ch'i links spirit and substance. Light ch'i floats as air; heavy ch'i sinks to form matter. "Ch'i is extensive and vague. Yet it ascends and descends, and moves in all ways without ever ceasing. That which floats upward is the yang that is clear, while that which sinks to the bottom is yin that is turbid."*

Ch'i follows the patterns of Tao, changing, condensing, and expanding, inhaling and exhaling. At times it is mass; at other times vapor.

In Chinese, the character *ch'i* has two meanings: one cosmic, one human. Heaven's ch'i encompasses air, steam, gas, weather, and force. Man's ch'i includes breath, aura, manner, and energy. The two types of ch'i are far from separate. Man's ch'i is strongly influenced by the ch'i of both heaven and earth.

The land most influenced by ch'i, the Chinese claim, is the most habitable: Flowers, trees, and grass grow fastest, animals are the fattest and most useful, and people are the happiest, most comfortable, and prosperous.

As Lin Yun describes it, ch'i spirals around and around in the earth, ever-changing; sometimes "exhaling" toward the crust, sometimes "inhaling" toward its depths, always pulsating and

---

*Wm. Theodore De Bary, ed., *Sources of Chinese Tradition* (New York and London: Columbia University Press, 1970), vol. 1, p. 468.

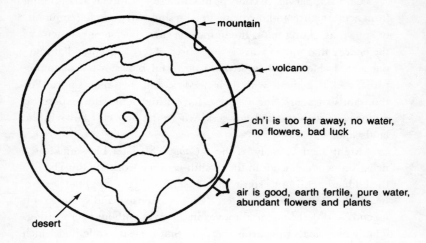

*Ch'i and the world.*

manifesting itself in different ways: a high mountain, a deep ravine, a flat desert. In the course of its turning, ch'i may rise near the earth's surface, creating mountains. It may expand so strongly as finally to escape, erupting into a volcano. And if ch'i recedes too far from the earth's crust, the land will be dry, desertlike, and flat. The best situation occurs when ch'i nearly brushes the earth's surface, causing mountains to form, trees to grow tall, grass to be green, air to be fresh, water to be clear, clean, and accessible, flowers to bloom, and man to live comfortably and contentedly. When ch'i is too far away, no water flows, pollution and sickness thrive, and there will be bad luck.

Atmospheric ch'i molds human ch'i. Ch'i must flow smoothly and near a person to improve his ch'i. It must be balanced. If the current is too strong or too weak, it can have negative effects.

From the fetal stage, human life is said to be closely linked to cosmic ch'i. This ch'i, in a sense, is a person's destiny. At conception *ling* (tiny airborne particles of ch'i), having entered a woman's womb, gives the fetus a spark of life. This is the embryonic form of the baby's ch'i. Ch'i pervades the whole body, determining a child's physical characteristics, movements, and mental state.

As with mountains and streams, the Chinese say, the human body is carried by ch'i, a central energy. Ch'i moves us, it causes contractions in muscles and tendons. The ch'i flowing out to the arms allows us, for instance, to bend our elbows, grasp and carry a cup, and sense hot and cold, thus warning of scalding things that might burn us.

Ch'i must flow smoothly and steadily through the body. If ch'i is too weak, we can't move. If it can't flow through an arm, that arm will be paralyzed. If ch'i doesn't circulate through the legs, they won't be able to walk, and if it doesn't reach the heart, then, without a beat, death will follow.

Human ch'i unites mind and matter. Ch'i is not just a signal telling us to move—*ch'i actually moves us.* Chinese painters stress the importance of the ch'i, or, roughly, the strength of the brush stroke. This creative ch'i flows through the body, the arm, along the brush, and then onto the paper or silk, linking artist with creation.

Ch'i, this breath of life, is man's aura, man's real self, his energy and soul. It can be seen by some. It propels us through life and affects our interaction with others. Because all people possess ch'i, every human movement influences both the self and other people. We have been said to give and receive all sorts of "vibes" and "chemical reactions." We are drawn together and repelled as magnets attract and repel. Whatever it is, we are sensitive to others' movements and manners, picking up intuitive information without words. In feng shui, people are also sensitive to the ch'i of their environment. Atmospheric ch'i shapes human ch'i, casting man's destiny. Feng shui practitioners try to direct a smooth, good current of ch'i to a person and divert or convert harmful ch'i.

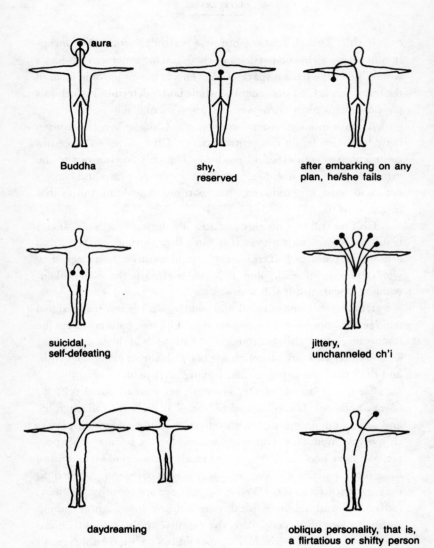

*Human ch'i variations.*

# *Origins*

People possess different types of ch'i, producing various character traits, problems, and reactions. The most desirable is an even distribution of ch'i throughout the body and channeled through the head, creating a halo similar to the Buddha's topknot or Christ's aureole. Another ch'i might be less developed, hiding timidly in the body. Some people have slanted ch'i rising out of their shoulders—the ch'i of an extrovert, or someone continually distracted by his surroundings and opportunities.

A very pretty woman who walks into a crowded room but is not noticed has muted ch'i or presence, while a not-so-pretty woman with slanted ch'i in the same room would create a stir wherever she turned, striking other people's awareness (ch'i) with her ch'i and sending out strong vibrations.

Ch'i, although rooted in a person's body, may at times be directed toward a different time or place. The Chinese call that state, "The body is present, but the mind is not." We'd call it daydreaming. Those whose ch'i rises up to the throat, but no far-ther, can neither speak up, overcome trials, nor endure hardship. One whose ch'i comes out of the mouth before getting to the brain may talk too much without thinking about what he is saying. Another person's ch'i may be unchanneled, coming out from every which way, indicating a jittery, nervous disposition—a person who is frenetic about what he does without having any real impact or direction. Others may have good intentions, but when they enter society and the world, they fail—their ch'i rises toward the heart and falls limply out of the side of the body. Those with a downward moving ch'i will be self-defeating and suicidal.

Lin Yun begins to analyze people's ch'i by telling them to "look left, then right." Some people move just their eyes, others their heads, others their whole body. Some move smoothly but slow-ly, others in jerking motions, while others look left, then stop for a second, then look right. After diagnosing their ch'i, Lin Yun tries to help them "untangle" the knots inhibiting their happiness and effectiveness.

The Chinese admit feng shui has its limitations. Lin Yun says he can manipulate a person's destiny, but he can't change its general course. He says:

> Everyone has a potential and a fate. People are born being basically lucky, unlucky and medium lucky. That is fate. Sometimes you can't do anything to help a person—they may be slated to die. But usually, you can improve your lot to a point through initiative, discipline and feng shui to actualize your potential. So that a medium-luck businessman with drive and an auspicious office lay-out and building can financially surpass a good-luck businessman whose work space has less beneficial surroundings.

According to feng shui masters, buildings, trees, and sun all affect the quality and flowing of our ch'i, but do not increase or reduce the amount of ch'i in a person.

Feng shui's goal is to tap the earth's ch'i, just as the goal of acupuncture is to tap a person's ch'i. The feng shui adept must find a place where the ch'i flows smoothly and the principles of yin and yang are balanced. If this isn't possible, feng shui offers methods of bringing the environment into harmony. In divining the potential of a landscape, house, tomb, or room, feng shui experts discern if ch'i is expanding or receding and make suggestions accordingly.

The Chinese distinguish between yin and yang dwellings—the houses of the dead and the places of the living. Yin structures are morgues, mortuaries, and tombs. Yang builders include residences; offices; schools; shops; companies; public works, such as parks, airports, ferry piers, harbors, and train stations; urban planning features, such as bridges, roads, and buildings; and prospective projects with developmental possibilities, such as oil wells, factories, racetracks, and casinos.

Examining the feng shui of a building or grave generally requires a house call or visit to the tomb site. Like doctors, feng shui men will discern ch'i circulation and pulse. While some use cosmic compasses, others merely know where and how to look, sensing the luckiness of a site.

One seventeenth-century feng shui theorist wrote that recognizing an auspicious site requires special senses—a trained eye and a keen sensitivity.

> There is a touch of magic light... It can be understood intuitively, but not conveyed in words. The hills are fair, the waters fine, the sun handsome, the breeze mild; and the sky has a new light: another world. Amid confusion, peace; amid peace, a festive air. Upon coming into its presence, one's eyes are opened; if one sits or lies, one's heart is joyful. Here ch'i gathers, and the essence collects. Light shines in the middle, and magic goes out on all sides.*

*Andrew March, "The Winds, the Waters and the Living Qi," *Parabola Magazine* 3, no. 1 (1978), pp. 32–33.

# *Three*

# RURAL FENG SHUI

## THE EARTH

To the Chinese, earth and cosmos comprise one "living, breathing organism."* Feng shui men ascribe to nature not only cosmic breath—ch'i—but also animal and human characteristics. A moun-

*Ernest Eitel, *Feng Shui: or the Rudiments of Natural Science in China* (Hong Kong, 1873), p. 20.

tain can be an awesome but benevolent dragon. An overhanging cliff might be a tiger's jaw. An hourglass-shaped rock might be an *amah* (nurse) or a maiden. Indeed, an entire branch of feng shui, the so-called school of forms, interprets the landscape by detecting shapes suggestive of animals or objects.

Feng shui is a language of symbols. And within feng shui vernacular, nature is a vast simile, an animal park with beasts wandering across it. The environment thus takes on a metaphorical quality: mountains can be watchdogs, tigers, or dragons; rivers can be dragons or serpents. But the metaphor continues, too, stressing the causal link between man and nature. Man is affected by these animallike earth masses, and these earth forms are endowed with the powers and attributes of the things they resemble. Nature imitates life: a dog mountain may guard, a tiger hill may threaten. Around one Hong Kong grave, a geomancer spotted elephant, snake, tiger, phoenix, and dragon mountains. The Chinese take this very seriously (we in the West also recognize mountains as representative of other objects: Camelback, Scarface, and even Nippletop).

The mere shape of a nearby mountain can cast an imprint on a person's life. In feng shui, like often produces like, and life can imitate nature. A mountain shaped like a calligraphy brush rest might spur scholarly success. A cliff on Lan Tao, an island off Hong Kong, resembles a naked man with an erection and is said to prompt exceptional flirtatiousness in the girls of a nearby village.

Shapes not only affect a person's character but can also threaten an area's prosperity. In the nineteenth century, crops repeatedly failed for several years in an area of China's Kwangtung province. Geomancers traced the source to some nearby hills resembling a rat, which they said was devouring the crops. Construction of a huge rattrap gateway was advised—and no sooner built than the crop yielded grain in abundance.*

*Maurice Freedman, "Geomancy," Presidential Address, London School of Economics and Political Science, 1968.

*Mountain dragon.*

ragons, the most frequent mountain symbol, protect many Chinese villages. Different parts of the mountain mass embody aspects of a dragon. A line of ridges leading to the summit link the vertebrae. Ridges running to either side spread into arms and legs. Mountain streams and underground springs are veins and arteries pumping the earth's ch'i, the "dragon breath" or "dragon vapor." And to find ch'i one merely has to trace ridges of green foliage.

One Chinese commentator noted:

> The magic dragon writhes and changes . . . and the mountain ridges that have life breath will start to run east then suddenly turn west, or begin to run south then suddenly head north. . . . Off they go in all directions. . . . It is said, if it [the landscape] has permutations, call it dragon: if it has none, call it barren mountain.*

It is no accident, then, that dragons figure largely in Chinese legend, art, and symbol. During the Ch'in dynasty, they became official imperial emblems, carved into thrones and embroidered on silk robes. The emperor, semidivine himself, was always termed a dragon: Many legendary emperors purportedly descended from dragon fathers. And with similar powers, mountain and water dragons rule their domains, warding off sickness, famine, and ill luck, and serving as creators and destroyers.

Hong Kong locals trace the name *Kowloon*, "Nine Dragons," to the unwitting self-sacrifice of the last Sung dynasty emperor. Legend has it that when the Mongol hordes invaded China, a seer advised the emperor to search in the south for nine dragons and there rebuild his empire. Arriving at the appointed place, he counted only eight mountains. In despair, the imperial dragon threw himself into the sea—having failed to include himself in the count.

*Andrew March, "The Winds, the Waters and the Living Qi," *Parabola Magazine* 3, no. 1 (1978), p. 29.

Though descriptions differ, the Chinese dragon is an odd mixture of several animals. One ancient claimed it had "the head of a camel, the horns of a stag, the eyes of a demon, the ears of a cow, the neck of a snake, the belly of a carp, the claws of an eagle and the soles of a tiger."* It is a versatile creature that can grow miles in length or shrink to the size of a bookworm.

But metaphors are more than mere figures of speech. The dragon embodied in myth the awesome forces of the landscape, most typically mountains, water, and wind. Hatched from precious stones called dragon's eggs, they served as both preservers and destroyers. They are an early attempt to explain not only natural forms but also natural forces on which the Chinese depended for their livelihoood and life. A water dragon, for example, when controlled, was the source of fertile fields; when unchecked, the source of death and destruction. Water dragons had the power over weather, tides, and water levels. To bring on nourishing rain, they merely flew to the clouds. The Chinese credited them with natural phenomena and disasters: An eclipse was caused by a dragon eating the sun and the moon; a storm was a dragon battle; a drought, a sleeping dragon; a flood, a wrathful one. To keep dragons happy, solicit their support, and thus control nature, Chinese traditionally sacrificed to rivers. Until the Han dynasty, young girls were thrown annually to river dragons as brides. The dragon image was so vivid in the Chinese mind that one was sighted as late as the sixteenth century. During a disastrous flood, one reportedly entered a home in northeastern China and escaped by bursting through the house wall, leaving a devastating hailstorm in its wake. The extent of dragon veneration grew to wasteful and absurd extremes: Po Chu-yi, a T'ang dynasty poet of the ninth century, and a governor known for his water-control projects, spurned dragon worship

*Donald Mackenzie, *Myths of China and Japan* (London: Gresham Publishing, 1939).

enough to write a satirical poem, "The Dragon of the Black Pool."[*]

Mountains and water are eternal in the Chinese mind. As landscape features of extreme beauty, they were havens transcending a fickle political world. Poets, painters, and scholars retreated to mountains and rivers. Turning away from upheaval and court intrigues, they looked to the landscape—translated as "mountain-water"—to find solace in Tao and contentment in nature's beauty. In city gardens, they withdrew from the outside world to the quietude of a miniature man-made landscape: Pools were lakes and rocks were hills, condensed forms of powerful mountains. As Tu Fu, an eighth-century poet, wrote, "The state may fall, but hills and streams remain."[†]

A country's feng shui depends on mountains and rivers. Lin Yun divides the earth into plains and hills and rivers and lakes: "By studying these resources, we can understand a nation's destiny," translated as "mountain-river."

Feng shui experts see mountains and water as interdependent: the keys to a Tao-like harmony within the earth, creating perfect vehicles to pump beneficial ch'i through the earth's veins. Mountains (yin or passive) are balanced by water (yang or active). Earth needs water to nourish crops; rivers need hills to avoid floods.

Mountains and water are thus two crucial features in feng shui. And the earth, of course, presents feng shui men with an endlessly varied terrain. In siting anything—a house, a village, a grave—they survey the shapes of the surrounding landscape. They examine the contours of mountains and the courses of streams. They look for specific good features such as orientation, trees, and rocks. They follow certain very basic rules and several classically auspicious settings.

[*]For the text of the poem, see Arthur Waley, *Translations from the Chinese* (New York: Alfred A. Knopf, 1941), pp. 166–167.

[†]David Hawkes, *A Little Primer of Tu Fu* (New York: Oxford University Press, 1967), p. 48.

Mountain peaks are the points where earth and heaven meet and from which all directions emanate. Temples and shrines dot Chinese mountains like telegraph stations to the gods. From the beginning of the Chinese empire, rulers made dynastic sacrifices on Mount Tai, the largest mountain east of Sian. They thus took possession symbolically of all quarters of the realm. A Han dynasty history, typically anxious to establish the Hans' right to rule, chronicles Ch'in Shih Huang Ti's failed attempts to ascend Mount Tai. It notes that because storms drove him from the peak, Emperor Ch'in was thus proven unworthy to rule. In contrast, the Han emperor Wu made several successful ascents.

Mountains served as axes in orienting houses and graves. This had its practical side. The north of a mountain is windy and shady; the south, calm and sunny; the east brings early morning sun; and the west faces the glare of dusk.

Hills have figured prominently everywhere in the world. The Chinese say that a house on the south or east side of a mountain is best; both house and vegetation will prosper under the sun's warm rays.

Auspicious spots also tend to lie close to the veins of subterranean ch'i, delineated by points—dragon pores—of rich green foliage and vegetation. These dragon veins usually run down the ridges and backs of mountains following the nerve network.

Certain topographic features make for bad feng shui. A flat riverless plain is devoid of ch'i. The Chinese warn against building a house on the tail of a dragon, because the dragon is in the habit of moving it, creating an unsettling situation. A house on the dragon's head can be risky: living on its brain is good, but a slight miscalculation could put the residents dangerously close to the beast's mouth, the source of strong ch'i and a huge appetite. Dwellers of a house sited under an overhang, or tiger's mouth, will always live in fear of being gobbled up, disappearing when his upper jaw drops.

A hill resembling a wide couch will bring early violent deaths to male offspring. A mountain shaped like an upside-down boat will bring illness to daughters and jail sentences to sons. The worst mountain forms range from turtles to baskets, from "eye of a horse" to ploughshare.

When natural contours are lacking, thoughtful altering of the earth is encouraged. Straight rivers, threatening life, money, and prosperity, can be turned to a more advantageous direction.

A protective mountain dragon, of course, needs plenty of clear water to drink. Lao-tse wrote, "The highest good is like that of water. The goodness of water is that it benefits its 10,000 creatures."* Such advice encouraged people to imitate the clear, pure properties of water. A large stream or river meandering along the earth's contours is integral and desirable to the feng shui landscape, dispersing smooth, advantageous ch'i. Water, often synonymous with money, is the life source not only of dragons but also of tigers, phoenixes, and tortoise mountains. The yang element in a landscape, water, according to Lin Yun, is moved by ch'i.† Ch'i rolls a river's waves, determines its course and currents, and defines its clarity and depth.

By merely looking at the flow of water, feng shui experts like Lin Yun can discern the nature and strength of ch'i. The shape of a lake, the twists and loops of a watercourse, and the speed of its current are all vital signs in discovering aspects of ch'i.

The Chinese have countless rules about the shapes and orientation of waterways. For example, a house built near the confluence of streams will prosper. Water should be balanced, not flowing too swiftly or too slowly.

But lifegiving water can also be destructive to feng shui. According to the ancient *Water Dragon Classic*, "Water must not be fast or straight. . . . If water pours out [of the site] it drains off, it is hur-

---

*Traditional Chinese feng shui books say, "Wind disburses ch'i, water retains it."

†Arthur Waley, *The Way and It's Power* (New York: The Macmillan Company, 1958), p. 151.

ried. How can it be abundant and wealth accumulate? If it comes in straight and goes out straight it injures men.'' If water runs fast and straight, not only will the area fall victim to arrowlike ch'i or ''killing ch'i'' but also the land unscathed by the river's ch'i will not enjoy much ch'i because it whizzes by so fast. Ch'i influence, in that case, is confined and directed to the current's line of fire. Sharp bends also project arrowlike ch'i.

Trees further improve a feng shui landscape, protecting against malign winds (or killing ch'i) and fostering good growing ch'i. Feng shui trees, specially planted, tend to be large and old. In Chinese poetry, the evergreen symbolizes longevity. Lin Yun says the greener the tree, the stronger the ch'i of the area. In rural quarters, abundant foliage signifies prosperity and is a sign to farmers of fertile soil. Stones, too, can be important. The Chinese sometimes feel the destinies of certain individuals are wrapped up in particular stones. These stones are large and oddly shaped and are often adorned with petitions to the gods.

What, then, makes the classic feng shui site? Most experts agree that the protective ''armchair'' hill formation, also known as

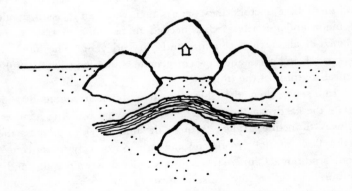

*Classic mountain formation.*

"dragon-protecting pearl" or "mother-embracing-child," is ideal. The armchair might be composed of a pack of powerful earthly beasts: the green dragon, the white tiger, the black tortoise, and the vermilion phoenix. The best site is backed by a high black tortoise mountain, flanked to the right by the fierce white tiger and to the left by a slightly higher green dragon—to keep the tiger's appetite away from the site—and, facing the lower vermilion bird, a sort of footstool to the armchair formation. The tortoise, tiger, dragon, and phoenix, in addition to retaining and emitting their own ch'i, snare the good ch'i flowing over the phoenix. Ideally a house would be built halfway up the black tortoise mountain, neither too high (yang) nor too low (yin), and looking over the phoenix with a commanding view.

Human needs and desires often conflict with ideals of natural harmony. Altering the land in any way—building a road, installing a well or swimming pool, constructing a house—can disrupt the currents of ch'i.

In premodern China, any changes to the land required feng shui men. Like doctors, they determined where an incision should be made and described what needed to be done to restore the balance of all earthly elements and yin and yang. The aim was always to bring earth and new constructions into harmony with the natural rhythms of the universe.

In a sense, then, the Chinese were early environmentalists; to violate the earth was heresy. They would avoid building a superhighway tunneling straight through the hills. Besides piercing the earth's flesh, straight roads conduct ch'i too quickly for anyone's good. Traditional Chinese roads thus wander slowly along the land's contours, avoiding any disturbance to nature's balance and tranquility.

One man's "balance," however, can easily be another's "blasphemy." Twisting and winding along every earthly deviation to avoid rupturing the earth, the Great Wall itself seems a classic of feng shui. Yet some saw the stone boundary, snaking 2,300 miles across China to the Himalayan foothills, as counter to feng shui's principles.

In the last days of the Ch'in dynasty (221–207 B.C.), when the emperor died and the succession came into question, the honorable General Mêng T'ien and the heir apparent were stationed out in the western reaches of the Great Wall, then only recently completed. Uninformed of the ruler's death, they received a forged letter, purportedly from the emperor. The letter, a product of the dead monarch's eunuch adviser, Chao Kao, who sought to establish his own puppet, accused Mêng T'ien and the heir of treason, and demanded their deaths. Imperial records tell of a parting soliloquy, in which Mêng T'ien bemoans the unjust accusations, then realizes he indeed had betrayed his country by overseeing the construction of the wall. In severing the veins of the earth, he put his country agriculturally and politically in jeopardy. Indeed, a few years later, the dynasty fell.

But if roads or construction work upset the balance of yin and yang, the flow of ch'i, and the currents of wind and water, feng shui can, for the most part, restore them.

The Chinese are fiercely protective of their surroundings, and this has often made problems for Western colonialists. Take the fate of poor Señor Amaral, a nineteenth-century governor of Macao, the Portuguese colony forty miles west of Hong Kong. Señor Amaral, it is said, combined a passion for road building with a contempt for Chinese superstitions and especially feng shui. He doubtless interfered with many Chinese tombs, but when he finally severed one too many dragon's feet, his own head was lopped off by an assassin. (The murder, the Chinese claimed, was the revenge of feng shui.)*

Feng shui, as it was practiced by Chinese peasants through the

---

*Eitel, *Feng Shui,* p. 2.

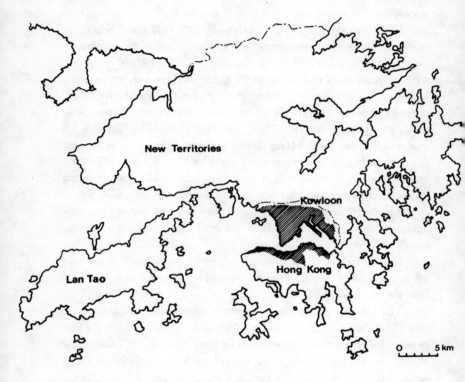

New Territories

Kowloon

Lan Tao

Hong Kong

0    5 km

*Map of Hong Kong
and the New Territories.*

centuries, is still very much alive in Hong Kong's New Territories. Today, the Hong Kong government seems acutely aware of feng shui, especially in the rural areas. Before beginning housing projects, factories, and public works, or resiting villages or graves, district officers or corporate planners consult with village leaders. This derives primarily from the nature of Hong Kong's New Territories. Leased to the British in 1898 for ninety-nine years, the 400-square-mile area is probably the only large section of the China mainland openly to maintain a traditional rural Chinese way of life. Squeezed between ragingly capitalist Kowloon and the stridently communist People's Republic, the New Territories areas have somehow escaped both New China's four modernization programs and—for now—Western urbanization.

While Hong Kong and Kowloon—together one of the British Empire's last outposts—are technically as English as Kew Gardens, the New Territories has remained traditionally Chinese and essentially autonomous. For more than eighty years, the British have carefully maintained a "hands-off" policy. Officials defer to village elders, the clan heads who still make most major decisions. While the Red Guards were destroying Taoist and Buddhist temples just across the border, New Territories families such as the venerable T'angs, who trace their local roots to a Sung dynasty princess who fled there in the eleventh century, retained much of the architecture, customs, and beliefs of old rural China. (In light of recent Chinese-British talks about the Chinese reclaiming the New Territories after the lease runs out in 1998, rural feng shui might well become ancient history.)

The day-to-day problems in the New Territories are not unlike those of General Mêng T'ien, albeit on a slightly smaller scale. They range from altering the landscape for the worse to cutting off feng shui site lines to disturbing graves and their resident spirits.

Building roads is a particular problem. The government or developer can't blithely clear land and cover it with asphalt, because he just might cut a capillary of a dragonlike mountain.

In 1963, at Taipo's Plover Cove, where the British first raised the Union Jack over the New Territories in 1898, construction on a mountainside caused great complications. Digging into the earth revealed red soil, which to the villagers was the raw flesh of a wounded dragon. "When it rained," remembers John Warden, Secretary of the Home Office of the New Territories, "it was particularly unnerving to have blood-like mud gushing down from the hill-side wound." In similar cases, villagers had cut branches and brush to dress earthly wounds. This time, to calm the distraught villagers, a 100-by-200-foot fence was constructed, a bandage to spare them the gory sight. Sound odd? Well, maybe, but in the West, community groups band together to protect their environment. They raise a storm over development projects that might damage local trees and hill scarp. Instead of feng shui, it's often called "zoning."

Feng shui often seems logical to Hong Kong bureaucrats. Robert Upton, Assistant Regional Director of the New Territories, says: "From our point of view it also makes good sense to preserve park space as a wooded hill in the center of town. The villagers' insistence becomes our willing concurrence. What they're saying is sensible but it's a slightly different approach."

Sometimes even building techniques are altered to avoid feng shui conflicts. In one New Territories area, the builder used concrete blocks instead of driving stilettolike piles into the earth to construct a house.

The wonder is that anything gets accomplished. Most projects in the New Territories are preceded by an elaborate Tun Fu ceremony, an all-purpose ritual to placate any dragon or tutelary spirit in the area. Villagers say that without this something bad could happen.

In 1972, for example, because of a road the government proposed to build over their guardian mountain, villagers threatened to move from an area inhabited by their ancestors for ten generations. They explained: "If the dragon's neck of our feng shui is cut, our good fortune will vanish, then bad luck will come." More than forty-five years before, they noted, the people of Ting Kau village were all killed because the dragon air there was destroyed.

So every year the colonial government of Hong Kong doles out tens of thousands of dollars to appease not only local spirits but also villagers concerned over construction projects, swimming pools, roads, latrines, to mention a few. Most of the money goes into the Tun Fu ceremony. Taking a hard line, Mr. Upton says, "We give them a standard rate of about U.S. $1,500 and tell them to get a feng shui *lo* ["priest" in Cantonese] of your choice and say we'll be back next week with 'dozers." Often the government checks up on the town to see that their feng shui contribution is put to good use. A typical one was detailed by a Mr. Grout (see Appendix 1).

Sometimes, though, the Tun Fu isn't enough. After a winding path was terraced into a mountainside in Saikung Park, several local residents died. In a panic, the villagers called the Hong Kong government, complaining that the path had cut into a dragon. The government covered the path with turf, and all was well.

Cries of dragon molesting can sometimes be mere feng shui blackmail. Government officials say that the standard rate for Tun Fu ceremonies is sometimes an incentive to villagers to be feng shui hypochondriacs. Says Mr. Warden: "A large part of the Tun Fu money goes into the pockets of the village elders. Still some have objections of feng shui out of genuine fear. Yet feng shui is an indefinable thing people use as a ploy to squeeze the government out of money."

Eventually the government officers become pretty savvy about detecting such extortion. "You'll come across a villager who will say, 'Look, I don't want to hear about money, but my ancestor's grave is there and it's staying there.' That sort of thing," explains Mr. Upton. "On the other end of the scale, they'll say 'Can't be moved,' so you say, 'U.S. $1,200.' 'Can't be moved,' '$1,400.' 'Can't be moved,' '$1,600,' pause, '$1,700?' 'Done!'"

Mr. Upton says he and his colleagues caught on after a while to some basic feng shui rules. Analyzing natural forms, for instance, isn't difficult. With a slightly trained eye and an active imagination, the uninitiated Westerner can discern dragons from the landscape. In fact, many Chinese and British government officicals in Hong Kong have become amateur feng shui los.

In 1977, when the government presented a New Territories village with a road proposal, the villagers balked. The road, they said, would chop their dragon's toes, making him uncomfortable, irritable, even vengeful. An official well versed in the subtleties of feng shui noted that if the villagers inspected the map closely, they'd see the road would not sever the dragon's toes, but merely clip its toenails, thus doing both the dragon and the locals a great service. The road, he said, would ultimately improve their feng shui.

As a compromise, the government agreed to build an altar on a hill overlooking both the village and the road. Such shrines generally enhance the feng shui, not only for their spirit-placating value but because their shapes harmonize with the landscape. Pagodas, indeed, are said to serve as lightning rods for cosmic ch'i.

One government architect is considered something of a feng shui wizard. In a park on Hong Kong Island, he designed an octagonal hilltop pagoda that, in addition to summoning the powers of the *I Ching*'s eight trigrams, is also said to disperse the exceptionally strong and harmful ch'i that blows from the north. His pagoda is credited with a business boom that occurred shortly after.

The Chinese see houses as important additions to the landscape. Pagodas of varying scales, replicas of a balanced universe, enhance their gardens. Landscape paintings generally depict a mountainside retreat—sometimes large temple complexes—lodged among mountains and waterfalls. Indeed, feng shui shared this tradition, as long as the dwelling not only fit into the environment but also enhanced the natural patterns.

Ironically, protective feng shui can also cause death and destruction. One feng shui stone sat in a river in China, wrecking countless boats every year. The locals wouldn't move it or diminish its size, fearing worse calamities might ensue.

Often feng shui stones get in the way of progress and enterprise. As George Stevenson, a Hong Kong solicitor, explains,

In Saikung, New Territories, there was a rock on a village elder's land and someone tried to move it. Very soon afterwards, his eldest son drowned at sea. So it gathered an aura of bad joss. When we came along and tried to buy the land and offered to move the rock to another place—so we could build a multi-level carpark—he just wouldn't budge. He said if we moved it his next son would die, so we had to go around it.

Sometimes even houses can be less important than preserving feng shui. Problems arose when the New Territories administration wanted to widen a small road into two lanes. "But, there are lots of old buildings close to the road," says Mr. Upton.

So at one stage we wanted to bring one lane down south, leaving part of the village in a loop, that way we didn't have to knock down any houses. A neat plan. But, woe and disaster, we found we were right in the middle of a feng shui area—a little wooded knoll, a stream, a little shrine and even a feng shui rock. The full gamut. We couldn't avoid it. So the road alignment reverted to the original proposal which meant knocking down people's houses. We've lost at least six months and several hundred thousand dollars [Hong Kong dollars], and if we have to move more than a few houses, it may be in the millions. Needless to say this wouldn't be the way it is done in England.

Siting is generally very important. Living in the wrong place may bring disaster. Back in the early part of this century, one entire village resited itself because no village male had ever attained the age of forty-five years and no chicken would live there; obviously, the feng shui was bad. Although the villagers were very poor, they expended a lot of money, time, and labor. Through their own effort, they moved from one side of a valley to the other side. After they moved, the men lived to ripe old ages and the chickens never strayed far from their coops.

Feng shui has its scientific basis. The value of watercourses dates to around 3500 B.C., when the Chinese became the world's first rice cultivators. To the rice farmer, a meandering river is a natural blessing, providing better irrigation and a more fertile soil silt than a straight rushing torrent. Such conditions produce larger, perhaps tastier, crops, allowing a family to be healthier and more prosperous—the origin of feng shui's link between water and money.

Using north-south orientation, the feng shui man takes advantage of solar power to heat homes. In China, entire Neolithic villages often faced south. The Chinese traditionally protected the houses against north winds by nestling them against the natural windscreen of a northern hill, or by building a wall with no northern gate. In Hong Kong's New Territories, villages today still generally follow these rules. The one modification is that most are not sited on mountains, but rest at the foot of the hills so workers can be closer to crops. In those cases, a band of special feng shui trees may separate the village from the hill.

Although an area may be totally deforested, often a grove of trees is left standing for feng shui reasons. The trees either serve as a wind barrier or assume potent mystic meaning. This tradition is so strong that even in the People's Republic, where officials say feng shui is "backward" or "superstitious," such trees are an important fact of life and livelihood. Throughout the countryside of Guilin are barren hills stripped of trees by lumberers. Here and there, however, stand fully treed hillsides, always with a farm at their base. A Chinese guide pointed this out as evidence of feng shui, saying the farmers refused to let the government cut the trees. This practice is actually useful since it provides fine protection to the houses. It prevents soil erosion and dangerous mudslides from the hill, and acts as a windscreen to homes and crops. This same situation can be found in other more modern farming communes throughout China.

Practical value aside, though, feng shui trees are also guarded, often for centuries, to avoid the disasters that might follow any damage. So strong were such feelings that, in late nineteenth-century China, the high price of camphor wood used in shipbuilding was directly blamed on feng shui:

> The population from among whom the timber is procured is influenced to so great an extent by the feng-shui superstition that large offers are necessary to induce them to come forward with supplies. (*Peking Gazette,* January 1, 1877)*

Rural feng shui is riddled with superstition. Some trees and stones gather a mystique and are worshiped as wayside shrines. In Hong Kong, the branches of an old evergreen will often be festooned with petitions to the gods. Such trees are also found in Singapore, where massive urban-renewal programs often stop for nothing. In the middle of Singapore's old Chinatown stands an ancient gnarled tree. Although the area has been cleared for renewal, amid the rubble the tree remained, tended by an old man and covered with red paper and incense sticks. Says one Singapore resident, "There was a great hue and cry, so the bulldozers carefully circled the tree. They flattened everything for hundreds of yards around, but left it standing like an oasis in a desert. They're perfectly happy to knock down thousands of people's houses, but they wouldn't touch that tree."

In Hong Kong, sometimes feng shui trees aren't old, but are grown as protection against newly created malign spirits—tall buildings, smoke-belching factories, roads—or as a village boun-

---

*Stephan Feuchtwang, *An Anthropological Analysis of Chinese Geomancy* (Vientiane, Laos, 1974), p. 128.

dary and a hedge for privacy. Often when factories of new highrises are built near a farm or a town, the locals react by growing trees to block out the towering building's ill effects, or to neutralize pollution or bad ch'i.

(In some feng shui practices, however, trees and plants can be undesirable. They are seen as havens harboring malign spirits that are waiting to snare a person's health. On Cheung Chau, one of Hong Kong's outlying islands, a Western journalist returned to his newly rented cottage to find the surrounding trees and flowers chopped down, replaced by a layer of cement. His landlord, who lived upstairs, explained that the vegetation was a breeding ground for the evils that might befall his family.)

It is not unusual for a feng shui man to use rudimentary science to find a good site, then clothe his selection in mysticism. In siting a brick kiln, a feng shui man decked out in a saffron-colored robe set up a table with wine, burning incense, and religious paper. Despite the mystical trappings, the priest was actually divining the site not through communion with the gods, but by careful use of the scientific method. He discovered by watching incense smoke the general direction of the wind, then calculated the angle needed to blow it away from the village. By lighting religious money, he could estimate how high ashes flew and determine how high the stack should be.

Orientation eventually became more sophisticated and mystical. The world's first compass was invented in China not for navigation but for geomantic purposes. Some feng shui men today use an intricate version of this same compass, with all the elements of the Chinese universe charted in, sometimes as many as twenty-four concentric circles around a lodestone. The outcome, putting it simply, is the harmonizing of the perfection of the universe with the earth.

This way of siting can be very exacting. Take the Tin Hau Temple in the center of Tsuenwan village in the New Territories. The 200-year-old structure obstructed the Mass Transit Railway tracks. Villagers insisted the temple was Tsuenwan's good feng shui, and that because of it the town had developed quickly into a prosperous area. A compromise was struck: While the temple would be moved to let the railroad be built, it would later be reconstructed, brick by brick, in the same place, facing the same direction (west). The price: U.S. $400,000.

Although the compass is a traditional feng shui tool, today some geomancers find they can do without it. Says Lin Yun, "I have internalized the compass."

## GRAVES

Hong Kong graves seem to sit on the best plots of land. Hundreds of graves populating Hong Kong's mountains enjoy views of lush greenery, the South China Sea, and islands that seem to rise abruptly out of the glimmering water like the backs of whales playing in the bay.

For thousands of years, the Chinese, from emperors to field laborers, have applied great thought and money to the selection of gravesites. They believed that unless the deceased were properly buried the descendants would suffer. The offspring of an ancestor with an exceptionally good grave, it is believed, will be rewarded with wealth, health, lots of sons, and perhaps even a high position.

Graves, insists Chen To-sang, a feng shui man in Hong Kong, are the most important feng shui considerations. He blames the deaths of John F. and Robert Kennedy, for instance, on "an ill-placed grave—definitely a grandfather's tomb has bad feng shui." Using the same line of reasoning in 1979, he predicted that Teddy Kennedy would never be elected president.

Gifted with hindsight, Lin Yun traces the United States' myriad problems to the relatively insignificant-looking grave of its founding father, George Washington. Besides being sited too low into the foot of a hill at Mount Vernon, the tomb's entrance is shaded by a large tree planted several feet in front; thus lack of sun and limited ch'i flow hinder the country's development.

The feng shui of graves is wrapped up with the age-old Chinese practice of ancestor worship. The rewards are the impetus to maintain the ancestor's grave. One nineteenth-century missionary denounced the practice as un-Confucian and selfish.

In siting a grave, feng shui men use many of the living siting methods. The area's outside influences must be surveyed: whether the grave is close enough to a body of water; whether the orientation is correct, with the green dragon to the left and the white tiger protecting the right flank, the black tortoise in the back, and the red phoenix in front. Burials have been delayed for months while the perfect site was sought.

One geomancer retraced Sun Yat-sen's rise to his mother's well-placed grave in Clearwater Bay, New Territories. The grave follows the classic feng shui strictures. It sits on the south side of a tortoise looking out on the blue water of the South China Sea. To its left is a mountain, the green dragon; to the right sits a lower hill, the white tiger. Besides the embracing hills, the view and the site of a water body, symbolizing money, are also important. Some people buy up land in front of their graves to ensure against buildings blocking off its access to wealth.

Mountain shapes can influence the deceased's descendants. A misshapen mountain can bring misfortune. One Chinese-born American links literal deformity to a cleft in a hill facing the ancestral gravesite. "Since we started burying there," she explains, "each generation gave birth to one child with a harelip."

Sometimes, in grave siting, a grain of science exists. The area north of Loyang has long been famous as a burial ground, principally because the low water table kept the corpses dry and prevented decomposition, thus, the descendants thought, preserving family fortune and wealth.

Stories and legends proliferate about the marvels and power of feng shui graves. Back in the Ming dynasty, they say, a man became emperor by hanging his father's coffin in a mountain cave—the mouth of the dragon—so the father literally became the dragon's tongue.

Besides its offspring, the fate of a nation depends, it is said, on the correct burial of the ruler. When ill befalls a country, the source may be not the economic or political policies but a wrong siting of a ruler's grave. Some Chinese say Taiwan's political problems, especially the United States' recognition of the People's Republic of China in 1978, are linked to the incorrect placement of the generalissimo's grave: on a living dragon instead of a dragon for the dead.

People are not beyond using the dead to hurt their enemies. About fifty years ago in Taiwan, people attributed the rise of a rich family to the good placement of the father's grave by an artful feng shui professor from China. The family prospered and had lots of sons, who in turn prospered until the feng shui man's son came to Taiwan and was ill-received by the family. To punish their ungratefulness, he bought the land in front of the grave and planted a semicircle of bamboo trees with a road joining the ends of the grove and another perpendicular road aimed toward the grave, like a bow and arrow. Strangely, the gravestone cracked in half. Within three years, the family went broke and many of them died. So they hired another feng shui man from China to see what had gone wrong. He discerned the problem, and set it right by replacing the headstone and placing two stone rabbits on either side of the grave with their hands out, ready to catch the arrow (rabbits are quick). In a year, all was well.

Graves are the oldest surviving example of feng shui in China. Like the Egyptians, when burying dead royalty the Chinese took great care to create an environment where the dead might rest forever as peacefully and comfortably as possible. The grave of Ch'in Shih Huang Ti, the first emperor of China, is a man-made mound of earth arranged along a north-south axis with a life-size army flanking the tumulus. In fact, a palacelike design was re-created in the vault. The product of 700,000 laborers, the tomb interior represented the harmony of the universe, with heavenly constellations painted on the ceiling and the earth's topography complete with mechanically run quicksilver rivers and oceans on the floor. (In earlier dynasties the safety and comfort of a dead ruler were ensured by burying human attendants, chariots, horses, and decapitated enemies.)

If the grave escaped looters, the inside would reveal favorite artifacts, frescoes of both courtly and religious processions, and coins, bronzes, and mirrors. Today, the Chinese carry on this earlier tradition of sending treasured objects to the spirit world by burning mansions, Lear jets, cars, servants, clothes, toilet articles, pots, pans, money, and sunglasses—all, of course made of bamboo sticks and paper. Other favorites of the deceased, such as cigarettes, are placed in the coffin.

A sort of immortality—a perennial pursuit of the ancient Chinese—was achieved in some imperial graves. In one Han dynasty princess' tomb, the geomancer must have found an adequately dry place to preserve for 2,000 years not only her body but the silk robe she wore on her funeral day.

One grave in the New Territories was so auspiciously placed that it remained intact for 300 years. Modern buildings have been constructed on lesser plots around it, and the horseshoe-shaped T'ang grave remains sitting on several acres of choice Tsuenwan real estate with a feng shui siteline to the sea. (The grave's shape itself is considered lucky, mimicking the mountain armchair formation.) The placement of graves in the New Territories has rewarded offspring financially. When government or private contractors want to construct a building or a road, they often have to pay high grave fees for exhumation and relocation, or sometimes they must even divert public projects.

Graves in the New Territories are like booby traps. Burial urns seem to mine the entire countryside. In Yuen Long, when the government wanted to surface a road "purely for the benefit of the villagers," they found a lot of burial urns containing dried and scoured bones. The descendants insisted that that road section not be disturbed, that it remain unpaved. Today the asphalt road has a rough ten-foot-long earth track.

Feng shui men grapple with siting graves even in Catholic and other Christian cemeteries. In all cases they must divine how best to use ch'i. The plot shape, according to Lin Yun, is important; it must attract and bring in ch'i. A square plot is best. It is also good to have a narrow inner part and a wide entrance.

A narrow entrance causes problems. "If the narrow section is at the entrance and the wide part at the back, this drastically influences the life, the career and financial opportunities of the sons and grandsons. Their road will become more and more narrow." The area must not have a closed, claustrophobic feeling.

As for the headstone, it must be placed like the grave's headboard. Maintenance, says Lin Yun, is important. Sometimes the gravestone can change color. If it blackens, catastrophe will befall the family. "If white comes out of the stone, the family within two or three years will have a white happening," claims Lin Yun. (White is the Chinese color of deepest mourning.) So, Lin Yun advises, you can either scrub the white or black off—a rational solution—or, even better, "use the *chu-shr*, transcendental way, and rub the white streak with either *jusha* [a red powdered medicine] or *jusha* wine."

A yin site should be drier than a yang site, so the body and coffin won't rot quickly. For this reason Lin Yun says a family should make sure the plot has good drainage to siphon off the rainwater and that the neighboring graves' drainage doesn't run into the plot.

# Four

# TOWNSCAPE FENG SHUI

### The Valley Wind

Living in retirement beyond the World
Silently enjoying isolation,
I pull the rope of my door tighter
And stuff my windows with roots and ferns.
My spirit is tuned to the spring season:
At the fall of the year there is autumn in my heart
Thus imitating cosmic changes
My cottage becomes a Universe.*

*Lu Yün (262–303). Waley, *Translations from the Chinese*, p. 79.

Feng shui has its roots in the very beginnings of society. With plenty of sites to choose from, the first men to build houses naturally sought the easiest and most comfortable spots. Facing south, safely above floods, and sheltered from the north wind, man and his flocks thrived among warm sun, water, and abundant plants. Those with the best eye for such locations prospered.

In towns and suburbs, and even in the densest of cities, rural feng shui rules can—and do—work. The search for ch'i and the balancing of yin and yang are still the prime goals in the placement of houses. The Chinese in Hong Kong are quick to point out that previous colonial governments, knowingly or not, observed basic feng shui principles. Every feng shui man I consulted agrees that the governor's mansion, standing high above the heart of Hong Kong's financial district and Victoria Harbor, occupies one of the colony's most propitious spots. They say much of the colony's financial and political success can be traced to this seventy-year-old white building. Built when Hong Kong was no more than a small port town, the mansion's entrance faces not the harbor side, as one might expect, but the botanical gardens on the uphill side. This is said to help the governor make judicious and balanced policy. Says Chen To-sang:

> If he faced the water, it wouldn't be as good. You see, on the right side of the house is Victoria Peak—a dragon whose spine runs along through the garden to the entrance of the house. So the governor enjoys ch'i that practically goes to his doorstep. And as if this isn't good enough, another mountain arcs around so that, with the Peak, it protects the house, cradling it like the arms of an embracing mother.

With civilization encroaching on the landscape, inevitably some old beliefs must be discarded. The construction of roads, the disruption of graves or burial urns, or the moving of a certain stone—all crucial to village or farm life—become less important. The modern feng shui man faces a new environment. As more people move into an area, the number of choice spots inevitably declines: not every house can have a sea view, or be backed by a hill; defined plots and regular streets require new rules and variations on old ones. To all of this feng shui men have adapted. They must reconcile and exploit not just the traditional forces of mountains, trees, wind, and water but also the host of modern man-made forms: roads, sewers, plots and house shapes, neighboring houses, and even such esoterica as zoning.

As man's hand comes to dominate a landscape, architecture also plays an increasing role in the workings of feng shui. Despite all the talk of natural forms, traditional Chinese buildings did not, at least by Western standards, fit harmoniously into the landscape. In fact, from the second millennium B.C., Chinese homes, temples, palaces, and even whole cities followed formal geometric lines—a U-shape building complex squared off by a screen or surrounding walls. These rules were far from being arbitrary—they were symbolic and sacred. On one hand they might be seen as angular imitations of mountains, refined representations of the feng shui ideal generally set on a north-south axis. A good example is Erh Li-tou, a Shang dynasty (1766–1123 B.C.) palace in Henan province. The main building lies in the north part of the compound facing the entrance gate and therefore the sun. This layout might have been derived from the protective, archetypical formation of the mountain animals: red phoenix, black tortoise, green dragon, and white tiger. It sheltered residents from harsh northern winds.

Until recently throughout the empire, Chinese, be they prince or pauper, built houses along this same model with only slight deviations, using bricks of the same uniform measurements. If a family grew in size, they merely built on another square unit. Sometimes compounds encompassed half a dozen of these units.

Even contemporary, Western-trained Hong Kong architects admit to using basic feng shui concepts. Eric Cumine in designing the Hong Kong Country Club dealt not only with the property's man-made boundaries but also with its surrounding landscape, a mountain in back and the sea in front. "I tried to disguise the property lines and work with natural boundaries, balancing the area with bushes here and trees there." Thus, in relation to the plot, the clubhouse is askew, in line with only the natural elements. Says Mr. Cumine: "The best measured building drawings are unequal. Symmetry isn't necessary to have balance. Nature isn't symmetrical; our faces aren't symmetrical, our hearts aren't symmetrical."

## HILLS

Hills have figured prominently in the development of towns everywhere in the world. While the West often used them to center towns and forts, for the Chinese they have traditionally been welcome barriers, defenses against Mongol barbarians and cold northern winds. Hills—or, in flat areas, mounds of dirt—were also believed to supply heat, making winter life more comfortable. As modern architects will confirm, they also retain coolness in summer.

The shape of a hill, which is a product of the powers of wind and water, is crucial in town feng shui. Seen as earthly outcroppings formed by good ch'i, hills present rich, useful imagery normally associated with rural areas: dragons, tigers, phoenixes, and the rest. (Unlike the countryside, though, Chinese towns and suburbs long ago surrendered to the man-made alterations in the landscape. Residents rarely erupt in protest or demand Tun Fu ceremonies at the first sight of a bulldozer.) The worst possible location for a building is featureless ground—a flat plain with no ch'i-formed undulations—probably because in ancient China such a house would be threatened by floods during spring thaws or heavy rains.

Looking at hills from the side, the Chinese see three basic shapes: round, square, or triangular. The gracefulness of a rounded hill and gentle valley is naturally the most preferable, offering a continuous rolling quality in its contours. Square buttes, with the house

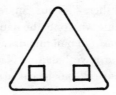

*Triangular hill or plot:*
*Put house on the muscle of this*
*shell-like shape to hold in ch'i and money.*

on top, will protect the house from floods, but expose it to cutting, harsh winds. Triangular land is inhabitable only if terraced, or if the house is sited at just the right place. If by chance a triangular hill resembles a mussel or clam shell, Lin Yun suggests building a house not on the hill's side, but in the place of the animal's tenacious muscle to hold in ch'i and money.

According to tradition, a Chinese house should be built in a commanding but well-sheltered place: midway up a hill facing south to the sea is the classic. In this case feng shui principles coincide with Western ideas of good location. "Some people who don't know about feng shui," comments Lin Yun, "still choose a good place to live." (Not surprisingly, these are often the rich, with beach houses facing the sea and backed by a mountain.) Best of all, though, is an armchair-shaped hill arrangement protecting the house on three sides—the so-called azure dragon, white tiger, black tortoise. A bad situation, on the other hand, might be under a bulge or an overhang—a "tiger's head" or "lion's head." It would be unwise to tempt such a beast by placing one's house under its mouth.

The preference for a protected site rather than an exposed hilltop has deep roots in the Chinese character. Unlike Westerners, who seem to try to dominate nature, feng shui followers seek to use it. Hong Kong Island with its thrusting mountains shows both sides of the dichotomy. To resident expatriates and some Westernized Chinese a symbolic hierarchy exists: The higher one lives, the better one's station, with the Peak itself the pinnacle of prestige. Many Chinese are amused at the wealthy corporate directors and diplomats residing in mansions, luxury highrises, and consulates on the Peak 1,500 feet up, usually shrouded in damp mist and buffeted by drafty wind, and a long trip from most offices and stores. Many wealthy Chinese prefer, instead, the comfort of mid-level flats, nestled against the mountain, often with better views, greater convenience, and protection from typhoons. (Lin Yun adds, though, that a house might be built on a hilltop, but only on a spot exceptionally well endowed with ch'i.)

In feng shui terms, of course, development often unbalances nature. Roads cut through mountain veins or high knifelike buildings plunge into the earth's flesh. In these cases, the keen eye of a feng shui expert has proved indispensable. Hong Kong architects, engineers, and contractors often seek their advice. Feng shui experts look beyond immediate landmarks for signs of danger or good luck. On Po Shan Road in Hong Kong, developers cut into the mountainside creating a flat terrace to build some luxury apartments. In 1975, a feng shui man perusing one of the flats warned its occupants they must move out right away: "There is a dangerous frog crouching on top of that slope," he said pointing to an overhang. "At any moment it might pounce." The family did indeed move, and a week later, after heavy typhoon rains, a "frog" of mud slid down the steep slope, burying their old building, and killing eighty neighbors.

Sometimes, though, the geomancer can improve the feng shui landscape. If a hill resembles a headless animal, a house built at the neck would place the residents in the position of thought and control. The house, by creating the head, not only completes a natural design, but also brings harmony to the landscape, enhancing its ch'i and the ch'i of the residents.

## WATER

In town siting, as in rural feng shui, the topography of water, symbolizing money, is crucial. There can be too much or too little, and both are equally bad. A house at the head of a round bay is best because the water is round and money is balanced and flowing in; houses on the end of a point may have trouble, with nothing to hold the water/money in. Another good place for a house is above the confluence of streams. But a stream running through a yard, close to the house, emits bad ch'i and can carry away a family's fortune.

Ponds, lakes, or rivers in front of a house are generally good, bestowing ch'i on residents. But Lin Yun cautions that one must see if the waters are "alive"—clean and moving, activating pure and good ch'i—or "dead"—dirty and stagnant, damaging health, diminishing ch'i, and, incidentally, breeding mosquitoes. Dead water may also influence the way residents make financial ends meet by predisposing them to move toward tainted money. The Watergate complex, Lin Yun points out, is well placed in Washington, overlooking the Potomac River and its financially beneficial ch'i. Because the river water is polluted, though, the money could be sullied and various nefarious activities could occur.

As with all feng shui, a garden pond or pool must be balanced: It should be close enough for the house to benefit from the water's ch'i, but not so close as to be destructive or dangerous. Ch'i from the latter sort, says Lin Yun, will leap quickly from the water, hitting the house like a gun blast and causing "unfortunate occurrences." To lure in distant waters, Lin Yun prescribes hanging a mirror that acts as a magnet for ch'i. To modify the ch'i of a pond too close to the house, Lin Yun suggests lengthening the distance by laying a winding pathway from the pond to the house. This is similar to the meandering paths and archways and zigzag bridges in Chinese and Japanese gardens that prolong the spatial and temporal interval of getting from one point to another, artificially lengthening the land-

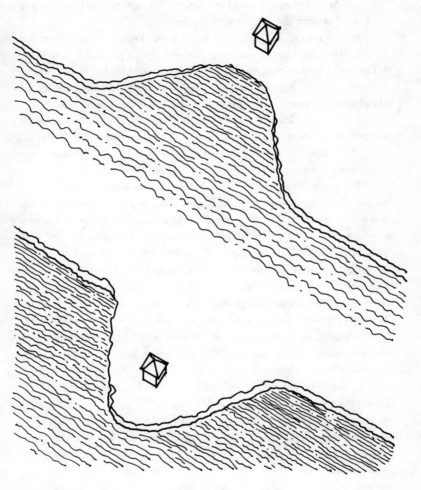

*Water shapes: A house at the head of a bay is best, water and money flow in. A house on a point can be bad with nothing to hold money in.*

scape vista and giving a small garden the appearance of being larger and symbolizing the universe in microcosm.

Size is also important, and should the pond be larger than the house, its ch'i may overwhelm the residents. Explains Lin Yun, "The most important aspect of the land should be the house where the people live, not the water. They are the hosts and the pond should be the guest. The guest shouldn't be larger than the host." To correct an awkward situation, Lin Yun will use a lamp, a rock garden, or a tree at the end of the yard opposite the pond. This, he says, balances the area, extending the domain of the house and disbursing the pond's excessive ch'i.

From ancient times, the Chinese stressed the water body's shape. The ideal was a quarter-moon-shaped pool circling away from the house. The feng shui of household wells is discerned through yin-yang analysis: well water (yang) ripples in the well (yin); people (yang) move through the house (yin). Therefore, in the digging of a well and filling it with water, yin is taken away and replaced with yang. In the house, the repercussion might be the illness or death of a person (yang) to balance the loss of yin outside. Lin Yun, in fact, says that the creation of a new well or window can bring sickness or death to a family. But he adds that, fortunately, old wells in existing houses are usually fine, provided the residents have not been having troubles.

A stagnant, poorly maintained well may become what Lin Yun terms "a reservoir of sorrow and bitterness." One cure is to place a plant on top to bring up bad ch'i and make it more positive. Sewers are also malevolent, but a cover near a house can be offset by placing a flowerpot filled with rice on the cover so the family will grow and eat well.

## PLANTS AND TREES

Plants, as in rural areas, provide keys to the nature of an area's ch'i. Says Lin Yun: "Some have light shades, others are vibrant green, like newly sprouted grass. You can usually trace a line connecting all the bright green plants." Such lush stripes are often termed "dragon veins" or "green ribbons." Buildings sited at points along them enjoy first-rate earth ch'i, tapping the landscape's most positive energy. Similarly, an ivy-covered house almost always outshines one with only a scattering of foliage.

Trees can be both good and bad in town feng shui. For a house on the roadside, they hedge against pollution, noise, and bad ch'i from passing traffic. Especially when planted to the west, they will block the worst heat of the summer sun. But too close to an entranceway, trees can break up the flow of incoming ch'i and inhibit that of residents passing by.

Because of their tie-in to the flow of ch'i, trees are often viewed as omens. Indeed, some have traced Taiwan's ejection from the United Nations to the death of a huge oak, one of two that had guarded the front of its official residence (suitably named Twin Oaks). For more than a decade, the ambassador fretted, but took no action, as the tree slowly withered. Just when the tree finally had to be cut down, the embassy was asked to close in favor of the rival People's Republic. As Lin Yun comments: "If I had known of this then, I would have advised them to plant a larger, more expensive, and better oak in the dying tree's place."

## ROADS AND STREETS

The feng shui access to a house should be cordial, not direct. The ideal is a pleasantly meandering approach, or at least a house off to the side of the road. By far the worst is the terminus of an arrow-straight dead end, the fast-flowing conduit of notorious "killing ch'i." Residents of houses skewered by straight-road ch'i may fall sudden victim to strange accidents and unexpected illness. Their friends will be untrustworthy and secretly critical, "stabbing" them in the back and "pointing" accusatory fingers. Such awful sites—and their cousins, the intersection of two perpendicular streets—suffer markedly in value in a Chinese town. In Singapore, for example, a house under the gun of a dead-straight street brought $50,000, $10,000 less than its virtually identical roadside neighbor. Ed Hung, managing editor of the *Hong Kong Star,* had a problem with a one-way road running down a hill straight at the entrance of his house. "The road was bad," he explains, "because headlights rushed at our gate like tigers stalking in the night." To defend themselves from the malign effects of the charging cars' killing ch'i, the family installed a fish pond in the small yard between the road and the house. Lin Yun adds that if a fountain or waterwheel were added, making the water ch'i rise, it would disburse even further the road's killing ch'i.

But a kind of opposite, draining effect can also damage a house's feng shui. Even a propitious house midway up a hill can have problems if its entrance drive leads straight down from the front door, allowing ch'i (and thus, money) to roll out. Another source of trouble is a too-narrow driveway, restricting the influx of ch'i. Far better is one that tapers toward the house, with the widest point where it hits the street to sweep in ch'i like a dustpan. John Chu, owner of a Hong Kong interior design store, is a connoisseur of street feng shui: "A fellow I knew lived at the top of a long hill, just the thing for money to flow out—and hardly the place for a bank manager. In the end, he was caught for embezzlement and killed himself jumping from the fourteenth story." Mr. Chu's own shop sits along a sloping road, but he sees no serious danger: "If you're in the middle, you can catch the money coming from stores farther up."

To lessen financial fallout from a hilltop home, Lin Yun suggests either moving the entrance to the side or installing a patio in front of the entrace. Even driveway shapes and directions are considered. One tapering Hong Kong driveway pointed straight toward its house like a dagger threatening its occupants. At the end of the driveway, they placed a white light to stabilize and equalize the ch'i flow. (The light, they confided, might steal their neighbor's ch'i so it would shine on them instead.)

## NEIGHBORS

Nearby houses, like hills or bodies of water, can seriously affect feng shui. Happy neighbors, of course, are always a good sign, and even the best feng shui men will try to check them out. But as Lin Yun explains, crowded suburban neighborhoods can also bring problems:

> As other people discover the beneficial setting of a house with good feng shui, they too flock there, building their own homes. As more houses crop up, these buildings affect each other—one may be much higher or larger than another, another may obstruct the sunlight or view of its neighbor. As the surroundings of the original house change, the dwelling loses its peacefulness and security; it becomes unbalanced and the occupants may suffer.

The shapes of neighboring houses often present problems. A wealthy Chinese in Hong Kong—a self-made man with vast financial holdings, some in the United States—raised a hoopla over a local American family building a house right in front of his residence. Immediately cries of feng shui arose. Although the new house blocked part of his view of Hong Kong harbor and its money-giving power, the main offense was the new house's chimney. It was, he insisted, a nail being hammered into his coffin-shaped driveway, causing his financial downfall. Solutions were sought. He tried un-successfully to buy the house; the expatriate neighbors even con-sulted a feng shui man and offered to relocate the chimney, only to be turned down. "You would have thought he'd change his driveway shape," remarked the new neighbor. But, as they discovered, he was only looking for a scapegoat. "His son told us not to worry—that the old man had simply overextended himself financially and needed an excuse for his setback."

The neighbor problem cropped up for a Hong Kong jockey who couldn't win any races after moving to a new house. A horse owner's wife, very keen on feng shui, sent over her feng shui man. Just above the place, he noticed a very modern house, a white struc-ture with brown glass around it. It resembled, he said, an open-mouthed frog—terribly bad luck. The feng shui man hung a mirror to reflect back the bad vibrations, and at the next races, the jockey managed two wins.

## THE ALL-PURPOSE REMEDY

Mirrors are the aspirin of feng shui. Whether the problem is weak ch'i, or too much bad ch'i, nasty neighbors, a wrongly shaped room, a threatening highrise, menacing ghosts, or the infamous ar-rowlike road, the cure is often no more than the polished bottom of a wok or a bit of shining glass.

The mystic appeal of mirrors runs deep in Chinese history. Worn on the breast or shield of a feudal warrior, they were amulets to ward off enemies and demons. Hung inside and outside a house, they kept malign spirits at bay. Chinese archaeologists have found hundreds of mirrors buried in ancient imperial tombs. During the Chou dynasty (1122–256 B.C.), bronze mirrors were said to reveal not just faces or things, but much more: "The brilliance of the mir-ror represented the light of the sun and the moon combined: communicated the intention of the powers of earth beneath and the spirits in heaven above."*

Mirrors today serve more prosaic uses. In Chinese communities throughout Asia and the world, they are the all-purpose solution to a vast range of feng shui ills. Most often, their use is defensive, an everyman's solution to easily visible threatening forces. In police stations, they are often hung to ward off corruption. For an expert, though, they can also be subtle, and Lin Yun places mirrors to balance poorly shaped rooms and even attract positive ch'i. Trial and error, though, is the way most people begin.

In a pinch, practically anything even halfway shiny will do. The ubiquitous *ba-gua*—a small, round mirror embedded in wood—comes plain (with I Ching trigrams only) or fancy (trigrams plus a menacing warrior god). Woks are a perennial favorite, apparently continuing to function even when covered with rust. Broken bits from an old medicine chest lack class, but will often get the job done.

Aware of reflective powers, people get very upset when evils are deliberately sent their way. Mirror wars are the result, and some have nearly ended up in court. One story starts with a Hong Kong family whose house had a feng shui deficiency. The solution was deemed to be a mirror with two menacing prongs sticking out. It was aimed, though, at a neighboring mansion, whose owners apparently had enough bad spirits already. They retaliated, installing a larger mirror with three prongs. For years the battle raged, each side putting up more and more mirrors. Finally the issue was decided by the police, who deemed the battlefield a hazard to nighttime motorists and ordered the armaments removed.

*Florence Ayscough, *A Chinese Mirror* (Boston: Houghton Mifflin, 1925), p. 9.

## FENG SHUI

## THE LAST RESORT

When absolutely nothing works—often because development has totally destroyed any chance of natural harmony—even the most imaginative feng shui man may give up and simply recommend getting out.

Lin Yun, though, is not traditional. His Black Hat mystical feng shui has evolved what he says are remedies for even the most hopeless cases. These "secret ritual practices" are mystical methods of manipulating and correcting feng shui. Unknown to traditional feng shui experts, these cures follow a transcendental, irrational, and subconscious healing process known as *chu-shr,* or that which is outside our realm of experience or knowledge. Whether chu-shr, by chance, makes sense or not, many Chinese swear by it.

To the extent that it can be understood, chu-shr feng shui works through three basic techniques:

1. The "connecting ch'i method" ties in ch'i that is too far from a house or too deep beneath the earth's surface. A simple, stopgap variation is to plant into the earth a hollow pole with a light at the top to siphon up the ch'i.

2. The "balancing ch'i method" rounds the environment into harmony with itself and its surroundings. If, for example, a house is awkwardly shaped, a landscape or architectural feature might be added to achieve equilibrium.

3. The "outstanding methods" either increase or modify the flow of ch'i. These can churn and activate weak or stagnant ch'i, circulating it through a house with a bright light, a fountain, or a bubbling fishtank. Strong and dangerous ch'i can be dispersed by moving, musical gizmos such as windmills, wind chimes, and bells.*

*Joseph M. Backus, "Lin Yun, Geomancer," *The American Dowser* 19, no. 3 (August 1979), pp. 118–119.

## PLOTS OF LAND

Feng shui men consider individual parcels of land. In town areas lack of choice sometimes presents only oddly shaped plots formed by poor planning or natural boundaries such as rivers or hills. In such cases feng shui can balance the asymmetrical angles and give purpose to and enhance awkward shapes.

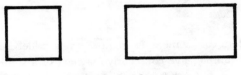

*Good plot shapes.*

A rectangular or square shape is best. The south side should be open, allowing the sun's rays to enter and warm the house. If the plot is large, the backyard can be a bit higher than the front. But if the garden is small, it is best to have it level rather than sloping. (The latter would let ch'i roll downhill too quickly, like a flood sweeping the family off its feet, taking with it health, social standing, and money.)

In dealing with strange property shapes, Lin Yun says, a feng shui expert must use intuitive talent—strong imagination, common sense, and psychic knowledge—in other words, chu-shr feng shui. "I look at land plots from all angles—whether they are high or low, long or short, square or round—to see what the shape may resemble—be it a fish, animal, or object. Then I add something to activate it into a vital organism pumping good smooth ch'i." In one case, he suggested installing a water fountain to make oddly angled land look like a wind or water wheel, constantly churning and pulsating ch'i. His frequent suggestion for a sloping plot is to balance it with a hollow lamppost, whose light also serves as bait for additional ch'i.

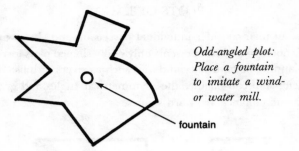

*Odd-angled plot: Place a fountain to imitate a wind- or water mill.*

fountain

Odd plots can sometimes require even odder remedies. In Taipei, for example, five consecutive owners of a squiggly shaped plot lost money and failed in business. The spot, not surprisingly, became widely known for its bad feng shui. The next owners, wanting to open up a restaurant, called in Lin Yun, who made the land represent an auspicious symbol. He advised placing a hollow red pole with a light on it at the narrow end of the plot, with two red poles at the receded entrance, making, among other things, the access wider. And, voilà, it became a scorpion with stinger. (Chinese concepts sometimes differ markedly from Western ideas—bats, for

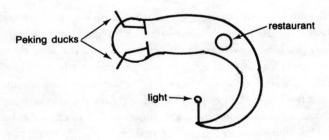

*Scorpion-shaped plot for restaurants.*

example, are considered lucky. The scorpion is good for a restaurant or a store since it might aggressively pursue its prey, and the owners will thus catch a lot of business.) Lin Yun suggested they continue the metaphor by hanging two Peking ducks—scorpion pincers—outside the entrance. Today the restaurant is a popular Taipei hangout; its owners plan a counterpart in San Francisco.

In another instance, Lin Yun turned a crescent-shaped piece of land into the likeness of a shrimp by advising the owners to install two hollow green lamp poles at the wider end. The family prospered. However, they later painted the poles vibrant red, which

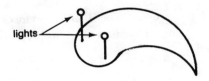

*Shrimp-shaped plot: Lights painted red are bad, because red is the color of cooked shrimp. Green lights are good, the color of live shrimp.*

under most circumstances signifies good luck to the Chinese, but in this case they lost money. So they called Lin Yun back. He said, in a word, that they were cooked. The problem was the lamppost's red color. "It should be green—red is the color of steamed shrimp." So they painted the lamppost green and all was well.

Even otherwise fine rectangular plots can sometimes have feng shui problems. In Taiwan, for example, a Mr. Chou lived next to a Mr. T'ang, on tracts of land that were virtual mirror images. Mr. Chou one day bought an adjoining plot, lengthening—and unbalancing—his land: It had too much backyard. As his business began to decline, Lin Yun was called in. He suggested a tall, red light post at the long end of the property, and it quickly had the desired effect. When he saw his neighbor's good fortune, Mr. T'ang also installed a similar red lamppost. But, in feng shui, one man's

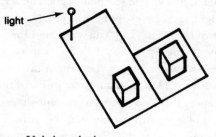

*Unbalanced plot:*
*If plot is too long, balance it with a light.*

cure can be another's catastrophe: The T'angs' finances quickly worsened. Explains Lin Yun: "The lamp tilted his property, which originally was balanced."


## THE FENG SHUI HOUSE

With the notable exception of Buddhist/Taoist temples, few buildings today go all out to achieve the ancient feng shui ideals. From the ground up, the traditional Chinese house was a universe in itself. Timbers rose from a foundation of stamped soil, symbolically linking heaven and earth. Behind high surrounding walls, a garden court presented all nature in microcosm. And around it, the building itself mimicked the most auspicious feng shui arrangement: the U-shaped, dragon-tortoise-tiger armchair hill, protecting the center and ideally facing south.

The ideal of the garden was both central and simple: No matter how far a house lay from a truly pastoral countryside, its residents must never lose touch with the elemental universe. Nature was made an integral part of the building, just a step away through a courtyard or a glance through a latticework window. Rocks were

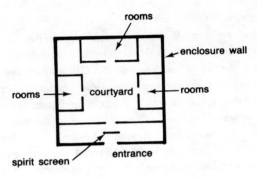

*A traditional Chinese compound.*

mountains, fish pools were oceans, and bonsai, of course, were old gnarled trees. Against the geometric regularity of a Western garden like Versailles—where man sought to control nature by imposing order on it—Chinese garden courts were irregular, imitating nature in miniature.

The rooms surrounding a garden court embodied the notion "within yin there is yang." Intertwined with Taoist philosophy, the design turned inhabitants away from roads, other people, and the working world toward an ideal of simple nature. (It also supplied both a steady influx of ch'i and excellent ventilation.) The paradox of formal architecture surrounding spontaneous nature was a pleasure rather than a problem. Over the course of thirty centuries, to be sure, elements of out-and-out superstition have crept into Chinese design. Some Chinese saw screens inside of doorways as shields against malign spirits or demons. It was said that demons only flew in straight lines so the screens would repulse them. Often a yin-yang symbol decorated the screen as a protective talisman. An I Ching trigrammed mirror (a ba-gua) might adorn the screen to be placed above the door so that when a demon charged, he would be greeted by his own fierce face, and presumably flee in fear. Painted images such as warlike door gods were hung by the entrance to menace would-be intruders.

The origin of China's traditional sweeping, up-curved roof is unclear. Some say it derives from nomadic tents, others that it mimics a spread of branches or the Chinese character for "tree." Others say it is purely aesthetic. Less scholarly sources insist it is designed to keep devils away. When a devil pounced or fell from the sky, he would slide down the roof and be sent skyward again, and if he fell again, the spiked eaves would impale him. But whatever the explanation, the ornamented roofs also serve a practical purpose: Their eaves allow maximum winter sun to enter, but let in only a minimum of summer sun. (Roofs are more peaked in south China to keep the hot sun out, lower in the north to allow wind to flow over unobstructed.)

Practical concerns were in fact fundamental to much of traditional Chinese design. For thousands of years, the Chinese arranged buildings in such a way as to subject natural forces to human convenience. Aside from carefully calculated roofs, wind screens and masses of earth were used to regulate heat and cold. Ancient palaces had cooling systems with water running down between double walls. And ch'i, of course, was rigorously controlled, using screens, walls, staggered windows, and labyrinthine doors. Even today, many Chinese are uncomfortable with three or more windows or doors lined up on the same axis—the flow of ch'i, they say, is too strong.

### Modern House Shapes

Modern architecture and life-styles have, of course, largely ruled out traditional Chinese house design. The task of the modern feng shui man is to create or restore old-style harmony and integrity, normally within a conventional twentieth-century framework. Many layouts are possible, but some are very clearly better than others.

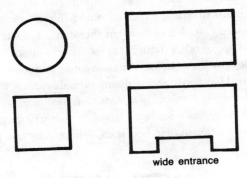

*Good house shapes.*

As with plots of land, the best house shapes are the most regular: rectangular, square, or even round. A small entrance courtyard, an interior court, or even just a chimney will let ch'i permeate the house. Provided there are no serious problems with the house's location, the result will be a fine structure in which to build solid income and a steady life.

Any of the almost infinite number of odd or irregular shapes can bring trouble. It might be something seemingly innocuous: A

*"Small-nosed" house shape: If the front is too small, plant shrubbery or flowers.*

small entrance foyer or a "nose" jutting from the house front can choke the influx of ch'i and thus encourage money problems. An arrowlike, sharply angled corner can threaten inhabitants, requiring pools, gardens, or other fixtures to create harmonious balance. On a larger scale, any unbalanced form can cause problems, with various L-shaped or U-shaped arrangements probably the worst offenders.

In ill-shaped houses, placement of the various rooms often decides the occupant's destiny. Feng shui men pay most attention to the location of the master bedroom, where most people spend at

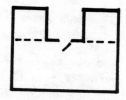

*U-shaped house: Place guestroom or gambling room in the wings.*

least a third of their lives, and the kitchen, where food is prepared, influencing health and, indirectly, wealth. With a U-shaped house, for example, if the front door is in the concave part with the kitchen behind, then the family, especially the husband, eats out all the time, staying away the entire day. A similarly placed master bedroom would also be a "dangerous situation": The husband will feel like he is sleeping outside, and might in fact end up spending nights elsewhere, symbolically locked outside of the house and family. Other troublesome side effects might include chronic headaches, surgery, failure of careers, frequent changing of jobs, or even getting fired. For such a situation, Lin Yun recommends constructing a screen or wall across the entrance to complete the rectangle and make it seem whole. If the bedroom were instead in one of the wings, making it into a guestroom would at least ensure short visits.

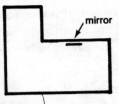

*Boot-shaped house: Don't put bedroom on the sole, or hang a mirror to draw it away from the sole.*

With the shoelike variety of **L**-shaped houses, a bedroom along the sole may "trip up" a family's fortune or cause residents to feel "downtrodden," resulting in headaches. Far better is the "ankle area," the juncture for power and energy. For boot-shaped houses, Lin Yun recommends balancing: "On the heel side, plant flowers or vines so the house is never quite stepping down and its weight does not press heavily on the master." This also prevents the entire family from "tripping up" in life. Another solution would be to add a pond, fountain, or artificial river to square off the **L**, making the house appear complete. With any **L**-shaped or **U**-shaped home, the unsettling factors can be modified by placing a mirror within the house to reflect the disconnected wind, thus drawing it into the main part of the building.

Perhaps the most precarious arrangement is a house shaped like a cleaver—doubly so if the bedroom lies against the "blade."

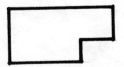

*Knife-shaped house: Don't put bedroom on the edge, put it in the handle.*

Always "on the edge," an occupant may be exposed to illness—perhaps fatal—or loss of job or money. In such cases, Lin Yun advises moving the bedroom to the handle area, the controlling part and the locus for the power, to become fiercely successful.

# *Five*

# URBAN FENG SHUI

In financially and industrially sophisticated Hong Kong, a city which perhaps more than any other devotes itself single-mindedly to the amassing of wealth, people are still having feng shui experts ritually bless and arrange their homes and offices. Feng shui has even infiltrated Westernized sectors of Hong Kong. A real estate ad that ran in an English-language Hong Kong newspaper not only boasted plush, newly built luxury apartments with balconies overlooking the South China Sea and convenient transportation but also promised ''excellent feng shui.''

To understand urban feng shui, one must first look to the beginnings of a city. Urban feng shui probably grew out of rural practices and became more sophisticated in the hands of imperial court diviners. When they built cities, they considered surrounding natural shapes, orientation, and the auspiciousness of a site.

It was a long process, beginning with divination of a site. In the ancient *Book of Songs,* several poems, including one about the legendary founder of the western Chou dynasty, King Wu, mention observance of feng shui.

> Omens he took, our king,
> Before the building of the capital at Hao:
> The Tortoise directed it:
> King Wu perfected it.
> Oh, glorious King Wu.*

Practical considerations in choosing a site were also important. In one poem describing a first-century A.D. city, good landscape features bring power and good fortune.

> In abundance of flowering plants and fruits
> It is the most fertile of the nine provinces.
> In natural barriers for protection and defense
> It is the most impregnable refuge in heaven and earth.
> This is why its influence has extended in six directions
> This is why it has thrice become the seat of power.†

Once the Chinese chose a site, they set an order on the city's form and hierarchy. Through a symbolic design system, they linked urban planning to other cultural entities: politics, astrology, religion, art. Special attention was paid to capital cities, on the assump-

---

*Arthur Waley, *The Book of Songs* (New York: Grove Press, 1978), p. 264.
†Quoted in Arthur F. Wright, "Symbolism and Function: Reflections on Chang-an and Other Great Cities," *Journal of Asian Studies* (1964), p. 669.

tion that the nation's well-being and the emperor's effectiveness depended on proper alignment with the most potent elements of the universe. So palace and capital layout were patterned after strong natural images and along stellar routes. Because of the emperor's arbitrating position between heaven and earth, the Chinese thought it critical that he sit at the hub, not only of the capital, but also of China—the middle kingdom—and the universe itself. His throne was placed where "earth and sky meet, where the four seasons merge, where wind and rain are gathered in and where yin and yang are in harmony."*

A city's shape is essential to its feng shui. Two forms of urban design arise out of feng shui: One derives power from surrounding natural forms, the other from symbolic shapes.

Hangchow, for instance, China's southern Sung capital, harmonized with the landscape, following the contours of lake and mountain. Reflecting rural influences, its layout responds to natural forces (dangers). Dating back to the Han dynasty (206 B.C.–A.D. 220), Hangchow was a town periodically threatened by floods. Built around a tidal estuary, which became West Lake, the city lay victim to high tides that during equinoxes produce tidal waves. In attempting to rein in the water flow, city governors—among them two renowned poets, Po Chü-i and Su Tung-po—enhanced the scenery's aesthetics and its feng shui with two landscape-gracing dikes.

Symbolic shapes were most prevalent for larger cities. Legend has it that one Ming dynasty plan for Peking's Forbidden City —where the emperor had resided from the twelfth century onward —was human-shaped, with important buildings and halls placed where vital organs should be.

Since the Chou dynasty (1122–256 B.C.) the Chinese have built cities, especially capitals, in square shapes mimicking their image of

---

*Quoted in Roderick MacFarquhar, *The Forbidden City: China's Ancient Capital* (New York: Newsweek, 1978), p. 72.

the earth, which they thought was square. These geometric cities were generally built on a grid of north-south, east-west roads running along a strong central axis. Peking's precise geometric layout struck Marco Polo, the Venetian voyager, as a "chessboard." Centuries before Peking was even a town, the Chinese built Chang-an, the first Chinese capital (c. 200 B.C.), along a north-south axis. Chang-an, modern-day Sian, became a prototype of sorts for later Chinese cities. (In fact, it was designed so auspiciously that the Japanese built two of their ancient capitals, Nara and Kyoto, along the same lines.) During the time of Chang-an, various traditional urban feng shui features were established. To the north lay the market, to the south, the palace. In the center stood the bell tower, which was moved several times as the city grew or shrunk. Government buildings and temples were also auspiciously placed.

Walls were an integral part of a city's feng shui. South of the Great Wall lay many more walls. Thousands of miles of walls surrounded farms, temples, homes, and cities. Both a defense and a definition of the town, walls were built to deter barbarians, harsh winds, and malign spirits. At one point in the Ch'ing dynasty, Westerners petitioned to open Peking's south wall to allow the Peking-Hankow railroad to pass through. The Chinese resisted, claiming Peking was shaped like a dragon: The central south gate was his mouth, the flanking gates his eyes. After the railroad proponents won, the losers warned that the dragon had been wounded and city money (dragon's blood) would seep out.

Mountains were another important feature of urban feng shui. Mountains were huge earth shields that protected the cities from harsh winds and barbarians who swept down from the north. At times mountains were even manufactured. Such was the case of Coal Hill, a 300-foot-high artificial mountain directly north of Peking. Coal Hill's origins can be traced to the thirteenth century, around the time the Mongol chieftain Genghis Khan was born. Chinese geomancers predicted that a hill to the north possessed a "king-making vital force" that would ultimately destroy them. Attempting to forestall this threat, they lavished gifts on the northern Mongols in return for their allowing the Chinese to tear down the hill and move its earth south to Peking, where they piled up the new hill. Shortly after the Chinese completed this huge endeavor, wasting men and money, the Mongols attacked, setting up their own capital and dynasty.

These mountain screens, obviously deriving from rural rules of orientation, reflect a near-obsessive Chinese aversion to the north. The emperor resided in Peking, sitting on his dragon throne with his back to the north, shielding China from the myriad evils emitted from the north. By facing south he also benefited from sun and sea, while governing over his kingdom. Not only was this position good for the emperor personally but it was also auspicious for China. (Because of the south-facing of China's rulers, all maps were drawn opposite to ours, placing the south at the top and the north at the bottom.)

In siting a city or town, the Chinese generally avoided flat, featureless plains where winds and floods could whip through streets. When the British, French, and German "foreign devils" encroached on Chinese soil and demanded trading outposts, the Chinese emperor and governors bowed, giving with perhaps a slight smirk the low sections of Shanghai, Tientsin, and Hankow, not incidentally with the worst feng shui and riddled with malign spirits. (The foreigners, to the amazement of the Chinese, improved the settlement area's flat feng shui by constructing tall, mountainlike buildings.)

Hong Kong Island itself was spurned by the Chinese. In 1842, after the first Opium War, they ceded it to the British, figuring that with its bad feng shui, it was sort of a Trojan horse. Devoid of beneficial ch'i and plagued by pirates, it was called the "barren rock." The British initially encountered problems in developing the island, and instead of improving the feng shui, they made it even worse. They began building the first commercial trading center in a low area, ironically named "Happy Valley," a mile away from the ports. To create their business center, they built roads that the Chinese claimed maimed the guardian dragon by severing his feet. The British leveled hills and filled in lakes, thus wiping out chances for financial opportunity. The resulting low swampland became a breeding ground for malaria-carrying mosquitoes. After several people became ill and died, the Chinese workers boycotted the development as bad feng shui, and the trading center was more auspiciously relocated in Hong Kong central, where it thrives today, backed by mountains and looking out on water.

## CITY LIFE

Today some town feng shui principles can be and have been applied, if unwittingly, to certain city-planning concepts. Parks, no matter how small, and tree-lined streets bring ch'i and its beneficial effects to local residents. Apartments or offices with river views, gardens or balconies, and space or southern exposure are also good. (In Peking, the rent for apartments with southern exposure is a third higher than those facing the north.)

When Lin Yun visited New York City in 1978, one civic-minded friend took him up in a helicopter to check out the city's ch'i. His insights were not surprising. Those living around Central Park with its grass, trees, and reservoir enjoy the best ch'i, while those living on Roosevelt Island—"a barren, featureless rock surrounded by too much water"—have the worst. He said that the amount of ch'i penetrating the island's rocky terrain was so small that the Roosevelt Islanders might be hard-pressed to retain their jobs or positions, much less succeeed professionally. He added that while the Midtown area is good, the United Nations' ch'i suffers under the oppressive influences of the towering Citicorp building, making the international organization sluggish in acting on important issues.

Naturally, urban ch'i differs from town ch'i and even more from country ch'i. Lin Yun explains:

In the country, life is more stable and calm. But remember, good feng shui in the country depends on good earth ch'i: If ch'i is good, life will be smooth, prosperous, and happy. If ch'i is lacking, life will be more troublesome. Ch'i fluctuates more in the city than in the country. It can be particularly good, or exceptionally bad—there is a greater potential for unusual occurrences, such as making a million dollars a month or losing it, or falling prey to senseless, extreme violence. The variation of people's fates and fortune is greater.

Even if a city's ch'i is good, many things can alter it. An area endowed with excellent, balanced ch'i doesn't necessarily make for good feng shui: Corners, roads, buildings, or other construction works might destroy the harmony. Because of this, city planning and awareness of the urban environment are important.

The site of a tree, the bend in a river, or the shape of a hill, however, often makes little difference. The overall urban environment is determined not so much by natural landscape features as by man-made structures. In the cityscape, high buildings replace mountains, roads are scrutinized as rivers once were. So the urban geomancer pays attention to the size, shape, and even color of skyscrapers, the direction and turns of overpasses and roads, and the angle of a building's corner.

Street patterns, for example, play a greater role in urban feng shui. A house above the confluence of roads is fine. Living below, however, where the streets seem to point like arrows, can be as dangerous as living at the point of a knifelike road. Increased traffic—cars racing down knifelike urban roads—is particularly lethal and disruptive, dispersing harmonious ch'i. The occupant of a building facing oncoming traffic may not only be a victim of continuous stabs from strong, killing ch'i and fierce winds, but may also be bombarded with the sounds of car horns and motors and the sharp screeches of tires.

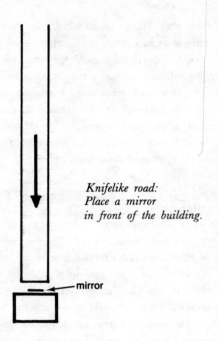

*Knifelike road:*
*Place a mirror*
*in front of the building.*

The proliferation of gambling, drugs, and prostitution in one Kowloon building was blamed not on poor law enforcement but on bad feng shui—the roads joining together in an arrowhead pattern gave it a deadly atmosphere. The repercussions are often serious. One Hong Kong businessman explains: "It's proven to me. It's bad to have an apartment facing oncoming traffic. One friend moved into one such flat. Six months later his girl friend died. After another six months he was fired. It affects your physionometry."

The shape and position of government buildings are still credited with a country's or city's harmony. Chinese still base Hong Kong's successes and failures on the siting of government buildings

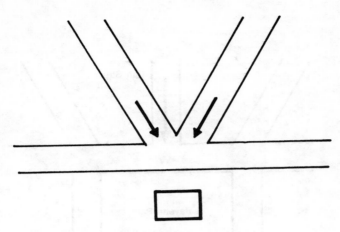

*Bad building placement.*

and land shapes. They trace the colony's financial success to the correct position of the governor's mansion. On the other hand, they blame Hong Kong's high crime rate on the fact that the central courthouse sits on a good site, thus encouraging crime to thrive. One planner in the Hong Kong government suggests that a further blow to the colony's law and order fell from a knifelike airport runway built out into the harbor. Arriving jets continually stab the belly of one of Kowloon's nine protective dragons. A remedy, he proposes, might be to disguise the saber strip by filling in the harbor on either side of the runway.

The Chinese use feng shui to interpret the destinies of other countries. Looking out from the Washington Monument, Lin Yun noted that some American presidents' problems and tragedies of the country itself could be traced to the siting of the White House. A president must reside in an auspicious place both for the country to be strong, rich, and lucky and for the man himself to be a wise leader. On one hand, the president enjoys good feng shui from the strong curves of the Ellipse and the White House lawn in back of the

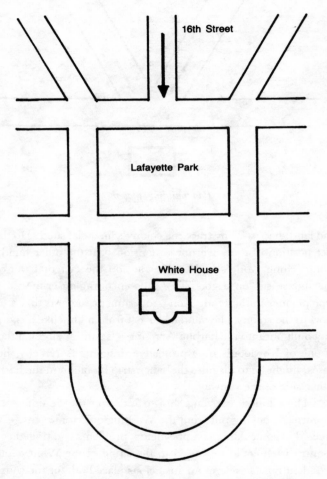

*Knifelike road: aerial view of the White House.*

executive mansion. These lawn formations, he notes, represent the nation as a whole unit full of smooth-flowing ch'i. (An ellipse evokes the wholeness, the coming together of opposites of the symbol *tao*.) The problems, says Lin Yun, stem from the arrowlike quality of 16th Street, which shoots "killing" ch'i right to the heart of the executive mansion's entrance. The straight road's impact, he says, causes divisiveness in the nation and blasts away the area's positive or smooth ch'i, so that the president cannot govern to his fullest potential.

The cure for the White House's disruptive avenue, says Lin Yun, would be to install a water fountain or windmill to disperse the strong ch'i, making it spread out, like positive ripples, throughout Washington. Monuments, such as the Lincoln and Jefferson memorials, are, in general, good feng shui, helping a nation's luck by bringing up earth ch'i. Monuments, however, can also portend the country's future. When he looked up at the Washington Monument from outside, Lin Yun commented on the two shades of the obelisk, as if it were a national thermometer registering and forecasting the country's future. He interpreted Washington's ch'i by reading the monument. The lighter shade at the bottom third of the stone needle indicates a strong, healthy ch'i, he said—with perhaps more hindsight than foresight—meaning rapid development, prosperity, and power for the United States. But the ch'i, or light shade, rises only so far and then stops. He said that the United States had recently hit a leveling-off period, the dividing line of lighter and darker shades. For several more years the country will seem to be slumping, almost sliding back, in all fields—military, economic, scientific. The United States will eventually forge ahead again, but it will never progress at the velocity of its earlier years.

Lin Yun says Washington's ch'i is losing its vitality. The capital needs something to attract and activate good ch'i again. Lin Yun suggests using a chu-shr method—constructing a heavy monument or building somewhere around the Ellipse or slightly outside Washington city lines. Another, more simple method, he says, would be installing a large bright light in that area to create and attract ch'i.

The significance of the placement of a government building extends even to a city capital. During a New York City mayoral campaign in 1977, a Vietnamese geomancer was asked which candidate would win. On checking out City Hall's alignment, he said it really didn't matter—the building's feng shui was so miserable that whoever won would have to face an overwhelming assortment of feng shui problems. It was a no-win situation.

## BUILDING DESIGN

Many urban feng shui problems come from the shapes, heights, and juxtaposition of nearby buildings and structures. In city feng shui, the earth seems ignored to the point of being abused. Indeed, earth dragons are trampled and suffocated by the weight of high buildings and then skewered by their knifelike shapes, while arrowlike roads puncture their flesh. Water dragons are diverted or dammed up. So the design of buildings is crucial.

In Hong Kong, people point to the ultramodern Connaught Center, which houses a lot of foreign companies, as a prime example of faulty feng shui. As local Chinese watched the circular-windowed building rise fifty-two stories above Hong Kong's waterfront, they nicknamed it "Sing Chin Ko Szee Fat Long," "the House of a Thousand Assholes," ostensibly for the porthole shape of its windows, but also, some suspect, for its tenants. The $80 million highrise's problems didn't end at name-calling: Expensive Italian tiles started falling off its outer walls; water main breaks caused four successive floods; and elevators began blitzing out, sometimes trapping their riders, sometimes plummeting several stories past their destinations—leading some Western bankers to dub the building "Hancock East" after the problem-plagued John Hancock Insurance Building in Boston, Massachusetts.*

Call it what you may, the Chinese trace the Connaught Center's unforeseen structural problems not to poor cement or bad engineering, but to feng shui, saying it lacks ritual balancing of the natural elements. They criticize the contractor's disregard of the winds, water, and the placement and design of the building.

Several explanations tend toward the graphically death-oriented, such as: The round windows apparently resemble the circular photographs of the deceased on Chinese tombstones; the headstonelike building is aligned with the Peak Tower restaurant, which looks like the urn in which incense sticks are burned as an offering for the dead. Some occupants conveniently blame their financial woes on the fact that the building looks like a crab cage pulled out of the harbor, with water—symbolizing money—pouring out of the holes.

The Chinese see a direct relationship between the symbol of

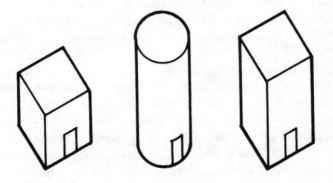

*Good building shapes.*

*Veronica Huang, "Hong Kong's Tower of Assorted Trouble," *Wall Street Journal,* October 12, 1976, p. 1; and Roy Rowan, *Fortune* (October 1977), p. 191.

their buildings' shapes and the destinies, welfare, and behavior of their occupants, much as Chinese in the country say mountains shape their lives and fortunes. Uncomplicated square-shaped, cylindrical, and rectangular buildings are fine. Some shapes can be downright auspicious. The Hong Kong/USA Asian Trade Center in Oakland, California, is a consortium of octagonal buildings imitating the ba-gua symbol of the *I Ching*. The project, drawing from the mystical resources of the *I Ching,* is totally eight-sided—skylight, tiles, fountain, flowerpots, benches, kiosks, towers.

This idea draws precedent from early Chinese architecture. The Temple of Heaven, south of Peking, where the emperor annually sacrificed animals to heaven, was built in a propitious shape. Leaving the square (earth) plaza, the emperor mounted round (heaven) steps, auspiciously numbered in multiples of three and nine, to pray for a lucky year, good harvest, and reaffirmation of the Mandate of Heaven, his divine right to rule.

The most potent fear, an old feng shui carry-over, is death-oriented symbolism. In Hong Kong, modern housing complexes glisten with woks and mirrors that residents place outside their windows to ward off the bad luck of church crosses. A Chinese minister explained: "They think it is the cross of death and we believe it is the cross of love."

This philosophy was the bane of Western missionaries in China. In the nineteenth century, the missionary-scholar Reverend Edkins described feng shui as "one of the great obstacles to the progress of civilization," which, he wrote, "checks the efforts of missionary zeal." In the nineteenth century, missionaries were forced to remove the earth-impaling crosses from their churches. But the Chinese didn't single out Christians, insisting Moslems also remove minarets from their mosques.

Throughout Asia, the Chinese avoid living directly across from a church or a Buddhist temple. One family living across from a church in Hong Kong fell ill—a liver problem, a strange high fever, and so on. The dread cause was the coffin-shaped hexagonal church windows.

Other fears evoked by churches range from the overbearing, formalized religious architecture to the harmful draw and power of the building, which, the Chinese insist, can drain good ch'i from a building it faces. Even in New York City, the Chinese will board up windows and change entrances to thwart the draining of ch'i from their offices toward a church.

Because of the strong association of funeral parlors with death, most Chinese avoid living or working near them. But with the lack of space and choice in a city, often commercial and residential sectors must mingle. This can be disturbing if you happen to live across from a funeral parlor. The rental rates of an apartment house went down when a funeral home went up beside it. Said one tenant, "No one likes to be reminded of the dead."

Feng shui symbolism often reflects the actual potential of a design. In Mei Foo Sun Chuen, a large housing estate in the New Territories, some of the tens of thousands of residents interpreted a nearby incinerator as portending death. They said it would hurt local feng shui because its three 100-foot-high chimneys rose like incense stacks, billowing smoke and ash, making their own buildings resemble tombstones. In this case, the symbol imitated the detrimental potential outcome of the incinerator's pollution.

The heights of surrounding buildings, no matter what shape, can oppress an apartment's ch'i, hampering personal and financial growth. The occupant will constantly feel overshadowed and overwhelmed. A Hong Kong businessman explains: "My own factory business wasn't doing well, because a cinema towered over and oppressed it, so we hung a mirror and business improved until we had a bad month again. I looked up one day and noticed the mirror was broken. So we replaced it and now things are going well again."

Another case is the apartment of Lin Ke-fan, a violinist. When Mr. Lin arrived in Hong Kong from China, he could afford only an apartment reputed to have bad feng shui. Soon his luck soured, his money ran out, and his work failed. He called in Lin Yun, who divined that the problem lay in the juxtaposition of Mr. Lin's second-floor walk-up surrounded by highrises.

The skyscrapers apparently oppressed Mr. Lin's ch'i, not allowing him to perform to his full capabilities. All this was changed by the simple expedient of hanging a red hexagonal mirror outside one window. The mirror, bordered with the I Ching trigrams, blocked the overbearing qualities of taller buildings and reflected them back. This, however, raised a perennial feng shui problem: The tactics that benefit one person may be the demise of another. One nearby family developed sudden, inexplicable illnesses, and to appease his desperate neighbors, Mr. Lin removed the mirror from outside. (Unknown to the family, the mirror hangs inside, still facing in their direction.)

Besides the hexagonal mirror, another effective panacea for a building's inferior height is to place a pool of water on the roof. Lin Yun says this works particularly well not only because it reflects the taller structures' oppressiveness back at the buildings but also because the images mirrored in the water are standing horizontally, as if they have collapsed. The pool also allows ch'i to circulate and rise in the building.

Another good distortion of a Goliath-size building is the convex mirror, reflecting the perpetrating highrise upside-down.

A building's symbolism can affect the lives and business of its tenants. Knife-shaped and boot-shaped buildings are to be avoided. In Singapore, some businessmen link the failure of a modern shopping mall to its coffin shape. Feng shui men initially vetoed the plan but it was built anyway; now the shopping center is commercially dead, a self-perpetuating prophecy.

If an apartment building has towers that give it the shape of a meat cleaver, the occupant may be eating, sleeping, and working on the edge. Living in the tower, the handle of the knife, on the other hand, can improve the residents' ch'i, giving them a sense of con-

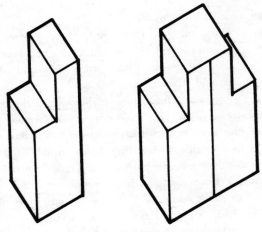

*Meat-cleaver-shaped buildings.*

trol. A mirror hung on the wall opposite the edge wall will bring the occupant and his/her desk, bed, or table away from the blade to safety.

Chinese residents of Hong Kong refused to buy apartments in two tall, luxury harborside towers. A cloudy future, they said, stems from flashing red lights on top of the buildings to warn away planes: At night, the buildings look like lighted offertory candles or incense sticks used at funerals or in ancestral shrines. Many Westerners embrace this way of thinking because cries of bad feng shui lower the high rent and occupancy rates; thus, they lease these luxury apartments for considerably less money than normal.

Urban feng shui adepts consider not only where to live, but how high. Lin Yun, applying principles similar to those of town placement on a mountain, says an apartment dweller must find a balance—living not too high or too low—somewhere between Scylla and Charybdis. Living on the top floors isn't the most stable situation. Although the view may be expansive, strong winds disperse ch'i, buffet the building, and rattle windows. A very tall building can also sway a bit with the wind.

The lower floors, on the other hand, are oppressed by the height of other buildings and the weight of higher floors. Less sunlight gets in. They are also more susceptible to the bad influences of traffic, pollution, and street noises.

A building's entrance is important. It should be wide enough to let in a healthy stream of ch'i. It should not directly face trees or columns, both of which obstruct ch'i from entering as well as oppressing the ch'i of those exiting the building. In the initial design for the multimillion-dollar Hong Kong/USA Asian Trade Center in Oakland, California, a Texas architect had a support column blocking the main entrance to the complex. Explains one employee of Gammon Properties, Ltd., a Hong Kong real estate concern: "The architect paid little attention to feng shui. When the boss saw the column in front of the main door, he said, 'This won't do at all.'" So they moved the entrance, and knocked out a new one unhindered by a pillar. A rounded pillar, however, won't hurt the occupants as much as a square one, because ch'i can move smoothly around it, and no corners jut out to harm it.

Businesses follow their own feng shui rules. It is best to have a store sited where the ch'i can easily enter. Applying rural river concepts, a store at the confluence of roads will get a steady stream of business and money. An American banker at Hong Kong Citibank joked that much of the success of the international banking concern in the region came from the building resting right where several roads meet. A store in the middle of a long arrowlike thoroughfare will not fare as well. As Tao Ho, a Harvard-trained architect, says:

> As an architect, when I talk about environmental design, in fact I am talking about good feng shui. . . . A shop at a corner has very good feng shui, because a lot of people are walking from different sides and also because of the stoplight. You take away the stoplight and people must rush across the street ignor-

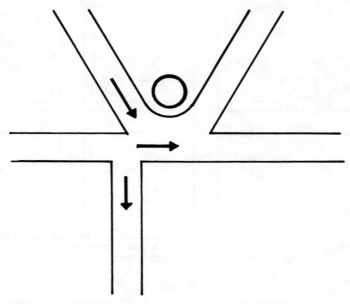

*Citibank in Hong Kong: An example of good building placement.*

ing the shop. If the light is red every few seconds, people will stop and buy. If there isn't a light, business won't be so good, people won't stop. There's a lot of sense to feng shui and that's what today is called planning to human needs.

Often the Chinese make a corner shop, hotel, or bank entrance slanted so that access to business is widened and ch'i, people, and money are all drawn in. For years these slanted doors were used mostly by gambling operations, as they still are in Macao's casinos. When a Hong Kong bank opened a branch with a slanted entrance a few years ago, many Chinese were alarmed at the symbolic allusion to the way the bank might be actually handling their money—cutting corners to make cash.

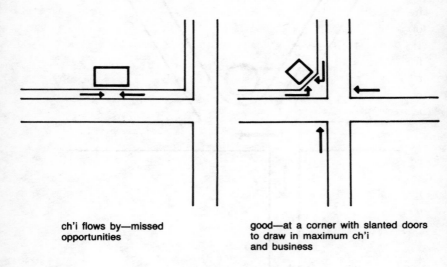

ch'i flows by—missed
opportunities

good—at a corner with slanted doors
to draw in maximum ch'i
and business

*Store sites.*

The slanted door's financial benefits are derived from the door's relationship to the street. Good ch'i, and therefore money, will be drawn in, affecting the ch'i of the other cross streets so they, too, are directed toward the door. When Lin Yun did the feng shui of Ywe Hwa, a large store selling only products from the People's Republic of China, Lin Yun suggested they install slanted doors at a corner for an entrance—and business is booming. Indeed, the slanted door allows greater access to the bank or store, making entrance easier for more people from a variety of directions. The slanted door not only blunts what might have been a sharp corner but also creates part of a ba-gua symbol, adding even more auspiciousness to the door formation.

Water is an important element in making money. In business, the Chinese say, it is so important to the feng shui of the Hong Kong and Shanghai Bank that the institution gave the colonial government money to build a park and a low-lying garage so that its view of Victoria Harbor—or access to water—would not be interrupted. Lin Yun says that when water bodies are not available, outdoor fountains are good, simultaneously bringing up good ch'i. Pointing to a large fountain in Hong Kong's Sha Tin racecourse, Lin Yun once said that it was good for the raceway's business, bringing money back to the track, ensuring that people will return another day.

The Chinese use the words *feng shui* as slang for gambling. According to Lin Yun, the presence of ocean water on the Atlantic City shore presents "a lot of opportunity to make money." But because the water is less than pristinely clear, not surprisingly, "the chance of intrigue exists."

While villagelike claims of feng shui incursions and subsequent extortion seldom happen, some bogus feng shui claims arise from a face-saving mechanism. According to an American lawyer in Hong Kong, one elderly Chinese businessman used feng shui to save his sons' face. The sons had drawn up a contract to buy a large hotel in the southwestern United States. Seeing that his sons had made a mistake and the hotel wasn't worth the price, the old man complained that the building in question lacked the correct balance of wind and water and that under such circumstances, he would not buy the hotel—thus extricating his money and his sons' honor from a foolish business deal.

Stories of feng shui deception abound in Hong Kong. According to Hong Kong legend, in the 1930s a feng shui priest warned a Mr. Eu that he would live as long as he built houses. So for years Mr. Eu added castlelike wings and turrets onto his already sprawling mansions; there were three in all—Euston, Eucliff, and Sermio. When the Japanese invaded in 1941, building stoppped and Mr. Eu—as prophesied—died shortly thereafter. Some Hong Kong residents say the feng shui man and the architect were in league.

Some people, on the other hand, go so far as to equate their well-earned prosperity with good feng shui. No matter how wealthy they are and how many mansions they may own, their official address will remain in a run-down section of Hong Kong where they first made their fortune. They see themselves not so much as self-made but as men whose money was destined to come to them because of their auspicious home or office. They keep the house as we might keep a rabbit's paw. The theory is: as long as his official address is this place where he got his start, then good luck will follow him.

One amah will not allow her employers, the Edgars, to move, saying their Hong Kong apartment brought them eleven relatively lucky years—no ill occurrences, no bad health. But, more important, the Edgars' mid-level home is *her* "good luck" flat. "Our luck is OK," says Sylvia Edgar, "but everything our amah does turns out well; she'll buy land in Lan Tao and the property costs will double. Everything she touches turns to gold. Although she has property and land, and is probably wealthier than we are, she likes living in our flat. She says it gives her luck and if luck is what she has, she has a lot of it."

## *Six*

# INTERIORS: ARCHITECTURE

Apartments and offices have the greatest impact on city dwellers. The inside is the base of a city person's life, determining and shaping ch'i. Interiors with good feng shui nourish the residents' ch'i, so they will both thrive in the outside world and handle hostile circumstances ranging from gun-point robberies to cutting tongues. On the other hand, to live in an ill-designed interior is asking for trouble. Bad feng shui hampers the occupants' potential, causing stress, irritability, and, ultimately, unhappiness. If the inside is not balanced, a good neighborhood will be of little help. According to

Lin Yun, "If people live and work in surroundings that harm or stunt their own ch'i, nothing will succeed. Other places will develop, but an area with unbalanced residents will degenerate." Thus, in cities, modern feng shui men stress inside ch'i.

Although the country generally offers better ch'i, a city dweller can remedy urban ills—lack of space, sunlight, trees, and water—by using feng shui antidotes and thus control his or her environment. Nevertheless, interior rules also apply to rural and suburban homes.

Lin Yun uses chu-shr methods to give meaning to spaces and to activate ch'i; to resolve hostile surroundings; to balance unharmonious habitats; to channel the energy in rooms to improve occupants' energy and thus their performance in the world. Feng shui staples include mirrors, lighting, symbolism, wind chimes, and plants.

A house resembles a body because it has its own metabolism. Ch'i must flow evenly throughout, pumping smoothly from hall to room. Windows and doors, the house's "noses" and "mouths," separate inside ch'i from outside ch'i. Once inhaled, ch'i is ideally channeled from space to space by doors, walls, screens, halls, corners, plants, and furniture. The occupants, a house's vital organs, are nourished by a healthy, balance flow of ch'i—not too strong and not too weak—to operate to their fullest capacity.

The door size, for example, should be balanced with the house. A proportionately small entrance is like having a tiny mouth: It doesn't allow enough ch'i to get in to circulate, thus diminishing chances of health, wealth, and happiness. On the other hand, if the door is too large, too much ch'i will enter. To remedy a small door, place a mirror on the top or on the sides of the door to give the effect of height and width. If the door is too large, install a wind chime in the front hall to disperse harmfully strong ch'i currents.

## DOORS: ENTRANCES

Good feng shui often depends on entrance doors' shape, size, and orientation. If the front door's feng shui is wrong, disaster may befall the household. Because of this, some people enter only through their back doors. A famous Hong Kong actress walks through the servants' quarters to enter her elegant apartment. A Chinese housewife living in Shek-O, a posh section of Hong Kong island, was told that all good things were going out of her front door, so she blocked it off despite protests from her European husband. Nonetheless, everybody from servants to guests entered through the back door. And their luck changed—so much so that when the husband later moved his offices, he called in a feng shui man who told him he needed two doors. After making the necessary adjustments, he fared very well.

The entrance sets the tone, the "vibes," of a house. As Lin Yun says, "If you are sensitive enough when you enter a house, you have various feelings—some give you a happy feeling, some make you uncomfortable and depressed." Traditionally hospitable, the Chinese arrange an entrance, the protection from the outside and the threshold into an inner world, more for the resident's benefit than for the visitor's. A faulty entrance barely affects the visitor. But to the resident it is one of many house features that can mold or program ch'i. If ch'i is continually sparse or withdrawn, then residents will become more timid, almost self-destructive. Their ch'i will retreat and their movements will be reserved. If ch'i is balanced and flows smoothly, on the other hand, residents will prosper. Thus, light and dark, distance and nearness, solid and space must be complementary, a balanced base from which to embark on a successful life course.

The ideal is to walk into a wide, light room or lobby with an expansive, happy feeling. This will encourage residents' minds, movements, and emotions to be expressive, unburdened, and constructive. Make sure doors open to the broadest area of an apart-

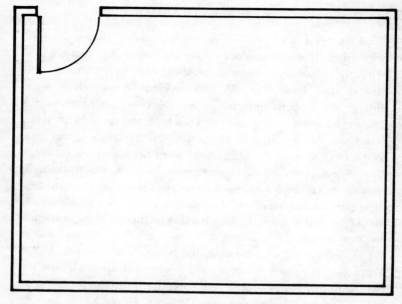

*Entrances: ideal entrance—maximum view.*

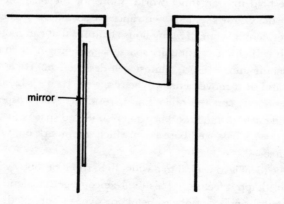

*George Hsu's entrance.*

ment or room for maximum view of the interior. Some Hong Kong businessmen have had the hinges of all their office doors reversed for this reason.

There should be no obstacles to ch'i. A lobby or an entrance hall can affect both the building and the occupant. If the hall or lobby is too narrow, ch'i can only trickle into the house, causing health and development problems. Like an undersized windpipe, it will suffocate the tenants' luck and choke their careers.

Take, for example, the foyer of the residence of George Hsu, the Hong Kong representative for General Electric. On entering the apartment, the Hsus were first greeted by a narrow, dark tunnel of a hallway punctuated by a beam that hovered low, further obstructing ch'i. This, claims Mr. Hsu, caused his children to be constantly ill, and, ultimately, his wife to die in childbirth. Distraught, he sought feng shui advice. To widen the narrow foyer, he placed a wide mirror on the hall wall visible from the entrance, thus adding apparent depth and allowing ch'i to expand through the obstructing wall. Mr. Hsu then installed a false translucent glass ceiling lit by overhead lights, thus obscuring the beam and encouraging his ch'i to rise toward the light.

Similarly, a wall directly in front of the entrance also can confine ch'i, making the occupant feel defeated, as if he were constantly coming up against a literal brick wall.

The solution to confined entrances, whether to a room, a hall, an apartment, or an office, is to hang a mirror on the offending wall, extending the visual area so the wall does not obstruct the movement of ch'i. For an oppressive wall parallel to the door, hang an appealing picture or poster of, say, a landscape to draw forward the person's ch'i. A bright light in the hall will draw up and expand ch'i. When the bulb goes out, replace it with an equally bright or even brighter light, never a dimmer one.

Ch'i that flows too strongly can inhibit residents' ch'i. To modify ch'i flow, the Chinese traditionally avoid having three or more doors or windows in a row. This arrangement—reminiscent of

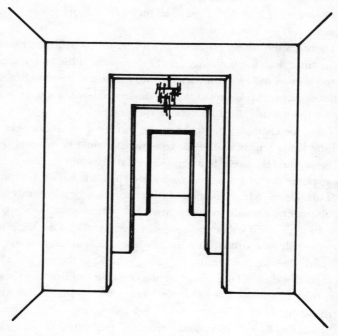

*Three doors or windows in a row: Hang a wind chime or mobile to disperse ch'i.*

arrowlike rivers and roads—funnels ch'i too quickly. It can cut the house in two, causing differing opinions within the household. A draft, itself a subtle physical barrier, can cause subconscious emotional walls affecting family relationships. The draft's invisible force can also carry away money and threaten family members with possible surgical operations deriving mostly from internal problems along the center vertical line of the body.

The Chinese traditionally place a screen between the doors to fend off strong ch'i and to thwart demons, who tend to fly in straight lines. Another antidote to domestic divisiveness is to have all bedrooms on one side of the hall. This, however, is a bit risky, subjecting the family to extreme changes in fortune that can be sometimes good, sometimes disastrous. The best overall cure is to hang a wind chime, a mobile, or a beaded curtain in the door's line of fire to disperse the strong ch'i current evenly throughout the house.

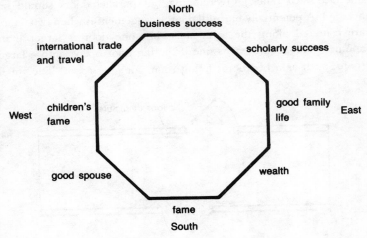

*Bed and door I-Ching positions.*

Unused or "dead" doors can also cause internal bickering. They inhibit the current of ch'i. A mirror hung on a "dead" door will cure the situation and give apparent depth to the door.

A door's orientation can help determine destiny. One orientation method is based on the octagonal I Ching symbol: Doors facing any of the eight possible directions bestow different fortunes. A door to the north brings good business, to the south means fame, to the east brings good family life, and facing the west bestows fame on offspring. A door facing northeast means scholarly success and intelligence, to the northwest promises family members will travel far and develop interests outside the home, to the southeast means wealth, and to the southwest a good spouse.

### Door Alignment

Door alignment is crucial. Doors should face each other directly, and should not overlap. (Two bathroom doors, however, should not face each other.) Overlapping but parallel doors should be avoided. A potentially harmful door arrangement is when two doors are centered along the same axis, but one door is larger than another. This alignment is fine if the big door opens onto a large room, such as a bedroom, living room, or guestroom. The small

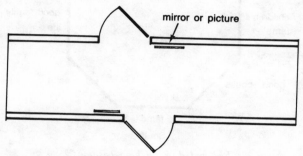

*Door alignments: Overlapping parallel doors and different size doors on same axis.*

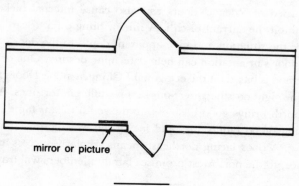

door should open to a small room—a closet, a kitchen, or a bathroom. Because large overpowers small, a large door opening onto a bathroom can cause health and personality problems—big doors should lead to big things. If it opens onto a bathroom, then the residents will always be there, either sick from indigestion or vainly preparing their faces. Hang a mirror or pretty picture outside the large door to draw residents out. Also to be avoided is having two doorknobs knock together when the doors are opened, causing family arguments. Either rehinge the door or paint small red dots at eye level on each door.

Worst of all is when two doors are slightly out of alignment, though not apparent to the eye. This can harm health, career, and family peace. Imitating a bad bite, two family members will always

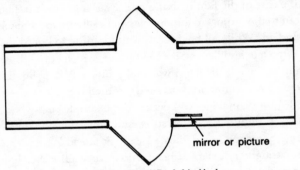

mirror or picture

*Door alignment: ''Bad bite'' doors.*

be at odds, arguing and differing in opinions. This ''bad-bite'' door alignment can unbalance residents' ch'i with its knifelike corner. It also presents an uneven vista. If a person is constantly confronted with two views—one quickly ending at a wall and the other looking long-range into the next room—his or her body's inner harmony and ch'i flow can be disturbed. The situation is similar to wearing eyeglasses with the wrong prescription; the wearer will feel disassociated and unfocused with and without the glasses.

Antidote to uneven doors: Either hang a mirror to give the impression of extended space on the nearer wall, or place something attractive on the wall, something pleasing to the occupant. For example, a picture of a favorite child on the wall will direct attention and ch'i toward the child. A businessman might mount a $100 bill. So the occupants' perspective on life and the world will be balanced, directed, and in focus.

### Slanted Doors

The most dangerous door is the slanted door—one on a bias or under a slanted ceiling. A slanted door can destroy good feng shui, bringing on an unusually horrible, unimaginable occurrence.

Slanted walls, beams, or doors can cause fluky catastrophes. Take the case of the family living under a slanted beam: Their child went out to the airport to join his classmates flying to England where they studied. While all his friends were on time to board the jet, he arrived too late and flew on the next plane, which crashed. Although the child survived, his hand was badly injured. Explains Lin Yun, "If you have something slanted, something slanted—oblique, warped, unimaginable—will occur. For example, if I work hard in business, I should be quite successful, but the outcome will be different. Someone less dedicated will get ahead."

To straighten a slanted beam, door, or wall, either hang from the beam, door, or wall a pretty awninglike curtain edged with small silk tassels or add wood, flowers, or plants. Another method is to build a complementary slant on the thinner side of the beam, to fashion a ba-gua symbol.

## WINDOWS

The window's shape and style can determine ch'i flow. It is best to install a window that opens completely—outwardly or inwardly—

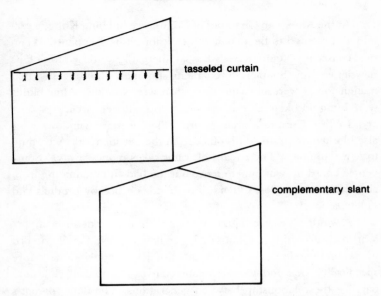

*Slanted structures: Hang a red, tasseled curtain or wood beam to even out slant, or build a complementary slant.*

instead of one that slides up or down. An outward-opening window is best. It enhances the occupant's ch'i and career opportunities because the maximum amount of ch'i can enter and circulate inside. The movement of opening stretches the occupant's ch'i outward. Some inward-opening windows, on the other hand, can hurt ch'i and thus careers. No obstacles should be in the way to interfere with the ch'i flow and the flow of the opening process.

If a window opens halfway, as do many in old New England homes, this causes the resident to give a false impression to others, because they get only half the ch'i.

Chinese sometimes spurn a good view, blocking off windows for feng shui reasons. Usually, that window looks to the west, the source of oppressive late afternoon sun glare, which can interrupt work and bring on headaches.

At the American Chamber of Commerce in Hong Kong, a certain seat seemed to be a chair of death for all its occupants. When two consecutive employees who sat there died, the editor of its newsletter, June Shaplen, hired a feng shui man who suggested that malign forces were entering through a west window. After blinds were hung and kept shut in the afternoon, all went well.

In Eric Cumine's architectural office, western windows were also blocked off to shield his office from the outside road. According to Mr. Cumine, "The stream of traffic takes money away." Some people board up windows to fence out the bad ch'i emanating from churches and temples. Others draw blinds on nearby brothels and sailor bars.

A window's size and juxtaposition with interior doors is important in determining the house's inner flow of ch'i. Family accord hinges on the relative size and number of doors and windows. More specifically, the window-door relationship is like that of child and parent—the relationship between generations. The door (parent's mouth) must be more impressive than the window (child's mouth) or else the children will be rebellious.

The ratio of windows to doors also affects family harmony. While one window is fine, three or more can lead to family arguments—too many tongues lead to too many options. Too many windows mean that sons and daughters will criticize and argue with and even talk back to their parents. Family unrest can also occur if the window is larger, because the child won't listen to the parents. It is fine, however, to have a large window with smaller sections or panes.

The cure is to put a bell or wind chime on top of the door or where an opening door can ring it. The window (child) may be so big it won't mind the door, but when the door opens and constantly makes a sound, the window must pay attention.

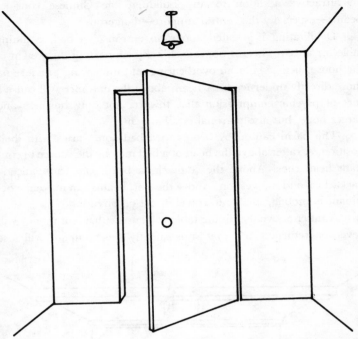

*Door-window ratio: If windows outnumber doors 3 to 1, or if the window is larger than the door, hang a bell or wind chime so the door rings the wind chime when it opens.*

## BEAMS AND PROJECTIONS

Low-lying beams and rafters, burdens to prosperity and growth, should be avoided. Beams not only oppress the ch'i of those underneath them, but also impede ch'i circulation throughout the house. Although exposed rafters in Western homes and beams held together with exquisite joinery in Chinese temples and pavilions are an attractive addition to any building, the Chinese consider beams—especially the central support—dangerous.

Debilitating if situated above an entrance, a bed, a dining table, or a stove, beams oppress ch'i. By supporting the weight of the house, beams emit an overbearing and unnerving pressure on those directly underneath. A beam above the entrance will cause a sort of psychic compression that thwarts not only business and career hope, but also personal development.

The harm caused by beams in a bedroom varies with their position. A rafter above the head of a bed may be the source of constant headaches. Above the stomach, a beam can cause ulcers, backaches, and indigestion. Above the feet, beams can make the occupant immobile, unable to travel or act on anything.

A rafter above the dining table will ensure that lent money will never be returned and that subsequently the occupant will lose

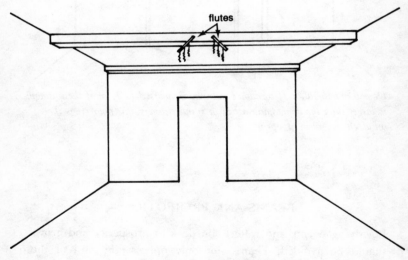

*Beams: Create a* ba-gua *(octagonal) symbol by hanging two flutes with tassels. The flutes pump ch'i through oppressive beams.*

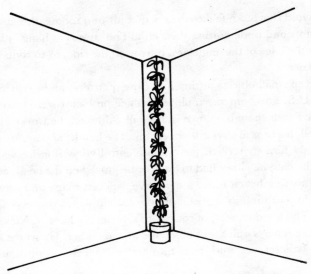

*Projecting corner: Install a mirror or a vine to soften edge.*

money in other ways. As a result, less and worse food will be set on the table. A rafter over a stove also affects wealth, curtailing financial opportunity.

Antidotes: Either move the bed, stove, or table out from under the beam, install an overheard mirror to allow ch'i to penetrate up through the beam, or place a firecracker above the beam to symbolically detonate the oppressive structure. Another, more mystical cure would be to hang two bamboo flutes slanting toward each other with red silk tassels or ribbons hanging down. Not only does this arrangement imitate the auspicious ba-gua formation—an image that corrects all wrongs—but because each flute is hollow, it becomes a purveyor of ch'i, symbolically rising through the beam. The flute is knifelike and if correctly aimed protects the occupants, chasing out evil spirits and tragedy.

In a hall, installing a false ceiling of translucent glass, lit by overhead lights, allows ch'i to circulate smoothly.

Avoid sharp, knifelike corners that jut into rooms, threatening occupants and undercutting their ch'i. The cure is to hang either a vine at the edge of the angle or a mirror on the side, or to round out the corner.

Even small objects jutting into close quarters can be detrimental. A U.S. government employee's office problems were traced to an attic handle hanging down in his hall. Although he worked hard and well, his boss always criticized him. The handle apparently programmed him to receive poor treatment: Every time he walked down the hall, he either had to duck or be grazed on the head, eventually molding his ch'i into a defensive, uneven shape and causing people to pick on him. Subconsciously the employee was asking for abuse. The antidote was, of course, to shorten the handle. Now, the employee reports office and home life are smoother. He works less, but his boss respects and treats him better. "I feel in control of my life."

## STAIRS

Stairs are the house's conduits, pumping ch'i from one floor to the next. They should not be too confined. Graceful and rounded stairways curving into a main hall are best. (The Chinese avoid stairs running down straight toward the front door—this would allow good ch'i and financial opportunities to roll away.) Banisters with sharp angles can also hurt ch'i. Similarly, poorly lit low-lying ceilings over the stairs oppress ch'i, choking and inhibiting its flow upstairs. To enhance ch'i circulation, place a mirror on the ceiling, heightening the otherwise confining situation. Bright light can also activate stair and hall ch'i.

## LIGHTS

Lights, symbolizing the sun, are auspicious. Dark rooms and halls oppress ch'i. Brightness stimulates a person's ch'i, bringing yang to a yin situation. The light should blend well with surroundings. For example, chandeliers both activate ch'i and distribute strong ch'i evenly around a room. If hung too low, or in the way of people's actions, however, they can harm the residents' ch'i.

## MIRRORS

On Long Island, the Pans hang a mirror in the dining room not for design reasons but to improve feng shui. They want to draw the river water—money—into their home and onto their dining table, thus blessing their food and their lives. While mirrors, a frequent feng shui cure, are traditionally used to deflect evil spirits and bad feng shui formations, Black Hat feng shui uses mirrors in five additional ways: to draw in positive forces, such as water and mountain ch'i, and to refract light; to allow good ch'i to pass through unused doors, nourishing the apartment and the family; to reflect intruders when the occupant's back faces the door, preventing surprises that might disperse ch'i; to combat the oppressive effects of a close wall, thus creating a healthy visual sense of distance, so ch'i can circulate freely; and symbolically to bring inside the house a room that projects outside the front door.

Mirrors, no matter what the use, should never be hung so they cut off the top of the head of the tallest person in the family; otherwise, that person will be prone to headaches and his ch'i will be lowered. Similarly, mirrors should not be hung too high.

## PLANTS

Plants provide an attractive panacea for many interior feng shui problems. They provide a symbolic reminder of both nature and growth, evoking nature in miniature. Placed in a corner, they allow ch'i to rise and circulate and not to linger. Placed at a protruding corner, they shield the room from sharp edges. Growing above the head of a bed, they elevate the sleeper's ch'i. Plants themselves, besides conducing ch'i, create and purvey it. They add a growing, lively feeling to a house. Often plants can curb malign affects, transforming it into smooth positive ch'i, such as restraining heavy ch'i doses that enter through large windows.

## WATER

The presence of water in homes, offices, businesses, and restaurants draws in money. Some lucky companies with views of rivers, lakes, and harbors can hang mirrors to reflect water's money-giving ch'i into their businesses. Others, however, must supply their own water by installing fish tanks. (Ones with bubbles rising through them particularly stimulate ch'i circulation.) Water should always be clean and fish should be healthy.

Washrooms also are crucial to avoiding business going down the drain. At Lee Travel Service, the back door of the salesmen's office opened onto the entrance to the ladies' washroom. The office was advised to keep the door closed and to hang a half-length mirror to improve sales and to open up a symbolic new road.

In one Hong Kong business, the owner moved the washbasin—sink, pipes, and all—next to the accounts secretary. "Every time someone washes his hands," he explains, "more money comes in."

## COLORS

Another aspect of good feng shui is color. To the Chinese, one's destiny can be shaded by the color of one's house, clothes, office, and so on. In the West, colors describe moods: seeing red, painting the town red, green with envy, feeling blue, white knight. Often one dresses in a color representing one's state of mind and feelings. Advertisers can often manipulate a person's emotional and psychological responses to a product by color choice. Similarly, color affects the feng shui of a home. Red, to the Chinese, is the most auspicious color, connoting happiness, fire or warmth, and strength. Shrines, clothes, and envelopes—the sort given to children on New Years or presented to geomancers for feng shui favors—are particularly special if they are red. A Chinese bride sports a scarlet cheongsam, the father of a newborn son hands out red eggs. Many of Lin Yun's patients wear red ribbons around wrists, waists, and necks to channel and retain ch'i.

Deep red and purple or plum—the "heart" of red—is an equally vital color, inspiring deep respect.

Green emits tranquility and freshness. It is the color of spring growth and a sign of healthy earth ch'i. Chu Mu, the movie director, lives in a green world surrounded by green upholstery, green rug, and plants. He even drives a green Mercedes. His reasons are more than just peace of mind. Explains Mr. Chu: "I was born in the year of the Ram and what do rams eat and thrive off of but grass, and the healthiest grass is green." So, living among green, Chu Mu hopes that his years will be fat and his opportunities will develop.

Yellow, the color of the sun and brightness, signifies longevity. A golden yellow was reserved for the imperial family in their clothes and ceramic tiles. Buddhist monks traditionally wear saffron-colored robes.

The most fearsome color to the Chinese is white. White is the deepest color of mourning: what black is to Western culture. At traditional Chinese funerals, the deceased's family shroud themselves in simple unbleached muslin robes as a sign of humble grief. Some say white dulls the senses. Stark, fashionable, white-on-white rooms signify death to the Chinese. When Lin Yun inspected an all-white artist's loft in the SoHo section of New York, he suggested that the door be painted red. Otherwise, he explained, "It's like a hospital or a sick-room—eventually family members will fall ill. You should have color." Many white interiors checked out by Lin Yun sport red flowers, red dots, red doors, green vines, or colorful rugs to offset a "white occurrence"—meaning death, failure, and sickness. In one Hong Kong dental clinic, attendants shunned the white uniform and agreed to work only after its color was switched to green.

One feng shui–fearing developer refuses to use white or blue—a cold, secondary mourning color—in his buildings, sticking to more auspicious greens and reds. (Blue is not always avoided.)

Black is also avoided. It signifies bad luck, dark happenings, the loss of light as the coffin door is finally closed.

Often color arrangement and outcome are quite specific. For a young man who wishes to marry, Lin Yun suggests a chu-shr cure: using pink sheets on the bed.

## ROOM PLACEMENT

Room juxtaposition also affects feng shui. The closer the kitchen is to the dining room, for example, the better. The kitchen should also lie at a distance from the front door. The Chinese say if the guest enters and right away sees the kitchen, then the residence will constantly be used by friends dropping in only to eat. In such a case, keep the kitchen door closed with a mirror hung on it.

The siting of bathrooms is crucial. House plumbing seems to

affect the resident's internal plumbing and expenses, since the bathroom is the place where water—money—escapes from the house. Kitchens and bathrooms should be placed at a distance from each other. Otherwise, health and finance will be bad and earned money will seem spent or lost in no time. (Food money will be flushed away.) Keep the dining table closer to the kitchen.

If the first sight on entering a home is a bathroom, both guests and hosts will suffer from bad health. Also, the host's money will dwindle as finances get flushed away. Cure: Keep the door closed and hang a mrror on it.

A bathroom at the end of a long corridor is bad for a family's health, as it is right in the line of the arrowlike hall, conducting swift ch'i. Ch'i entering through a door or a window will shoot into the bathroom, affecting the family's biological systems. In one such household, the wife could not have children. A feng shui expert suggested, among other things, that she hang a beaded curtain in the corridor to disperse the ch'i. (A wind chime or mobile would also work.) A year later, she was a happy parent.

A toilet should never squarely face the door, but sit out of the main line of the door.

## MAINTENANCE

House maintenance is crucial to the smooth flow of ch'i and the balance of yin and yang. A house in good shape best affects residents. Ch'i can alter as house fixtures—cracked windows, leaking roofs, cluttered halls and rooms, clogged plumbing—break down or wear out. The effect is similar to an aging or sickly body: If blood and breath cannot circulate, the rest of the body will be unhealthy. Upkeep is essential. Residents may suffer comparable ills. An unrepaired hole might fester, infecting residents who might then have to have an operation. Boxes and shopping bags piled up in a hall or behind a door may inhibit ch'i, thus blocking physical movement and career goals.

Door maintenance is important. A door must open easily. If the occupant must continually push to shove the stuck door open, the ch'i of his body becomes unbalanced. Doors must be well oiled. Shrill screeches of rusty hinges not only disperse interior ch'i, but also pierce the residents' ch'i, causing not only jumpy nerves but ill health. Doors must not bump into each other like gnashing teeth.

The condition of windows—the house's eyes, ears, and nostrils—can affect the occupant's health, particularly his orifices. If the window is broken or covered with paper, the occupant's ears, eyes, and nose will be uncomfortable. Childbearing will be difficult.

Bathroom upkeep is crucial. In Hawaii, a couple suffering from intestinal problems asked Lin Yun to look at their house. He noticed the bedroom did not have a door dividing it from the bathroom. The sink drain in the bathroom was clogged. He suggested that they unclog the sink and install a door, and once they had made these two repairs, the intestinal problems disappeared.

# *Seven*

# INTERIORS: FURNITURE ARRANGEMENT

The Chinese resolve a multitude of interior problems, ranging from awkward room shapes to impractical kitchens, offices, and bedrooms, by rearranging furniture. Different arrangements give different impressions—furniture clustered together creates an intimate mood, a geometric array seems formal, other layouts seem homey. But the Chinese change their settings for other reasons, too, such as to harmonize unbalanced rooms and to alter both ch'i flow and, ultimately, the residents' destiny.

## APARTMENT AND ROOM SHAPES

Apartment and room shapes follow rules of house and land shapes. Squares, rectangles, and circles are best. A shape can imply an innate destiny for residents. Death-oriented images are to be avoided. When a young couple moved into a new Hong Kong flat, they consulted a feng shui expert who advised them to move again because the living room walls were unparallel, connoting a coffin. The expert said unless they moved they would die. They ignored his advice, and shortly after, their Volkswagen plunged into a lake, killing both of them.

With unusually shaped apartments, the Chinese pay close attention to room placement. The bedroom, kitchen, and dining room should be within the main part of any house, and not in a wing projecting outside the front door. Avoid locating bedrooms and kitchens along the edge of a cleaver-shaped home or in the toe of a boot-shaped room.

Boot-shaped rooms and apartments can trip up occupants and suppress ch'i. In the summer of 1978, house-sitters had a feng shui expert over to the New York apartment of Gig Young and his wife. When he entered the apartment, he recalls, "I was overwhelmed by a sense of impending disaster. Several elements were awry." Not only was the apartment boot-shaped, but the bedrooms rested in the toe that projected outside the main door—a situation that en-

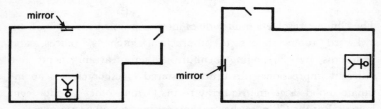

*Knife-shaped or boot-shaped room: If the bed is against the edge or toe of these rooms, a mirror can draw the bed away from the dangerous wall.*

courages disassociation in the family and the absence of the occupants. Moreoever, the bed itself rested right in the toe, resulting
in the stubbing of fate and career opportunities. The house-sitters
moved the bed out of the corner, but they left it in front of the door,
still in the wrong position. And, today, they blame the Youngs'
curious deaths on the mysterious workings of bad feng shui.

With a cleaver-shaped house or room, a bed, stove, or desk
should not be placed on the cutting edge. However, if furniture is
strategically arranged in the handle—the controlling part of the
knife—the occupants will be in greater charge of their own lives. For
example, proper manipulation of a cleaver-shaped room can give

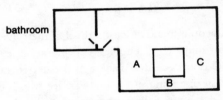

bathroom

| A | | C |
| B | | |

*Mah-jongg room.*

those who never seem to win at games, be it poker or Parcheesi, an
edge over opponents: The cleaver shape of a mah-jongg room in the
house of actor Patrick Tse and his actress wife Debbie Lee means
good luck for some players and bad luck for others, depending on
where they sit. Miss Lee explains: "One friend always wins. Usually, he sits in seat B. Last time he won $800. Then he sat in seat A
and lost half of it. In seat C, he lost more." Apparently, seat A is the
worst because it rests on the cutting blade, inhibiting its occupant's
ch'i so he/she plays poorly. One antidote is to move the table out
from the blade wall. A chu-shr guarantee for Miss Lee to win is for
her to go into the bathroom (the handle of the knife) and wash her
hands, thus ritually acquiring control of the money situation.
Another strategy is to let the table, bed, desk, or stove rest against
the blade, and to hang a mirror on the opposite wall to reflect the
furniture away from the edge.

The Chinese also avoid strange-angled rooms. A room with an angle smaller than ninety degrees is unbalanced with an uneven ch'i flow. Such an angle will trap ch'i, causing business to fail and creating a dead end for luck. To remedy this, install a tree or flowering plant in the corner to allow ch'i to go through the plant, because plants give life to otherwise dead ch'i and recirculate it.

## FURNITURE PLACEMENT

### *Bedrooms*

Because most people spend at least a third of their lives in bed, the bed position can shape ch'i. The first consideration is the bed's juxtaposition to the door. Always place a bed cater-corner to the bedroom door so that one lying in the bed can see who is entering. (The Chinese avoid having a bed's feet aim at the door, which resembles coffins in mortuaries, thus evoking forebodings of death.) If the cater-corner arrangement is impossible, hang a mirror to reflect any intruder who might startle the occupant and disperse his/her ch'i. Avoid overhead beams and knifelike corners that overhang or point toward the bed. A headboard should be higher than the footboard.

Large bureaus and armoires, if placed next to or near the foot of the bed, can also imbalance the occupant's ch'i, inhibiting body

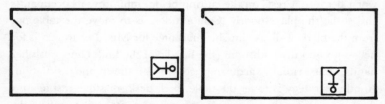

*Ideal bedroom: Bed should be cater-corner to the door.*

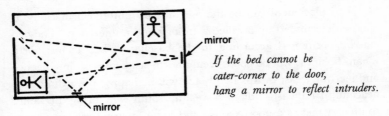

*If the bed cannot be cater-corner to the door, hang a mirror to reflect intruders.*

movements and disturbing internal harmony. The effect on children can be more severe. For example, in the crowded quarters where three sisters slept—a double-decker bunk and a cramped cot—a feng shui man asked the girls, "Who broke her arm in the past few months?" It was the girl in the cramped bed.

In the room of a Western journalist's son, a heavy bureau flanked the bed. The feng shui expert asked about a recent broken arm. And the couple said yes, he just broke his arm, and the next week, their son broke his arm again.

The Chinese feel the shape of a bed can mold a marriage. A bed with rounded corners can take the edges out of a rocky marriage. A communal large mattress is better than two twin-sizes lying side-by-side. One American journalist took heart when a feng shui man said the rifts with his wife could be patched up by replacing their twin beds with a king-size mattress. By getting rid of the crack between their beds, the expert said, the chasm of their conflicts would be bridged.

Beds should generally rest against a wall. Otherwise, the occupant will feel unstable with nothing to lean on in life.

During pregnancy, to avoid miscarriages, don't move or dust under beds. According to the chu-shr view of conception and birth, the universe is full of *ling,* or spirits. Each ling has a character and seeks out chances to enter the woman's womb to give life-breath to the fetus. When the child is born, the spirit will be the child's breath and aura (ch'i). These ling float under beds, waiting for the moment to enter the womb. If the woman is always arranging things and cleaning, ling will scatter and the fetus will be lost.

Bed placement can be the outcome of minute calculations. It can be determined by detailed astrology and numerology. The bed can be positioned according to the ba-gua: A bed facing north means business will be good; facing northeast brings on intelligence and learning; east means family life will be happy, rewarding, and peaceful; southeast indicates wealth; south will bring in fame; southwest means a good spouse and happy marital relations; west promises fame for future generations; northwest indicates travel far and wide. Charles Dickens always slept facing east, in order to catch the most positive cosmic flow.

Other mystified Westerners have come around to using feng shui in bedrooms. One British woman married to a Chinese says: "We moved into a house in Bangkok—which has its own brand of feng shui—and everything went wrong. You couldn't put your finger on it but we said, 'Here we are, a happy couple, yet nothing is happy around us'—arguments, relationships, all were going wrong. So a feng shui man told us: 'Ah, your bed is in the wrong position.' But we didn't change it." Five months went on and things got worse. "Then one day my husband marched into the bedroom and moved the bed into the corner of the room. It was an extraordinary experience—perhaps it was merely in my mind—but, suddenly, everything went right."

Sometimes rooms can be cursed with multiple problems. Dr. Liang, for example, practicing Western medicine in Hong Kong, could not sleep. "I'm not comfortable in bed," he said. "Does the bed have a problem? Should I change the mattress? Is it too soft?" None of the above. A beam running lengthwise over the Liangs' bed made them feel something was going on over their heads, making them anxious. A feng shui man suggested hanging two flutes in a ba-gua arrangement on the beam. In addition, outside the building runs a road that aims at the building and then curves around it, appearing to enter through one window, run over the bed, and go out another window. Dr. Liang asked, "Should I keep the windows closed?" To disperse the unsettling road ch'i, the feng shui expert suggested wind chimes be hung at the center crosspoint of the room.

## Living Rooms

Living rooms are less complicated, as they are receiving rooms for guests. However, they should be light and large and devoid of feng shui ills such as beams, oddly shaped corners and angles, or three windows or doors in a row. The host's favorite chair should face the entrance.

Living rooms should contain certain shapes, pictures, and doodads imbued with symbolic powers with which the resident identifies, such as ba-gua–shaped rugs or rounded tables. Chu Mu went "whole-hog" in this department. Not only are the corners and bed edges rounded, but also his desk, dining table, stairway, and couch—even a moon door that he claims can stop disaster. "Rounded decor to Westerners may be interior design, but to Chinese it is also feng shui," explains Mr. Chu. "If prosperity comes, it could go out the front door. This way wealth circulates through the house."

Chinese homes, restaurants, and stores also hang watercolors of flowers and plants, such as peonies, which symbolize peace and long life.

In the doodad department, Chu Mu's living room is infested with good luck paraphernalia. There rests a pantheon of fat smiling Buddhas to improve the ch'i throughout the flat and to attract wealth; an Eiffel Tower and a seashell schooner to ensure travel to far places and wide-reaching distribution of his movies; a knife fashioned of old Chinese coins, strung together with red string, to protect Mr. Chu from misfortune; and a trio of ivory Taoist sages to attract luck, fame, and money.

## KITCHEN: HOME AND RESTAURANT

The Chinese pay attention to the kitchen, especially the placement of the stove and rice cooker. Stoves are the symbolic sources of fortune because food is cooked there. (The Chinese word for food, *tsai,* sounds the same as their word for wealth.) In addition, food affects health, emotions, and behavior, so gastronomic satisfaction is crucial. Says Lin Yun, "From our food comes health and effectiveness. If it is well prepared and of good quality, we will do well in the world, earn more money to buy even better food." This food-money cycle, however, can turn the other way. "If you are poor, you eat worse, then fare poorly in the world. You might perform so poorly that eventually you get fired." The Chinese aren't the only ones to feel this way. As Virginia Woolf wrote after a less-than-agreeable meal: "One cannot think well, love well or sleep well, if one has not dined well. The lamp in the spine does not light on beef and prunes."*

The stove should not be in a cramped corner, inhibiting the cook's ch'i, but should allow the cook room to work. Otherwise, the chef might constantly hit her elbow, unbalancing her ch'i. In this case, mirrors can visually extend the space.

Above the stove, many Chinese hang a picture of the kitchen god who watches over the family and the hearth. A sort of spy for heaven, every New Year's he makes a journey up to the skies to report on the family. Before he embarks, he is bribed with food offerings and his mouth is smeared with honey so he will say only sweet things about the family.

Other kitchen hazards are angles pointing dangerously at the cook. In this case, hang either a mirror or something growing, such as a vine, to soften the edge.

*Virginia Woolf, *A Room of One's Own* (New York: Harcourt, Brace & World, 1957), p. 18.

The best stove site is where the toiling cook can see all entering the kitchen. Interaction is thus smooth. If a cook faces away from the door, health, wealth, and domestic harmony will suffer. Surprises disperse the cook's ch'i, making him or her jumpy, and the meal disappointing, thus affecting the whole household. "It makes sense," comments a Chinese-American State Department employee. "The husband comes home and surprises the wife in the kitchen; she might snap at him and a senseless fight will ensue." One precaution is to hang a mirror above the stove so the cook can see—Annie Oakley–style—any intruder, or to hang a bell or wind chime near the door so that before the visitor enters, he knocks against it.

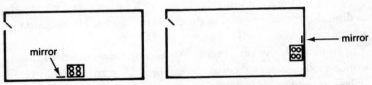

*Stove sites: In the kitchen, avoid having the cook's back to the door. Hang a mirror to reflect intruders.*

This is particularly important in restaurants. If the chef is surprised, a nervous chain reaction is set off, affecting everything from his performance to the waiters' attitudes to the customers' satisfaction. If ch'i circulation is smooth, it improves the quality of the dishes and the amount of business. (In one New York restaurant, however, the chef declined to have a feng shui mirror installed above his stove because, he said, it made him dizzy.)

Throughout Asia and the United States, Chinese restaurants use feng shui. Some of New York City's choicest Chinese restaurants—David K's, Hunam, Peng's, to mention a few—have been scrutinized and sanctified by a feng shui expert. The approach is both culinary and business-oriented. In 1978, the part-owner of Peking Park, Lawrence Chow, sent Lin Yun a round-trip Hong Kong–New York ticket to check out his restaurant's feng shui. Not only had business been poor, but a review by Mimi Sheraton, the *New York Times* restaurant critic, bestowed only a one-star rating. "I can't understand it. We have first-class chefs," remarked Mr. Chow. Hoping to stem his restaurant's losing streak, Mr. Chow invited a feng shui man, who divined that the restaurant's problem lay in the position of the cash register. They moved it closer to the door to improve the flow of money. Less than a year later, Gael Greene gave the restaurant a two-star rating in *New York* magazine.

Ch'i flow affects a restaurant's business. A feng shui rule is to create a good atmosphere for clients: angles, for example, abuse customers and create financial obstacles for owners. In Washington's House of Hunan, owner Johnny Kao covered a row of square columns with mirrors to allow ch'i to circulate evenly and to diminish the sharp effect of the columns' angles. He also installed round bar-counter ends.

In general, the cash register should be cater-corner to the entrance so the cashier faces the customers. A mirror should be installed to ensure the influx of business and money.

Restaurants can benefit from symbolic decor. Many Chinese restaurants choose the auspicious mixture of red and gold, symbolizing good luck and fortune. Their walls are festooned with pictures of Taoist sages and gods, flowers and landscapes—images that connote longevity, peace, and prosperity. Often these are enhanced by "double happiness," "long life," and "prosperity" written in gold characters on a red background. Other symbolism can be more subtle: fish tanks, meaning money, or plants, meaning growing ch'i. At a popular New York sushi bar, Lin Yun noted that the appealing decor of hollow vertical bamboo stalks helped the restaurant thrive. "Like large flutes they channel up and activate ch'i." In New York, David Keh, owner of David K's, added several large fish tanks to improve ch'i and to drum up even more business.

## STORES

Shopkeepers in Asia and the United States also use feng shui. Some stores sport small altars with pictures of the god of wealth. The Hong Kong and Shanghai Bank painted a god of wealth high above its old trading floor. In Sunnyside, Queens, Julie Wu invited a feng shui man to look at her newly bought cleaning store. She explains, "For twenty-eight years, the former owners weren't prosperous." The problems came from a slanted door and the position of the cash register. After hanging a mirror behind the register, putting a wind chime near the door, and placing plants by the slanted door and corners, business improved.

Stores also follow domestic feng shui rules. A jewelry store proprietress in Hong Kong hangs a plastic vine on a dangerously sharp corner in her shop to both smooth the corner's edge and siphon up ch'i.

Plastic, silk, and paintings of plants also improve surroundings and business. While walking through Saks Fifth Avenue, in New York, Lin Yun commented that a display of fake trees that appeared to grow out of sales counters increased the department store's business. "Trees give the feeling of springtime, when all is blooming," he said. "So the store will develop and prosper." He added that they elevated and helped ch'i circulate, making people flock to shop there.

## STUDIES AND OFFICES

In studies, desks should sit cater-corner to the door with the occupant facing the door. If one prefers looking out on an inspiring view, which precludes facing the door, a mirror may be hung above the desk angled to reflect any intruder. In Hong Kong, a reporter thought his work would improve if he hung a mirror above his desk

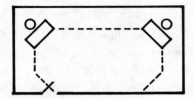

*Two desks in a study create a ba-gua symbol.*

that looked out on the South China Sea—in addition to attaining the ch'i of the water outside, his own ch'i would not be hurt from being startled, so he could retain his train of thought.

If two people have to work in one room, as academics C. C. Lee and his wife do, the desks can be placed to create a ba-gua shape with the wall. A plant and a bright lamp in back of the desks may create an aura to improve ch'i.

Next to the home, office arrangement is the most essential in determining a person's fortunes. Throughout Asia, many businesses, both Chinese and expatriate, call on feng shui experts to inspect their premises. Among them: Chase Asia, American Chamber of Commerce (Amcham), Citibank, the *Asian Wall Street Journal,* Jardines, and so forth. Some multinationals are known to auspiciously position each employee's desk according to astrology to encourage higher productivity and greater prosperity. When the *Far Eastern Economics Review* moved into a new office, they enlisted the help of a feng shui man. He said three desks were inauspiciously placed. Derek Davies, the *Review*'s managing editor, writes:

> One belonging to the receptionist Helen Tung, who had been feeling off-color since the move, was switched around and adorned with a "good luck" character—and she immediately perked up. "Focus" editor Donald Wise, who has otherwise hardly known a day's illness but who had been struck down with pleurisy and gout (twice!) since the move, trundled his desk across the editorial floor—and also recovered.

Other desks facing east, south or northeast were duly adorned with red porcelain horses or dark marble flower pots, filled with water but no flowers. I rotated my south-facing desk 15 degrees clockwise.*

The first consideration in any office is the manager's desk. Applying the theory that a country's destiny is determined by the feng shui of the emperor's palace, especially his throne, the Chinese feel the entire company's fortunes rest on the good siting of its president or manager. Some Hong Kong residents say Jardines encountered problems when a new director took over but failed to have his office adjusted by a feng shui expert.

The manager should reside in the most commanding position to assert his authority over his employees. Authority generally emits from the corner office farthest from the entrance. American office

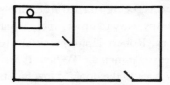

*Ideal office and seat for manager.*

arrangement also coincides with feng shui. In *Power!*, Michael Korda writes: "Generally speaking, offices are based upon a corner power system, rather than a central one. . . . the closer one is to the center the less powerful one is."† However, in feng shui not any corner will do. The manager of the Lee Travel Service in Kowloon, Frank Kwok, moved his office from the north to the south side—an old conference room—so that he would sit in a position fitting his rank. His second-in-command moved into his old office, and a wall

---

*Far Eastern Economics Review* (February 2, 1979), p. 27.
†Michael Korda, *Power!* (New York: Random House, 1975), p. 75.

was knocked down enabling her to oversee workers in an adjacent room.

Offices often follow apartment rules: avoiding knifelike corners, beams, columns, long dark hallways. Offices sited at the end of a long corridor—peering into the dragon's mouth—are undesirable. In such a case, move desks away from the dragon's mouth or install a screen to fend off the strong ch'i. Sometimes, screens can cover up for inside corruption. A Taiwan construction manager added a mirror to the screen, symbolically discouraging workers froom double-dealing behind his back.

Desks should sit cater-corner to doors. As Michael Korda explains, "Even among the highest and most securely protected of the executive elite, it is usual for the desk to be positioned so that its occupant can look up and see the door, not so much out of politeness as because nobody likes to be caught unawares."*

In feng shui terms, being startled from one's work unbalances ch'i, making one jumpy, easy to upset, and partially distracted, thus impairing one's work. Robert Upton, assistant regional director of the New Territories, comments, "When I first moved into my office, I sat with my back to the door." Now he sits where he can see everyone entering. "They tell me it gives me 'killing ch'i,' so I am better equipped to handle matters, and in fact, things *are* much better." (This position is further defended by a ba-gua mirror on his window, deflecting malign forces from the adjacent police station.) There are, however, exceptions: His boss, David Akers-Jones, is quite content to officiate from a seat chosen by a feng shui expert—with his back to the door.

Most offices should have doors on them. A windowed door is a disadvantage: Everyone entering can see the occupant first, thus putting him or her on the defensive. If a desk cannot be cater-corner to the door, hang a mirror to reflect anyone entering. (Some carry

*Ibid.,* p. 79.

their symbolic search for superiority too far, with high seats for them and low chairs for visitors. Deals and bargaining edges have been lost by a visitor making the mistake of sinking into a fluffy sofa.)

In Hong Kong, stories proliferate about feng shui men picking out a "hexed" seat where an occupant died or failed. One such case happened in the architecture office of Eric Cumine. "I had a feng shui man in before office hours. He said there was one very bad seat—a jinxed seat." Mr. Cumine found this quite remarkable because the seat's last occupant, his son, had died only two months before. (The next occupant of the jinxed seat didn't believe in feng shui, even after his aunt and sister died suddenly.) The geomancer pointed to two seats, saying they were never "warm." And, indeed, those were the seats of trainees who would stay with the firm for a year, then quit to join the government planning office or another firm. Mr. Cumine noted he and his partner sit in the best seats—the way it should be.

Often, however, feng shui is a convenient excuse for doing poorly in business. The son of a Chinese film producer commented that his father always blames his box-office failures on bad feng shui and credits his smash business successes to his own talent. A man working for Chase Asia blamed feng shui for his poor performance at the bank. When the bank refused to relocate his desk, he left in protest—some say he was going to be fired anyway.

Some businessmen follow their feng shui expert's every word, occasionally to their own loss. One expatriate businessman married to a Chinese woman fared very well financially and was therefore in awe of his geomancer. One day the geomancer overheard the wife asking, "Why do you always follow that feng shui man's advice? You're European—I'm Chinese and I don't believe in that rubbish." So when the husband consulted with the geomancer, the geomancer said, "You are a very lucky man. You have lots of money and a good business. However, you could be twice as rich as you are. One thing stands in your way—your wife. To fulfill your great destiny you must send her away for six months every year."

---

So the wife, against her wishes, was shuttled off on safaris, tours, and shopping sprees for half a year. And for a while the husband thrived. But, eventually, his luck—not to mention his marriage—failed.

At times, office feng shui maneuvering can create tense office politics. When Unicom, United Press International's commodity wire service, set up office in Hong Kong, its American manager called in a feng shui man. He said that in the office Unicom shared with trouble-ridden UPI—one editor had broken an arm, others suffered marital problems, people left, others got sick—the bad ch'i emanated from the acting bureau chief's office. To deflect this, the manager hung a large mirror that caused further office problems: UPI's Chinese teletypists claimed the evil spirits were reflected in their direction and hung three octagonal mirrors fortified with hexing forks facing Unicom. Applying rank, the manager insisted the teletypists' mirror be removed.

# *Eight*

# HOUSE SPIRITS

Moving into a house or an office is like stepping into the previous owner's shoes. A desirable house is one in which the former tenant prospered and was content. Even better is one in which the family's fortunes were so good that they moved into larger and grander quarters. In such lucky cases, feng shui men claim, the next residents might well follow in their footsteps, aligning their fortunes with their predecessors'. Often new residents will repeat what happened to former tenants within two or three years.

This hand-me-down destiny has its obvious pitfalls: A former tenant may have died, gotten divorced, lost money, or argued with his family. And the resonances of these experiences may linger and affect the new occupant.

When moving into a house or an office, the Chinese investigate its past—who lived there and what happened. One puzzled New York real estate agent commented that some Chinese clients took great interest in houses' histories and—to be safe—avoided old ones, where the chance of a death in former households was greater. (Indeed, like a cookie cutter, bad interior feng shui—an ill-placed bathroom, an arrowlike corner, or a drafty hall—will re-create problems.)

In these cases, a feng shui man or a Buddhist priest is often consulted. These experts are purportedly endowed with a sense about previous owners and events. Beyond offering practical advice—furniture arrangement, door and window alignment, orientation—which may well have a scientific base, they explore an additional intangible aspect, the house spirit. This dimension is harder to define and prove than the effect of an oppressive beam; it addresses such nonverifiable realities as the sensations people get from a house.

## CONSECRATING A HOUSE

Any dwelling or building, whether it is old or new, well-placed or not, needs a moving-in ceremony, a consecration. A feng shui priest is called in to perform, with the aid of incense and chants, the first rites of the company, home, or shop. The consecration serves as both a cure for problems ranging from poor finances to bad architecture and a ritual warding off of potential ills and evil spirits. Often the ceremonies serve to attract clients, letting locals know a company is open for business. The Hong Kong and Shanghai Bank stages Dragon Dances when opening a new branch, even at the

World Trade Center in New York. As one bank official comments, "Who are we to fly in the face of superstition?"

House consecration dates back to the Shang dynasty, when dogs, humans, cows, and so forth were sacrificed and placed under a shrine or stele to spiritually guard a home, village, or palace.

One modern example is the Chase Asia building. For years, wags in Hong Kong joked that Chase Asia, Chase Manhattan Bank's merchant banking arm, was far less successful in its financial transactions than its rival, Citibank, due to feng shui. The Citibank building is well positioned at the confluence of two roads. At first, people blamed Chase's problems on the old Chase Asia building, not only because it was nestled in formerly malaria-infested land and had a graveyard as a next-door neighbor but also for the building's six-sided windows which bore a close resemblance to coffins. In 1978 the company moved to a new building. (It is unclear exactly why they moved, though some locals suspect a feng shui motive.)

But Chase's problems increased. The building had never been consecrated by an appropriate priest. After Chase Asia lost four big deals in a row and then lost a senior executive in a plane crash, it enlisted a feng shui expert. The two trouble spots, he said, were in the executive director's office and a manager's office. The director was quoted as saying of the solution, "I don't mind. It means I get fresh red flowers every day on my desk to chase away the devils." The other manager? "He got goldfish. They keep dying, but they're supposed to—to keep the devils busy." The fact that the company has since been prospering is "purely coincidental."

Even Dow Chemical does not hedge its bets, as UPI reported:

> At Dow Chemical, a feng shui expert held the opening ceremony of a plant during a week of pouring rain. A threatened deluge held off until after the outdoor extravaganza for 300 guests. The executive who organized the event, Dean Wakefield, the marketing communications director, was congratulated by Chinese executives—not for avoiding soaked dignitaries but for the downpour that followed. The rain

signified that "the money can't wait to pour down on you." Mr. Wakefield said that the venture has been successful beyond the company's expectations.*

One Black Hat feng shui method of mystical housewarming to establish ownership and right to the apartment space is to place nine orange, lemon, or lime skins in a bowl or pail. Fill it with water. Then splash the citrus water on all floors—where there is wall-to-wall carpeting use an atomizer—cleansing the place of bad ch'i and evil spirits. (A Western-educated Chinese said whenever he moves into a new apartment, he turns on the radio full blast as if saying, "There, spirits, I'm here now and you can kindly leave.") On the first day of moving in, take a flute, symbolizing a sword, and a flower vase, symbolizing security and peace, with a red ribbon wrapped around its neck. Enter the house carrying the vase and the flute. Walk through each room to establish one's presence.

Firecrackers should be used all over the house, especially in the front entrance. (When a member of a household dies, his offspring sets off firecrackers at the entrance to shoo away the deceased's ghost.)

After moving into a new house, avoid sleeping on an old bed. If this is impossible, however, buy new sheets and bedspread to give a fresh feeling for a good start.

As times change, so can the feng shui of a house. This depends on how the patterns of ch'i fluctuate. Sometimes a house's ch'i may become more auspicious or it may sour. As in the Chinese concept of the universe, a home's ch'i will also vary. Although one hundred years ago a house might possess good ch'i, the constant fluctuation of the universal tides, outside events, and development and depletion of environmental resources can inhibit the strength and flow of ch'i and a family's luck may go downhill.

*Suzanne Green, United Press International, September 1977.

Lucy Lo, a cooking instructor and Hong Kong philanthropist, explains, "About ten years ago, there were so many deaths in my family. After the first one, I didn't take notice. Then my mother died, then my brother. I started to get nervous, then came the fourth death." So she consulted the family feng shui scholar, who said, "Your house already has fifty years of good luck, from now on the luck is finished," and advised her to move.

At first Ms. Lo didn't believe him and didn't move. "But, then, my father-in-law died, so all the old folk had died. The young people decided to move. So I moved, too."

The fear of ghosts is a factor connected to a house's feng shui. The Chinese believe in a parallel world in which spirits exist at the side of the living. Chinese ghosts have power over the living, so various festivals, such as grave-sweeping, or the festival of the hungry ghosts, are devoted to keeping them content and out of trouble. Places where the Japanese are known to have imprisoned, tortured, or killed people have acquired the stigma of bad feng shui. Although the spirit-placating Tun Fu ceremony is mostly limited to rural areas, this odd exorcism still occurs in more developed sectors. In Indonesia, when one American-owned company suffered financial setbacks, local company officials insisted the factory was haunted. However, after the Americans agreed to sacrifice a sheep and roasted it on the plant's steps, it appeared that the problem was less ghosts than money being spirited off by employees.

Some Chinese believe the Hong Kong government is not immune to "hauntings." In 1974, the Murray Road Carpark was the scene of an exorcism rite financed by the colony's transport department. The bureau's headquarters were to be housed above the parking lot. The building, workers said, rests on a site where Japanese tortured people in World War II. So thirty years later a parade of seventy Buddhist priests, chanting and burning incense, pacified their spirits. As reported in the *South China Morning Post*, the Reverend Koh Kwang, president of the Buddhist Association, claimed, "The service will not only be able to pacify spirits, but also be able to extend its blessings to the smooth operation of transport without any major accidents."

The fear of haunted places often affects house prices and rents. In a lovely area of Singapore known to be a site of World War II tortures, a large house will rent for U.S. $750 per month. Only Westerners dare to live there. Prime real estate and beautiful old houses in crowded Hong Kong, where space is a precious commodity, lie fallow because of either ghosts or mere bad feng shui. Prospective buyers are often tempted by low prices, but usually think twice if the house possesses bad feng shui or ghosts.

On Hong Kong Island, one old mansion sited on expensive land remained abandoned for years. The story: Soon after an amah drowned in a bathtub, residents heard strange noises, a chair started rocking on its own, and objects were mysteriously moved around at night. The family moved. The house was eventually bought by the PRC, but, locals claim, even they called in an exorcist. Despite this gesture, however, amahs will work only during daylight hours.

# *Nine*

# CONCLUSION

Feng shui covers a vast area of human endeavor. Along with directing the destinies of countries, families, and individuals, it also deals
with the minutiae of everyday life. At this level, feng shui can be
highly personalized, depending on individual needs, desires, and
criteria. It may deal with names, astrology, numbers and a concept
called the five elements (see Appendix 5). When home and office
rearrangements are insufficient solutions, the chu-shr mystical cures
are often called for: In New York, a young writer placed his
manuscript on a high armoire to ensure a book contract; the owner

of a popular New York Chinese restaurant jiggled his full cash register to shake up even more business. A bank employee rubbed a mixture of wine and a Chinese herbal powder on her sole to heal an ailing liver. Even former Vice-President Spiro Agnew has been seen in the company of a feng shui man, presumably seeking advice. Chu-shr cures number in the thousands. Their potency comes from being transmitted orally only after a red "lucky money" packet is presented to the feng shui man. To maintain the cure's mystical powers, the "client" must not reveal details of the cure until success is achieved. Any "leaks" or secret-sharing diminish the power.

Feng shui is still a mystery. Sometimes it may parallel modern ideas of physics, self-fulfilling prophecy, medicine, and even just plain good design. At other times, however, logical explanations fall short. With a bit of his own brand of irrationality, Lin Yun asserts that in feng shui, ru-shr at best achieves 10 percent success, while the results of transcendental chu-shr can be as high as 120 percent. For example, if a couple is embroiled in a marital crisis, the normal advice is to show respect, be patient, and be more loving and considerate of each other. This is ru-shr—reasonable, logical, and easy to accept. But, as much as people would like to be considerate and work things out, the results are only 10 percent effective. In using chu-shr, a couple might reverse or adjust their bed a bit. Although it seems illogical and irrational, an act of mere faith, the impact will be far greater than the results from ru-shr.

With an approach that is both sensitive and knowledgeable, Black Hat feng shui encompasses both ru-shr—this-worldly, rational, and logical—and chu-shr—transcendent, irrational, and illogical. Similar to ru-shr, feng shui includes everything within our scope of experience and knowledge: scientific discoveries, facts, and understood events. And similar to chu-shr, feng shui is also the great expanse outside our known world: What is yet to happen, to be discovered, understood, or seen.

# Appendix 1

# THE TUN FU CEREMONY

Details of Tun Fu ceremony performed at Pak Wai village, January 17, 1960, as reported by G. C. W. Grout, a government officer in the New Territories. The geomancer's name was Cheung Yuen Chong and he comes from Kwangsi Province.

"He started by placing the incense, the cups and the rice bowl and red packet on a table. . . . The incense was then lit and water placed in the rice bowl. Two pieces of joss paper were then lit, placed in the rice bowl of water, and the nail put into it. He then took up one of the pieces of wet bamboo, passed it over the burning incense and wrote certain secret inscriptions on it, copying out of the book, and passed it over the incense again, the written side down.

"This was repeated for each piece of bamboo. Then the red cloth was cut into strips and tied with red string, and gilt leaves to the top of the inscribed bamboos. The inscriptions seemed to be in pairs, three pieces with different writing on the right and again three on the left, similarly written.

"After this was done, wine was poured into three cups and tea poured in the other three, the candles lit, and the geomancer took up his position at the head of the table and started his incantations.

"After about five minutes of prayer he seized the young live cockerel by the head in his left hand, and taking hold of the nail from the rice bowl, plunged it into the cockerel's eye. On the impact the young cockerel almost struggled free, fighting so hard that the geomancer had to tighten his grip and to push the nail in its eye once more. With a crunching noise he pierced the nail right through the cockerel's head and out of the other eye. Thereupon, the cockerel ceased struggling and lay limp, as if dead.

"Still holding the cockerel with the nail through its head in his left hand, he ordered the V.R. [village representative] and his assistant to place the bamboos in the two pots with sand, three in each pot with a cup of tea. He sprinkled some of the blood from the cockerel's eyes on the bamboos and then nailed the cockerel on to a tree, suspended by this nail through its eyes. Joss paper was then burnt under the tree, wine was poured on the ground in front of the tree, and crackers were fired.

"The geomancer then took the cockerel off the tree and more crackers were fired. Holding it in his left hand, he pulled the nail out with his right, and put some water from the rice bowl in the cockerel's blinded eyes with his finger. Crackers were set off again. The limp cockerel was placed on the ground and the geomancer then filled his mouth with water from the rice bowl and blew on the cockerel twice, hitting it on the rump at the same time. Surprisingly enough, the cockerel got up and started staggering about, not knowing where to go, as it was still dazed and couldn't see.

"One of the pots with the three bamboos was then taken up by the V.R. on the geomancer's instructions. They brought it to the end of the village and placed it under a tree chosen by the geomancer. The assistant then went with a pick and started digging into the hillside behind the village at intervals of about 10 feet. Then the other pot with the other three bamboos was taken to the other end of the village and similarly placed.

"Lastly, the geomancer declared that work could start in three days' time and said the ceremonies were over.

"P.S. The V.R. came into our office two days later and I asked him about the cockerel. He said it was quite healthy and could see. I said I didn't believe him and asked to see the victim that afternoon. He had a good laugh and explained that the nail was stuck in the eye socket in such a way as to avoid the eye. I still insisted and arranged to see it that afternoon. It looked quite healthy and appeared to be the same one. On closer examination I found that one eye was blinded. Apparently the geomancer fumbled a bit."

# *Appendix 2*

# NAMES

As Shakespeare once asked, "What's in a name?" A great deal, according to many Chinese. They attach great significance to the literal and implied images of place names. They named hills and mountains, of course, after their shapes. But names can change as man transforms his landscape. A place in Hong Kong used to be called "Green Dragon Head" because the landscape resembled a dragon. About one hundred years ago, the story goes, a farmer discovered a pair of round, glasslike rocks buried under the earth. He dug them out and yellow water gushed out profusely. Locals say the farmer had offended feng shui. Soon after, he fell ill and died. From then on, locals referred to the area by an updated name, "Blind Dragon."

Chinese is a homonymous language; names and words constantly evoke portents and symbols that the Chinese fear will eventually become reality. For example, a newlywed couple living in a New Territories area with a name originally translated as meaning "twin trees"—which through years of British mispronunciation of Cantonese sounded more like "separated lovers" or, even worse, "twin corpses"—were advised by a feng shui expert to move, for fear of their lives and marriage.

Historically, place names have caused problems for Westerners. When the British wanted to introduce telegraph lines linking Hong Kong and Kowloon to Canton, the people at the Cantonese end were not amused by this development. They said the telegraph wires would mark the decline of Canton and bring possible disaster. Canton, alias the City of Rams, would be tethered and led by the leashlike telegraph lines right to the mouths of nine hungry dragons (Kowloon).

Even the Hong Kong Tourist Association credits the Chinese name of Bruce Lee, the late king of kung fu movies, with his untimely death in 1973. At the time of his death, Lee, whose Chinese name was Lee Shao-lung, "Little Dragon," lived in a Hong Kong suburb called Kowloon Tong, "Pond of the Nine Dragons." A Tourist Association press release notes, "Had he consulted a feng shui master before moving in, it is likely that he would have been warned against tempting fate. For in the mythological survival of the fittest, the little dragon must eventually give way to the combined might of the nine full-grown creatures who dominate the legendary pond."

Reports say Lee knew of the bad feng shui and sought to deflect it by hanging the octagonal ba-gua mirror outside his front door. But people say that the mirror was blown off during a typhoon shortly before the actor's death, leaving him undefended against the inevitable.

The Chinese devoted great thought to selecting the name for a capital. The Chinese empire's first capital, Chang-an, "long peace," lasted nearly a millennium.

# *Appendix 3*

# NUMBERS

To the Chinese, as to other cultures, numbers possess magical powers. Renaissance poets such as Edmund Spenser arranged lyrics and syllables in numerological schemes to bring a subconscious sense of harmony to the reader. In the West we have three wishes in fairy tales, the Christian Trinity, and the sacred restorative powers of pyramids (four triangles). Seven and nine also recur as numbers in magical ceremonies throughout the world.

As in the West, the Chinese traditionally used what they considered auspicious numbers in their architecture. For example, in a chapter on "Building Artisanship" in the *Rites of Chou*, a book on Chou dynasty ritual practices, the repetition of particularly auspicious numbers further sanctified a capital city. "The capital shall measure nine *li* (a Chinese mile) on each side and on each side there shall be three gates. Within the city, there shall be nine north-south streets and nine east-west streets. The north-south streets shall accommodate nine chariot ways.''*

Other architectural examples range from the imperial palace in Peking, which is based on "magic squares," and the Temple of Heaven (*Ming Tang,* literally translated as "cosmic house"), which has steps built in variables of three and nine.

The Chinese took great care to measure and build their temples according to the strict numerological calculations of geomancers. Miscalculations, they believed, would jeopardize not only the temple's sacred powers but also the worshiper's fortunes—some temples were abandoned because of slight slips of the ruler.

"Nine" and "one" are the most auspicious Chinese numbers. Nine connotes fullness, it is the largest number. One signifies the beginning, the birth.

The Chinese in Hong Kong and Taiwan interpret even more meanings into numbers than traditional magic. The sounds of numbers, as of names, are associated with other meanings. Homonyms add a special significance to Chinese numbers. A parallel to this would be if Americans started to identify *won* with the symbol *one*.

This practice extends to many areas of life in Asia. A Hong Kong artist picked a date to open her painting exhibit because the numbers added up to nine, which in Mandarin means "long life." A real estate developer could not sell certain office lots in a multimillion-dollar development because they ended in four, which in Cantonese sounds like "die." Chinese buyers particularly shun number 424: "die and die again."

*David Lung, "Heaven, Earth and Man (Master's thesis, University of Oregon, 1978).

# Appendix 4

# CHINESE ASTROLOGY

Doing the right thing, whether it is moving into a house or office, having a funeral, or marrying, at the right time is crucial to the Chinese. Some executives will not hold press conferences, break ground for buildings, or travel abroad unless the moment is propitious. To determine the correct day and hour for an event, Chinese throughout Asia either consult a feng shui man or fortune-teller or peruse an almanac offering not only assessments of the future but also helpful hints on subjects ranging from farming to face-reading. Feng shui men and fortune-tellers can charge from a couple of dollars for good travel days to hundreds for a ground-breaking date. Chinese more often do it themselves, seeking the aid of the almanac. One Chinese-American employee at the State Department said his wife consults

# APPENDIX 4

the almanac on when to make a bid for a house or when to sell their car. "It's amazing," he comments. "Things always work to our advantage."

This all ties in, of course, with Chinese astrology. Marriages were once arranged according to complementary birthdays. Still, today, some Chinese pay attention to the astrological congeniality of their partners. Unlike Western astrology, which stresses months, the Chinese method is based on the twelve animal years of the Chinese lunar calendar. Each year represents an animal that bestows certain general character traits on those born in that time span.

*The Rat* (1900, 1912, 1924, 1936, 1948, 1960, 1972, 1984) possesses attributes ranging from charming and humorous to honest and meticulous. The Chinese say those born in these years make good and wise advisers, yet they can never decide for themselves, and change directions constantly. However, rats at times hunger for power and money, leading some to be gamblers, others to be manipulative or petty. Their greed can lead them into a destructive trap.

*The Ox* (1901, 1913, 1925, 1937, 1949, 1961, 1973, 1985) works hard, patiently, and methodically. These people enjoy helping others. Behind this tenacious, laboring, and self-sacrificing exterior lies an active mind. While their balance and strength inspire confidence, oxen can seem rigid, stubborn, and slow. They must labor long hours to accomplish little. The Chinese say the time of year and day an ox is born is important in determining life-style. One woman in Hong Kong bragged that she would always be financially provided for with minimal effort on her part because she was born on a winter night. Oxen have little to do during the winter months, she explained, because the sweat of summer and fall harvesting is over and it is up to the farmer to feed and keep the oxen warm so they'll have strength for spring planting. Oxen born during agricultural months, however, are sentenced to a life of hard labor.

*The Tiger* (1901, 1914, 1926, 1938, 1950, 1962, 1974, 1986) is courageous, active, and self-assured and makes an excellent leader and protector; tigers attract followers and admirers. However liberal-minded tigers may be, they are passionate, rash, and resist the authority of others. Chinese say tigers born at night will be particularly restless, for night is the time they scavenge for food. The Western term for a particularly fierce woman is "dragon lady," but the Chinese call her an "old tiger lady." And for this reason some Chinese avoid having children in the Tiger Year—for fear of having a daughter.

*The Rabbit* (1903, 1915, 1927, 1939, 1951, 1963, 1975, 1987) is quick, clever, and ambitious. but seldom finishes what he starts. The rabbit is a social creature, tactful, cool, and sensitive to others. Yet, this calm can become aloof; the sensitivity can be quirky and thin-skinned; and the intelligence can become dilettantish. The rabbit is lucky: With brains and only a little hard labor, the rabbit can go far.

*The Dragon* (1904, 1916, 1928, 1940, 1952, 1964, 1976, 1988), to the Chinese, is born in the most desirable year. The imperial family adopted the all-powerful dragon symbol as its royal insignia. Possessing magical powers, the versatile dragon is capable of soaring to the highest heavenly heights or diving to the depths of the sea. On one hand shrewd, healthy, and full of vitality, the dragon also possesses a mystical side, intuitive, artistic, and strangely lucky. Dragons, however, can plunge pretty low, becoming irritable, stubborn, and impetuous. The dragon's mystical allure may become a bit too other-worldly, making him/her difficult to get close to. The dragon's unsatisfactory love life leads to a string of loves and marriages.

*The Snake* (1905, 1917, 1929, 1941, 1953, 1965, 1977, 1989) in Asia prefers to call himself "little dragon," indicating this, too, is a lucky year. Snakes are wise, philosophical, calm, and understanding. They are receptive and physically alluring, often fickle. Success and fame come easily to snakes. If crossed, they spit venom and can be selfish. They can be lazy and self-indulgent. Their innate elegance can at times be ostentatious.

*The Horse* (1906, 1918, 1930, 1942, 1954, 1966, 1978, 1990), charming and cheerful, is an extremely likable character. Hard-working, self-possessed, and sharp, the horse skillfully acquires power, wealth, and respect. However, the horse's sometimes appreciated frankness can be tactless. The horse's impatient pursuit of success may become selfish and predatory. Horses can be obstinate.

*The Ram* (1907, 1919, 1931, 1943, 1955, 1967, 1979, 1991), endowed with innate intelligence and artistic talent, will fare well in business. These people are good-natured and altruistic. However, their successes are limited to money; in family matters they will flounder. They can be a bit too wishy-washy, undisciplined, and irresponsible, and at times show a morose, misanthropic side.

*The Monkey* (1908, 1920, 1932, 1944, 1956, 1968, 1980, 1992) is lively, likable, and witty. Inventive and intelligent, those born in these years can solve most problems quickly and skillfully and are able to accomplish much in business. Often, however, monkeys are too clever for their own good and can be mettlesome, opportunistic, and unscrupulous to the point of being tricky and manipulative. They tend to be lazy, concentrating on small matters while ignoring more important issues.

*The Cock* (1909, 1921, 1933, 1945, 1957, 1969, 1981, 1993), hardworking, resourceful, and talented, is a self-assured person. Unlike our Western stereotype of chickens, the Chinese cock is courageous. In groups, they are vivacious, amusing, and popular. But cocks can be a bit too cocksure—strutting their stuff brazenly can be particularly annoying to relatives and close friends.

*The Dog* (1910, 1922, 1934, 1946, 1958, 1970, 1982, 1994) makes a faithful, honest, and courageous friend, has a deep sense of justice, and inspires confidence. These people tend to be both magnanimous and prosperous, yet they can also be dogged, guarded, and defensive. They accomplish goals quickly. But the dog never really relaxes. Despite appearing calm and at rest, his heart and mind are always jumping.

*The Pig* (1911, 1923, 1935, 1947, 1959, 1971, 1983, 1995) is sensitive, caring, and indulgent. Not only intelligent and cultured, the pigs also have a streak of bawdiness and earthiness. Their various indulgences can verge on gluttony. Unlike the conniving Machiavellian pigs of *Animal Farm,* Chinese pigs tend to be helpless and insecure. During fat spells they suddenly lose all and are unable to defend themselves, much less attack others. Pigs in general are lucky but lazy.

The Chinese have charted approximate marital compatibility:

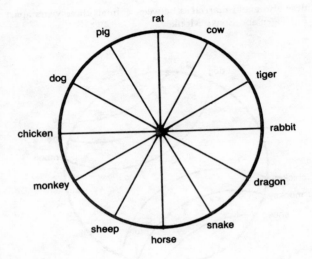

*Bad marriages.*

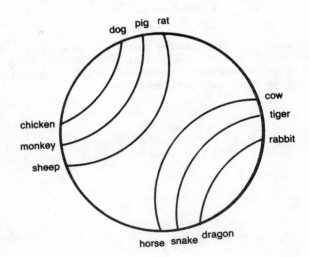

Chinese also avoid marriages between animals three years apart, except for Pig-Tiger and Snake-Monkey.

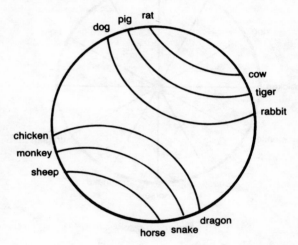

*Good marriages.*

Chinese astrology is in practice much more exacting than these generalities. In fact, one British woman married to a Chinese joked she had cesareans so her children would be born at an auspicious moment, thus pleasing her feng shui–conscious mother-in-law.

# *Appendix 5*

# THE FIVE ELEMENTS

The Chinese hope to improve their ch'i and fate by examining their five elements. Out of the interplay of yin and yang come five manifestations of ch'i: wood, earth, fire, water, and metal. Like yin and yang and ch'i, the five elements are not physical substances but powers or essences describing all matter and attributes. The Chinese associate these elements with time, space, matter, senses, colors, and psychological moods. For example, they assigned the element wood to spring, the color green, and the East. Fire heralded summer, the South, and red. Earth, positioned at the center, was mid-autumn and yellow. Metal is autumn, white, and the West. While water governs black (the deeper the water, the blacker it gets), the North, and winter.

The five elements have relative effects on each other, creating and destroying one another in a fixed succession. The cycle of development goes like this: Fire produces earth (ash); earth produces metal (minerals); metal creates water (although water rusts metal, this order derives from the observation that when water is in a metal cup, water forms on the outside of the vessel); water feeds wood (trees need water to grow); and wood aids fire. The chain of destruction is: wood harms earth; earth obstructs water; water destroys fire; fire melts metal; metal chops down wood.

Human ch'i can be divided into wood, earth, metal, water, and fire. Lin Yun says each person's nature possesses varying quantities of these corresponding natural elements. Each of the five human elements, he says, can be divided into seventy-two different types or amounts.

> Everyone has the five elements.* If someone is deficient in an element, this isn't necessarily bad. You first must check out the other elements to see whether they are well balanced. The ideal situation is to follow the mean, not have too much or too little of an element. On a scale of 1 to 72, the average 36 is the middle road, the most harmonious of natures. But if you have a lot or a little of an element, neither has a good or bad connotation, you simply must see all the elements in relation to each other.

The element wood, for example, stands for the Confucian ideal of benevolence, loyalty, and forgiveness. If a person possesses only a little wood, he is like a green leaf floating on a lake. When the east wind blows, he goes this way, when the west wind blows he goes that way: He is easily influenced. So whatever he hears, he agrees with or repeats. He doesn't have his own opinion.

A person with type-36 wood is like a growing tree: Under the influence of the wind his leaves flutter—meaning in the small things he is flexible—he bends but still has roots. When others say something, he listens, ponders all sides, and then makes his own decision. If he has a great deal of wood, he is like an old sturdy tree. When the wind blows, he isn't swept along. He doesn't listen to others (only to himself). He can be so inflexible that under a strong typhoon gust, he might break. He is prejudiced and just plain can't learn from others. No matter how long people talk to him, he still holds to his set position.

Metal, also translated as gold, stands for righteousness. People with little metal seldom speak, are very meticulous and careful, appear aloof and

---

*Traditional Chinese belief has it that males possess combinations of all five elements but that women should always be minus one element. If a woman has all five elements, she will not bear sons.

arrogant, strange and isolated. Little metal can also be the essence of a very independent person. A person possessing the mean of metal is fair, speaks the right amount, and always says the correct, appropriate thing. If someone is wrong he will criticize, but not overdo. In contrast, the person with a lot of metal tends to be unfair and self-righteous, leaping on any chance to gossip, criticize, and put his nose into others' business. He is argumentative and prone to complain. On the other hand, he can fight for principles and help and care for others. In Hong Kong, when a very talkative woman stopped her marathon monologue to ask Lin Yun about her five elements, he replied with a puckish grin, "Ah, you have an inordinate amount of gold/metal." This pleased her sense of self-righteousness and amused the bored and annoyed initiated who had listened to the soliloquy.

Fire is the element of wisdom, reason, and etiquette. When angered (literally "produce ch'i"), the person possessing little fire swallows his pride (ch'i) without expressing himself. When he is criticized, he doesn't speak up and ask for proof or defend himself. He is meek, with little passion to expend except for self-pity. The 36-person's anger is based on principle and logic. He knows how and when to put his foot down, but after he finishes stating his point or criticizing, he stops. The person with a maximum amount of fire can flare up without reason. He can be loud, unreasonable, unheeding, and highly critical of others.

A person short on earth, the element assigned to honesty and faith, will be an opportunist and a cheapskate. He'll easily scan a given situation and use it to his advantage. He has an eye out for good opportunities. He can be narcissistic, selfish, and slick. He may be a procrastinator and a cheater, always looking for shortcuts. People with a medium amount of earth are honest and dependable, very frank, and helpful to others. People who have lots of earth are like our aggy or hick. They are backward, old-fashioned, and unfashionable. Although something might be done to improve a situation or help themselves, they are scared to venture because people might criticize them, so they maintain their old customs. They do, however, like to help others to the point of self-sacrifice.

Lin Yun explains:

> If three friends, one with little earth, one with a medium amount, and another with lots of earth, go to a restaurant, the first two have $10 each, while the last has only $5. When the bill comes, the one with little earth will say he has only $5, the next will offer to lend the difference, and the third will offer to treat them all, though he's short on cash.

Lin Yun divides water—the element of insight, motivation, and social contacts—into living (or flowing) and dead (or still). Each person possesses both kinds. Flowing water is a person's drive and effectiveness in society. Still water reflects a person's clearness of mind. Lin Yun identifies seven of the seventy-two possible types of flowing water.

Of the moving variety, the smallest amount is valley water, which trickles down from a small mountain and then disappears (evaporates or seeps into a cave or a crack) before reaching level ground. These people are agoraphobic—they don't like to go out and are uneasy in open spaces. They prefer to spend time in the country and around the familiar sights of home. They also have a hard time mixing in society.

The second type of moving water is the fountain springing out of the ground, appearing glamorous, strong, and controlled, but in fact fountain water rises only to return to its pool and rise again. These people run around, expend a lot of energy, but get nowhere. Habitually, they go to the office, work, and return home. Lin Yun characterized a vivacious former actress as being a fountain. Every day she energetically performed chores for her family, entertained her husband's business associates and friends, and ended the day feeling tired and dissatisfied, only to replay her routine the next day.

The next is the stream whose activity is wider and whose progress may be meandering but ultimately has direction. When faced with an obstacle the stream may be set back for a brief interval, but it always finds a way to get around it and continue its course.

The rivers (the mean) are still more powerful and directed. They enjoy wider and unhindered social contacts and activity—seeing and making friends during vacation.

The large river has a lot of drive, but can flood over its shores or drag things along in its path, sometimes leaving chaos behind without being affected by it. He always accomplishes tasks efficiently. This is the prototype aggressive person.

The sea has a network of connections everywhere and travels a lot, touching people in different countries and different walks of life. It is the way of the jet-setter, or a social and political creature.

The ocean, although it has high and low tides, belongs on any shore. He is unpredictable, going in every direction, but attractive—all rivers flow to him.

The first type of the seventy-two varieties of still water, Lin Yun says, is the well water with limited vision and no movement in thought—a stagnant mind. The second type is sewer water—a person with unclear thoughts who clings to the wrong opinions and who is polluted from outside sources. The third type is troubled water, an unstable, hysterical person's assessment of things. The fourth type is muddy water, or someone with innate understanding who is nevertheless inarticulate and unclear. Pool water, on the other hand, has a clear knowledge that is learned and not instinctive. A person with pond water may have a clear understanding at home, but when he enters society his thought may be polluted by nearby roads (ideas), causing misunderstanding and poor decisions. Lake water stands for pure knowledge. As the sun and the moon rise and set, the middle of the lake shows the reflections. As things happen, the person reflects them like a mirror. He clearly knows what is going on and can intuit the essence of people and things around him.

Lin Yun's Tantric mysticism offers solutions to regulating and developing the five elements. Because the five elements are in fact five different manifestations of ch'i, the solutions are exercises and symbols to let ch'i adjust itself into the most balanced distribution. The exercises are the same for both quantities of too much or too little of an element. Lin Yun's solutions are not necessarily the most logical (for these cures to work, he says, they must be orally transmitted after the feng shui man is presented with a red ceremonial envelope). When people with too much metal are too talkative, logically we'd tell them to speak less. But Lin Yun maintains that this method is only cosmetic. For the best result the talkative should use breathing exercises. "This is a mouth problem," he says. "So you breathe through the mouth. In the morning when you get up, first inhale—but don't let out—one deep breath, then exhale it in nine short blows. The last breath should be the longest. Do this nine times for nine days or twenty-seven days if necessary."

For too much or too little wood, Lin Yun prescribes that, every morning right after arising, give the bed three or four shakes. Do this for nine days.

For an imbalance of earth, find a mole on the body nearest the heart. Then for nine days, on getting up, rub a cosmetic moisturizer on the mole, massaging in circular strokes the same number of years as your age.

To balance fire, carry something soft on the body—Lin Yun suggests suede, silk, or jade—jade's texture is cool and soft. Wear the object until your next birthday.

To balance water, Lin Yun prescribes a sort of chain-letter approach to control or further one's personal network of friends, one's activeness, and the amount of social contacts and judgment. For nine or twenty-seven days, you should meet or contact, by writing, calling, or seeing, nine new friends.

Traditional Chinese practice is more literal. In Hong Kong, a rich and intelligent man discovered when consulting a fortune-teller/feng shui expert during a business lull that he was short of fire. To correct this, he arranged in his entrance parlor an altar with an image of a fire god lit by a red electric light bulb. Supposedly, to the day he died he kept it lit in his front hall and business was always good.

The other five elements' antidotes are even more graphic. One longtime Hong Kong resident explained:

If you're short of wood then buy a wooden door or bed. If you're short of water, put a fish bowl or water basin in your room and office. (Water is especially important for businessmen because water is slang for money.) If you're short on earth, then you must be closer to the ground, and not live on a top floor of a highrise. Pick a bungalow with foundations next to the earth and have a lot of flowerpots filled with earth and plants. If you're short on gold, well, that's easy, you wear gold next to you.

Everyone's ch'i reacts to a color. Not all colors, however, affect everybody the same way. Some colors enhance a person's aura and others detract.

To assess a person's best color, first analyze his ch'i to discern his strong element—earth, fire, water, metal, wood. All five elements represent colors: wood is blue/green, fire is red, earth is yellow/brown, metal is white, water is black. These colors follow the five element cycles of mutual growth and decay. Once the element is found, use the cycle of development to see which element's color will enhance it. For example, people with a lot of wood should wear black (the color of water), while white (the metal color) will generally be bad for luck. Someone with lots of water should wear white and avoid yellow (the earth color). This can also work for buildings and interior design. Lin Yun said the United States' luck might well improve if yellow flowers were planted around the White House.

# BIBLIOGRAPHY

Ayscough, Florence. *A Chinese Mirror*. Boston: Houghton Mifflin, 1925.

Bleibtreu, John. *The Parable of the Beast*. New York: The Macmillan Company, 1968.

Boyd, Andrew. *Chinese Architecture and Town Planning 1500 B.C.–A.D. 1911*. Chicago: University of Chicago Press, 1962.

Burkhardt, V. R. *Chinese Creeds and Customs*. 3 vols. Hong Kong, n.d.

Capra, Fritjof. *The Tao of Physics*. New York: Bantam Books, 1977.

De Bary, Wm. Theodore, ed. *Sources of Chinese Tradition*. 3 vols. New York and London: Columbia University Press, 1970.

# BIBLIOGRAPHY

Edkins, Rev. Joseph. *Chinese Buddhism*. London, 1893. Reprint. New York: Paragon, 1968.

Eitel, Ernest. *Feng Shui: or the Rudiments of Natural Science in China*. Hong Kong, 1873.

Eliade, Mircea. *The Sacred and the Profane*. Translated by Willard R. Trask. New York: Harcourt, Brace, 1959.

Feng, Yu-lan. *A Short History of Chinese Philosophy*. Translated and edited by Derek Bodde. New York and London: The Macmillan Company, 1948.

———. *The Spirit of Chinese Philosophy*. Translated by E. R. Hughes. Boston: Beacon Press, 1967.

Feuchtwang, Stephan D. R. *An Anthropological Analysis of Chinese Geomancy*. Vientiane, Laos, 1974.

Frazer, James George. *The Golden Bough*. New York: The Macmillan Company, 1951.

Graham, David Crockett. *Folk Religion in Southwest China*. Washington, D.C.: Smithsonian Institution Press, 1961.

Hawkes, David. *A Little Primer of Tu Fu*. New York: Oxford University Press, 1967.

Hitching, Francis. *Earth Magic*. New York: William Morrow, 1977.

*I Ching, or Book of Changes, The*. 2 vols. Translated by Richard Wilhelm, rendered into English by Cary F. Baynes. Princeton, N.J.: Princeton University Press, 1950.

Keswick, Maggie. *The Chinese Garden*. New York: Rizzoli, 1978.

Korda, Michael. *Power!* New York: Random House, 1975.

Lee, Sherman. *Chinese Landscape Painting*. New York: Harper & Row, 1971.

Lip, Evelyn. *Chinese Geomancy*. Singapore, 1979.

Liu, Wu-chi, and Yucheng Lo, Irving. *Sunflower Splendor*. Bloomington, Ind.: University of Indiana Press, 1975.

Lung, David. *Heaven, Earth and Man*. Eugene, Oregon, 1978.

MacFarquhar, Roderick. *The Forbidden City: China's Ancient Capital*. New York: Newsweek, 1978.

# Bibliography

MacKenzie, Donald. *Myths of China and Japan*. London: Gresham Publishing, 1939.

Meyer, Jeffrey I. *Peking as a Sacred City*. South Pasadena, Calif.: E. Langstaff, 1976.

Needham, Joseph. *The Shorter Science and Civilization in China*. 2 vols. Cambridge, Eng.: Cambridge University Press, 1980.

Plopper, C. H. *Chinese Religion Seen Through the Proverbs*. New York: Paragon, 1969.

Reischauer, Edwin O., and Fairbank, John K. *East Asia: The Great Tradition*. Boston: Houghton Mifflin, 1960.

Saso, Michael. *Taoism and the Rite of Cosmic Renewal*. Pullman, Wash.: Washington State University Press, 1972.

Sickman, Laurence, and Soper, Alexander. *The Art and Architecture of China*. New York: The Viking Press, 1978.

Sullivan, Michael. *Arts of China, The*. Rev. ed. Berkeley, Los Angeles, and London: University of California Press, 1979.

*Village as Solar Ecology, The*. East Falmouth, Mass.: The New Alchemy Institute, 1980.

Waley, Arthur. *The Analects*. New York: The Macmillan Company, 1938.

———. *The Book of Songs*. New York: Grove Press, 1978.

———. *Translations from the Chinese*. New York: Alfred A. Knopf, 1941.

———. *The Way and Its Power*. New York: The Macmillan Company, 1958.

Watson, Burton, trans. *Cold Mountain: 100 Poems by Han-Shan*. New York: Grove Press, 1962.

White, Suzanne. *Suzanne White's Book of Chinese Chance*. New York: M. Evans, 1978.

Woolf, Virginia. *A Room of One's Own*. New York and London: Harcourt, Brace & World, 1957.

Yang, C. K. *Religion in Chinese Society*. Berkeley and Los Angeles: University of California Press, 1967.

Yoon, Hong-key. *Geomantic Relationships Between Culture and Nature in Korea*. South Pasadena, Calif.: E. Langstaff, 1976.

Sarah Rossbach has lived, worked, and studied in Asia for two years. She was graduated from Barnard College and Columbia University Graduate School of Journalism where she received the Far East Asian Journalism Fellowship. Her articles have appeared in the *New York Times*, the *Asian Wall Street Journal*, *Travel and Leisure* and *Art & Auction*. She now lives in New York, where her desk and bed are in lucky positions.